GENTLEMEN IN BLUE

GENTLEMEN IN BLUE

The History of No. 600 (City of London) Squadron
Royal Auxiliary Air Force
and
No.600 (City of London) Squadron Association
1925 -1995

by

HANS ONDERWATER

LEO COOPER
LONDON

First Published in Great Britain in 1997 by
LEO COOPER
an imprint of
Pen & Sword Books Ltd
47 Church Street, Barnsley, South Yorkshire, S70 2AS

British Library Cataloguing in Publication Data
A catalogue record for this book
is available from the British Library.
ISBN 0 85052 575 6

Dedicated to
Her Majesty Queen Elizabeth the Queen Mother,
Honorary Air Commodore,
to No.600 (City of London) Squadron,
to all who served with it from 1925 onwards
and
to those who kept the spirit of the Squadron
alive through its Association.

CONTENTS:

CLARENCE HOUSE
S.W. 1

600 (City of London) Squadron was formed over seventy years ago. It was very much a family unit with many of the air and ground crews drawn from the City of London which proved to be a great strength to the Squadron in times of peace and war. The skill and initiative of the early pilots and the courage and fortitude of those who served in World War II will always be remembered.

Since I had the honour of being appointed your Honorary Air Commodore I have visited the Squadron on numerous occasions and I have always greatly cherished my close links with the famous '600'.

Despite the Squadron being disbanded in 1957 the comradeship of those who served in 600 Squadron has been retained through the Association, and I send you all my greetings and my best wishes for the future.

ELIZABETH R
Queen Mother

THE RIGHT HONOURABLE THE LORD MAYOR
SIR JOHN CHALSTREY MA MD DSc FRCS

THE MANSION HOUSE LONDON EC4N 8BH
TELEPHONE 0171-626 2500

Britain's military history abounds with stories of the role of the volunteer. The City of London has always been proud of its contribution, from the raising of the Trained Bands in medieval times to the modern day and the brave contribution of No: 600 (City of London) Squadron.

The Squadron was raised in 1925 and had its headquarters in Finsbury barracks on the fringe of the City. Initial recruitment came from the great City institutions such as Lloyds and the Stock Exchange. The Squadron rapidly reached a high peak of efficiency and, on the outbreak of the Second World War, it was able to mobilise as a fully operational unit.

After a distinguished war record the Squadron re-formed in 1945 and continued as a "Territorial" Squadron until its disbandment in 1957.

The City of London is proud of the achievements of the members of this Squadron which was very much in keeping with the traditions of many of the military Units associated with the Capital.

I commend this book to you in the words of Greta Briggs' poem:

"I, who am known as London, have faced stern times before,
Having fought and ruled and traded for a thousand years and more;
I knew the Roman Legions and the harsh voiced Danish hordes;
I heard the Saxon revels, saw the blood on the Norman swords.
But though I am scarred by battle, my grim defenders vow
Never was I so stately nor so well-beloved as now."

John Chalstrey

PREFACE

BY PROFESSOR R.V. JONES

It is good that the history of No. 600 Squadron of the Royal Auxiliary Air Force has now been written, and even better that the book is the culmination of a profound act of gratitude by Hans Onderwater in recognition of the Squadron's part in being the first British Squadron to go to the aid of the Dutch people on the 10th May 1940 after German forces invaded Holland from which attack 600 suffered heavy casualties when five of the six Blenheims of the Squadron failed to return to base. At that time 600 Squadron's Mk1F Blenheims were operating in a day fighter role. These aircraft were too slow and poorly armed to compete with the German fighter of the day.

My own contact with the Squadron started in 1941 when I met Peter Stewart, then a Group Captain, We were the Assistant Directors of Intelligence on the Air Staff, his responsibility being photographic reconnaissance and mine scientific intelligence. Previously he had been in charge of the Air Ministry War Room and it was from him that I first learned about No. 600 Squadron, of which in pre-war days he had been Commanding Officer. Although he never 'shot a line' about what an honour that must have been, it was a source of quietly intense pride to him as I saw continuously over the years until his death parted our ever-growing friendship in 1968. Through him I came to appreciate the pride, even élan, with which the members of the Squadron wore the 'A' on their lapels, signifying their status as volunteers in the Royal Auxiliary Air Force. In the post-war years I was privileged to be invited to many of their functions such as Squadron and Association dinners and the bazaar to support the Squadron Church of St. Bartholomew-the-Great in London. I vividly recall the happy informality of those occasions including one in which the after-dinner session was going so well that some of us were fearing that our last trains home were already departing and our fears were quelled by Douglas Bader gathering up the Honorary Air Commodore, Her Majesty, the Queen Mother and saying 'Come on, Ma'am, it's time you went home!' and waltzing her out while she waved and we all sang 'If You Were The Only Girl In The World!'

Despite my long friendship with Peter and my Honorary Membership of the Squadron Association from 1958 onwards, I never heard any boasting about the proud record of the Squadron in being founded as one of the first Auxiliary Squadrons in 1925 and its achievements and sacrifices in the Second World War. In fact it was news to me when I read Dr. E.G. Bowen's book 'Radar Days' in 1987 that the Squadron has been so involved in the early days of AI airborne radar; and as radar technology evolved, the crews of the Squadron were welded into the most successful night fighter Squadron of the whole of the RAF. Dr. Bowen, to whom Britain owes much for the early development of airborne radar, had at first been taken aback by the cavalier approach of what he described as 'an elite Squadron made up of prominent bankers and brokers . . . if the truth be told, many of them had a private telephone connection from their caravans to the office in the City and in between flying duties they continued to do a little business on the side – strictly picnic fashion and in the best amateur tradition'.

But their resilience to their losses and their recovery to continue the Squadron's brilliant record of service – with its deep patriotism and warm comradeship – earned his lasting admiration, as it does mine.

Reginald V. Jones.

INTRODUCTION

BY HANS ONDERWATER

In October 1917, with the Great War still raging, provisions were made for an Air Force Reserve as well as an Auxiliary Air Force in the Air Force Constitution Act. Two years later Sir Hugh Trenchard, the Founder of the RAF, wrote a memorandum suggesting the formation of a Reserve Air Force on a territorial basis. It was not until 1923 that the Salisbury Committee recommended the formation of no less than 52 Squadrons to form a Home Defence Air Force. In October 1924, Sir Samuel Hoare, as Secretary of State for Air, was able to pass the law that finally led to the formation of the Auxiliary Air Force. The target strength for the Auxiliary Air Force was twenty Squadrons, being 38% of the Home Defence Air Force. When in August 1939 the Auxiliary Air Force was embodied into the Royal Air Force, this aim had been achieved. And when the Battle of Britain began about 30% of the RAF Squadrons taking part in this epic fight were Auxiliaries, accounting for about 30% of the losses of the German Luftwaffe. This meant that these auxiliaries were as effective as their regular colleagues. Many years later Viscount Templewood said: "Trenchard envisaged the Auxiliaries as a corps d'élite composed of the kind of young men who earlier had been interested in horses, but who now wished to serve their country in machines. He conceived the new mechanical Yeomanry with its aeroplanes based on great centres of industry. Esprit de corps was to be the dominating force in the Squadrons and each, therefore, was to have well-equipped headquarters, mess, and distinctive life of its own"◊. Social meetings between Squadron members were to be encouraged and on no account was any Squadron to be regarded as a reserve for filling up regular units. The experiment was successful from the beginning. The forebodings of the doubters and critics were soon proved groundless. So far from the non-regular units damaging the reputation of the regular units, they actually added some of the most glorious pages to the history of the Royal Air Force during the Second World War. The Squadrons of the Auxiliary Air Force were numbered from 600 upwards, while the Squadrons of the Royal Air Force Special Reserve were numbered from 500 upwards. At first six Auxiliary Squadrons and seven Special Reserve Squadrons were formed. However, neither No.500 nor No.600 Squadron were the first. Starting 15th May 1925 Auxiliary and Special Reserve Squadrons were formed:

15th May 1925	No. 502 (Ulster) Squadron ≈
12th September 1925	No. 602 (City of Glasgow) Squadron
14th October 1925	**No. 600 (City of London) Squadron**
14th October 1925	No. 601 (County of London) Squadron
14th October 1925	No. 603 (City of Edinburgh) Squadron
05th October 1926	No. 503 (County of Lincoln) Squadron ≈
14th October 1928	No. 504 (County of Nottingham) Squadron ≈
14th June 1929	No. 501 (County of Gloucester) Squadron ≈
17th March 1930	No. 604 (County of Middlesex) Squadron
17th March 1930	No. 607 (County of Durham) Squadron
17th March 1930	No. 608 (North Riding) Squadron
16th March 1931	No. 500 (County of Kent) Squadron ≈
10th February 1936	No. 609 (West Riding of Yorkshire) Squadron
10th February 1936	No. 610 (County of Chester) Squadron
10th February 1936	No. 611 (West Lancashire) Squadron
01st June 1937	No. 612 (County of Aberdeen) Squadron
01st June 1937	No. 614 (County of Glamorgan) Squadron
01st June 1937	No. 615 (County of Surrey) Squadron
01st November 1938	No. 616 (South Yorkshire) Squadron
01st February 1939	No. 613 (City of Manchester) Squadron

Many jokes have been cracked about the Auxiliary Air Force versus the Royal Air Force and its personnel. Wasn't the Auxiliary a gentleman who tried to be a soldier, while the Regular soldier tried as desperately to be a gentleman? Weren't there vicious and often costly battles the moment an Auxiliary Squadron arrived at an RAF base? Wasn't the mess full of dashing youngsters who arrived in sports cars, bringing their own champagne and brandy, spending more money during their Summer Camp than a Regular would during a whole year? Wasn't the Annual Summer Camp one long orgy of wine, women and song, with young gentlemen misbehaving in the service of the Realm? Indeed some of the Auxiliaries were well-to-do young men, some arrived in sportscars, keen to show the regulars that they were to be reckoned with. But many others were common men, albeit with a great interest in aviation and a dedication to their country. From simple airman to Commanding Officer, they all gave time, loyalty and if necessary their lives for that magnificent force "in blue".

This book tells the story of No.600 (City of London) Squadron, the second Auxiliary Air Force Squadron to be formed. During the defence cuts of the mid-fifties they were disbanded on 10th March 1957. For forty years after this No.600 (City of London) Squadron Association keeps the memory of that proud Squadron alive. Indeed a proud unit it is, having produced from its ranks men like MRAF Lord Charles Elworthy, who became Chief of Defence Staff, AVM Sir Desmond Hughes, a great night-fighter pilot who became Commandant of RAF College Cranwell, AVM "Ted" Colbeck-Welch, Air/Cdre C.J. Mount, who flew as a fighter pilot during the Battle of Britain and who successfully took a group of Hurricanes from an aircraft carrier to Malta. "Micky" Mount served in North Africa as a Wellington pilot and a highly regarded Squadron Commander and finally became an Air Commodore until he retired from the RAF. Many served with great distinction. More important is that Officers, NCOs and Other Ranks kept an Association together with disregard for rank and status. They never forgot their less well-off comrades and the Welfare Officer is a haven for those in need of help. The gathering of members and their ladies was and still is a source of great pleasure and immense comradeship. The Squadron itself not only won fame by its fighting exploits, but also it is the only Squadron to have two crests, the City of London arms, or, as some like to call it the "Dustcart Crest" and the second, a crescent moon, with a sword in the bend, remembering the days when No.600 Squadron was the 'fright of the night' over the skies of North Africa and Italy. It was the highest scoring night fighter unit in the allied air forces, thanks to the total commitment of air and ground crews alike. After disbanding in August 1945 in Italy, the Squadron was re-formed in England ten months later. It proudly served as a day fighter unit flying Spitfires and Meteors. In its history No.600 had the distinction of being a bomber, as well as a night-fighter and day fighter Squadron.

The author has the honour of being one of the Honorary Members of the Squadron Association, finding himself in the company of no less than HRH Prince Bernhard of the Netherlands and Prof. Reginald. V. Jones, the great scientist who, during the Second World War played such an eminent part during the "science war" against the Germans and who, through his intelligence and wisdom was instrumental in many fields. By the way, "R.V." also is a very good player of the mouth-organ! I owe him my sincere thanks for being helpful on the matter of Airborne Radar and for putting me in touch with one of the founding fathers of the practical use of it, Prof. R. Hanbury Brown, who was so kind to give me extensive and fascinating "gen" on A.I and "600". I cannot but thank two other prominent Gentlemen in Blue, both Navigator/Operator Radar in the Squadron during the Mediterranean Campaign. I wish to thank them for their amazing memories and their total dedication to help me write this book. They are Group Captain Norman Poole and Squadron Leader Laurie Dixon. They have written long letters, using their logbooks and diaries to describe life in 600 during that time. And without forgetting the help I received from so many other ex-members I cannot but say: "Thank you both, mission accomplished, job well done, Norman and Laurie".

This book does not tell all the stories that are worth telling; this proved an impossible task. Therefore the author has tried to give a fair view of more than seventy years of dedication, patriotism, courage and comradeship. Gentlemen in Blue honours all the men who served in No.600 (City of London) Squadron and especially those who, in the Squadron Association, keep the memory of the "Dustcart Squadron" alive.

God bless the Gentlemen in Blue.

Barendrecht, October 1997
Hans Onderwater

1) Leslie Hunt: *Twenty-One Squadrons; the History of the Royal Auxiliary Air Force* – Garnstone Press 1972
2) No.502: Converted to an Auxiliary Air Force Squadron on 1st July, 1937
   No.503: Converted to an Auxiliary Air Force Squadron on 1st May, 1936
   No.504: Converted to an Auxiliary Air Force Squadron on 18th May, 1936
   No.501: Converted to an Auxiliary Air Force Squadron on 1st May, 1936 (City of Bristol until 1 May 1930)
   No.500: Converted to an Auxiliary Air Force Squadron on 25th May, 1936

TO BE AN AUXILIARY

It should perhaps be explained what was expected from an Auxiliary, apart from loyalty to his Sovereign and preparedness to fight and if necessary lay down his life for his country. The term of enlistment for Auxiliaries was four years. On its completion the government granted extensions. Aspirants for the ranks of the Auxiliary Air Force were recruited as "Aircrafthand under training" in the trade they chose and the process of remustering, reclassification and promotion was exactly the same as that existing for the Royal Air Force. To the Regular NCO fell the task of instructing the Auxiliary airmen in their trades and the Auxiliary Officers in ground subjects such as maintenance, administration, signals, bomb aiming, engines, photography, gunnery and rigging. Last but not least the NCO in charge of Squadron Discipline enlightened all Squadron members as to the intricacies of the AP818. On inauguration of the Auxiliary Air Force volunteers for commission as a pilot had to be in possession of the civilian Pilot's "A" licence prior to his appointment. This particular rule was later waived, and applicants needed to have no prior knowledge of flying. Instruction was carried out on the standard lines of a Royal Air Force Flying Training School starting with "ab initio" dual and solo on training aircraft and graduating to dual and solo on Service types, followed by the necessary tests and examinations prior to getting their wings. In no instance whatsoever was an Auxiliary pilot given "a break" compared to his Regular colleagues. All had to comply with a Service flying course. In the early days this often extended over a period of eighteen months to two years, owing to the fact that flying instruction could only be given during weekends, the fourteen days "Annual Camp" and odd evenings during summers. Regular adjutants who served in Auxiliary Air Force Squadrons needed unbounded patience and an extreme sense of humour, but to the credit of all concerned damage was very rare. Esprit de corps was great in the Auxiliary Squadrons. Officers, NCOs and ORs, felt a strong bond of comradeship and dependence on each other's responsibilities in the Squadron itself. This allowed Associations to blossom after Squadrons were disbanded. Both officers and airmen had to make a certain number of attendances at the Squadron Town Headquarters or Aerodrome each year. Besides this they had to attend the Annual Camp period unless special leave was obtained. Included in these scheduled attendances were a number of weekend camps, as distinct from the normal weekend "exercises" on Saturdays and Sundays. The Auxiliaries were to remain in camp over the weekend and conform with Service routine. Sometimes Flights from Regular RAF Fighter Squadrons were attached for Interception Exercises and Camera Gun practice. If any Auxiliary desired to go to a Regular unit which specialised in a particular subject, short courses for the period of time they could afford were arranged for them, and, donning their uniform away they went, Regulars in all but for the letter "A" which was worn by the officers on their collar lapels and by the airmen on the shoulders of uniform jackets and greatcoats. The results of various examinations gave proof of the keen competitive rivalry amongst all ranks; failures were very rare. The experience of some of the older Auxiliary Air Force personnel was quite extensive, the early Squadrons started with AVRO 504Ks and either DH9As or Fairey Fawns, but were later equipped with AVRO 504Ns and Westland Wapitis, and in some Squadrons the Wapitis were in turn replaced by Hawker Harts.

When recruiting first opened for the Auxiliary Air Force, the Squadrons could have been manned to full strength in the first six months, so numerous were the applicants. But a system was adopted whereby none but the best type of recruit was accepted for a rank or trade.

Enlisting only the best types was in itself an assurance that the men would take their new "hobby" seriously and at all times be a credit to their "Mother Service", whose uniform they were to don, and also, that they were not enlisting for the personal monetary gain with no other object in view. This slow process of enrolment ensured that at no time during its existence would the Auxiliary Air Force Squadrons be below a 50% strength of trained personnel. Had the Squadrons been fully manned in the first six months, an efficient Auxiliary Air Force could never have been built up, for the tenure of service of the personnel would have expired practically all at the same time, and no sound objective would have been achieved.

The First Squadron Badge.

Of course after the Second World war broke out the percentage of Regular and RAFVR members of the Auxiliary Squadron increased. It was quite amazing to see that today even the Regulars still remember their time with the Auxiliaries as a climax of their entire RAF career. The loyalty and devotion with which the Auxiliaries took their hobby to war, the wonderful esprit de corps among all ranks and the degree of efficiency already attained made them a part of the Royal Air Force of which these Regulars were justly proud.

CHAPTER 1

IT IS FAR BETTER THAN HORSES.

FROM THE FORMATION IN 1925 TO 1930

"It was announced last night by the Air Ministry that arrangements have been completed for the establishment this year of the first four Squadrons of the new Auxiliary Air Force, which will form part of the Home Defence force, and be administered by local Territorial and Air Forces Associations. The Squadrons forming immediately are City of London, County of London, City of Glasgow and City of Edinburgh Bombing Squadrons. Among the commanders appointed is C.N. Lowe, the famous rugby international. The date on which recruiting of airmen for each unit will be opened will be announced later, but the County Associations are now prepared to receive applications from gentlemen who wish to be considered for commissions in the new units. It is the intention to fill the commissioned ranks, with the exception of the senior appointment, from among candidates who have no flying service experience". In August 1925 it was great news. It allowed young men, who were willing to give time to the defence of the Realm, an opportunity to join the world of aviation. They were to form their own Corps, fly and service their own aeroplanes and, above all, it would not cost the government too much.

"The honour of being the Father of the Auxiliary Air Force, as Sir Hugh Trenchard was of the regular Royal Air Force, fell to the Rt. Hon. Freddie Guest, PC, CBE, DSO, MP, who too is considered that of No.600 (City of London) Squadron", wrote N.P.Henderson about the first years of the Squadron. Henderson served as a pilot in RFC and RAF. He was the first "historian" of the Squadron. In his partially hand-written record he described the happy life of the "Gentlemen in Blue". And indeed, gentlemen they were. Most members worked in the City of London, with Lloyds or at the Stock Exchange, in financial firms and legal institutions. They all believed that the City of London had to have its own Aeroplane Squadron. Besides it seemed far better than horses. Flying was the young gentleman's new pleasure and the sky his new hunting ground. Henderson also remembered how the Auxiliary Air Force had begun its life as a fighting force in Great Britain. The idea behind the Auxiliary scheme was sound: in case of an emergency young men able to fly an aeroplane could be called upon to serve their country. As long as there was no necessity for their services, they would earn a living in civvy street, thus not costing the government more than a few pounds during the annual camps. They were expected to be good patriots, keen volunteers, dedicated ground crews, very experienced fliers and, above all, gentlemen. A Squadron was to have its own Squadron Association, directly connected with the County, City or Town as the case might be. Each Squadron was to have its own Town Headquarters and a peacetime aerodrome, within easy radius for the men, thus facilitating their training. In wartime each Squadron would occupy its own war station where it was expected to form a valuable "Auxiliary" to the regular RAF.

On 15th October 1925 the Squadron was officially created and became known as No.600 City of London (Bomber) Squadron, raised and maintained in accordance with Section 6 of the Air Force (Constitution) Act of 1917 and in conjunction with the Auxiliary Air Force and Air Force Reserve Act of 1924. It was affiliated to the City of London Territorial Association, a body whose activities and help it was hoped would greatly assist this new and embryonic branch of the Services. Part of Finsbury Barracks was renovated and handed over to the Squadron as the City Town Headquarters, whilst Northolt became the aerodrome as a peacetime flying station. Finsbury Barracks, on the fringe of the Old City of London, had been built originally as a defence of the City. The old turrets and the architectural structures dating back to the Middle Ages had of course since become surrounded by houses and buildings of the 20th century and some questions were raised if these surroundings would prove to be popular for the Squadron's Town HQ. In his book Henderson wrote: "Here then we find the home for our new Squadron and from which the various affairs of the unit were destined to be directed for some time to come. The Drill Hall, rather a more recent addition to the building, was quite a good and spacious hall and apart from its official purpose appealed to one as having encouraging possibilities for festive gatherings on the Squadron in the near future . . . ."

Avro 504N J8676 of No.600 Squadron pushed out for a sortie. The City of London crest can be seen on the right hand side of the fuselage just ahead of the cockpit.

Early in October 1925 the first appointment to No.600 (City of London) Bomber Squadron was made. F/L The Hon. James H.B. Rodney MC became Adjutant and Flying Instructor. He commenced flying training after being posted to the Royal Flying Corps in November 1915. Having served in Egypt, Iraq, England, Palestine and as a Staff Officer until his demobilisation in March 1919, he was considered to be the right man to lead the Squadron. Rodney received the Military Cross for valuable work in the Middle East. He was also Mentioned in Despatches. He proved to be an excellent man to build a new unit from scratch. Recruiting for the Squadron began on the 2nd November 1925, in a temporary office at Finsbury Barracks in the City of London. One week later the Squadron Offices in the Town Headquarters were taken over. From the date of formation of No.600 Squadron to 21st May 1926 Regulars were engaged in preparatory work of making the necessary equipment for the training of future recruits. The ultimate goal was to have a proper hangar at Hendon with Squadron offices, a

workshop, a plant, an armoury, photography and lecture rooms
and a number of transport sheds. As a temporary measure half a
hangar at Northolt was allotted to No.600 Squadron. Regular personnel of the Squadron consisted of one Flight Sergeant, three
Sergeants, two Corporals and eighteen airmen. Between 14th
October and the end of November they were busy at work at
Northolt. On 16th October the Squadron transport arrived: a
Leyland lorry, a Huck's starter, a Crossley tender and a P&M motor-
cycle with sidecar. Two weeks later the first aircraft arrived. Two
Avro 405K biplanes, with serial numbers H6631 and F8811, were
flown in from Henlow by F/Ls Rodney and Coleman. The next day
Rodney collected a third Avro 405K, J7837. Nine days later F/O
Adams, a wartime pilot who had served in South Africa and at
Headquarters RFC in France, began as Stores Officer. The first
official public appearance of the Squadron took place on 9th
November 1925. As in the next seventy years, the Lord Mayor's
Show was the perfect occasion. F/L Rodney commanded the reg-
ular personnel. It was a proud day for the new Squadron.

The distinction of being the first Auxiliary Officer gazetted to
No.600 Squadron fell to W/C James MC, who was appointed
Commanding Officer from 17th November 1925. He had been in the
15th Hussars when the First World War broke out. Via a posting with
the 3rd Hussars he transferred to the Royal Flying Corps in March
1915 and became an observer in No.16 Squadron. His job was
artillery spotting and observation work. After graduating as a pilot
he joined No.5 Squadron, then went to No.2 – the oldest fixed-wing
Squadron in the world – and ended the war as OC 6 Squadron. When
the war ended James went to GHQ, then commanded Digby RAF
Station before being posted to Cranwell as Chief Instructor of the
Cadet College. In 1923 he went to India to command No.60
Squadron. Two years later he relinquished his command and
returned to civilian life. But as was the case with many airmen, James
could not forget the time of his flying and became an Auxiliary. The
first Squadron flight was from Northolt on 18th December 1925. F/L
Rodney and AC Clarkson took up Avro H6631 for a test flight which
took fifteen minutes. By the end of the month the first DH9a arrived
from Henlow. Again F/L Rodney was at the controls. At the end of
1926 a move was made from Northolt to Hendon, where the
Squadron was to remain until the outbreak of the Second World War.
With the coming of 1926 No.600 Squadron had finished the posting

in of its regulars and recruitment of the first batch of Auxiliaries had been completed. Hendon had been bought from Claude Graham-White in 1925 and it was to be the Squadron's home. The Regular and Auxiliary Squadron members were:

Regulars:

F/S Harrop W – Discipline
F/S Wilson J – Flight
Sgt May F W – Flight
Sgt Pritchard O F – Town HQ
Sgt Donaldson S R – Stores
Cpl Easton C F – Orderly Room
Cpl Ryall G – Flight
Cpl Gray G P – Medical
LAC Galloway W – Cook House
LAC Chamberlayne S.H. –
Orderly Room
LAC Moore W J – Hut Orderly
LAC Smith W – Batman
LAC Page R W – Flight

LAC Myers S Y – Flight
LAC Haskell A B – Flight
LAC Durbridge – Flight

LAC Rogers W D – Town HQ
AC1 Rich W D – Flight
AC1 Clarkson J – Flight
AC1 Rowbottom – Flight
AC1 Caynes H G – Flight
AC1 Evans A H C – Flight
AC1 Utz H G A – Flight
AC1 Wolff H E – Dining Hall
AC1 Pollard A – Runner

AC1 Hall J J B – Transport
AC1 Blanche A E – Transport
AC2 Henton R – Orderly Room
AC2 Chapman H G – Officer's Mess
AC2 Vousden W J – Hut Orderly
AC2 Hughes E W – Flight

Auxiliaries:

AC2 Warrel J W	AC2 Wood W J T	AC2 Greenwood F
AC2 Berry N A	AC2 Ashton W S	AC2 Bias F
AC2 Hibbins G	AC2 Bass F	AC2 Martin E J
AC2 Allen A W	AC2 Payne A S W	AC2 England P F

Soon a new member was posted in as a Medical Officer. His name was N.P.Henderson. He became a very keen diarist for the Squadron and had been a soldier during World War One before he managed to join the RFC. Early in April 1926 the Drill Hall at Finsbury Barracks received its finishing touches and was now ready for use and drills. Also about that time the workshop there was equipped with vices and stripping stands for Mono and Liberty engines so that both the 405K and the DH9a could get regular servicing by the Squadron itself. On 1st May the first Squadron Routine Orders appeared.

Further Orders were issued on a regular basis, twice a week, beginning on 3rd May.

The Auxiliaries were very keen to learn all about aviation; NCOs lectured on many subjects.

Lectures were given and slowly all Auxiliaries felt more and more confident that they were "the right stuff". But the Squadron was to perform a duty previously unknown to airmen. When on 3rd May 1926 a general strike was declared the Squadron was ordered to form a company of the Civil Constabulary Reserve for the period of the strike. The Company was accommodated at the Town Head-quarters at Finsbury Barracks with W/C James in command. F/O Henderson and Mr. Foot both became Inspectors. Airmen Wood, Barry, Martin, Greenwood, Bass and England were appointed "Special Constables". Together with thirty civilians they were issued with truncheons, tin hats and armlets. Part of the men were detailed to protect food convoys going from Poplar to the West End. Their duty was to guard the food stuffs against possible attacks from the mob, but fortunately no violence happened and when by the Wednesday evening the news filtered through that the end of the strike was near, the Squadron was stood down and returned to its weekly duties.

A great event, of course, was the first weekend camp at Northolt. From 22nd till 24th May the following officers and men took part: F/L Rodney, F/Os Adams and Henderson and airmen Greenwood, Berry, Hibbens, Bass, Chester, England, Murton, Leary, Lang, Payne, Martin, Allen and Warrell. They received ground instruction in the various branches of aviation. F/O Henderson, after 50 minutes dual instruction on an Avro 504 with F/L Rodney, flew solo for 65 minutes, repeating his exploits the following day for 1 hour and 25 minutes. Not having flown for at least seven years, Henderson showed that "the art of flying once acquired" was not readily forgotten. New officers arrived. F/O Jenyns arrived in July 1926. He now worked at the Stock Exchange and had been a German prisoner of war during the war, after having been shot down over the Vosges Mountains. Unfortunately captured while trying to return to his own troops he was sent to East Prussia to "sit out" the war.

The next exercise was the 1926 Bank Holiday Camp in August at Northolt. Parachute descents from a Vickers Vimy bomber were the reason for great excitement. F/L Rodney showed that being pulled off the wing of a Vickers Vimy could be great fun and really was nothing to worry about. F/S Harrop, one of the No.600 Squadron volunteers, decided he was going to do the same. At about 1000 feet the brave F/S pulled the ripcord and landed safely, though looking a bit bewildered when photographed after the event. Another feature mentioned by Henderson was that 30 flying hours were achieved during the weekend. He wrote: "F/O Jenyns almost required his meals served up in the air". During this camp the first DH9a (E8666) was in full use. On 3rd August P/O Wallcousins joined the Squadron. After only 2.50hrs dual flying time he went solo and looped his Avro to the utter delight of all present.

By the end of the month two new officers joined, F/O Lamplugh and P/O Matheson. In September the big day came: the beginning of the very first Annual Camp, the highlight in the life of each and every member of an Auxiliary Squadron. Manston was chosen as the place where it all was to happen. Being the Headquarters of the School for Technical Training for Men it was a fine place to teach the Auxiliaries the fine art of aviation. Days before the Camp the first Auxiliaries arrived. Jenyns flew in with the Avro of the Squadron on 26th August, bringing in a second aeroplane the next day. Then the CO arrived with the Medical Officer, by rail, while P/O Wallcousins travelled by road. The other participating officers were Messrs.

Dalton, Lancaster, Massey and Hackett. On 28th August nineteen Auxiliary airmen arrived by train. When the Camp began the CO had nine officers and forty three airmen at his disposal. Seven officers and nineteen airmen were Auxiliaries, the others all Regulars. Flying began immediately and proceeded continuously throughout the rest of the stay in Camp. F/L Rodney was extremely busy, being the Adjutant as well as the Flying Instructor. He added considerably to the numbers of hours actually flown during the training. F/Os Dalton and Jenyns spent most of the time airborne. P/O Lancaster went solo. Dalton and F/S Harrop gave many hours of instruction on aerial navigation, gunnery, bombing and photography. F/O Henderson joined S/L d'Arcy Power as an Assistant Medical Officer. F/O Adams ran the stores as if it was his daily business and organised football matches. Unfortunately No.600 Squadron was beaten twice by the Regulars of No.9 Squadron. However, at the third match they managed to return victors. Another very important thing was the Air Ministry Swimming Test for Special Certificates. These tests were carried out at the Station Swimming Pool. Many Auxiliaries took part and qualified for the certificate. The airmen prepared aircraft, carried out inspections and did minor repairs. In addition the excellent facilities of the Technical Training Centre were made available to the Auxiliaries. They had superb opportunity to carry out practical work under skilled instructors. At the end of camp a thorough inspection was made and on 12th September all men returned home. A small group stayed behind to fly the aeroplanes back to Northolt, the others travelled by road (Regulars) or train (Auxiliaries).

The Camp received a lot of attention in the national press. It was a first class chance to show the general public what a great people the Auxiliaries were. Photographs were taken by the correspondent of the "Times", who published an article on 6th September. A "Daily Mail" photographer came to the camp and took very good pictures. A further article appeared in the "News of the World" and last but not least the "Gaumont Graphic Cinema Company" made a film with the promise to show it in the various cinemas all over the country. Henderson wrote in his diary: "All this publicity was considered good for recruiting". The article in the "Daily Mail" was only 23 lines. The "Times" and the "News of the World", however, wrote long articles about the "Auxiliary Airmen" ("Times") and "Air Territorials" ("News of the World"). As recruiting concentrated at the City Institutions of Lloyds (Insurance Brokers and Underwriters) and the

F/O Jenyns shows the Auxiliaries how to pull the ripcord of a parachute when standing on the ground. Doing it from the wing of a Vickers Vimy bomber would be a different thing. Some of the volunteers made their first parachute jump during the 1927 Bank Holiday Camp.

Stock Exchange, more and more people with a financial background joined the Squadron. Most of them came from the financial world. They were bankers, underwriters, insurance brokers, stock brokers, etc.

In November 1926 W/C James left the Squadron. His successor gave a great boost to the Squadron's morale. From 19th November no other than S/L the Rt. Hon. Freddie Guest PC, CBE, DSO, MP, a very popular man in political circles and a fervent supporter of the Auxiliary Air Force, assumed command. At the turn of the century he had served in the 1st Life Guards and had been Mentioned in Despatches. He had fought in the Boer War, and also served as ADC to Field Marshal Sir John French on the Western Front. There, he again had been Mentioned in Despatches. Then he had been posted to East Africa, returning with two DSOs. He also served as private Secretary to Churchill. As a Permanent Secretary to the Treasury from 1917 to 1921, Chief Whip in the 1917-1919 Coalition, before becoming Secretary of State for Air from 1921-1922, Liberal MP for Bristol North since 1924 and Chevalier of the Légion d'Honneur, he was to give 600 all it needed to rise to great heights. The Squadron felt extremely fortunate to have him as their CO. A week after he assumed command the new CO invited the Squadron officers for a dinner at his house at 7 Alford Street, Park Lane. Other guests present were the Secretary of State for Air, Sir Samuel Hoare and Lt. Col. "Billy" Bishop, VC, DSO, MC, DFC, the famous "ace" of World War One.

In December that year another important decision was taken to ensure comradeship and good standing in the Squadron. A Committee was formed to proceed with the organisation of Sports and Entertainment. F/O Henderson was elected President, with F/O Adams as Sports Advisory Member, F/S Pritchard as the Secretary and F/S Harrop and AC Berry and Greenwood as members. The committee took its task very seriously for immediately after it had been formed a Squadron Dance at Town HQ was organised for 23rd December. A band of five performers was arranged, flags and other decorations procured, cloakrooms and refreshments provided. All present had a marvellous evening. The Committee immediately organised other activities in January: darts, billiards and Ping-Pong. They even organised teams to play football (soccer and rugger), cricket and tennis for the coming season.

Aerial gunnery lectures were given, such as here by F/L Dalton, before air gunners would be allowed to take to the air and do "the real thing".

The New Year of 1927 was commenced with a lecture on 6th January, the subject being "The Home Defence Scheme". More interesting was the lecturer, an officer called S/L Park, whom all would get to know during the Battle of Britain as Sir Keith Park, AOC No.11 Group, Fighter Command.

The new year also saw the Squadron moving from Northolt to its own airfield Headquarters at Hendon, where 600 was joined by 601 (County of London) Squadron. The Flights were reorganised and now consisted of a HQ Flight with S/L Guest, F/O Henderson and P/O Wallcousins; A-Flight (F/O Jenyns, P/Os Earnshaw and Hackett); B-Flight (F/O Lamplugh, P/Os Massey, Vaizey and Larking) and C-Flight (F/L Dalton, P/Os Lancaster, Young and Courtis). In March P/O Stewart joined No.600. He was to become one of the most prominent members of the Squadron. An official rugger match was played against a team of Messrs T. Cook & Sons, Bankers. The team of 600 consisted of: P/Os Earnshaw, Massey, Young and Wallcousins and ACs Annan, Branigan, Galloway, Clarkson, Johnson, Durbridge, Berry, Caynes and Evans.

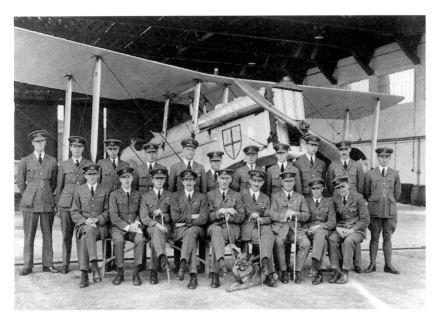

600 Squadron officers in front of a DH9. Standing from left to right: P/O Coates, P/O Ferguson, P/O Burton, P/O Stewart, F/O Vaizey, P/O Brown, P/O Earnshaw, P/O Hackett, P/O Montefiore, P/O Bonner and P/O Larking. Sitting: F/O Massey, F/O Wallcousins, F/L Henderson, F/L Rodney, S/L Guest, F/L Russell, Hon. S/L Grey, F/O McKinley-Hay and F/O Courtis.

It was a disaster for the Bankers' Team; they lost 14-0 and Jenyns wrote: "All thoroughly enjoyed the game and suggestions for another at an early date was made." More serious undertakings also called for the attention of 600. On 28th March P/Os Massey, Young, Wallcousins, Courtis and Stewart went to Eastchurch for a course in "Aerial Gunnery and Bombing". After 27th April a new feature of the Squadron's life was introduced: periodical flying every Tuesday and Thursday evening at Hendon, apart from the weekend flying. Being a member of the Auxiliary Air Force meant one had to spend a lot of free time for the Auxiliary Air Force's and one's own benefit. This included regular tests by the Trade Test Board. At times these would cause disappointment among men who did not meet the standards. On 3rd June six AC2s, who scored 55% and less were remustered to another trade group. In cases where the obligations to the Squadron did not coincide with the demands of one's employer, it also meant resigning one's commission, as did P/O Lancaster in June 1927.

Hendon became "a humming hive of workers" while preparations were made for the great RAF Display staged for 2nd July that year. Now being a "real" Service station, many useful additions and alterations were carried out. Chief amongst them was the appearance of a new Grandstand capable of holding between two to three thousand people. Numerous railings and enclosures had been arranged for the various sections of the public as can be seen on the official map of Hendon. A crowd of about 100,000 people witnessed a most attractive programme, which started with the presentation of the Sassoon Cup at 1100hrs in the morning. The programme took until about 1600hrs. The programme included a message pick-up demonstration, the Air Ministry Race, the RAF Reserve Officers Race, individual aerobatics, an altitude race, an air dog fight, more individual aerobatics, day bombing, air manoeuvres to music, night bombers flying off, crazy flying, a parade of new experimental aircraft, attack and destruction of a kite balloon, parachutists jumping from the wings of a Vickers Vimy, an air battle and the departure of the participating aircraft. All kinds of aircraft were present. A Handley Page Hinaidi, Fairey Foxes, Siskins, DH9a's, Brisfits, Moths, Virginias, Grebes and Gamecocks, ensured a marvellous display. However, as far as the Squadron was concerned, the best part of the show was the last event, in which the men were to play a part. The scene was as follows: "A native town where a small community of European traders has long been established peacefully pursuing its activities. A church has recently been completed. A wave of unrest is sweeping the country, and patrolling aircraft from concentrated air forces are searching the countryside on the lookout for signs of violence by the native populace against isolated white European communities. The time is dawn. A patrolling aircraft observes such an outbreak in a town where the Europeans have been isolated in an old mud fort, and are sending up distress signals; the aeroplane calls for assistance by radio-telephony from the nearest aerodrome (this call was broadcast to the crowd). Meanwhile, the Europeans manage to break out of the fort and under cover of rifle fire by the men the party succeeds in crossing a bridge over the river, and the women and children flee across the open country away from the town. The men follow gradually, holding up their pursuers with rifle fire. At this moment a Squadron of Fairey Fox aeroplanes arrives on the scene and attacks the town and pursuing natives with bombs and machine-gun fire. The attacks are carried out by flight after flight until the bridge is destroyed and the town in ruins, with the exception that the church escaped. Meanwhile aircraft of the two London Squadrons, Auxiliary Air Force (Nos.600 and No.601), arrive and drop food, water and ammunition by parachute to the European refugees. Shortly afterwards a relief force arrives in two troop carrying aircraft (Victorias) which land and deplane reinforcements with machine guns and light howitzers. This force attacks the village by fire from the ground and kills or drives off the few natives who have managed to cross the river. The Vickers Victorias emplane the women and children and convey them to safety". The episode concluded by the sounding of the "Cease Fire" by trumpeters of the RAF, while the town was seen burning in the distance. Four Squadrons took part, No.12 Squadron from RAF Andover, flying with Fairey Foxes under S/L Salt DFC, No. 58 from RAF Worthydown with Vickers Victoria Bombers. This Squadron was commanded by S/L A.T. Harris OBE, AFC, who was to become a man of great fame when he was in charge of Bomber Command during the Second World War. The two Auxiliary Squadrons based at Hendon aerodrome were No.600 City of London Bomber Squadron under S/L The Rt. Hon. Freddie Guest and No.601 County of London Bomber Squadron under S/L Lord Grosvenor. Both bomber Squadrons flew DH9As with Liberty engines. In this event No. 600 Squadron sent up three aircraft, flown by F/Ls Rodney and Jenyns, and P/O Wallcousins. The Squadron planes arrived over the North Western end of the aerodrome in single line and punctually to the scheduled time reached the native town on the aerodrome and then dropped food, water, medicine and ammunition to the refugees, according to plan. It definitely was an excellent demonstration of what well-controlled aircraft could do to protect Europeans from the vicious attacks of brutal natives. It should keep the public reassured that all over the Empire brave aviators were ready to protect Britain's interests. The men of No.600 Squadron were very proud indeed when a letter from Air/Cdre Hearson commended the Squadron's good work and reached S/L Guest shortly after the Display:

> "My dear Guest,
> In addition to the various official telegrams of congratulations which have been published in my orders, I have received a personal letter from the Commander in Chief, in which he says: "The accuracy with which the Auxiliary Squadrons dropped parachutes showed a high degree of training which was remarkable on their very first appearance at the Display". The part taken by your Squadron in the Display this year was only a small one, but in my opinion, it could not have been carried out better than it was, and I feel confident that the bigger part your Squadron will take in future years will be equally successfully accomplished and will earn you a similar well deserved praise to that which I quote above. My own congratulations to you on this success,
> Yours sincerely
> J.G. Hearson

As this was the first year of the Auxiliary Air Force participating, all those who had been responsible for the new Air Force were pleased with what Jenyns called "the value of our part in such wonderful and impressive performances of air supremacy". After the first Display a lot of changes took place in the Squadron. Regulars came and went as part of the policy of posting personnel. Leading Aircraftmen were promoted to Corporals who proudly had their wives, mothers or girlfriends sew their newly won badges of rank on their uniforms. Even romance needed the attention of the Squadron: LAC Hill married (with permission) Edith Emily Jones (Spinster). Others excelled in rather dangerous undertakings: AC1 Evans attended a Parachute Course at Henlow. The same year another Air Pageant took place. It was at Birmingham and F/O

Henderson was asked to supervise the Medical Services of the local General Hospitals on duty during the Pageant. Unfortunately thick fog made it impossible for him to fly any further than Daventry. Not being allowed to land on the drome the following morning he proceeded overnight by road. Some units decided it was suicidal to fly on, or even attempt to fly to Northolt. This time the Birmingham Air Territorials, as the programme called No.605 Squadron, carried out the same sortie as Nos. 600 and 601 had done at Hendon. Again the natives were shattered and the Europeans saved.

The 1927 Annual Camp for both 600 and 601 Squadrons was at Lympne in Kent. The Squadron again started a thorough preparation and an advance party proceeded to Lympne from Hendon on 2nd August to arrange things before the Squadron's arrival four days later. At Hendon on the morning of 6th August there was a lot of excitement permeating the air. Machines were out all ready to fly to Lympne. Lorries were loaded up with the baggage and other essentials needed at Camp. For those travelling by rail or road the weather was not much of a problem, but for the pilots it could mean delay and disaster. A fairly heavy ground mist clung around the country and the earlier weather reports had been quite unfavourable. Everything was ready for a start and when at last the "all clear" signal was given all went off. The Squadron Avro formation proceeded first, led by Henderson, then came the two DH9A-Flights, led respectively by F/L's Dalton and Jenyns. The adjutant brought up the rear as "beater up". All went well until they reached the hilly district around Biggin Hill and almost without a warning they were forced to descend to only a few hundred feet, over country strange to many and some of the pilots with only a few flying hours to their credit. Some of the DH9a's climbed above the clouds and proceeded by compass direction and then descending again found themselves fighting the elements. The Avro's continued at low level and endeavoured to pass down the valley of the railway cutting through Biggin Hill with the intention of striking the main Southern Railway line running direct to Ashford. At this time, in parts the fog was right down on the hill tops and only the valley itself was clear. To make matters worse soon after entering the valley it started to rain and visibility was now very poor, in fact only a few hundred feet. Therefore it was hardly surprising that four Avro's were forced down. The pilots needed skill and determination to ensure that no aircraft were lost due to the adverse weather conditions.

Flying to Lympne in poor weather P/O Hackett ran into trouble. He soon found that he would not be able to reach the aerodrome. Hackett tried to land his plane near Crowborough. The Avro 504K, one of a batch of 100 built by Hewlett and Blondeau Ltd, came down in the tree tops. P/O Hackett got out without a scratch and after hard work by the ground staff the aeroplane flew again within two weeks. Of course the incident was great news, as could be read in an article by a special correspondent the next day.

P/O's Hackett, Curtis, Earnshaw and Young had to use all their wits to achieve a safe landing. Hackett made a landing in a tree top in a Kentish cottage garden near Crowborough and escaped unscratched. For the press, the trip from Hendon to the South was something like a hero's undertaking and the following day vivid reports were written about the Squadron's achievements:

THE POSTMAN AS AN AIR BOMBER
London "Terriers" fly in the fog
A TREE-TOP LANDING
From our special correspondent, Lympne-Monday

"London's Territorial airmen, they are referred to, unofficially, I believe, as the Airedale Terriers – are having their jolliest time of the year in camp at the aerodrome here. I met my postman in one of the great hangars. For a fortnight he is an airman. In camp are No.601 County of London Squadron, commanded by S/L Lord Edward Grosvenor and No.600 City of London Squadron under S/L F.E. Guest. Among the airmen are Bank clerks, insurance clerks, manufacturers' agents, civil servants, tailors' cutters surveyors, and piano salesmen. "It was a thrilling time coming down", said S/L Guest, "and the journey showed just how valuable the training is that the men are getting. One pilot, who a year ago knew nothing about aircraft, showed wonderful judgement in a very difficult situation. The fog forced him to fly at a height of about 700 feet, and then, unexpectedly, he came across a hill near Crowborough. There was no time to do anything. He had to choose between crashing into a house or settling down on the tree tops. He made a remarkable landing in the top of a tree and escaped injury, although the plane was somewhat damaged. The other three aeroplanes which made forced landings were not. The great feature of training is that there is no drill. Of course, our men know how to form fours and how to handle a rifle, but beyond that we do not worry. We are concentrating on becoming the most efficient people in handling aircraft. During the time we are in camp now every man will go up in the air. They will be taught aerial gunnery and will receive instruction in wireless". In one corner of the hangar I saw a bank clerk, who is now an experienced rigger, in oil-bespattered dungarees, smiling and whistling "I am an airman" while he put the finishing touches to the tuning of a wing. Examining a great 400 h.p. engine was a garage mechanic, who for the rest of this year has to be content with putting oil in a 2-seater car. Imagine the gleam of joy in his eyes as he produced the roar from this monster engine".

As reported in the article, the other three pilots came down safely.
Earnshaw picked on Haley Morris' Estate. Henderson, after a good
deal of compass flying, struck the coast near Bexhill. Later it was
discovered that his compass had not been "swung" which explained
the error of navigation. After a landing at Bexhill and a cigarette, he
arrived in Lympne a little late for lunch. The DH9a's safely reached
Lympne. However, Vaisey, on landing there, had some conflict with
a ridge and swept off his undercarriage. Jumping out, he walked to
the tarmac. As if nothing had happened the Squadron began its
training. However, the weather decided to play a part. Southern
England had never before been the scene of such terrible weather!
It was so horrible that the newspapers reported about it with big
headlines.

The Evening Standard said:

"WILDEST SEAS OF A WILD SUMMER!!
Bathing stopped and beach cleared of
holiday makers.
AMAZING COAST SCENES.

For the men of the Squadron this meant little flying and much
waiting. Little else remained but to listen to what was taught during
courses and the Squadron diarist knew little else to do but describe
how Lympne had changed since he first visited it: "Lympne is a
familiar name to many of us being an old wartime station, recalling
memories of the days when we used to put in there during the war
before leaving from the last "opping orf ground" in England to
proceed overseas. Many changes have taken place at this station
since those days. The old hangars have been pulled down and fresh
ones put up at the south-west side of the aerodrome. The 'drome is
equipped with red lights and lighthouses for the guidance at night
of various air liners that may have to call in for petrol or other neces-
sities. From the aerodrome situated on the top of a little plateau one
has a fine view of the coast as far as Dungeness to the West and
Eastwards to Hythe, Folkestone and Dover, inland the wooded
countryside of Kent. Such were our surroundings and a great place
for a camp even in wet weather!"

The press wrote heroic stories about the daring exploits of the
dashing Auxiliaries. Air enthusiasts and men with great knowledge
of aviation came to witness what the Auxiliaries were capable of.

Another mishap occurred when P/O Vaisey landed his DH9A at Lympne on 6th August 1928. He did not notice a ridge, came in too low, lost his undercarriage and subsequently made, what was called "a perfect belly-landing".

Major Turner wrote a half page article in the Daily Telegraph of 9th August: "LONDON AIRMEN IN CAMP. Good flying in Difficulties. Auxiliary Force Progress". A journalist of the Times vividly reported on 10th August: "THE AUXILIARY AIR FORCE – London Squadrons at Lympne". He described the "severe tests" the men had to endure and explained with great zeal that in spite of the atrocious weather the airmen took to the air almost every day. The Evening News of 22nd August was duly impressed by the courage of the men when he wrote: "CLERK-PARACHUTISTS, London's men training as airmen", and informed his readers that the men spent one day doing parachute descents. He said: "So keen were the officers and other ranks that there was a queue waiting to go up. These City clerks showed no fear when they took up their position on the wings of the planes and waited for the pilot to give the signal to go after he had got more than 1000 feet up. Twenty parachute descents were successfully made". During the camp the Squadron was visited by Fairey Foxes from Andover which had come to Lympne to fly under-secretary of State for Air Sir Philip Sassoon from Lympne to Manston and back. Diarist Jenyns recorded an amusing incident that took place with one of the sleek Foxes: "This machine and its pilot had earlier in the day endeavoured to reach Tangmere aerodrome but was forced to return to Lympne owing to very thick weather. While at tea a machine suddenly shot out of the mist over the aerodrome and all ran out to see who it was. It turned out to be one of our Auxiliary Air Force pilots back from Tangmere on a cross country. Our Fairey Fox pilot was the next to shoot across the aerodrome and set off for Tangmere. Such is only related to show the spirit of this new force and the efficient manner in which the personnel endeavour to perform their duties". During the week in camp the Squadron organised a visit of A-Flight of Avro's to No.605 Squadron, who had their camp at Manston. The pilots flew to Manston where they had lunch and were entertained by No.605. On the return journey that afternoon they ran into very thick weather and from Dover onwards flew over the sea below the tops of the cliffs. All aircrew enjoyed the trip very much. A return visit was made by No. 605 Squadron the next day. At the camp F/L Henderson ran his Medical Centre. Sick parades were recorded: 29 auxiliary and 14 regular airmen. P/O Courtiss had to be admitted to sick quarters for ten days after he bashed his head in a crash. Only one leg injury had to be taken to Shorncliffe Hospital. All officers were found to be up to medical standards during their annual Medical Examination. Considering the very poor weather it was gratifying to record that no serious illnesses occurred. The many civilian and military visitors were impressed with Henderson's Medical Section.

Sport competitions between members of the Squadron were an integral part of the camp and various games were played. Physical fitness was very important for all. It enhanced comradeship between the Auxiliaries and showed the men the importance of competition. Besides it was a great social event with the ladies (Officers') and wives (NCOs' and ORs') present to cheer the men and take part in some of the games. Sports allowed men of all ranks and trades to compete as equals and it would not make any difference if the lowest form of airman beat the Commanding Officer in a fair game. On 17th August was the Camp's Sports Day and according to the diary it was a very important event. The event was meticulously organised and a group of officers, NCOs and Other Ranks ensured fair play. Strict rules were made and high ranking officers acted as officials. Some of the games asked for physical fitness, others for good co-operation and in a few cases it was important to do some clever thinking. The programme showed many different challenges:

Auxiliary Air Force Sports, Lympne 17th August 1927 at 3 p.m.

Officials: S/L Lord Grosvenor and S/L Guest, F/Ls Bowen and Rodney. Stewards: Sgt Collins, Cpl Ryall, AC Wallbridge, LAC White. Clerk of Course: F/O Adams. Starter: F/S Pritchard.

1   100 Yards Handicap.
2   Wheel Barrow Race.
3   Ladies and Gents Cigarette Race.
4   1/2 Mile Inter-Squadron Relay Race; Gents to act as Chariots, Ladies as Drivers.
5   Blindfold Chariot Race 150 yards; 30 yards (put on boots), 30 yards (put on tunic), 30 yards (put on cap), 60 yards (run in).
6   High Jump.
7   First Man on Parade 150 yards.
8   Blindfold Squad Drill (Inter Flight): 4 airmen, 1 instructor to form a squadron. Movements on parade number, quick march, about turn, right form, forward left form, forward halt. Marks will be given for best formation movements to be made by word of command only.
9   Officers Relay Race (Inter Squadron): 1st Competitor to run 50 yards in flying clothing and hand baton to second competitor, who will put on flying clothing and race proceeds as No.1.
10   Throwing the Cricket Ball.
11   Tug of War (Inter Squadron teams of 10 Catch Weights)
12   Open Relay Race to HM Forces 2-220 and 2-440 yards.

The games were a great success and much laughter was heard while men tried to overtake each other, driven by ladies as experienced wheelbarrow drivers.

With the end of the Camp came the Annual Inspection. The Squadrons were inspected by high ranking officers. They were Air/Cdres Felton Holt CMG, DSO, Air Officer Commanding the Auxiliary Air Force, John Hearson CB, CBE, DSO, and Gerrard CMG, DSO, who had succeeded Hearson as AOC AuxAF. They witnessed and judged the results of the exercises. An interesting extra at Lympne was the coming and going of many British and foreign passenger aeroplanes. A Dutch KLM Fokker, an Argosy of Imperial

Air/Cdre John Hearson AOC Auxiliary Air Force walking with S/L The Rt. Hon. Freddie Guest, OC No.600 (City of London) Squadron. Guest commanded No.600 Squadron from 1926 to 1931. After handing over command he was asked to become the first Honorary Air Commodore of No.600 Squadron. Freddie Guest served in this capacity from 1931 – 1936.

Airways and a French airliner. As far as No.600 was concerned the highlight of the Camp occurred when S/L Grosvenor and the rest of No.601 Squadron set fire to their own mess tent. During the last week of the camp a Squadron Guest night was held and a few days later a Station Guest night. At the latter the principal guest was no less than Sir Philip Sassoon himself, who commenced the after-dinner period of speech making and who was followed by OC 601 and OC 600. Then virtually each and every officer was made to speak about anything. A very wild evening ensued and, wrote Jenyns "we finished up by surf-riding in baths, towed around the aerodrome by motor cars". Indeed the Auxiliaries were perfect gentlemen! On 21st August the Auxiliary Squadrons returned home; Hendon became what was recorded as a seething hive of hungry folk. Adjutants of both 600 and 601 were seen smiling again now that their flocks had returned home safely and they were about to be relieved of the responsibility for some time. A photograph of the Squadron with S/L Guest and the Squadron dog in the middle was the visual reminder of a marvellous camp. Another important day in the history of No.600 Squadron was the Lord Mayor's Show in the City of London. On 9th November 1927 the Squadron, as a unit of the City sent a representative contingent. The fuselage of a DH9a was drawn in the procession by the Auxiliary airmen. S/L Guest commanded the Auxiliaries while the Adjutant F/L Rodney took charge of the Regular personnel. The papers said it all: "The Air Force contingent marched with a bearing that in itself was an inspiration". Two days later, on Armistice Day, 11th November, F/O Stewart and four airmen went to the London Troops' Memorial at the Royal Exchange and represented the Squadron.

Sports was an important feature in the Squadron and the Sports and Entertainment Committee worked hard to organise as many games as possible to forge the bond between the men. On 3rd December a rugby football match was played against Barclays Bank. A date was set for next year's Squadron Dinner and members were allowed to bring a guest to be paid for by the person concerned. It was decided to raise a cricket team. In the December issue of "Air" S/L Freddie Guest wrote a foreword to an article by F/L Dalton. Observations were made by Guest, who said: "I feel sure the readers of Air will not fail to notice the salient point of this article. They are the entire absence of fatal and even serious accidents, which speaks volumes for the way in which enthusiasm is tempered by adequate

The annual Lord Mayor's Procession allowed the City of London Squadron to show itself to the public of the City. Here Auxiliaries of the Squadron pull the fuselage of one of the Squadron DH9As through the City. F/L Rodney is in command of the group.

instruction; secondly, the very important part which the Auxiliary Air Force can play in the national system of Air Defence; and thirdly, the need which still exists for additional recruits and for the building up for each Squadron of the Auxiliary Air Force of a permanent organisation comparable to that existing in territorial units in the Army. I should like to add one more vital consideration, namely that the training of the Auxiliary Air Force offers to those patriotic enough to join them opportunities which will undoubtedly have increasing value to those in civilian life. Civilian flying is a new profession, the possibilities of whose development are almost infinite, and in this profession the plums will be for those who have the courage to be pioneers".

After the Christmas vacation the first parade took place on 5th January 1928. The results of the remustering trade test board, held on 20th December 1927 were now known. Two volunteers failed due to lack of experience and were told to study hard for a second try. Internal postings were carried out and some of the regulars left. So did F/O Lamplugh who resigned his commission on appointment to the Reserve. Lamplugh owing to business reasons found that he was unable to carry out the many duties required by the Auxiliary Air Force and reluctantly left. AC Blanche married Mary Mountford and Cpl Rowbotham forged a bond with Lily Gregory. Sgt Donaldson became the very proud father of a daughter called Nancy. Some of the men volunteered as aerial gunners and A.B. Ferguson joined the Squadron as a P/O. Enlistments were quite satisfying for within a couple of weeks ten recruits had joined.

Squadron DH9As ready to take-off from Lympne for a demonstration in formation flying.

In March 1928 His Majesty King Amanullah and Her Majesty Queen Souriya of Afghanistan visited Great Britain. As Their Majesties intended to see a special air display at Hendon the officers of No.600 Squadron received permission to come if they came in uniform. The display was carried out by the RAF and the King left much impressed by the manoeuvres of the aircraft. One sight particularly thrilled the Royals from that far away land: one bomber, having been hit by a fighter, came roaring over with a long trail of black and grey smoke. It was done so professionally, said the papers, that it seemed the aircraft would crash right on the royal dais. Suddenly however, the machine was zoomed and shot up into the sky. His Majesty expressed His great pleasure and appeared tremendously honoured by the fact the British were willing to shoot down an aircraft to amuse Him and his entourage.

On 6th May 1928 the first serious accident in the Squadron took place when P/O Young had a bad crash at Mill Hill in a DH9a. Young had not yet done much solo flying on this type of aircraft and on this particular occasion was carrying out formation flying in the vicinity of the aerodrome. It appeared that he stalled his machine and went into a spinning nose dive. Just as he was near the ground he righted his machine, but owing to lack of height he was unable to get her over the hill. A crash followed and the aircraft burst into flames. As a result of the prompt and gallant action of four Roman Catholic priests, Young was dragged from the wreckage and eventually taken to Hendon Hospital. His injuries were shock, burns to the face and part of the body and a broken ankle. This was exceedingly unfortunate for Young who was liked by all. Of course the local press jumped on the story. "SAVED FROM A BLAZING PLANE! Pilot dragged off wreckage in Mill Hill accident. Student rescuers driven back by the intense heat and fumes!", it said. Photographs of the four priests next to the scarred remains of the aircraft, with a small picture of Young inset in the whole scene made sure that the reader knew how the clergy had saved this airman from certain death. The reporter wrote: "Dressed in their cassocks, with red sashes, they rushed out into the field and one, Brother Streiber, tried to pull the pilot off the burning wreckage on which he had fallen. The heat was so intense that he was driven back, but three others, including Brothers McGough and Van Couteren, joined in the rescue and managed to pull the pilot clear. The rector of the college phoned for the police, ambulance and fire brigade, and more than a mile of hose-pipe was run across the field to the scene. Two doctors who were passing saw the crash and, leaving their motorcar, rushed to the scene". Towards the end of June the Squadron machines were again busy preparing for their part in the Royal Air Force Annual Display which again was to be held at Hendon, on 30th June. In the meantime P/O Young was making good progress to recovery and was in a condition to be moved to Uxbridge RAF Hospital. two days later he went to Osborne House, East Cowes, Isle of Wight for 28 days sick leave. This meant he was not present at the Display to which all members of the Squadron were looking forward. And, as his recovery took much longer than anticipated he was also to miss the greatest event of the year, the Annual Camp.

An even larger crowd than a year earlier attended the Display. Their Majesties the King and Queen were there and no less than six reigning Princes from India attended as well. Six aircraft of the Auxiliary Air Force took part in the show. They were to carry out an aerial attack on structures built on the North side of the aerodrome representing oil wells. Three machines were from 600 and three from 601 Squadron. The 600 Squadron officers taking part in the attack were P/O's Massey, Vaisey and Wallcousins. All three aircraft recorded direct hits. In the programme booklet a vivid description was written about "Event No.12, 5.40, attack on an oil refinery". It read: "A British Aircraft Carrier, which is co-operating with the fleet in enemy waters, has received orders to despatch sufficient aircraft to carry out an effective raid on an enemy oil refinery situated about 20 miles from the coast of the hostile country. The refinery in question is responsible for producing the bulk of the enemy air force's fuel supply, so it is consequently heavily guarded by anti-aircraft guns, and a Kite Balloon for observation purposes. Orders have been issued to an advanced shore base to co-operate in the destruction of the oil refinery. The attack is carried out in the following manner: – A Flight of the Fighters is despatched to carry out a surprise raid on the enemy's anti-aircraft defences, with a view to disorganising them before the arrival of the Bombers. In order to escape observation the Fighters approach the target at an extremely low altitude, but in spite of this manoeuvre an enemy Kite Balloon observes them when they are about a mile away and signals their approach to the ground. Before the Balloon can be hauled down the Fighters arrive and shoot it down. They now carry out a machine-gun attack on the anti-aircraft gunners, inflicting heavy casualties. Meanwhile A-Flight of Fleet Reconnaissance aircraft, armed with high explosive bombs, have left the carrier; on arrival they bomb the target, breaking it up badly and causing one or two small fires. Bombers from the shore base then arrive on the scene, and dropping high explosive and incendiary bombs cause a general conflagration. The raid having been successful, the aircraft disperse, the Fighters bringing up the rear to ward off any possible attack by hostile aircraft. The units taking part are: 405 (Fleet Fighter) Flight, 443 (Composite) Flight, 600 (City of London) Bomber Squadron Auxiliary Air Force and 601 (County of London) Bomber Squadron Auxiliary Air Force."

The story ended with an interesting note: "*Owing to the possible*

danger from falling tackle and burning fabric, the observer in the
balloon is a dummy".

The Display was a great success for the Auxiliaries, 600 Squadron
scoring direct hits on the target. The observer was a dummy indeed!

Summer Camp at Lympne (1927). S/L Freddie Guest, his dog, his officers, NCOs
and Other Ranks. Note the officers with their canes, some wearing breeches and
puttees.

The Summer Camp was again to be at Lympne as in the previous
year. A visit to the aerodrome about this time, after convincing the
MP orderly at the gate that one really was an Auxiliary Airman, found
the regular personnel of the Squadron, tearing about here and there,
collecting this and that, all in readiness for the visit to Lympne from
4th to 19th August. Again the eyes of the press were upon the
Squadron. The Evening News wrote: "CITY CLERKS AS AIRMEN"
and "SKY-FIGHTING HOLIDAY BY THE SEA" as if 600 Squadron
was having a leisurely week or two. The paper also added that
"many of the airmen have arranged for wives and families to take
their holidays at Folkestone, or Hythe, or Sandgate – three pleasant
seaside towns near Lympne – so that they can visit them in the
evening when the day's work is over". When the Camp had finished
the Times of Tuesday 7th August 1928 wrote:

LONDON UNITS IN TRAINING; THE CAMP AT LYMPNE.

"The two London Squadrons of the Auxiliary Air Force are now in camp at the aerodrome having arrived during the weekend. There is no question that these two units, 600 (City of London) and 601 (County of London) Bomber Squadrons, are justifying the experiment of instituting Territorial airmen. After watching this new force from its foundation I was agreeably surprised today to find the progress made in three years in making military pilots from amateur club members and technical airmen from an assortment of professions and trades, ranging from civil servants to bank clerks and from clerks to shop managers. Today the Adjutant took the Squadron a stage further and led them out on Squadron formation practice for the first time, and later when they came high over the aerodrome I had a chance to appraise the piloting skill now reached. It was exceptionally good, far better than I expected. Considering that the Auxiliary Air Force has to get its practice more or less spasmodically at weekends it appears that machines embodying the most modern facilities should be allotted to them rather than those of the war period, which are certainly not so safe".

Tea in the hangar for the NCOs, Other Ranks and their wives.

The Times "Aeronautical Correspondent" of course was referring to the De Havilland DH9a aircraft the Squadron flew. At this stage of the history of the Squadron it is interesting to have a closer look at this "fighting machine". Peter Stewart, who flew this aircraft and who later became OC600 from 1934 to1937, gave a vivid account of the aircraft and its habits. The aircraft was fitted with a 500hp Liberty, water-cooled engine and remarkable as it might seem nowadays, the undercarriage suspension system and the tail skid depended on many strands of elastic. It was an easy aircraft for the pilot to get into, as the first step was not very high and the cockpit was fairly roomy and contained only a few instruments. The edge of the cockpit was upholstered with leather such as one would see in the old London Hansom Cabs. The view the pilot had was similar to that of a canary as one gazed through a sea of wires, landing wires, flying wires and incidental wires. In the centre section was a gravity tank containing some twenty gallons which was fed from the main tank of 500 gallons which all but sat on the pilots knee. The two feed pumps were intriguing in that they were two wind driven propellers in the centre section and the flow of petrol from the tank to the gravity tank was controlled by the pilot with a three-way cock. The pilot had ample knowledge that the gravity tank was full, as not only was there an intriguing little rod with a blob of paint which traversed a tube some 3" long projecting from the top of the tank, but there was an overflow pipe which threw a cloud of petrol over the pilot's head as soon as it had had enough. The ignition system, by modern standards, was elementary in that it depended on two batteries for the dual ignition system, and it was advisable when throttled back to run on one battery only, as there was always the fear that the batteries would have run down should one be called on for the emergency use of one's engine, and for this reason too the wise pilot always kept his gravity tank filled. On the rudder the aircraft responded quite reasonably and with the right use of tail trim the fore and aft movement was quite pleasant. A turn of the wheel allowed the weight of the engine to take charge, but laterally it needed the strength of Samson to move the aircraft at anything higher than the hangar base. The excrescences stuck on the aircraft, made it look rather like a Christmas tree. There was a parachute flare tube, a wireless aerial tube, a generator, a large exhaust pipe by the side of the engine and various other gadgets which were stuck on as additional requirements which a light day bomber would need.

The safety equipment consisted of a broad belt, and there was no Sutton harness. There was a ring in the middle of the floor of the rear cockpit onto which the Air Gunner clipped himself before attempting to manage the Scarff ring gun mounting. The aircraft was more than comfortable at all altitudes and when we were in the process of re-equipping the Wapiti the DH9a could, at any altitude, out-distance the Wapiti and with much greater comfort for the man in control. There was a small wind screen to provide some comfort for the pilot, but with no heating, dressed in a Sidcot suit, with flying boots, parachute, the movements of the pilot were seriously restricted. The means of communication to the brave men that ventured into the rear seat was by means of a Gosport speaking tube. However, if the chap at the back happened to be on wireless duty, the means of communication was by a cord tied round his wrist, which the pilot pulled and then handed a hastily written note. In air to ground fire to move the Lewis gun, clear the stoppage or

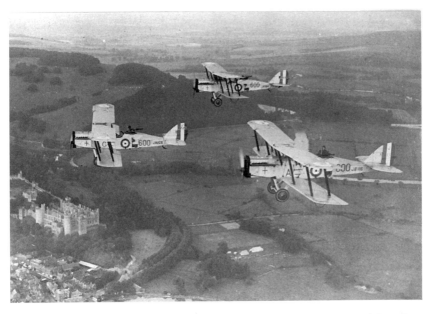

14. Three 600 Squadron DH9As in an immaculate formation over Arundel Castle – Sussex. The aircraft are J8116, J8223 and J8184. All three aircraft were part of a batch of 130, built by Westland (33), de Havilland (25), Short Brothers (18), Parnall (18), Saunders (18) and Blackburn (18). J8116 was built by de Havilland, J8184 by Parnall and J8223 by Blackburn. The number 600 is clearly visible on the fuselage. Two air gunners are behind their Lewis guns; the air gunner in front seems to have more interest in the photographer.

empty the collector box was almost a day's work. The poor fellow, also in Sidcot suit, flying boots and a parachute to his stomach, had to imitate an earth worm and squeeze himself down the fuselage in order to lie full length and gaze through the floor to get his eyes on the bomb sight. The camera was set on boxes of plates and was hand operated, the box of plates being changed in the air as necessary; continuous film had not yet been introduced. The method of flying in those days was from the moment of opening the throttle to expect a forced landing and to fly accordingly. It was an excellent school and those who remembered these days knew of no more satisfactory feeling than a perfect three point landing in a DH9a, when one was lucky enough to pull it off and did not give the elastic on the undercarriage or the tail skid too much work.

The most daring achievement of the Squadron during the Summer Camp at Lympne was an attack against the Air Ministry in London itself, which amazed the public by its audacity. The air defence of London was considered impregnable. The success of the Auxiliaries was great news. On 14th August the headlines in the Daily Express screamed:

DARING COUP BY THE "ENEMY".
BOMBS DROPPED ON THE AIR MINISTRY
VOLUNTEERS FEAT – EIGHT OUT OF TEN RAIDS REPULSED

"The greatest air manoeuvres in history, in which more than three hundred RAF machines are taking part, began at 6 p.m. last night, when "war" was declared between "Eastland", a continental power and "Westland", of which London is the capital. A spectacular coup was made by the "enemy" in full daylight within an hour of declaration of war. The Air Ministry, the nerve centre of the defence, was bombed by a Squadron which, helped by the clouds, had until then eluded the fighting Squadrons of the homeland. They were attacked as they approached the Ministry, but they claim success. This remarkable feat was accomplished by No. 600 (City of London) Squadron, one of the Territorial Squadrons, which are taking part in these operations for the first time. Twenty percent of the personnel are regulars, the rest are volunteers, clerks, brokers, and postmen."

At this point a story, depicting the typical Squadron spirit, should be mentioned. In the 1928 Air Defence of Great Britain exercises, instructions were given by one of the commanders of an Auxiliary Air Force Squadron that the aircraft were to be on the tarmac with engines warmed up by 0500hrs on the next morning. What a buzz of excitement followed for all ranks, for No.600 was to make its debut into the realm of the Bomber Squadrons by a mock air raid on London. The evening gave every promise of favourable weather on the morrow, and most of the Auxiliaries turned in early, as 0330hrs was the time set for the commencement of activities. But the morning weather was quite adverse to expectations, and a heavy drizzling rain prevailed, with banks of low cloud blotting out the aerodrome at intervals. At 0315hrs the Adjutant was expected to give his final decisions and all were anxiously waiting what the Great Medicine Man was to decide. So bad was the weather that all expected a wash-out, but the Adjutant in his infinite wisdom decided to carry on with the programme in the hope that dawn would bring an improvement. True to type the Auxiliary airmen duly mustered in the hangar at 0330hrs as originally ordered, but to the utter amazement of the Adjutant hardly one Squadron member was properly dressed. The great majority had shown up with their greatcoats over their pyjamas, anticipating to return to their bed within a few minutes. Asked why they had turned out in this rather strange outfit, the men gave three clear reasons. Firstly, being woken up and seeing the weather conditions they were sure that the programme would be cancelled, making it rather unnecessary to dress up in air force blue. Secondly, having left their beds anyway, they intended to drink their morning cocoa, rather than have it thrown away. Thirdly, by showing up, though somewhat irregularly dressed, they at least had shown their good intentions and not let their officers and the Adjutant in particular, down. On their being informed that the programme still stood as arranged, and that now there was no time for them to get properly dressed until after the Squadron had taken off, they just gave one rousing cheer, opened the hangar doors and had the aircraft out in record time. Another Auxiliary Air Force Squadron was housed in the next bay of the hangar and although the zero hour for their programme was later, some of its personnel arrived at the aerodrome in time to see their friendly rivals dashing around in mud-begrimed pyjamas. The chaff that followed can well be imagined. However, by dusk the following day fate brought the chaff to bear on the other Squadron and they of the pyjamas had their sweet revenge.

One Sunday morning in June 1929 Cecil Tedder was in the back seat of a DH9A taking off from Hendon with Peter Stewart as the pilot. With great difficulty they just cleared the Officers' Mess roof much to the relief of Tedder and no doubt to Peter's too, but worse was to follow. When they landed, they bounced twice, with dire results to the undercarriage – the elastic broke. Those who recall the DH9A will know what this meant and can probably guess the reason – the plane was still carrying the ballast, the weights carried on a bar abaft the centre section, carried of course, when flying solo to counteract the weighty water-cooled engine. The chippy rigger

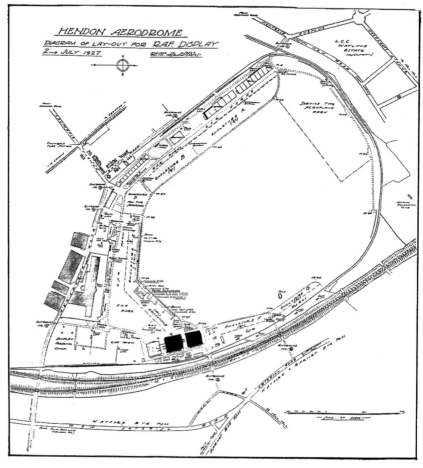

This diagram of lay-out for the Air Display on 2th July 1927 shows the hangars of Nos. 600 and 601 Squadrons on the East side of the aerodrome. The railway line which ran along the Eastern edge of the airfield at times caused a fit to the aircrew as well as the railway engine drivers if the approach for a landing turned out to be "somewhat low".

NCO, Cpl. Durbridge, had a few not very kind words to say of the crew. It was a silly mistake but one which Stewart would never make again in his flying career. In October 1929 the Squadron said farewell to its DH9a's and changed to the Westland Wapiti. The aircraft incorporated as many DH9a parts as possible. It had served well with No. 84 Squadron in Iraq and was expected to be the perfect aircraft for the Auxiliaries. It was a metal structured, fabric covered two-seater general-purpose biplane. The Wapiti had a 480hp Bristol Jupiter engine which was to give the aircraft a maximum speed of 135 and a cruising speed of 110mph. Its range was 360 miles and its service ceiling 20,600 feet. Armed with one fixed Vickers gun forward and a Lewis gun aft, carrying a bomb load of 500 lb., the Wapiti was to serve the Squadron in the years to come.

By the end of the Twenties the days of the DH9a were numbered. Soon a new aeroplane, the Westland Wapiti, became the new Squadron aircraft. Here F/O Hackett and his gunner Cpl Nicholson are ready for take-off. Note the large "600" on the fuselage behind the gunner.

CHAPTER 2

INTO THE THIRTIES.
1930 TO 1935

During the 1930 RAF Display 600 Squadron participated again. Flying was so perfect that no difference was visible between "Regular" and "Week-end" Air Force. This sometimes led to amusing incidents between the Services. Something like this happened at the Display and was recorded for posterity: "An airman of No.600 Squadron was rubbing imaginary specks from the engine cowling of a Wapiti, when officers of the RAF approached, obviously interested in the standard of maintenance of Auxiliary Air Force aircraft. Being questioned the airman informed the officers that indeed he was an Auxiliary airman as the officers had so rightfully assumed. Then followed a bombardment of questions as to his trade: 'Did he like the Auxiliary Air Force? Was he keen on flying?' And I suppose you Auxiliary fellows come in for a good deal of chaff from outsiders and other territorial formations?', to which the airman replied: 'Oh no, Sir, not at all, for you see we are so efficient that they think we really are RAF!', and with a pukka salute, he carried on removing further imaginary specks. The Regular officers walked away quietly, and pondering".

Reference to the RAF was a constant source of amusement and, at times, annoyance for the Squadron personnel. If any aircraft, Service or civilian, flew over poultry farms, piggeries, garden fetes, horse breeding grounds, manor houses, golf courses, baby shows, and the nearest aerodrome happened to be the home of the local Auxiliary Air Force, the poor adjutant was usually in for a terrifying time. He would be on the phone constantly, trying to pacify irate owners or sponsors who were threatening to use all their contacts with top brass or even both Houses or the Crown to have the RAF

CITY OF LONDON'S BOMBERS

1st May 1932. The "City of London (Bomber) Squadron of the Auxiliary Air Force held a church parade at St. Botolph's Bishopsgate yesterday. The RAF Central Band in dress uniform accompanied the members of the Squadron and is seen entering the church while the public watches the airmen".

disbanded within the next 24 hours if this practice was not to cease immediately. Such complaints usually came at a time when the Auxiliary personnel were at their civilian employment and their aircraft locked behind the hangar doors. On occasions, however, where the offender belonged to an Auxiliary Air Force Squadron, his lesson was complete by the time the Adjutant had finished with him. In one case a complaint during a weekend had an amusing climax. On being officially investigated, for the alleged "Giant Bomber" that had disturbed a brooding hen and shaken the chimney pot off the owner's house usually proved to have been a Moth from a light plane club.

S/L Will Cardew has had a very long connection with 600 Squadron. In one of the Association magazines he remembered the days when he became an Auxiliary airman. The cold and foggy morning of early November 1930 and the punctuality of the steam trains of those days were directly responsible for his becoming 800221, AC2 (ACH u/t) on the 8th of December that year. At Friern Barnet, amongst the other ten or fifteen people to be pushed into an already crowded carriage, was John Wright, an erstwhile school friend of Cardew with a "Flight" magazine tucked under his arm. Conversation in the train turned to flying. The logical outcome was mention of the Auxiliary Air Force and what it had to offer. While passing the police station at Bishopsgate he remembered having seen a poster depicting DH9a's in formation and advertising the Auxiliary Air Force, so he made inquiries. Will was directed to Finsbury Barracks. On arrival at his office Cardew phoned what he knew as the T.H.Q. (Town Headquarters) and spoke with someone who invited Cardew to call there at lunch time. This he did and in the process ascertained some surprising facts. The Flight Sergeant, by the name of Frank Pritchard, was a cousin by marriage to Will's managing director; No.600 Squadron was not anxious that he or any other chap who just popped in should join them but he might be considered eligible to join in one of the lowest categories. All this happened long before Selection Boards were formed and the applicants actually had to compete for vacancies.

On the evening of 8th December 1930 Will Cardew was duly sworn in by the Adjutant F/L Tim Healey, and welcomed by all, not forgetting those in charge of the bar and refreshments upstairs. He paid his first sub to the Sports and Entertainments Club and he remembers it took a long time to get the hang of things – whether the S&E Club was the Squadron or vice-versa. There was a game in progress at the bar the end of which foxed him. It was called "Pig" and the chaps were referring to each other as "Snake", "Stew" and "Hib". Curious was the jargon used by the men – "One Eye", "One Donker", "Paper" and, finally roars of laughter followed by "Come on, Bob, sign here!!" This seemed to be a happy brand of soldiering until a new face suddenly came round the corner and shouted: "On Parade!" Face and voice Will Cardew got to know only too well. With some other characters called "Erks" and other fancy descriptions, Cardew was handed over for basic instruction in filing and other forms of higher engineering to a regular known as "Ginger".

It appeared that T.H.Q. nights were Mondays and Thursdays whilst at weekends one was expected at Hendon. Directions to Hendon were casually given: "Take the tube to Colindale, turn left and follow your nose. You can smell the castor oil as you come out of the Station. Follow the smell and you are there". Cardew did and still can remember the inner excitement. On arrival at the gate he was directed to the 600 hangar but was saved a long walk when someone offered him a lift, a welcoming gesture which he was to meet everywhere on the Squadron. At the hangar he sought out "Ginger" who found him some overalls in the Stores, took him round the hangar to see the "kites" and explain their innards. Then Will Cardew was attached to a party of Auxiliaries who were assisting in the top overhaul of a Wapiti and pretty soon was learning how to remove a pot from the Jupiter radial engine, clean the piston crown and ring grooves. He was taught how to file decently in order to be able to fit the rings; meanwhile he was to get cracking cleaning the carbon out of the tar pot (cylinder). The Auxiliary Air Force was definitely more than Sports and Entertainment only! One Saturday afternoon in December Ginger told Cardew to put on a parachute for his very first trip in the Wapiti. His pilot was F/L Robert Faulds, who was to lose his life in a sad civilian air crash on 20th February 1935. The Wapiti took off and went up to 6,000 feet. What a fine sight it was for Cardew, fleecy cotton wool for miles and miles. He had even forgotten the warning before he took off: "Remember you will have to wash it out yourself", for he was so delighted that he never got sick. These were exciting days, no runways, no petrol pumps. In fact the Air Force had just changed from 2 gallon cans to 50 gallon hand propelled Bowsers.

Those were the days of plenty of fun taking off and landing on the often soggy surface. Pilots said that a landing was a bit like a controlled emergency landing. When Cardew was first warned for a weekend camp he had visions of crowded bell tents, but this turned out to be a mistake. A comfortable barrack room was provided. Those who went to the City on Saturday mornings arrived after lunch in civvies with a suitcase containing the fancy-cut riding breeches specially altered to suit their individual taste but not so as to outrage the Flight Sergeant. They wore jackets with stiff choker collars obviously designed to maintain the "'head up" attitude and those dyed discarded horse bandages called puttees. At some unearthly hour on a Sunday a chap called the Orderly Sergeant blew in, made one hell

Three Hawker Harts of No. 600 Squadron. These three aircraft were built by Vickers Ltd.

of a din on the empty coal container and bawled: "Wakey, wakey". Then followed a working parade, march off to the hangars and so to work. The highlight of the year undoubtedly was Annual Training. It was usually preceded some time before by speculation as to the venue and in 1931 it was again popular Tangmere.

About this time of the year the value of F/S Pritchard became obvious beyond doubt for it was he who used to write to one's employer, and to novitiates such as Cardew it was flattering that his boss should be given the impression that Cardew's services at camp were really quite indispensable for the efficiency of the Squadron nay, the very safety of the Realm. At camp the men would work like Trojans under the leadership of men like then Acting Corporal John Wright, who took Cardew to his first Camp at Tangmere in his old Citroen Cloverleaf with a piece of string attached to the accelerator pedal to ensure its return, as the spring was rather weak.

The Camp was, as said earlier, the highlight in an Auxiliary's life. All would look forward to two weeks on an RAF aerodrome at the coast; it was like a child promised a coveted present. During this

Tangmere, August 1932.
From left to right: F/O G.F. Anderson, F/L A.B. Ferguson , P/O Viscount Carlow, F/O J.B. Campbell-Orde, F/O N.T. Tangye, F/O G.H. Compton, F/L P.G. Stewart, F/O N.C. Singer, S/L S.B. Collett, F/L E.A. Healy, F/O G.P. Kerr, F/O G.C. Bonner, F/O R. Hiscox, P/O R.F.G. Lea, P/O P.S. Norris, P/O. J.M. Wells, F/O The Hon. R.N. Frankland and F/O W.H. Wetton.

period the Squadron came into its own – each man proving his particular abilities, and the Squadron as a whole its remarkable efficiency – for flying maintenance of aircraft, engines, guns, wireless equipment etc. Organisation of routine and administration were carried out entirely by Auxiliaries, with the RAF personnel of the Squadron remaining in the background in an advisory capacity, only acting when some large obstacle was met with, and of course filling in time when aircraft were flying or on dud flying days with lectures and ground instruction. Inevitably all good things came to an end after 15 days and the last day of each annual camp was looked on with deep regret by the Auxiliaries. For the Regulars, however, the last day was the signal that in a few days they would be away on Summer leave. Well earned indeed, for no Regular in the Service Unit was called upon to exercise so much self-sacrifice as the one who served with an Auxiliary Air Force Squadron. But to those serving, the knowledge that they formed the hub about which the wheel in the form of their Auxiliary Air Force Squadron revolves was ample recompense for their efforts. Auxiliary 800.101, AC2 C.W. Kirby, who joined the Squadron for the duration of four years with effect from 2nd July 1928, gave a vivid description of the annual camps that took place at Tangmere in 1929, '30 and '31: "We had our last camp with the De Havilland DH9a. I recollect the Adjutant, F/L Russell, pronouncing a valediction on the old DH9a to the assembled Squadron and expressing the sorrow of us all at the old lady's demise. At the same camp the same officer made less generous comments when, on the last day, the aircraft were being flown off one by one to Hendon. A sort of utility version of the 9, known to us as the Ice Box, was taxiing past the aircraft park when the wind caught it and virtually uncontrollable (no brakes in those days) it charged into the other kites. Unless you are personally involved in repairing the damage there is something quite fascinating about propellers chewing up bracing wires and canvas. The Adjutant's language rose majestically to the occasion, but sad to relate the spares had to be fetched from Barnham Junction station, where they had already been packed in a railway van, and some of us spent exceedingly busy hours on rebuilding jobs".

At Tangmere the Other Ranks had four accommodation blocks, each of two storeys and exceedingly comfortable by any standard. Allocation was one block to each of A, B, C, and HQ Flights. Each block was set in a grass island suitably embellished with flower beds and the layout lent itself admirably to inter-flight nocturnal warfare. It was in fact dangerous to leave one's sash window open on the ground floor, since it represented an open invitation for the decanting within the barrack room of the contents of a dustbin or fire bucket from the neighbouring block – usually the preliminary to a full scale attack. At the end of the camp there would be a "formal" display of the trophies "won". They were displayed on lockers and by the bedside. There was some evidence of vandalism – it is not easy to believe that a road danger sign could have been retrieved after genuine loss, or that spend-a-penny machines could have been acquired other than with the expertise of the Fitters. A big step forward at Tangmere, as compared to Lympne, was a dispensation which permitted the wearing of plain civilian clothes off duty. But the wearing of hats remained compulsory. It was a regrettable fact that the well-dressed citizen airman off duty might have possessed only a bowler and that this hat would take a lot of space in the issue kitbag. In consequence almost all the men were hatless. However, airmen working in the mysterious fastnesses of stockbrokers' offices and issuing houses were not easily foxed.

Pretty soon the Squadron cricket team had been persuaded to hand over their caps for the common good and in no time a system was organised whereby a gent in plus fours and cricket cap would clock out of the guard room and pass his hat back through a hole in the hedge for "next please". No wonder airmen did so well escaping from POW camps. Others went out over the hedge at Shripney Road, and back the same way. Authority met the crisis of the hats by inviting a hatter from Chichester to offer his entire stock of cloth caps to reluctant buyers at around 2s. 6d. a time.

In 1931 command passed to S/L Collett, who previously served in 601 Squadron. Flying time for the Squadron had risen to 1700 hours, flown on the Westland Wapiti, undertaken at weekends and during the annual camp. Annual training invariably coincided with the Air Defence of Great Britain Exercise, and naturally the Squadron participated. Pretty lethal they were with their rows of parsnips strung underneath the wings. It was no real hardship to be awakened before dawn with a cup of strong sweet cocoa, all ground crews

No.600 Squadron Rugby Football Team. Standing l/r: G.R. Hunter, S.J. Hennings, J. Eames, G.M. Beer, F.H. Kelly, Madle. Seated l/r: Lambert, L. Styles, Peter Stewart, N. Berry, F.H. Styles, G. Thomas, F. Swaine. On the ground J.A. Stewart-Garden and L.H. Styles.

were on the job to ensure that the Squadron could be airborne at first light.

There always seemed to be the early morning mist and the heavy dews which made the operation at times an overcoat job, and for the background music the very satisfying exhaust note of the Liberties swelling into a crescendo as one by one they were started and warmed up and then the climax, when all nine aircraft were airborne and individual exhausts were lost in the rumble of an aggregate horsepower of no less than 3,600. And so for the ground crews it was back to the barrack blocks to clean up for breakfast. It was in 1929/1930 that the Kestrel engined Hawker Fury and Hart appeared for the first time.

But it was a long time before these machines would enter service with No.600 Squadron. From time to time "new and modern aircraft" would fly over Tangmere. Kirby still remembers those days: "I was sitting up on the Downs one off-duty afternoon and watched a Squadron of Harts put to flight the attacking Bulldogs. The Bulldog was then our fastest fighter, good for 175 mph, and it was about to be succeeded by the Fury, which could clock 225 mph. I believe the Hart had a top speed of 185mph when first introduced". Much as the men of No.600 Squadron enjoyed Tangmere, nothing would induce anyone, unless on duty, to remain on the premises after the day's work. The evening saw a general exodus to Bognor or Chichester. The famous Mr. Butlin had even then a fun fair at Bognor, and it is a fact that an undeclared state of war existed between his attendants and No.600 Squadron. Butlins was subjected to a series of sporadic but highly co-ordinated raids for the express purpose of capturing the current collector arms of the Dodgems, in effect, of course, the enemy's colours. Surprise was the order of the day, one moment of relative peace, the next thing a grand mêlée with protagonists locked in battle on individual Dodgems. It became a tradition of Tangmere Camps for Other Ranks to hold mock parades on the beach at Bognor on the last Saturday evening. An AC1 would take the role of Parade Commander with all the gags in the book thrown in. On given the order to march off the assembled company headed for the town in single file, nothing being permitted to halt their inexorable progress. Ring-o'-Roses round the traffic cop or a bunch of girls, down one side of the public conveniences and up the other, the whole 100 odd of them, until suddenly they found their numbers wasting perceptibly as their itinerary reached the pubs and bars. Yes, Bognor knew when the Auxiliaries were on the move.

RAF Sutton Bridge, where one of the many Summer Camps took place.

With aviation said to be the "coming thing" some entrepreneurs in England saw good opportunities in aerial transport. Mr. Hillman, who ran a fleet of coaches in East Anglia, decided to add the business of an Air Carrier to his enterprise. His fleet consisted of DH84 Dragons, developed into the Rapide – or Dominie. Civil aerodromes were scarce, so Hillman without any hesitation built one for himself at Maylands, near Romford. There was considerable pressure for a larger airport for Essex and a day of junketing on 24th September 1932 was part of the propaganda, with open Air Displays at Maylands and a large meeting of interested people in Romford. The Lord Mayor of London, Sir Maurice Jenks, agreed to take a leading part, and to underline the aeronautical flavour he would arrive by air. As this was the first official journey for a Lord Mayor by this means the Squadron was invited to provide an escort, so eight Wapitis flew to Heston to accompany the party to Maylands. In the transport aircraft were the Lord Mayor and Lady Mayoress, the Sheriffs and the Director of Civil Aviation. The modern monoplane was a little fast for the biplane bombers of 600 Squadron, so the escort was at long range. Whatever they tried, the Wapitis proved unable to keep up with the airliner. Only six pilots of the Squadron were present on arrival of the Lord Mayor. The others had not made it in time. To mark the event Sir Maurice presented the Squadron with a handsome piece of silver, to be known as the "Jenks Cup", which since disbandment of the Squadron has an honoured place in the Lieutenancy Room at Finsbury Barracks. It may seem ungrateful to say it – but No.600 Squadron was not then a *BOMMER* Squadron as was engraved twice on the cup. In the fifties, when the Squadron disbanded, whenever possible the silver was returned to the donors or their next of kin. This particular cup went to the City Corporation where it forms part of the Mansion House Plate.

In the meantime great changes occurred in Germany. After winning the 1933 elections in Germany the new Chancellor Hitler took full control of the country. Raising the slogan that he had saved the country from communism, and with the aid of the SA and SS he soon had a free hand. Meanwhile, the rest of Europe, wrapped in its own economic problems, took little notice of what was happening in the Reich. In October 1933 Germany left the League

Five Westland Wapitis of No. 600 Squadron rehearsing for the 1932 Hendon Air Display. Wapiti J9606, with the City of London crest on the tail, is flown by Peter Stewart, who later became OC 600 and who was one of the gentlemen responsible for the founding of the Association after the war. Peter was the first chairman.

of Nations. From now on it expanded its military power at a dazzling speed. In the country itself a vicious purge started and anyone who dared to oppose the new regime disappeared into a concentration camp. Life for Jews became more and more unbearable and thousands, those who could afford it, left to begin a new life elsewhere. In Britain it seemed no one really wondered what Hitler was up to. The feeling of safety in the British Isles seemed to satisfy people that events on the Continent were of no real significance to the Empire. Great masses came to see the annual air display of the RAF and No.600 City of London Squadron was proud as always to play a part in it.

In 1934 a new device known as the "Ahrens Smoke Wind Indicator" was installed at Hendon. It was a heated tray into which waste oil dripped to produce a large volume of smoke to indicate the wind direction. It was a great improvement as in those days anything like a crosswind landing was considered suicidal. The apparatus was located in a brick-lined pit about 6ft x 6ft and the tray was heated by a flame on the Primus stove principle, the responsibility for operation being vested in the MT section since they had immediate access to transport and were used to traversing the landing area during flying operations. It may seem trivial to the reader that this contraption should be mentioned at all, but from being initially a source of amusement, then contempt and finally exasperation, in the memories of No.600 Squadron members who observed it, the Wind Indicator fully earned its reputation as the most diabolic piece of equipment ever used in the RAF. When the indicator was first installed the interest down the line from the CAS to the lowest ACH/GD was such as to make one feel elation in commanding the Section chosen to nurse this baby. The Prince of Wales, with his brother, the late Duke of Kent, made a special journey to view the masterpiece and even the Rt.Hon. Ramsay MacDonald, the Prime Minister, inspected it before leaving the country for the Stresa Conference. For the first 24 hours of its installation, secure below ground under an iron grating, the late Frank Moody used to watch the smoke drifting exactly as designed over the grass, and certainly it looked a winner. But then there was no flying and the benefits were somewhat academic. Soon the real test was to come when two days later on the Saturday the three Auxiliary Squadrons started their weekend flying activities.

It seemed that the pilots had decided to treat the indicator as a

Tangmere, August 1934. A-Flight No.600 (City of London) Squadron.
Back row, l/r: LAC Cardew, LAC Hennings, AC2s Pestell, Ratcliffe, Lillyman, Norris, LAC Page, AC2s Tedder, Hodson, AC1 Robinson, LAC Thompson, AC2 Madle, LAC Wordsworth and AC1 McHale. Centre row l/r: LAC McCombie, AC2 Williams, AC1 Archard, AC2 Styles, LAC Parry Jones, AC1 Stewart, AC2s Eames, Devers, Prickett, Hadland, Beer, Webster, AC1 Kelly, LAC Cuthberth and LAC Toghill. Front row l/r: Cpl Welham, Sgt J.F.M. Wright, P/O A.A. Vickers, F/Os J.M. Wells, I.R. Campbell-Orde, F/L P.G. Stewart, F/O The Hon. R.N. Frankland, P/O R.P. Braun, F/S J.Shone, Cpls Cowan and Elliot. In 1996, when this book was written, LAC (now a retired S/L) Will Cardew still was a proud and active member of the Squadron Association.

landing marker with the result that every direct hit or near miss either blew the flame out or spilled the oil off the tray when the whole lot would go up in flames. With continuous take-offs and landings it was a hazardous business to get to the equipment. The men responsible for it deemed it their duty to relight the flame-out. On occasions they were confined to the use of the Hucks Starter as the only available means of transport and anyone remembering the oddity based on a Ford "T" lorry chassis can visualise its erratic passage across the Hendon turf at a full and uncomfortable 20mph. At times Frank Moody wondered if the Hucks was really intended to be started up by an aeroplane instead of vice-versa. It was to the credit of the Auxiliaries at Hendon that this tiresome apparatus was finally abandoned, having regard to the time and trouble expended by the MT people to keep it going. If it went on fire it would be red hot by the time they reached it and this meant waiting until it had cooled off. A straight-forward relight after a flame-out took time so that in either case the operators were stuck in the middle of the landing area during flying operations.

S/L Collett, Officer Commanding 600 Squadron, was an experienced pilot when he took command. He died in a freak accident during the 1934 Air Display at Hendon, flying with F/O Lea as his pilot. It was said that the pilot accidentally touched the petrol cock with his knee, thus cutting off the supply of fuel. Collett was the son of the Lord Mayor of London. His nephew Sir Christopher Collett was also Lord Mayor of London in 1990.

Sadly during the 1934 Air Display a sad and fatal accident happened. During a display the aircraft in which S/L Collett flew as an observer spun in at low altitude, killing Collett instantly. By order of the Lord Mayor of London, his father, he was buried with full military honours after a procession through the City. No.600 Squadron of course took part and escorted its Commanding Officer to St. Paul's Cathedral, where a service was held. Needless to say that the death of such a prominent gentleman under such terrible circumstances received full attention from the press. Shortly after the accident there was a full investigation. A newspaper wrote, on 24th July 1934:

RAF PAGEANT TRAGEDY
THEORY THAT PETROL WAS TURNED OFF
INQUEST ON LORD MAYOR'S SON

"The inquest on S/L Stanley Collett, aged 38, son of Sir Charles Collett, Lord Mayor of London, who was killed while taking part in the RAF Pageant at Hendon, was resumed at Hendon yesterday. He was observer in a machine belonging to No.600 (City of London) Auxiliary Squadron, which he commanded. He was an assistant-secretary to the Great Western Railway Company. Robert Lea, of Southwood, Worcestershire, the pilot, said that he had flown solo for 220 hours before the accident.

The Coroner (Dr. G.Cohen) – Can you account for the accident?

Mr. Lea – I can not. The Coroner – Why did you leave the formation?

Because the engine failed. The Coroner – Were you hampered in landing?

In normal circumstances the space was ample, but I was in such a position as not to be able to use it to the best advantage.

Can you tell us exactly what happened in the air? When the engine failed I turned to the left and first thought of landing outside Hendon. However, I decided to turn to the aerodrome. I turned into the wind, and the machine lost speed and came down on its side. Major Cooper (AM Inspector of Accidents): Do you remember looking at the instruments when the engine failed?

Mr. Lea – Yes. Major Cooper: Was your petrol on? Yes. Are you certain on that point? Absolutely. Major Cooper said that examination of the wreck was carried out on the spot, and the engine was stripped and examined at the maker's works. There was no evidence of any defect, apart from the damage due to the crash and the fire. He was satisfied that no part of the engine failed or developed any trouble during the flight. Then the Coroner asked about the possible cause of the accident. Can you form any conclusions why the accident happened? Major Cooper replied: I have no hesitation in saying that there is no proof that the engine failed. I have formed the opinion- that the forced descent was caused by the pilot accidentally or unwillingly shutting off the petrol cock with his knee. This stopped the supply of petrol to the engine. This petrol cock was found almost completely turned off. My view is that if this had been caused by the crash they would have found it completely turned off. Subsequent investigations have shown that the position in which it was found can be caused accidentally by the pilot's knee catching it. This is partic- ularly so in the case of a tall pilot. Furthermore, there has been a previous case." The Coroner – Is there any way of preventing this happening? Major Cooper – Yes. It is one of those things that after an unfortunate accident like this will be taken in hand. The jury returned a verdict of accidental death and said there was no suspicion of blame attaching to anyone. They were satisfied with Mr. Lea's competency as a pilot.

In memory of S/L Collett's death his mother embroidered a Standard for the Squadron. Today this "Bomber Squadron Standard" can be seen on display at the RAF Museum at Hendon. It is only brought out on request for a really special occasion. The Standard carried annually at the Lord Mayor's Show is a copy of the official Standard presented to the Squadron at Buckingham Palace in June 1953. Collett was the first Commanding Officer to die while serving with the Squadron. To fill in the vacancy caused by the accident, F/L Peter Stewart was promoted to Squadron Leader and given command of the Squadron. Peter, in civilian life an underwriter at Lloyds, was a senior member of the Squadron from the DH9a days. He was to become one of the men who founded the Association and remained a great supporter of the Squadron until he died in the sixties.

CHAPTER 3

SOMETHING IS BREWING IN THE EAST.
1936 TO 1939

In 1935 the international situation grew more tense. The expansion of the RAF was finally under way with vigorous new training programmes. There were very good reasons for this. After orchestrating a Nazi uprising in Austria in July 1934, hoping thereby to overthrow Chancellor Dollfuss, Hitler now faced mobilisation of Benito Mussolini's forces and a speech of Stanley Baldwin, who warned the Führer that if he continued this way the Rhine might very well become Britain's frontier with Germany. When Hindenburg died in August 1934 Hitler combined the offices of President and Chancellor, becoming a virtual dictator. In January 1935 the Saar reverted from France to Germany. In March Adolf Hitler re-introduced conscription in open defiance of the provisions of the Treaty of Versailles. Little was done to show Hitler that the democratic nations would never accept his ideas. For the Führer this was proof that he did not need to fear. He felt safe enough to conclude a naval pact with Great Britain, which again disregarded Versailles. It made Britain look like a friend of the Third Reich and it threw dust into the Allies' eyes. Military activity in Britain increased. No. 600 Squadron put in more than 2000 flying hours for the first time. Drill and lectures at Town Headquarters and at the weekend camps were very well attended with officers and men showing great keenness. Among the lecturers were well-known aviators like S/L Reid, who talked on "Instruments", and F/L Johnson, the first men ever to make a blind take-off, who lectured about "Instrument Flying".

At that time only one out of six applicants for a commission were selected and of those interviewed for other ranks only ten out of

Hawker Hart Mk1 K2982 high over England. This particular aircraft was one of 65 built by Vickers Ltd. 16 aircraft were sold to SAAF and one to the Southern Rhodesian Air Force. Harts also served in India.

seventeen were accepted. The Squadron, which was destined to become one of the first-line night-fighter units during the Second World War, carried out the first night flying in 1935. It was done by F/O Sweeney in the Squadron Moth. It was in 1935, also, that His Majesty King George V reviewed RAF and Auxiliary Air Force at Mildenhall and Duxford. No.600 Squadron were present at Mildenhall but they did not fly at Duxford. An unfortunate incident took place on 26th May, when P/O Kellett flew to Eastchurch for an armament course. At front-gun practice he mistook the target-towing motor boat for the target itself. Fortunately there were no casualties and he caused little damage. Kellett, however, did not make many friends that day. To his credit it should be mentioned here that he improved his shooting considerably during the 1939-1945 war: In 1940 he was a Squadron Leader with the DSO, DFC and a Polish award shooting down five enemy aircraft. The high standard attained by the Squadron at this time was shown in a contest of front-gun drogue shooting held at Sutton Bridge in July 1935 when the Squadron beat the regular RAF Squadrons Nos. 29, 54 and 56. No.600 Squadron achieved a stunning total of 96.3% of hits. One of the best shots was F/O Peter Devitt, who was to become OC 615 Squadron after the war.

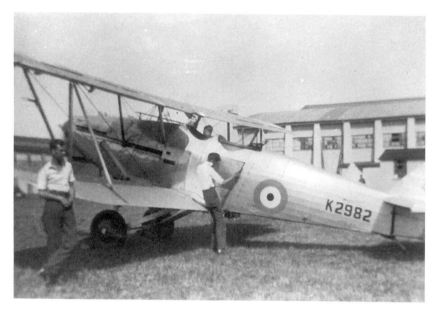

K2982 seen again, this time on the ground at Tangmere in 1937.

On 20th January 1936 at 2355 King George V died. The death of the Monarch sent a shock through country and Empire. Great efforts were made to give His Majesty a fitting funeral and the City of London Squadron too was to become involved in this ceremony. On 28th January 5 officers and 100 airmen of the Auxiliary Air Force took part in the funeral of the King. S/L Stewart was in command. The parade was split up into two parties. Fifty men and three officers lined the route and the other three officers and fifty men marched in the procession. The officers were in full dress uniform. Of the whole contingent 35 men were of No. 600 Squadron.

In May 1936 Mussolini invaded Abyssinia and Hitler sent troops into the Rhineland. Neither France nor Britain responded to this defiance of the Versailles Treaty. It might have saved the world from a global war if they had. The annual Empire Air Day of 1936 on 23rd May was rather tame for the Squadron as the Harts were unable to function. Two days earlier a message had been received that all flying in Harts was to stop immediately. At the Rolls Royce Works it had been discovered that their Kestrel engines showed excessive back-lash in the cam gearwheel. This caused extensive damage to the engines. Immediately Rolls Royce mechanics travelled all over the country to inspect the aero engines. The members of No.600 Squadron were not at all pleased. All they could do now was to form up with No.604 and fly nine Avros over the field. Two Hawker Harts from No.601 Squadron which had been declared safe were used for aerobatics by Blackwood and Campbell-Orde. On 26th May three Squadron Harts were serviceable again. Six members flew to Lord Cowdray's Landing ground near Midhurst, where they were met by Mr. Margetron and taken to the King Edward Sanatorium by car to visit William Burkitt, one of the pilots, who had fallen ill.

After a Camp there always was a formal inspection. Here five Harts of No.600 Squadron are lined up. In front of each aircraft stands the pilot, with behind him his gunner. Two ground crew members stand left and right of the undercarriage. The aircraft are K2988 and K2985

On 10th June 1936 nine aircraft, led by F/L Campbell-Orde (known as "The General") took off from Hendon. The pilots were S/L Peter Stewart, F/L Campbell-Orde, F/Os Walls, Devitt and Hiscox, P/O Mount and LAC Alford and Cpl Emler. They landed at Usworth for lunch, then flew on to Scotland. The home journey took them to Waddington on the following Sunday afternoon in very foul weather. However, the Squadron diarist was happy to record: "All came back safe, full of wonder at the magnificent manner in which Highlanders conduct their fun and frivolities". Two weeks later three Harts and six pilots flew to Netheravon where the passengers were to pick up three Avro Tutors and bring them to Hooton Park. The six pilots were F/L Wallis and Campbell-Orde, F/Os Devitt and Hiscox and P/Os Mount and Miller. The Tutor was the successor to the Avro 504. It was a good airplane with, however, one bad attitude: it was so "forgiving" that a student could make the most horrendous mistakes without chance of a mishap. It tended to make pupils overconfident and sometimes, while flying less forgiving aircraft, they would find out to their horror that flying an aeroplane was quite different from playing around in a Tutor. On 27th June it was Display Day. Misfortune overtook the Squadron during the day when a lorry containing no less than 21 parachutes, bedding and the private belongings of the men caught fire. Yet the Squadron carried out an immaculate combat demonstration when 9 Harts featuring as two-seater fighters repelled "enemy" bombers, trying to attack P/Os Clark, Maclachlan, Clackson and Mount. In the afternoon F/L Carlow and F/O Kellett took the Squadron Moth to Heston for dinner. After a very pleasant evening they returned home in the dark, which made the diarist write in the Operations Record Book: "This was the first known night cross-country for 600. From such small beginnings great things materialise".

1936 also was the year of the Berlin Olympics. Few people realised that the Games were being misused to show how peaceful and well-organised Germany was. People from all over the world were deeply impressed by the superb organisation shown by the German officials and the people. In February the Winter Games were in Berchtesgaden, followed by the Summer Games in August. Questions had been raised in Britain if athletes should take part. The British Olympic Committee waited from December 1933 to December 1934 to accept the formal invitation from the German Olympic Committee. Then they declared that sending a team to Berlin would serve the highest interests of sport. Countries organised alternative Games. In Tel Aviv there were Jewish Games in 1935. A Counter-Olympiad was planned at Prague and in Antwerp the "Workers Games" were prepared. The Soviet Komintern and International Labour Movement organised "People's Olympics" in Barcelona. But when the Spanish Civil War broke out these were cancelled. The Berlin Olympics gave the world an illusion of peace

Hawker Hart 1 K3028. The City of London crest is proudly exposed on the tail fin.

and people decided not to listen to opponents like Ellen Wilkinson MP, who declared that "if the Germans organised the Games like their latest elections, there would probably be only one competitor for each part of the game". For No. 600 Squadron it was business as usual. The Squadron went to Hawkinge for the annual camp whilst their "bitter rivals", No.601 Squadron, were at Lympne. It is on record that both ground and air raids were made on each other's camps with "a rare variety of missiles" which was soot and flour and other objects described as "having a very high length to width ratio". Continuing Squadron rivalry caused angry messages from No.8 Auxiliary Group and even from the Air Ministry. It was all part of the Squadron's social life, like the Annual Dinner of the City of London Lieutenancy Club which took part on 21st October that year in the Egyptian Hall of the Mansion House. The guests of honour were Viscount Swinton, Secretary of State, The Rt.Hon. Freddie Guest, Honorary Air Commodore of No.600 Squadron, Air/Cdre Quinnel (AOC 6 Group) and S/L Peter Stewart. Ten days later the Squadron had its own dinner and 40 members attended. After dinner the members went to a cabaret in Mayfair. The Squadron diarist reported that some of them had not had enough after this and "scattered in all directions to visit houses of many – including questionable – reputes". On 1st December, an important day for the Auxiliaries, the Squadron transferred from No.6 Auxiliary to No.11 Group of Fighter Command. After a little more than ten years the Auxiliaries were an integral part of Britain's Home Defence.

In 1937 Honorary Air Commodore Freddie Guest died and Lord Lloyd of Dolobran became his successor. Shortly before he passed away Guest had written a will. The moving document showed his deep love and affection for the Air Force and especially for "his" very own Squadron, No.600:

> *19 Berkeley Street W1* *18th February 1937*
> *To my executors Oscar Guest and James Swift.*
>
> *Dear Oscar and James Swift,*
> *I shall be glad if you will arrange for me to be cremated. Would you be so kind, also, to ask the Adjutant of 600 City of London Bombing Squadron if they will kindly scatter my ashes over the Welsh Harp, which has been such a wonderful landmark, and many times such a relief, to Squadron machines, which have been homing in bad weather for Hendon.*
> *Yours sincerely.*
> *Freddie E. Guest*

His last wish was granted and a Squadron aircraft did what their beloved Squadron Commander had asked. His ashes were scattered over the Welsh Harp reservoir by Squadron machines in an immaculate formation.

Soon a new Honorary Air Commodore was appointed, Lord Lloyd of Dolobran, who took over on 11th August 1937. His keenness was such that he learnt to fly and eventually went solo in a Demon in April 1938 at the age of 59. A year later he insisted upon flying dual on a Blenheim and taking night-fighter instruction. That year the role of the Squadron changed from bombers to fighters and therefore the Harts were replaced by Demons. The situation on the Continent was still very tense. In the spring of 1938 Hitler, for the second time, interfered in the internal affairs of Austria. But this time he would not stop at words. In the night of 11th/12th March Nazi soldiers marched into the country. Chancellor Seyss-Inquart, a fanatic Nazi, had asked Adolf Hitler to help the country and restore law and order.

Technically Hitler did not invade, he merely answered an official request for help. Seyss-Inquart would be rewarded for betraying his country, when in 1940 he became Reichskommissar (Governor) of Occupied Holland. For five years he ruled with an iron fist, assisted by two fellow Austrians, Rauter, who commanded the SS in the Netherlands and Fischböck, an economist, whose task was to rob the country of its wealth and resources. Seyss-Inquart's luck ran out in 1945, when he was arrested and tried as a war criminal. His crimes during the years he had been ruling Holland were considered so serious that he was condemned to death and hanged at Nuremberg. Rauter was captured by the Dutch and executed by a firing squad in 1946.

The Hawker Demon was the successor of the Hart. It entered service in 600 Squadron between February and May 1937. This aircraft, K5709, was one of 59 built by Boulton & Paul. It had a Kestrel VDR engine and carried a gunner. This aircraft has the shark teeth on the fuselage, as well as on the upper wing.

By the middle of 1938 Peter Stewart left the Squadron. He had been a much loved CO. In fact his standing with No.600 Squadron was such that it had even led to an adverse report from an Inspection Officer, who was annoyed to hear junior officers calling the CO by his first name. Reading the report Peter remarked with a smile: "I would rather be called Peter to my face than Stuffy, Sausage or

Ginger behind my back", referring to the nicknames applied to Air
Marshals Dowding, Cossage and Harris. S/L Viscount Carlow was
appointed the new CO. He took over at a time when war looked
very close indeed. Not satisfied Hitler now looked for another
trouble spot and soon found it in Czechoslovakia. For centuries
people of German descent had lived there. Now their leader Henlein
demanded autonomy within the republic. New tensions grew and
Hitler said he was ready to come to the aid of the "oppressed people
of German blood". It looked as if Europe was at the verge of war.
It meant that the Auxiliaries were to prepare for the worst. For the
first time in its existence No.600 Squadron was embodied. Men
hurried to railway stations. Camera guns were removed from the
Hawker Demons and machine guns installed instead, sighted for
targets at 200 yards range. The beautiful silver making the aircraft
so very good-looking disappeared under a pattern of dark earth and
green camouflage. 600 moved to Kenley and was brought to instant
readiness.

Hawker Demons. K5696, is still in the old Squadron colours while the one in front
has been camouflaged. This photograph was taken in 1938 during the so-called
Sudeten-crisis, which ended with a happy Prime-Minister waving a piece of paper
on which Hitler promised to pursue peace from now on. One year later Britain was
at war with Germany.

The Czechoslovakian government mobilised its determined, well-trained and well-equipped army. Thousands of soldiers marched into the fortifications built along the border with Germany. French and British diplomats hastily met for consultations. Lord Runciman was sent from London to Prague on a peace mission. There he heard Sudeten Germans chanting: "Lieber Lord, mach uns frei von der Tschechoslowakei" – "Dear Lord, deliver us from Czechoslovakia."

Lord Runciman was impressed and succeeded in persuading the Czech government to consent to Henlein's demand for autonomy for his followers in Czechoslovakia. But after visiting Hitler at Berchtesgaden Henlein suddenly changed his mind and now wanted nothing but a total cessation of the Sudetenland and a reunion with Nazi-Germany. Hitler made it perfectly clear that he was willing to wage war, and as both France and Russia were tied by treaty to help the Czechs, Britain was automatically involved since it was to help France if this country should go to war. To prevent this PM Chamberlain flew to Germany for talks with Hitler. After long, negotiations between Chamberlain, Daladier, Hitler and Mussolini, an agreement was reached. It dissipated the clouds of war, but it deprived the Czechs of vast areas of land. The Czechs were never asked how they felt about the agreement; they were told to accept for the sake of peace. And while other nations shared in the spoils – Poland occupied a part of Silesia and Hungary obtained bits of Slovakia and Ruthenia – the world believed Hitler when he said that this was the last territorial claim he had to make in Europe. As the scare died down, aircrews were stood down to twelve hour readiness until orders for disembodiment came through and all Squadron members were allowed to return home.

Yet, after this crisis events moved fast. A number of Squadron pilots were attached to other units for conversion to the twin-engined Blenheim. A few weeks before Christmas 1938 a trainer aircraft, the Airspeed Oxford, and the first Blenheims Mk1 arrived. The Auxiliaries felt very proud to be given this new aircraft. In those days it was the fastest aeroplane in Britain.

Designed in July 1933 by Frank Barnwell, the Bristol Aeroplane Company's chief designer as "Type 135", it was drafted as a small twin-engined cabin monoplane with two pilots and room for six passengers. Brought to the attention of newspaper tycoon Lord Rothermere, who wanted to own the fastest commercial aircraft in Europe, it had been re-designed as "Type 142 – Britain First" in 1935.

Pilots, air gunners and groundcrew of No.600 Squadron at Tangmere 1938. Standing in the back row (l/r) are Rufus Riseley (nr 6.), Montegue (10) and Harrison (13). In the middle row we recognise LAC Alford (5) and Jack Eames (7). Seated in the front row are l/r an unknown member, P/O Norman Hayes, F/O Micky Mount, F/O Mac Lachlan, F/L Peter Devitt, F/O Ian Campbell-Orde, F/L Ralph Hiscox, F/O Hugh Rowe, F/O Tony Miller, Sgt John Wright and Sgt Nash.

With Mercury rather than the original Aquila engines it could fly over 300 mph. The aviation world was amazed when it flew for the first time on 12th April 1935 at Filton. Being faster than any RAF fighter at that time, the Air Ministry felt somewhat odd. Subsequently the aircraft was presented to the nation by Lord Rothermere. The Blenheim was considered a state of the art fighter. Therefore the Air Ministry ordered 150 Blenheims in September 1935 and K7033, the first Service machine made its maiden flight on 25th June 1936. Everyone expected the RAF to be unbeatable once this wonderful machine had been fully introduced. One of the Squadron pilots, P/O "Mickey" Mount remembered how one day he flew over Kent in a Hawker Demon and to his utter surprise was quickly overtaken by a Blenheim which left Mount's front-line fighter standing still in the air: "While we were wondering what this incredible machine was and who the owner might be, it circled around us while we were flying at full speed. Do not forget that the maximum airspeed of the Demon was a mere 180mph., while the Blenheim did an easy 280mph. One can imagine our delight when we were told that this aircraft was to become ours. We were sure that from now on anything flying would be intercepted, overtaken and destroyed by the Blenheim". Few people in 600 Squadron believed that within nine months they were expected to fly it operationally and that their first war missions would be in the Blenheim, and with horrible results. Many remember the mnemonic "H.T.M. P.F.G" pilots were to recite: "Hydraulics, Trim, Mixture, Pitch, Flaps, Gills", to make sure that no lethal mistakes were made on take-off. Many air forces flew with the Blenheim MkI. About 1,280 served in the RAF, (Fighter and Bomber Command), Middle East Command, and Far East Command. Twelve went to Finland, while Turkey bought thirty aircraft. More than twenty saw a brief service in the Yugoslav air force. Later in the war, Blenheims which had been captured by German troops after having been abandoned by the RAF, were put into action with Axis friendly forces. Some were used by the Croats and Rumanians, while British Blenheims served in the air force of Portugal.

Early in 1939 S/L Carlow announced that he wished to give all the airmen the opportunity to fly and would present an aircraft for that

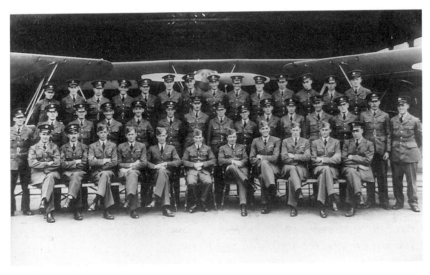

More officers, NCOs and Other Ranks of the Squadron, in front of their Demons. In the back row are John Squires, Arthur Butterworth Len Holt and Frank Cook. In the centre row are Cpl Des Farmer, Cpl Geoff Dobson, Norman Wheeler, Ron Haden, Eric Baker, Jack Cox and Gerry Alford . Seated on the front row are two unknown Flight Sergeants, F/O Smith, F/O David Clackson, F/L Ronald Kellett, S/L Viscount Carlow, F/L Jimmy Wells, F/O David Clarke, F/O Pritchard and an unknown Flight Sergeant .

purpose. A flying club was quickly organised and several qualified pilots offered to act as instructors. In due course the "Squadron's own private aircraft" arrived. It was an Aeronca 100 and soon it appeared flying over the railway embankment at Hendon and aerial activities commenced. It was a monoplane with a high wing wire-braced to the bottom of the fuselage and to a king post above the cabin. The engine was a two-cylinder JAP of about 36hp and the two seats were arranged side-by-side with dual controls.

The Squadron soon discovered that loading was a bit critical as only the lightest pupils could fly with Ben Bowring and Len Holt could be instructed only by the Assistant Adjutant, F/O Woodruff. The Aeronca achieved its maximum utilisation during Annual Training at RAF Manston in 1939 and there even with a light load it could sometimes not exceed the rate of climb of the aerodrome in an uphill direction take-off. The garage at the drome seemed to do a great trade in petrol during that fortnight as the club would some-times make more than one visit with a two gallon can in the afternoon. At 1/6d. a gallon for No.1 grade spirit it was heavy spending. When lying in the sun awaiting a turn to fly little did the men of 600 Squadron think that within six months they would be back at Manston as full-time airmen, with snow and ice enough to make it seem more of a polar region than the Garden of England. The ferry flight back to Hendon was undertaken by Bob Reed and though he took some maps there were not enough. After flying for some time he landed at Hornchurch to ask the way and borrow another map from Flying Control. At that time the Flying Control empire consisted of a "Duty Pilot" whose appointment was often the reward for a "black" and an airman on fatigues who was usually left on his own to carry on with the aid of a telephone, a doubtful weather report and a Verey pistol. There Bob decided to play safe and have his tanks topped up and when the giant-sized tanker was towed to the tarmac the quantity required was two gallons. Having filled up the usual number of RAF forms and handed over his 3/6d. (including Departmental expenses) he set off again and arrived at Hendon.

On return from Manston it was touch and go as to whether or not No.600 was to be embodied or not. This did not happen until mid-August when call-up papers were issued and the Squadron finally left Hendon aerodrome to go to Northolt on 25th August 1939 with 16 serviceable Blenheims. Soon after Camp the Certificate of

Airworthiness of the Aeronca expired and several weeks of intensive work for its renewal were put in during the stand-down but without result. There were reasons to expect a war to be fought and the battle task of the Squadron was of greater importance than its love for that strange under-powered flying machine. With the hope of making the airplane serviceable it was moved to Northolt and Hornchurch by road with the Squadron, but as prospects of flying it in the near future appeared to be nil, plans were made for long storage. Bob Reed made contact with a friendly farmer at Luton and suitably wrapped and inhibited against corrosion AEWU, as it was registered, was laid up in a barn for the duration. It stayed there until the summer of 1946.

By now Britain and France had given up the idea that Hitler was to be trusted. The armament production was speeded up in a desperate attempt to catch up with the Luftwaffe, which by now had become a force of tremendous power and experience. Many German pilots had flown in Spain, "volunteers" in the Kondor Legion, a unit that allowed the Luftwaffe to get familiar with what was to be known later as the "Blitzkrieg", the Lightning War. The men who were to lead the Luftwaffe into battle, men like Werner Mölders and Adolf Galland, got their experience in combat while flying against the aircraft of the Spanish Republic. In March 1939, with no word of warning Hitler marched against what was left of Czechoslovakia. President Hacha was forced to sign a statement in which he placed the country under the benevolent protection of Germany. The Czech army was disbanded, their armament put to good use in the Wehrmacht and the Luftwaffe. A few weeks later the first Czech immigrants arrived in England. A week after the rape of Czechoslovakia Hitler presented an ultimatum to Lithuania; Memel was "negotiated" into the Reich. Hitler's breach of faith aroused some indignation. Herr Hitler could not care less. The change from self-determination to domination was obvious. Even though no one believed that Hitler would actually attack France or Britain, His Majesty's government decided to be vigilant. The attempts to speed up Britain's re-armament programme which followed, provided Germany with a long awaited excuse for repudiating the Anglo-German Naval Pact.

Not at all satisfied with the world's reaction to outcries of alleged discrimination against Germans Hitler demanded the return of Danzig and the Corridor that separated Danzig from the Reich. Italy

The famous Aeronca 100 with Jap engine, No.600 Squadron's "private aircraft". It was a gift to the Squadron from the CO S/L Lord Carlow, it was used extensively to give groundcrew some flying experience. The aircraft was tremendously underpowered. In fact pilots could only take the smallest and lightest men with them. Yet, the aeroplane was great fun and many trips were made in it.

There could be mishaps when a pilot smashed the undercarriage in a rough landing

wanted new territory for his new Roman Empire, so in April 1939 the Duce invaded Albania. Hitler began a campaign of hatred against the Poles. In August he surprised the entire world: Germany signed a non-aggression pact with the Soviet-Union. Everybody knew now that peace in Europe was doomed. In the meantime the Blenheim Mk1 bombers had been converted to 1Fs with four .303 calibre guns in a box fitted below the aircraft. A single Vickers K gun in a hydraulically operated turret was to give rear fire cover. This to a large degree was thanks to the personal efforts of S/L Lord Carlow. First of all he had a considerable pull at Fighter Command and secondly he ran the Squadron like a private air force. He had been among the first to realise that the Blenheim was hopelessly under-armed and that it was useless as a night-fighter. He therefore had his own Blenheim equipped with the four .303s and finding the Air Ministry reluctant to pay for this modification he had it done at his own expense. Then they ordered armoured plates to be installed behind the back of the pilot and underneath their seats. Now the

With the improvement of communications many Auxiliaries received Wireless Operator training. Here volunteers of Nos. 500 and 600 Squadron pose at No.2 Electrical and Wireless School at Yatesbury in Wiltshire. Kneeling second from right is LAC Ray Aveyard, now President of the City of London Squadron Association.

aircraft was a "twin-engine long range fighter", the boffins said. The last of the gun boxes were fitted just before the Squadron went on its last peacetime Annual Training Camp – this time at Manston. During that fortnight extensive flying and air firing was carried out while in Germany more and more talk of war was heard. At Northolt they shared the aerodrome with Nos.25 and 111 Squadrons. Then, during the days before war was formally declared, all Squadron personnel were suddenly kept very busy digging slit trenches, laying field telephone cables, attending crash courses, testing out gas masks and dozens of other tasks to try and equip themselves for the task that lay ahead. The majority of the ground staff were still under canvas, but later moved into the now evacuated Married Quarters.

CHAPTER 4

ALL HELL BROKE LOOSE.
From 1939 to the Battle of Britain

In the years before the war, being able to intercept an enemy raider by night was virtually impossible unless by a great stroke of luck you got near enough to see the raider when he was illuminated by searchlights. There was also the possibility that you and a friendly fighter could also be illuminated by your own searchlights and hence become a target for both the enemy aircraft and gunners below. So until then plotting of incoming enemy aircraft was made on reports of the Royal Observer Corps phoning in to their nearest RAF Operations Room. These reports were used to "fix" plot the enemy aircraft's position. The same Operations Room was aware of the approximate position of the nearest RAF night-fighter aircraft and endeavoured to bring this fighter into close proximity to the enemy. Unfortunately the radio-telephone links at that time were not very good and frequently contact was lost. The night-fighter crew would keep a good look-out and were sometimes helped by seeing search-light beams searching for the raider and in some cases by anti-aircraft fire from the ground or even bomb flashes from the enemy. Searchlights and guns were assisted by the Army's sound locators, but it was commonplace for the searchlight beams and ack-ack fire to be behind the enemy aircraft. It could easily be a severe hazard to the night-fighter attempting to creep up on the raider. It was also common for the raider to be able to fly faster than the RAF pursuer. Science was to lend a helping hand to overcome this problem. "Radio/Radar" was expected to be the solution. An extensive research programme started.

As for all other Air Defence units, for the Auxiliaries the war began a few days before the actual declaration of hostilities. Under Lord

Carlow No.600 Squadron prepared for eventualities. On 25th August they were called out at less than one day's notice and immediately moved to Northolt with sixteen serviceable Blenheims. Only a training flight was left behind at Hendon. During the next period all members of the Squadron were very busy digging slit trenches, laying field telephone cables, etc. Sleeping conditions were very rough – twelve to a tent and not at all comfortable. Crash training courses were being given. LAC Ray Aveyard, a wireless operator, remembered how a Lewis gun course began at about midnight and continued until four in the morning. By that time each trainee was expected to be able to operate the Lewis gun, to clear any stoppages, to strip the gun down and reassemble it in almost total darkness. After the course some of the teams were put on guard duty on top of the hangars at 72 feet high as lookouts and gunners. The Squadron was ready and meant to use the few weapons available. At 0445, 1st September 1939 German troops crossed the Polish border from the west as well as from the north. Without a declaration of war "Case White" (Fall Weiss) began. The Russians followed

L1222 at dispersal at RAF Manston. It was one of 450 Bristol-built 142M Blenheim Is that were manufactured. Five of these were sold to Turkey and one, L1424, was the prototype.

from the east. An appeal on behalf of eight small nations by King Leopold of Belgium and Queen Wilhelmina of the Netherlands was brushed aside by the Germans. A protest by Roosevelt was ignored. Pope Pius XII tried to stop the bloodshed. Nothing could change Hitler's mind. The Second World War had become a grim reality. France and Great Britain discussed possible armed intervention. On the 3rd of September at 11am, Chamberlain spoke the words "that therefore a state of war now exists between England and Germany". A blockade by the Royal Navy of German ports was declared. It did not keep the German Navy from torpedoing the liner "Lusitania", killing 112 people, 28 of them Americans.

The Blenheim looked a strong, almost invincible aeroplane. Men of 600 Squadron proudly had their photograph taken in front of one of their aircraft. Standing from left to right: Farmer, Standring, unknown, Cox, Cook, Millborrow, Topping, Clucas, Clark, unknown and Harrison.

No. 600 Squadron was at dispersal, like all front-line RAF and Auxiliary Air Force units. Within a few minutes the Squadron was scrambled as air raid sirens sounded across the South of England. Sadly enough the war started with a bad omen. It was the day the Squadron suffered its first blow when P/O John Noel Isaac, aged 28, was practising approaches to Northolt and spun in on Hendon Old Town, not far from the Squadron's home base, while he tried a single-engine landing. Isaac died instantly. On 3rd September, 1939 with the 2nd World War only minutes old, he became the first Briton to die on active service. The story of his death went unreported because of the freshly imposed news blackout. Fifty years later his death was remembered by Alan Franks, a reporter, who met one of the eyewitnesses of the crash and wrote a story: "On that Sunday morning in Hendon, freakishly bright in the late summer sunshine, then cast into shadow by Chamberlain's broadcast at 11am, the episode was tinged with grotesque comedy. As a plume of black smoke from the Blenheim climbed into the sky, and gallons of fuel flowed in spate along the gutters, the neighbourhood could be forgiven for thinking that war had broken out in deed as well as word, and that it had started here in North London. Amazingly Isaac was the only fatality, even though three houses in Heading Street were destroyed. It took what seemed like an age for the emergency services to drive the half mile from the Hendon Borough Centre and there were dark mutterings perhaps attributable to start-of-war nerves about inefficiency. A witness that day was a boy of fifteen, Don Bridge, who lived in Sherwood Road. It was barely a mile from Hendon aerodrome, the birthplace of British military aviation, and the lad was used to the sound of Hawker Furies roaring in 150ft above the garden. But this noise was of a different order. The incident retains much of its immediacy since this was Day One of a daily diary which he was to keep for the next nine months. At 12.50 Don and his brother heard an immense boom. They ran out into the road, believing that the bombardment had started. This is how he describes it: The first that Isaac knew about the contents of the PM's broadcast was almost certainly at 11.40. He received a message from Hendon Aerodrome control telling him about the air raid warning below, and ordering him to return. But when the all-clear sounded minutes later, he was told he should continue his training flight. News of the war certainly did not unsettle him. It is possible that, like thousands of his generation, he was exhilarated, and glad that the long period of appeasement and the weekend crisis was now over. Perhaps he was thinking of the years ahead. In any event, at 12.45 he decided to try a single-engined approach on Hendon. He shut down the port engine and turned to the left. It was a crucial error. The Blenheim stalled. Isaac failed to open the port throttle which might have enabled him to regain control, and the aircraft spun in, crashing less than 100 yards away from St. Mary's School. Isaac was killed instantly. Of the unsung victim himself we know little, except that he was a bright young man with a second class honours degree in law from Jesus College, Oxford. He was born 18th December 1910, in Dinas Powis, Glamorgan, the only son of Wilfred John and Rosalind May Isaac, and before entering the university on a history scholarship had been a pupil at Magdalen College School. The archives of Jesus, a college with traditionally strong Welsh connections, give his address at his enrolment in October 1929 as 10 Fields Park Avenue, Newport, and his father's occupation as a fruit importer. By the time of his death the family had moved again. The records of the Commonwealth War Graves Commission give his parent's place of residence as Cardiff. Isaac was gazetted with No.600 on 12th January 1939. In July he and the Squadron travelled to Kent for a fortnight's training at RAF Manston. The investigation into the accident concluded that it was avoidable and that Isaac should have known not to turn the aircraft towards the dead engine.

After the start of hostilities a small group of ACH/GDs awaiting training as engineers at Northolt, were approached by F/S Fred Topping, the Discipline Senior NCO. He gathered twelve good men and marched them up to the main guard house. There they were halted and a rather large F/S Station Policeman came out and told the men to put on the SP armbands he held in his hand. Being airmen, this went down rather like a lead balloon. However the men had no choice in the matter and that was that. They were SPs. One of them was Bill Sills, who remembered: "We had a lot of duties, one of which I remember was to patrol around a hole in the aerodrome fence. This was a favourite way for airmen to nip out for an evening without a pass, which in those days was only for six hours anyway – not very generous. We thought this was a bit unfair and so did it our way. One moonlit night I was on patrol at about midnight, when I saw an airman casually walking up and down on the pavement outside. Now there was a very interesting bush quite near me, and having a sudden liking for botany, I spent some time examining it closely. When I finally looked up at the end of my inspection, the airman was nowhere to be seen. I did wonder what happened to him. Another time we, and the Air Ministry Wardens, were posted at the entrance to the WAAF site, on the other side of the road, opposite the guardroom. Our job was to split up airmen from the WAAFs and send the airwomen to their site., Now there was a hedge all round the WAAF site and down a path at the site was a gap in it. The airmen were duly split up, the airwomen sent in, and the airmen told about the gap in the hedge. Funnily enough they seemed happy with the arrangement. Good brotherly and sisterly inter-service relations, we thought. We even managed to train the "real" SPs in the gentle art of not putting poor airmen on a charge. There was a slip up one day however, when one of them apologised to us for having to do this fearful thing owing to an airman dotting him on the nose. I vividly remember a Station Dance at Bourne school. It was a requisitioned infant school which had been boarded up and included in the perimeter of Northolt. Among other things there were toilets built for toddlers and four feet high showers which all sizes of airmen had to use with comical consequences. It also had a large assembly hall with a stage at one end. We were to guard the doors with strict instructions from F/S Sam Storer that only Officers and Senior NCOs and their ladies were to be allowed out during the dance should they wish to stroll or otherwise enjoy them-selves outside, where there was a convenient playing field. Junior NCOs or airmen and their women were not to be allowed out under any circumstances, presumably in case they spoiled the enjoyment of their superiors. As soon as we were on our own we got together and reversed the orders. Do not forget we were still very much civilians in uniform and had not yet developed a proper respect for authority. As it happened, I was on the door when a stern looking Squadron Leader approached me with a female. On his attempting to leave I stopped him and told him that on F/S Storer 's orders, Officers and Senior NCOs and their ladies were not allowed out but Junior NCOs and airmen and their ladies were. Something seemed to happen to the Squadron Leader in that I thought he was going to have a fit. His eyes bulged and his face went a funny colour which was not improved when a Corporal came up with his lady and I told him that he could go out with her. The Squadron Leader turned on his heel and went back into the dance, muttering something I could not quite catch, but it did not sound very nice. The next morning we were all lined up outside the Guard-house and a funny looking F/S Storer spoke to us. Actually he was raving mad. He accused us of reversing his order, whereas we all replied that we had done exactly as he had told us. As a result we were discharged from being SPs. We were quite upset about it and it took us about two seconds to get over it."

A few days later P/O Woodruff flew all ab initio pilots to Wales, where they were to complete their training on the Blenheim. The Mark I in its original form was a fastish twin-engined monoplane and as such a pretty far cry from, the Hawker Demon biplane which it displaced. The version flying with No.600 Squadron had been adapted to the fighter role by fitting a box pallet, housing four 303 Browning machine guns beneath the bomb bay. The modification sets had been manufactured by none other than the Southern Railway locomotive works at Eastleigh.

All three units at Northolt, 25, 111 and 600 Squadrons shared day and night patrols of the first few weeks of the war. Then it was decided that the Blenheims with two engines, greater stability and longer range were more suitable than the Hurricanes. For several months the Squadron took part in what became known as the Phoney War, usually being airborne night and day. These night-fighter patrols were heart-breaking and the risks taken seemed to be out of proportion to the chance of success. One of the scientists involved in the development of AI was Professor Hanbury Brown, who vividly remembered No. 600 Squadron getting involved in the radar business. He first met the Squadron at Northolt in September 1939 when Lord Carlow was in charge. At first Hanbury Brown's job was to fit No.25 Squadron with AI at Martlesham Heath. He trained some of the operators and did much experimental flying with them. Incidentally it was the exercise he flew from Northolt which convinced him that AI would be totally useless unless Ground Control Interception (GCI) was developed. He wrote a letter to Professor Bowen which eventually brought about the development of GCI. No.600 Squadron watched what was going on, but was not yet involved. No radar coverage existed inland and before GCI came into use, the only plots of enemy aircraft available to the Controller were from the men of the Observer Corps. The night-fighter was plotted by radio fixes and the Controller attempted to intercept the enemy aircraft by vectoring the fighter, so that the Observer Corps plots of the enemy aircraft and the fighter radio plot came together on the Operations Room table. Due to the delays in the appearance of a plot, the Controller could never have had an accurate picture of the scenario. Therefore it frequently happened that the night-fighter aircraft crew seeing distant searchlights and AA gunfire knew that they were very distant from the enemy activity. The Squadron bashed away in its quest to perfect the art of night interception. On 2nd October it went to Hornchurch in Essex, continuing a few days later to Rochford for defensive patrols and searchlight co-operation. On 24th October F/L Miller, with S/L Seeley and Cpl Holmes crashed in BQ-O. They luckily survived.

November 1939 was a time of extremely poor weather and at times there was no flying at all. The atrocious weather conditions were a great danger to the aircrew. However, a sad loss to the Squadron was caused by engine failure rather than the weather. On the 16th at 2200 hrs, F/L Clark took off for a patrol. At 2345 Tony Vickers took off as well. While the aircraft gained speed people noticed the starboard engine spluttering badly. At about 200ft it cut completely and to the horror of all present the aircraft first hit a tree, then the ground, and burst into flames. F/O Vickers was killed instantaneously. The Squadron Operations Record Book said "The Squadron lost one of its most popular and capable officers". On 20th October S/L Lord Carlow, accompanied by F/L Hiscox, F/Os Lea, Frankland and Tony Tollemache attended the funeral service for Tony Vickers at Golders Green Crematorium. At 1800 hrs F/O Smith prepared to take off for a patrol. Unfortunately while taxiing he hit another aircraft and his sortie had to be abandoned. F/O Hannay took off to intercept an enemy intruder but he was too late to catch up with the German aircraft. While all this happened four Squadron pilots, F/Os Miller, Moore, Hayes and Sgt Ayres went to St. Athan to collect the new long-nose Bolingbrokes for the Squadron. The arrival of the aircraft was thought to be a real break. They were fitted with an air-to-air search radar, the very first Air Interception radar, developed by the famous Robert Watson-Watt. These AI aircraft were turned over to a special detachment, called X-Flight, under command of F/L Hiscox as non-flying captain and sent to Manston under absolute secrecy. AI had been under development since 1937. However it took until mid-June 1939 for a successful airborne installation to be ready to be tested. An Air Fighting Committee Report of November said: "It should be possible to navigate fighters by means of D/F intercept techniques to within 4 miles of an enemy – providing sufficient information regarding track and height of the enemy is available". The report also said that without the help of other means such as searchlights, it would be impossible to have a good intercept. In the months to come the Squadron gained tremendous experience, in spite of many failures and disappointments. The principle of operation of the Airborne Interception radar was and still is quite simple in that a directional pulsed transmission is made from the nose of the night-fighter and this signal is reflected back from anything but particularly metal objects in the "beam". The time from the occurrence of the transmitted pulse to the time at which the "echo" returned was measured and hence provided the range (distance) between the fighter and the target, whilst the angle of the returned "echo" gave the bearing of the target. The task of the AI operator was to assess the returned "echo" blips and to give instructions to the pilot so that the night-fighter was brought into a position behind and slightly below the enemy without being seen until the night-fighter pilot had visual contact and opened fire. In the early experimental stages it was found that with the night-fighter at a low altitude there was such heavy reflection from the ground and the sea (known as ground clutter) that any other target was obscured. It was only when the night-fighter and target were at 10,000ft or more that any aircraft target could be identified. Even so, this early design was very temperamental and unreliable. The Blenheim aircraft was not capable of great speed and therefore often unable to catch up with the enemy aircraft once it had released its bombs and put the nose down to make for its home base at speed. However, the night fighter crews worked very hard to practice interceptions and their experience in using the "night-fighter eyes" grew but it was not until the bringing into service of the Beaufighter with its greater speed and greater fire power of the four 20mm cannons and six .303 Browning guns all forward firing plus the greatly improved Mk.IV AI that No.600 Squadron came into its own and successes came thick and fast. On the 16th that month German bombers attacked British warships in the Firth of Forth. It did not look like a faraway war this time. The USA confirmed its neutrality, but the House of Representatives passed a law allowing countries at war to buy weapons from the USA on a cash-and-carry basis. It meant that Britain would be able to profit from the vast resources available in the USA, on the other hand it also would drain the British Treasury of substantial amounts of money.

Soon the Squadron found that serious problems endangered the use of the new Bolingbrokes. The internal wiring was incomplete and it took two full days to complete it. In the afternoon of the next day the CO tested the gunpack at the firing butts. It was found that when the guns were depressed as low as possible there was only 2 inches clearance between the line of fire and the bottom of the fuselage. On 25th November OC 600 received

The winter of 1939 was horrible and at times flying came to a standstill. aircraft stood parked in the snow and servicing them was quite an act of heroism. Here Blenheim BQ-V can be seen with BQ-W in the background. BQ-W was the aircraft in which F/O Moore and Cpl Isaacs were killed at Waalhaven aerodrome in Holland on 10th May 1940.

orders from AOC 11 Group to prepare three aircraft for operations against mine-laying aircraft. No.600 Squadron was told that from now on all Blenheim aircraft were to be entrusted with all night flying duties. The idea was to use the aircraft's' AI devices to stop He115 float planes from dropping mines in the Thames estuary, causing great danger to shipping. This order was received with mixed feelings. There had been very little time to gain experience with the new device As the German aircraft approached from almost sea level ground clutter completely obscured the "blips" on the radar screens. The Germans continued to lay mines and it seemed that AI would not be the answer to this problem. It was agreed that for the time being AI was of no operational value. However, seeing the possibilities, it was decided that training should continue. Sgt DeVroome, who was in the party, said that after the Flight was sent down to Manston it was committed to concentration camp conditions for security reasons. Every night Blenheims took off with crews hopeful to find, follow and finish off an enemy intruder. The Foreness Chain Home Low Radar Station played a vital role in the Squadron's experiments. One Blenheim would act as a target, coming from the sea for a mock attack on a destined target, while a second Blenheim waited on the ground until the crew was scrambled. The idea was that Foreness should "talk" the defender to the attacker until the attacker appeared on the AI screen. Then the operator should direct the pilot to the target for visual identification. The next step was a brief blast by the Vickers K-gun in the turret or the gun pack under the belly. All well and good; many hours were spent in freezing temperatures. It gave the boffins a lot of information, important for further research which later in the war formed the basis of an effective night-fighter force.

Ground crews and technicians were pressed hard to overcome the

Pilots of No.600 Squadron in front of the Officers' Mess at Manston. They are, from left to right: John Barnes, Hugh Rowe, Tony Vickers, Roger Moore, Michael Anderson, Tony Tollemache and Ralph Hiscox. Within six months after this photograph was taken Hugh Rowe would be a POW, Tony Vickers, Roger Moore and Mike Anderson dead, Tony Tollemache a "Guinea Pig", recovering from dreadful burns after attempting to save an army officer who flew as a passenger in Tony's Blenheim. Moore, Anderson and their respective gunners Isaacs and Hawkins remained "Missing, presumed dead" until the graves of unknown airmen in Rotterdam and Spijkenisse could be identified as those of the four missing airmen.

problems. The morning of 28th November was spent testing R/T. No
new orders were received in respect of the new modifications and
so no difficulty occurred. Just before lunch the CO took off and did
a short test which was not too good. Later that day he did a long test
and now the two way communications were excellent, even as far
as from Orfordness. Meanwhile AC2 Holland finished the wiring of
the new power pack which turned out to be incomplete on the AI
equipment of BQ-X. After lunch F/L Hiscox took off and flew over
Dover while S/L Pretty tried to catch the culprit. The bearing receiver
on the RDF was not too good and there was no interception, though
the "fighter" got close to the "bomber". The real trouble was that the
original track given to the bomber led him too far South and both
aircraft had to be called back just as they went over the French coast.
This of course was not the place to go with this new invention on
board. The following day F/O Le Rougetel ran into trouble when his
aircraft approached too low and struck one of the machine bays at
dispersal point, broke his starboard undercarriage, touched down
past the Chance light and swung rapidly to the right. The aircraft
crashed into the Watch Hut, demolished meteorological instruments
and completely wrecked the fire tender, also causing considerable
damage to the Watch Hut. Le Rougetel and his gunner Cpl Brown
walked away unhurt and fortunately there were no injuries among
the ground crew. It was an lucky escape. Poor Le Rougetel kept a
low profile for a few days, pending a Court of Enquiry.

The Winter of 1939/40 was horrible. A tremendous cold brought
life in Europe to a standstill. However, it did not keep the Soviet
Union from attacking Finland. To the utter amazement of all, the
Finnish army fought with tremendous bravery and several times
the Russians were defeated. It did not keep No.600 Squadron from
completing the move from Hornchurch to Manston. During that time
experiments on airborne radar continued. The importance of aircraft
able to find the enemy at night was obvious. Large listening cones
and searchlights alone would not do the job. To shoot down the
enemy he had to be caught where he was, in the air. Therefore two
aircraft from the Radar Flight at Martlesham were sent to Bawdsey,
while two of No.25 Squadron were ordered to join No.600 Squadron
at Manston. The Squadron flew Blenheims Mk.IV, although their
main strength comprised the Blenheims MkI. They were to co-
operate with Dover and Dunkirk RDF stations.

On 23rd December loading began and two days later all was ready

Blenheim BQ-G is pushed through the snow during the bitterly cold winter of 1939.

to be taken to Manston. Then came Christmas. Tight security was the reason that Christmas 1939 was to be spent under guard. The whole day was spent visiting one another: W/Os and Senior NCOs visited the Officers' Mess at 1130. At noon all the Officers went to the Sergeants' Mess and waited at the Airmen's Dinner. A Christmas party, organised for the Squadron became the talk of the town. It was Lord Lloyd's present to No.600 Squadron: an all-star concert of West End artists. One of the men present remembered in an article in the Association Magazine: "By good fortune one of the Territorials forming the airfield guard was Frank Lawton, of stage fame and husband of Evelyn Laye. Frank organised a marvellous concert with Beatrice Lillie, Frances Day, Charlie Kunz and other big celebrities making a hilarious night".

There were nine No.600 Squadron Officers present at the Christmas Dinner. A case of champagne from the City Mess was opened and much appreciated. In the evening a dance took place at the Sergeants' Mess and the CO's 30 gallon barrel of beer was by way of compensation and appreciated as well. But "there was a war on, you know"; patrols were flown over British convoys and when

Squadron Leader James Michael Wells was the son of Sir Richard and Lady Wells MP. Member of a family of eleven he was a keen pilot as well as an excellent ukulele player. He was a close friend of the famous British comedian George Formby and did the aerobatics in his successful comedy "It's in the Air". Note the "A" for Auxiliary on his lapels.

the first leave boats with British troops from France sailed home No. 600 flew overhead to protect the men from Luftwaffe attacks. After Christmas the Squadron went to Manston.

On 26th December all Squadron transport and an advance party under W/O Nicholson left Hornchurch for Manston. The next day at 1055 the air party left while the road party under F/O Anderson departed at noon in two London General Omnibus Company buses and a 35 seater coach. Kit and bedding followed by lorry. After a long trip to Manston the officers found accommodation at the Mess, while the airmen were put in huts. The huts were uncomfortable, cold and damp. Mattresses needed a very long time for drying out. Offices were difficult to come by, so the men of the Squadron found room behind "C" Hangar. The Detached Flight had become during their absence from the Squadron "very detached" and somewhat aloof. They used "X" Hangar for their aircraft but without sufficient room for any of the Mk1 Blenheims. These aircraft were now dispersed and some accommodated in "C" Hangar. Manston was not a pleasant place during the terrible winter of 39-40. It soon became apparent that it was never intended as an operational fighter station. The Operations Room, crew room and air gunners room were a long way from dispersal point and hangars. There was no furniture for the officers and although there were plenty of telephones in the rooms allotted, they were not connected. It soon became obvious that the question of fuel was going to be very important. The huts and offices were all fitted with stoves of various kinds, there being no central heating. There was a dearth of transport and it was increasingly difficult to obtain the requisite amount of fuel to keep the fires going. At times the entire field was 100% unserviceable. There were of course the lighter moments, as for example during a snow clearing operation of the road into Margate. It was a case of all hands to the pump and one airman was heard to remark, as he wielded pick and shovel, "if I thought this was ——'s (the Adjutant) coat I'd put my pick through it", after which a voice from behind said: "It is my coat, carry on!" Nobody was happy on Readiness: at night the Readiness Section and air crews suffered badly from the cold. The CO had to hire a car as his own had frozen up and the cylinder block cracked. P/O Bowring began the new year with a rather unfortunate landing. On 3rd January he pulled up the undercarriage instead of flaps. His aircraft was badly damaged and his skill was not commended.

Suddenly, when the Russians attacked the Finns, Carlow received orders to have the AI equipment stripped from his aircraft. Nine Blenheims were prepared to become part of the Finnish air force. It was a blow for the Squadron when their CO too was told to prepare for the Land of a Thousand Lakes, now all frozen and desolate. However 600 Squadron were not despatched to Finland, instead aircraft of 601 were sent there. After Viscount Carlow had left No.600 Squadron for the Directorate of Intelligence at the Air Ministry, pending his posting as an air attaché in Finland, James Michael Wells took over. Son of Sir Richard Wells, a Conservative MP for Bedford, and Lady Wells, he was one of a family of eleven, who lived at the family mansion The Grange. S/L Wells was a typical Auxiliary officer. Jimmy Wells joined 600 in the mid-thirties as a young and inexperienced Pilot Officer. He had become an out-standing flier, whose love for aerobatics was well-known. He excelled in sports. He had taken part in the Lent Races as well as in the Head of the River. He was a friend of George Formby, the famous comedian, and together they often played duets with Formby on the banjo and Jimmy Wells on the ukulele. He even took part in Formby's successful film "It's in the Air", doing the aerobatics for George. One of his stunts in the film was to actually fly through a hangar. Jimmy Wells was a passionate and accomplished airman, and a man with a promising future. Some day he was to take charge of the family breweries, for the Wells' were known as producers of excellent beers. With this in mind there was no reason why James Michael Wells should not become a superb CO. But fate often plays tricks on people. Sadly, Carlow, with the acting rank of Air Commodore, was killed later in the war, in a flying accident when his aircraft took off from Portreath in Cornwall for a long haul to Yugoslavia, where he was sent to make contact with Tito. He carried a briefcase full of golden Sovereigns chained to his wrist.

With little or no action over English territory, the war seemed far away. Yet, on a drizzly morning with low cloud, the gun crews' attention was drawn to the sound of a tri-motor aircraft. Was it a Ju52, the aircraft the Germans used as a transport as well as a bomber during the Civil War in Spain? There was a full alert and the AA-crews waited for the incoming hostile aircraft. At that stage of the war permission from the Operations Room was necessary before firing. This did slow down firing on aircraft that might be carrying out an attack, but it was very fortunate for the tri-motor and its passengers, a KLM Fokker, with Dutch officials flying to London for consultations with their British colleagues. They had a lucky day! "X" Flight, the "detached people", spent early 1940 testing IFF and AI. All tests were reported in detail, even though on many days flying was impossible due to the poor weather conditions. From 1st to 6th February "X" Flight was grounded, but on the 6th tests started again.

In the Operations Record Book they reported that Blenheims "X" and "Y" carried out trials. The IFF tests were a great success, a clear and obvious signal to saturation strength being received at Foreness every 6 seconds. The best feature of it was that it appeared on the tube even when no response was obtained from the aircraft. "This should prove invaluable when the signals fade", the Squadron diarist wrote. The following day Hiscox and F/O Frankland went over to Foreness again. F/O Smith took off to test IFF in "Z". But soon he landed again, as the cloud base was only 200 feet.

Blenheim BQ-N in better days. P/Os Haine and Kramer survived a forced landing South of the coast of the Dutch island of Goeree Overflakkee on 10th May 1940. Here the aircraft is in a better shape than it would be after coming down in Holland.

A couple of civilian technicians joined the Flight. Two of them, Messrs. Taylor and Ritson, very often took off to take part in the tests. On the 10th F/L Miller took Ritson for a test flight in "Z". Interceptions were carried out with IFF, giving a more sustained signal. For many, however, the new secret invention was a complete mystery. In the meantime great changes took place. More new men arrived and became crew members. These men would kneel down inside the fuselage of a Blenheim and peer at a little green light in a black box, near the feet of the air gunner. With the new "Operators", the crews had to get used to having a third crew member on board. Some of them did not look like airmen at all. Jimmy Rawnsley, an Auxiliary who flew with John Cunningham in No.604 Squadron, described the new arrivals: "First, they had neither distinguishing flying badges nor NCO rank, although aircrew had been made up to Sergeant some time before. Second, although they were expected to fly at all hours of the night and day, they hardly knew one end of the aeroplane from the other. They trod on all the wrong places; they picked up their parachute packs by the rip handle; they tried to walk into propellers. And since they were classed as aircraft hands or "clerks (Special Duties), neither technical tradesmen nor aircrew, they were easy prey for every Discipline Flight Sergeant who might be looking for hangar sweepers, ablution cleaners or extra guards. No wonder they wore a bewildered, harassed look. And I am afraid we air gunners did not help much. We rather resented the presence of these groundlings in the aircraft, and we treated them with scant courtesy and very little respect". Their value would be appreciated much later, when Nazi bombers came at night to attack British cities.

The Station Commanding Officer was at Foreness with Hiscox and in good visibility three runs were carried out. In the first, the "bomber" was out 25 miles and returned on reciprocal. A successful interception was made due either to the Controller saying 'Starboard' when he meant 'Port', or else the fighter pilot's absorption of the latter after lunch having confused the issue. Anyway he came up well behind the bomber by turning right on the order "port", at 8fi miles from the Station. On the second run the bomber went out 35 miles and returned with slight jinking, finally heading straight for the Station. The fighter was not off set early enough and so passed directly over the bomber at about an angle of 30°, finally taking up position about 1 mile to starboard and behind target, 14fi miles out. On the third run the bomber went out 20 miles and returned up the Thames estuary. About 9 miles from the Radar Station the fighter was brought directly behind the target at about 800 yards range. The Station worked excellently; all flying done at 1,500 feet".

On the afternoon of the 12th the future AI operators flew the Link Trainer, pictures of signals being placed before them and they gave instructions to the pilot. This proved very successful as far as it went. The procedure was repeated the following day and practices were

Blenheim BQ-R. The Vickers-K gun is pointing to the sky. S/L Wells flew this aircraft into battle on 10th May 1940. Wells and his air gunner Cpl Kidd were both killed, Wells' observer Sgt. Davis managed to bail out and save his life. One of the Squadrons members heard from Davis, when he returned to Manston, that the CO had virtually kicked him through the escape hatch of "R". He returned to England.

felt to have reached as useful a point as possible. What really was needed, however, was a pair of tubes with oscillators so that varying dummy signals could be given to the operator.

A shock went through the Detachment Flight when they were told by Fighter Command to hand the Bolingbrokes to No.248 Squadron at Hendon. F/L Hiscox did what he could to get the order cancelled, but to no avail. Even "X", an aircraft Mr. Taylor, the civilian, was working on, had to go. Taylor was unpleasantly surprised to see his hard work suddenly stopped and thought that he might be able to change the minds of top brass. He suggested delaying the stripping of "X" as much as possible while he went to HQ Fighter Command. Mr. Taylor too lost; the next day "Y" was stripped of aerials, AC generator and all wiring. The next day "X" followed. A day later HQ Fighter Command wanted to be informed what the reasons were for the delay in delivering the Squadron aircraft to No.248 Squadron at Hendon, as was previously ordered.

11th March 1940 was, in the words of someone who wrote about it, "a day of heroism unequalled in 600's history, although tinged with tragedy". F/O Tony Tollemache was airborne with LAC Smith as his gunner and Lt Sperling of the Welsh Guards as a passenger. The idea was to carry out a searchlight co-operation exercise. On completion of the sortie Tony's Blenheim approached the flare path. Then disaster struck. The aircraft hit a tree, crashed into a field and burst into flames. Witnesses later reported that a wing had been torn off and that the plane was already on fire before it hit the ground. Tollemache and Smith were uninjured and managed to free themselves from the blazing wreckage and get clear. But then Tollemache realised that Lieutenant Sperling was trapped in the aircraft. He ran back, tried to break through the forward hatch, completely ignoring exploding ammunition and the intense heat. He persisted in his brave attempts until his clothing set fire and he had to withdraw. His bravery almost killed him as his clothing was ablaze, ammunition exploding around him. All was in vain. Tollemache collapsed and was dreadfully burned. A farmer drove him and Smith to Manston where Doc Attwood treated the burns. The doctor had grave fears for Tony's life and had him transported to the Royal Naval Hospital at Chatham. Later he was moved to a convalescent home in Sussex where he met Colin Hodgkinson, who had lost both legs when his Albacore collided with a Hurricane and Richard Hillary, who would later write the book "The Last Enemy". Tollemache became one of Sir Archibald McIndoe's first "Guinea Pigs" at the Queen Victoria Hospital, East Grinstead and many operations were necessary before he was flying again. On 6th August he was awarded the Conspicuous Gallantry Medal, which was later changed to the George Cross, a very well deserved award for Tony and a great honour for the Squadron.

After the departure of Carlow and some experienced AI operators the personnel of No.600 had to be trained from scratch before they were able to operate AI with some degree of success. E.G. Bowen, who worked on the development of this new device, had to start the training process again and spent a great deal of April 1940 at Manston. He gave the new "Operators" instruction in the use of the equipment and demonstrated the interception techniques. Wells supported Bowen to the best of his abilities. During one of the flights a frightening moment occurred. Wells and Bowen were above cloud at 14,000 to 15,000 feet, doing a routine test interception on another Squadron aircraft when Bowen suddenly realised that a second aircraft had appeared on his tube, within range and closing fast. Bowen whipped his head out from under the black cloth that kept the light from interfering with his observations on the screen and looked around. There was a Hurricane racing in from the starboard side, clearly intent on getting the Blenheim in his sights. Bowen screamed to Wells to dive for cover; Wells did not hesitate for a second and hid in the nearest cloud just in time. The two decided to abandon the exercise. There was a reason for a Hurricane to try to shoot down a Blenheim. Rumours had it that the Germans had patched up several Blenheims that had crashed over Germany and were using them as intruders for reconnaissance of the Thames estuary and the London area. It was said that several "German" Blenheims had been spotted and the RAF was not taking any chances.

The Blenheim had three exits. One for the gunner, in front of the turret, one for the pilot, through a hatch above his head, and one through the side. Getting out from there was quite an undertaking on the ground; in the air it must have been virtually impossible.

The first real brush between the Squadron and the enemy came during the early morning hours of 10th May, when German forces crossed the borders of Holland, Belgium and France. The Phoney War had become a deadly serious war. At that time P/O Michael Anderson was on patrol near the French coast. Vectored by Control he spotted a Heinkel 111. When he prepared to attack the bomber his gunner LAC Baker, saw another He111, whereupon Anderson quickly turned to attack the nearest enemy. Then four other He111s loomed into view. A fierce battle developed and Anderson and Baker had to fight for their lives. The nearest Heinkel opened fire from 600 yards, while Anderson closed in, firing his guns from 400 yards. Bullets hit the Heinkel's fuselage and seemed to put the German gunner out of action. Anderson then dived so that Baker could fire his gun from the turret at 100 yards. The enemy turned back and headed for the East. Badly shot up the Blenheim managed to fly home, at sea level, and make a forced landing at Manston without wheels or flaps as the hydraulics had been shot away. This explained why Baker had not fired at the German. The intercom as well as the rear turret had been hit; Baker escaped without injuries.

CHAPTER 5

ROTTERDAM; DESPERATELY YET GALLANTLY.
10 May 1940

The Squadron was standing by the rest of the morning and the pilots had just gone to the mess for a quick bite of lunch when they were told to report to W/C Grice, the Sector Commander. He told them that since this morning the neutral Dutch had become allies and asked for immediate help in the Rotterdam area. No.600 Squadron received orders to fly to Holland to help the Dutch fight the powerful German forces now overrunning the country. German paratroopers and airborne infantry had attacked Dutch positions along a line going from the Moerdijk bridges in the South towards The Hague in the West. The Dutch air force had virtually ceased to exist, so RAF help was badly needed to counter German air power. The enemy had devised a plan, of great importance to their Blitzkrieg tactics, and used their parachutists and airborne infantry to disrupt the Dutch defences in the rear so badly that these troops would be tied up until a German armoured force had crossed the bridges at Moerdijk, Dordrecht and Rotterdam and pushed through to The Hague. Their aim was to arrest the Dutch government, the C-in-C of the Dutch Armed Forces and his staff and, above all, the Royal Family. Airfields were to be occupied, one of them being Waalhaven aerodrome, South of Rotterdam, one of Holland's two airports, now a military base with twin-engined Fokker G-1 fighters.

When the Germans attacked the field some of the Fokker G-1s had been able to take off with German bombs exploding around them. Unfortunately many others had been destroyed on the ground. The G-1, called "The Mower", having seven machine guns in the nose and a cannon in the tail cone, caused devastation among attacking German aircraft. But being too few in

Two Blenheims between blast walls at Manston. Such was the situation on 10th May 1940. The aircraft in the background is Michael Anderson 's BQ-L.

numbers against an overwhelming Luftwaffe, they were quickly outnumbered and shot down. While some of the G-1s returned to Waalhaven to refuel and re-arm, the Germans had occupied the field, in spite of a small company of young and in-experienced Dutch soldiers trying to keep them at bay. Completely surprised by the attack in the early morning hours, the Dutch were fighting desperately to chase the paras off the field, but the German reinforcement by airborne infantry had prevented the Dutch from doing so. There was only one way now to deny the Germans further use of the field, where Ju52 tri-motors were landing, unloading soldiers, ammunition and equipment. Waalhaven had to be made unserviceable for friend and foe. Fighter Command ordered "B" Flight of No.600 Squadron to fly to Waalhaven, destroy as many German aircraft as possible and cause such havoc that the aerodrome would no longer be suitable for use by the Luftwaffe. S/L Jimmy Wells and his men were to engage German fighters over the Rotterdam area and shoot them down. If there were no enemy aircraft, the Blenheims were to attack Waalhaven itself. They were told that it was of the greatest importance that Waalhaven should be rendered useless for the enemy.

One of the Fokker G-1 fighters was that of Lieutenant Noomen, a KLM captain. After taking off in the middle of the German attack he managed to shoot down a Heinkel He111 bomber. Landing at Waalhaven to refuel and rearm his fighter got bogged down and in spite of hard work under enemy fire by the soldiers it turned out to be impossible to take off again. Noomen had to abandon his aircraft, which was later requisitioned by the Germans and taken to Berlin for evaluation.

The more shot-up aircraft blocked the field, the better. It was believed that Blenheim fighters with their gun packs would cause tremendous damage. This idea ignored the fact that the Bristol Blenheim was used in a fighter role as the engines were underpowered and the armament was inadequate. Earlier warnings obviously had not taught Fighter Command that the crew of a Blenheim in the fighter role would be on a suicide mission. But for the Auxiliaries it was simple: This was what they had trained for, and now they had been ordered to show what they could do and they would meet the challenge. It would also prove that the weekend-fliers were as good and as determined as their Regular brothers-in-arms of the RAF. The Flight was ordered to fly to Holland at 1,500ft in two sections of three aircraft. To make navigation easier and allow the CO to concentrate on leading his Flight he was to carry a navigator, a Regular NCO by the name of Sgt John Davis. The Squadron flight to attack Waalhaven consisted of the following men and aircraft:

First section

	Pilot	Air Gunner	Navigator	aircraft
1.	S/L Jimmy Wells	Cpl Basil Kidd	Sgt John Davis	L6616 BQ-R
2.	P/O Norman Hayes	Cpl John Holmes	-.-	L1517 BQ-O
3.	P/O Dick Haine	P/O Mike Kramer	-.-	L1514 BQ-N

Second section

	Pilot	Air Gunner	Navigator	aircraft
4.	F/L Hugh Rowe	P/O Bob Echlin RCAF	-.-	L1401 BQ-K
5.	F/O Roger Moore	Cpl Laurie Isaacs	-.-	L1335 BQ-W
6.	P/O Mike Anderson	LAC Bert Hawkins	-.-	L1515 BQ-L

Left to right: LAC Bert Hawkins, Basil Larbalastier and Basil Kidd enjoying the sunshine. Basil Kidd died as air gunner of S/L Wells, while Hawkins lost his life as the air gunner of Mike Anderson. It was not until 1981 that the graves of two unknown airmen were identified as those of Hawkins and his pilot.

After the briefing Wells and his crews made their way to the aircraft. Men of the Squadron saw Wells and his crews leave and felt very anxious about events to come. The rumour machine had worked perfectly and some thought this was the last they were to see of their friends and officers. One of them was Eric Potter, a fitter. He saw P/O Michael Anderson and his gunner LAC Bert Hawkins off. Mike had been recalled from his honeymoon at Brighton the day before. When he said goodbye to his bride Ann, Mike asked her to return home immediately after she got a phone call from her husband. "Do not ask questions, Ann, just go", were the last words he said when he left Brighton. "After the morning brush with the He111s this chap should have been granted some rest", Potter thought. But in a serious situation like this there was no rest for anyone. Before climbing into the cockpit Mike Anderson put his hand on his gunner's shoulder and said to Hawkins: "If things get too hot, Bert, and you think it is time to bale out, do not wait for me to give the order, OK?". Then both men took to their stations, Hawkins in his turret, Anderson behind the controls. P/O John Barnes saw F/L Hugh Rowe and P/O Bob Echlin from Canada off. Having played the piano with Bob the evening before, John had no idea that this was the last thing they would do together. F/L Blackwood could not have known that he would never again see his best friend Jimmy Wells, godfather of his daughter Maureen, who had attended the christening of the little girl to please Blackwood.

At 1230 hrs. Jimmy Wells was the first to take off in BQ-R, followed by Blenheim BQ-N with P/Os Haine and Kramer. Someone took a snapshot of the pair racing by and gaining speed. It was the last picture taken of the CO, and his crew, and of the two aircraft. Followed by the other aircraft they gained height and set course for the target. Soon after take-off they formed up and flew to the East, at an altitude of between 3000 and 4000 feet. Over the North Sea they were to be met by a fighter escort. However no RAF fighters were seen. Later it turned out that both units had received different times for the rendezvous. Wells and his men circled around for almost an hour, in vain. Then the CO decided they were to fly on and carry out their mission. It will always remain a mystery whether Wells knew what awaited his Flight once they arrived over Holland. On 8th May ACM Hugh Portal had stated in a letter to the Air Ministry that he was convinced of the grave danger to use Blenheims as fighters. Immediately after their arrival the sky would be full of agile

enemy aircraft and, as Portal said, "we should be grateful if half of
our aircraft return". With this in mind Wells and his men entered
Dutch airspace and pressed on. In the distance they saw the huge
fires and the smoke in the Rotterdam area.

While Wells headed for Holland, twelve Messerschmitt Bf110
aircraft of Zerstörer Geschwader 1 took off from Kirchellen in
Germany. Commanded by Hauptmann Streib, one Section, 3./ZG1,
flew to the West, to attack enemy aircraft over Rotterdam. Streib had
been given an important task. With his Bf110s he was to escort eight
Ju52s, packed with airborne infantry troops to Rotterdam. One of
the Ju52 tri-motors carried no less than General Kurt Student,
Commander of the airborne troops. Before take-off Student had had
a brief conversation with Streib and the Captain had asked: "Tell me
Herr General, which aircraft is yours? I want to make sure that you
get the best protection." "Never mind", was the reply. "Your job is
to look after all aircraft". After the briefing the Messerschmitts took
off and once they met with the slow transport planes set course for
Rotterdam. The Section consisted of three crews. The pilots were
2nd Lieutenant Knacke, 1st Sgt Gildner and Sgt Müller. Behind
Knacke sat his gunner Kurt Bundrock. They had no idea that within
half an hour they were to clash with Jimmy Wells and his aircraft.
Many years later Kurt Bundrock vividly remembered his first real
aerial combat and how they clashed with the Blenheims of No.600
Squadron over the skies of Rotterdam: "We took off from Kirchellen
at about 1300 hours German time. The weather was good.

I sat with my back to Knacke behind my MG15 machine gun, on
which I had put a full magazine. We were to guard the sky over
Rotterdam, where our paratroopers and airborne infantry were
fighting the Dutch around that city. We were to make sure that our
Ju52 transport aircraft could land without being attacked by enemy
fighters. Below us was enemy territory. Strange; everything looked
so peaceful, almost lovely in the bright sunshine. Soon the peace
would disappear and hell would break loose. It was the first time I
really entered battle against strong and able opponents, the RAF. My
mouth was dry and I felt very nervous, for apart from opposition by
the small Dutch air force we expected Hurricanes or Spitfires.
Suddenly I heard Knacke in my earphones. "Bundrock, look over
there". Facing backwards I could not see a thing. Then Knacke
pointed down. Then I saw what he meant. Six camouflaged aircraft
passed about 1000 feet below us. Their roundels were clearly visible,

Waalhaven aerodrome, after Schiphol the most important civil aerodrome in Holland, was first devastated by German bombs. It was to be attacked many times between 10th and 14th May 1940. Bombed by the RAF, the Luftwaffe and the Dutch Air Force and shelled by Dutch artillery on the north bank of the Maas river it soon was useless. After four days it was littered with Dutch and German aircraft.

they were British. It looked as if the roundels said: "Look here, I am the enemy, I am ready for you". "Engländer", I shouted. Knacke replied: "Six Blenheim fighters, we can have them".

My heart started to beat faster. I stared at the British. All our aircraft now were in action. Our CO gave the order to attack and with the engines roaring twelve Bf110s jumped six British aircraft. The engines screamed when we accelerated. Like eagles two Messerschmitts at a time dived down. The steep dive pushed me out of my seat. I could hardly reach for my gun. When I turned my head into the direction we were flying I saw a Blenheim ahead of us. The distance was about 400 meters. We caught up with him and I sat behind my machine gun, which was pointing to our tail fins. "Have you cocked your guns, Sir?", I asked Knacke, who nodded. From that moment nothing was said. I grabbed a piece of bread from my knapsack. Chewing made me feel quiet. Knacke had switched on his gun sight. I saw the lights, circles and a cross.

A Messerschmitt Bf110 of ZG1. Aircraft of this unit bounced the Blenheims of No. 600 Squadron, causing a tragedy among the Auxiliaries.

Ahead of us flew the enemy. Suddenly I saw tracer flashing by. The Blenheim turned to the left, so did we. We closed in to about 150 metres. Then Knacke fired. The cannons and the machine guns spat their tracer towards the Blenheim. Cordite smell filled the cockpit. My body was thrown around, from the left to the right and back again. The Blenheim turned and turned. Another Blenheim crossed our path behind us. I fired with my machine gun and saw the tracer enter the enemy aircraft. The distance was 50 meters and pieces flew off the Englishman. The Tommy dived down at an angle of 45º. Turning the aircraft Knacke shouted: "I think he has had enough!" Then another Blenheim climbed very steeply and turned upside down. A man jumped out, his parachute opened. The aircraft spun down and crashed West of the docks. Flames and smoke showed where it had met its end. Gildner managed to catch another Blenheim. With a long flame and dirty smoke coming from its wing the enemy aircraft lost altitude and crashed as well. At the same time a single Blenheim kept on fighting, now virtually on its own. It shot at a Ju-52 that was trying to land. The transport plane was riddled and crashed right in the middle of Waalhaven. The Blenheim, chased by two of our aircraft, turned and turned and got away. I could not help admiring the Englishman. But they were no match for us. Their aircraft were old and slow; our nose guns caused terrible damage."

Hauptmann Reinhold Knacke (left) and his air gunner Kurt Bundrock, who both took part in the battle between the Blenheims and the Bf110s. Many years after the war Bundrock sent the author pages from his diaries, describing the encounter with No.600 Squadron.

On the ground Dutch people watched in horror as the RAF Blenheims were bounced by twice as many enemy aircraft. Within fifteen minutes four Blenheims had crashed West of Rotterdam, while a fifth limped back to the West, only to make a forced landing in the water South of the island of Over Flakkee. One single Blenheim slowly headed for England. It was all over. Eef Mak, a young man, saw how Anderson's "L" had fought gallantly. He recalled later: "The camouflaged aircraft with the glass nose was hit in the engine and flew very low. Black and grey smoke came from the aircraft and from time to time it seemed to disappear between the houses. Mak heard the rattling of its machine guns and the much slower and deeper sound of the German guns. Then the Blenheim came from the East and tried to escape in a Westerly direction. When it approached the Oude Maas river it had come so low that it flew into the dike rather than over it. The crew must have died instantly. After the smoke and flames had settled some people wanted to go to the wreckage and see what they might be able to do for the crew. Mak's father strictly forbade his son to join the men. Then Mak Sr. and Eef's eldest brother went with the group.

The scarred remains of a Blenheim; possibly Mike Anderson's L1515.

He returned shattered. Later Eef was told that the aircraft had been entirely destroyed. One engine lay about 120 yards from the fuselage. The gunner still sat in his turret, dead. The pilot was killed on impact. There was nothing the men could do. Early the next morning a small group of Dutch soldiers crossed the bridge at Spijkenisse, which was lowered only to allow them to pass. In a hurry they collected the bodies and carried them back. The only thing they could do was to ensure that these two men got a decent burial. All around them was fierce fighting. The Germans were patrolling towards Spijkenisse and the small Dutch detachment had to concentrate on the defence of the bridge.

Municipal Cemetery at Spijkenisse in 1946.
Two simple wooden crosses for two "Unknown Flyers". On top of the cross it reads: "Died for his country". At the bottom is the single word "Englishman". Beside them a Dutch soldier lies buried. He died during the battles around Spijkenisse on 12th May 1940. Note the fresh tulips around the graves. Since 1940, with a short interruption caused by the Germans no longer allowing "pro-Allied" demonstrations at the graves, during the annual National Remembrance in the early evening of May 4th, the citizens of Spijkenisse pay their respect to these three comrades in arms. Anderson and Hawkins were identified in 1982. Since then they have new headstones on their graves with their names inscribed.

German aircraft flew overhead and in the distance, some 5 miles to the East, the smoke from burning buildings at Waalhaven aerodrome were clearly visible in the blue spring sky. Due to the battle there was no possibility of identifying the bodies of the two men. They were buried as "Unknown Airmen". On the cross at Hawkins' grave was written "a Leading Aircraftman". Then the burial party left. There was a war to be fought. It would be 1981 after two long years of research and archive investigations before names appeared on the graves: P/O Michael Anderson and LAC Herbert Hawkins of No.600 "City of London" Squadron.

Corporal De Hoop, an Engineer of the Dutch Army was based near Piershil, about 5 minutes flying time SW of Rotterdam. He actually witnessed how Blenheim "K", the aircraft of P/O Rowe and P/O Echlin was attacked and shot down by a German fighter. After the Dutch surrendered on May 15th the Corporal wrote a sworn statement: "The twin-engined fighter was chased by a German aircraft. All the time they were shooting at each other. The light rattling of the British guns was quite different from the more heavy sound of the German guns. After a few tight turns the gunner of the RAF plane suddenly stopped shooting. That gave the German a chance to close in for the kill. Flames came from the British plane and it seemed to stagger in the sky. I remember that the German pilot was shooting constantly, even though it was clear that the Englishman was now defenceless and on fire. The pilot of the plane managed a belly-landing near Piershil. The plane came down billowing smoke and when it skidded across the farmland it threw dirt around. Then it made a half turn and stopped close to us. We left our building and ran to the aircraft as fast as we could, to see if we could do something for the men. The crew seemed dazed for neither of them moved. We smashed some of the windows in the glass nose and managed to pull the pilot out. His uniform was already on fire and his face looked terrible. But he was still alive. The man in the gun turret on the back of the aircraft was dead. He lay still over his weapon. At the same time the flames started to cover the fuselage and we felt the terrible heat when we tried to free him as well. As the flames grew fiercer our commander told us to forget about him and get the pilot away. Some of us tried to break the fuselage open with a pole to try and get his body out, for he should not burn as an animal. All was in vain; it was horrible to see, but we were helpless. While we watched, the body in the turret became engulfed in the flames; there was not a bloody thing we could do for the poor chap. One of our Sergeants said: "I hope that the poor bastard is dead" and we could not agree more. We had left the pilot on the grass, a stupid thing to do as this man was suffering terrible pains and needed immediate care. We gently lifted him and carried him to the road on a piece of wooden fence. Some civilians had come to watch and one of them was in a little truck. We commandeered the car and the pilot, who was moaning in pain, was taken to Oud-Beijerland, where we had a dressing station for the area. Our doctors gave him first aid and in spite of the continuous shooting between our own troops and the German invaders a civilian ambulance took him through the lines to the Rotterdam Zuiderziekenhuis where he would stand a chance to survive. The next day we got the gunner out and gave him a decent burial with military honours at the Reformed Churchyard of Piershil. They gave him a first class burial, in a nice spot of the church yard. It was the only thing we could do for this poor boy, who had died to help us. We were very upset, as it was the first time we actually saw a casualty of war. What a dreadful way to die. The Minister spoke a few words and I remember that in spite of our shortage of ammunition we fired a volley of live bullets, as of course we had no blanks."

In Canada, Hugh Rowe remembered: "I regained consciousness in a house where the Dutch army had a dressing station. Then I was taken to Rotterdam, and admitted to a hospital. For me the war was over, for after a few days the Dutch army surrendered. I did not notice much of it. However I was aware of the horrible bombing of Rotterdam as casualties were brought in, staff were very upset. Then one morning German army doctors came to the hospital. There was a lot of tension as the Dutch obviously hated the Germans for all they had done. They showed me to the Germans and there was a long discussion in German between the Dutch doctor and his German opponent. For the time being I was left in the care of the Dutch, who told the Germans that I was far too weak to be moved. Of course this could not go on for ever. After a few weeks the Germans knew that my recovery was suspiciously slow. A German doctor checked my burns and set a time for my departure. Hospital staff was made personally responsible for me staying in the building until I was ready to collected. Then, one morning I went to a POW camp as they believed me to be ready for travel. I still see that young Dutch nurse, who took care of me with such care and love, as if I were her own family. When the Germans moved me out she was terribly upset and in tears". About a year after this story had been published in a Dutch paper a letter from Spain was delivered at the author's address. It came from a lady by the name of Trudy de Bruin, who wrote: "In 1940, when the Germans invaded our country, I worked as a nurse in the Zuiderziekenhuis (Southern Hospital) in Rotterdam. I will never forget the young Englishman with burns who was brought in the second day of the war. His burns were horrible, his face was as black as a Negro's. But he never complained, even when we had to change his dressings, which must have caused a horrible pain.

After a few days our armed forces had to lay down their arms. Rotterdam had been bombed and the Germans threatened to bomb other cities as well if we did not give up. There was no way we could get the Englishman to his own country, for the Germans had been fighting in the streets not far from our hospital. We decided to save him from a prison camp as long as we could. We managed to keep him in our hospital ward for a couple of months, much longer than was really necessary. But the German doctors saw through us and took him away. I felt as if they had taken my brother from me. I can not remember having cried so bitterly as that day, when a German ambulance drove off, with my pilot inside".

People in Pernis saw the dogfights between Bf110s and Blenheims. Pernis being very close to Waalhaven soon became part of the battle as an eyewitness remembered: "We had some Dutch anti-aircraft guns in Pernis. The soldiers had fired at the Germans all morning, but when the English planes came they got rather confused and stopped shooting as they feared to hit an Englishman. The fight in the air took no more than 15 minutes. One English aircraft was hit and started to burn. The pilot pulled it up and we could see a man jump out. Then the aircraft came down in a gentle glide and crashed between Pernis and Heyplaat at the hamlet of De Hey. It fell on a house along the dyke, not far from the local milkman, Mr. Rasser. People found two bodies in the wreckage and buried them near the place of the crash. They placed a wreath and flowers on the grave with a miniature aircraft adorning the wreath. It was a simple yet moving way to show their feelings. For a long time one of the engines lay near the grave as some sort of a monument. People would bring fresh flowers and pull out the weeds.

P/O Robert Echlin (X), a Canadian, died in the flames. His pilot Hugh Rowe made a forced landing near the village of Piershil after the Blenheim had been hit and set alight. In spite of Dutch soldiers trying to free Echlin's body he did not survive. The Dutch buried him with military honours and since 1940 villagers of Piershil have tended his grave, the only war grave in the grounds of the Dutch Reformed village church.

A local artist witnessed Jimmy Wells' Blenheim coming down near Pernis. Some days after this shocking event he made this pencil drawing and kept it until he showed it to the author some fifty years later.

It annoyed the Germans quite a bit for they knew very well that we came there to show our affection for these men. On 31st August 1940 another British aircraft crashed not far from Pernis. Three bodies of the crew of that aircraft were buried alongside the other two. Later in the war the remains of the five men were taken to Crooswijk Cemetery in Rotterdam. The Germans knew that the graves were the site of "demonstrations" all over the country".

A Dutch policeman witnessed the crash of Blenheim BQ-W, the aircraft of Roger Moore and Laurie Isaacs. On the morning of 10th May the Burgomaster of Pernis told him to come to the townhall for an important task. The policeman was to take the cash that was in the townhall and deliver it to a bank in Rotterdam where it was hoped to be safe from looting Germans. With the cash in a large briefcase, the policeman took his bicycle and rode to town. At Waalhaven he was stopped by German paratroopers who were hiding near the perimeter fence of the airfield. Strangely enough, when the policeman told them quite sternly that he was on official business, the flabbergasted Germans let him go. When he mounted his bike again he saw the Blenheims roaring in: "With my briefcase pressed to my chest I dived for cover. The aircraft were British or French, for they had red-white-blue circles on their sides and on the tails you saw what looked like a French or a Dutch flag. I knew they were not ours, for Dutch aircraft all had big orange triangles on their wings and sides and their tailplanes were also painted orange. The aircraft shot at the German aircraft on the ground, but soon were attacked by German fighters. One British plane was hit and fell on the field. On impact it broke into two pieces. When there was a lull in the fight I hurried to Rotterdam to take the money to the bank. Frankly, I was pleased to hand it to the cashier. Returning to Pernis I was told that the men in the British plane had been buried on the edge of the airfield. Later in the war the Germans moved them to Crooswijk".

A Dutch boy in front of an engine of L6616, BQ-R, the aircraft in which S/L Jimmy Wells and Cpl. Basil Kidd lost their lives.

P/Os Haine and Kramer, hopelessly outnumbered by the many German Messerschmitts, tried to return to Manston. Their aircraft, BQ-N, had been shot up very badly. The port engine had cut and many instruments had been shot to pieces. Limping westwards the Blenheim quickly lost altitude. There was not a chance that they would ever reach England. Desperately trying to keep his stricken aircraft under control Haine managed to make a belly landing on the muddy South coast of Goeree-Overflakkee, one of the islands of the Scheldt estuary. It had not yet been occupied by the Germans. While people from Herkingen village hurried to the dyke to see if they could help, the two airmen climbed out of the aircraft and waded to the shore. A local farmer took them to his house, gave them bread, some pork and hot coffee. Soon a group of Dutch soldiers arrived, rifles at the ready. They first wanted proof that the men were not Germans. However, once the identity of the RAF officers was cleared, the soldiers took them to a local hotel where they could wash and sleep. The next morning, May 11th, an escort of Dutch infantry took them across the water to Numansdorp, a small town on the bank of the Hollands Diep River. The Dutch intended to take the two men to the French troops that were said to be advancing from Belgium in the South, to attack the German para-troopers who had occupied the bridges across the River and stop the German 9th Army from advancing to the Northwest. But the French troops did not show up. How could the Dutch know that the French attempt to go North had failed and that they were hastily retreating ahead of German tanks that were racing to the bridges to relieve their own men. The plan having fallen apart it was decided to try and take the two airmen to The Hague and get them to the British Embassy. After a long and adventurous trip on foot and by car, sometimes passing less than a mile from German positions, the two officers and their escort crossed the Nieuwe Waterweg River and were taken to The Hague

There they met S/L Adams, the British Air Attaché, and members of the crew of a No.76 Squadron Whitley shot down by the Dutch in March and who, after having been interned and released with the outbreak of hostilities, were doing a liaison job. S/L Adams asked them to proceed to Ypenburg airfield and try to fly a captured Heinkel He111 bomber to England for evaluation. However before this could be done they were told that the fierce fighting at the aero-drome would make a take-off impossible. The two spent the night

Local people from Pernis buried Wells and Kidd not far from the site of their crash. On 31st August 1940 a Blenheim Mk.IV, T1940, PZ-D of No.53 Squadron from Detling, with the Commanding Officer, W/C Edwards at the controls, and his crew Sgt Beesley (wop/ag) and Sgt Benjamin (observer) crashed. They were buried alongside Wells and Kidd. During the German Occupation the site became a place of regular remembrance and resistance. Flowers were put on the five graves, removed by the Germans and put back again the next day. Later in the war the Germans moved the five bodies to Crooswijk Cemetery, Rotterdam. Before that they put a simple shield at the grave: "Resting place for 2 English Pilots/Officers, fallen 10th May 1940 and an English crew of a Bristol Blenheim that was shot down by Anti-Aircraft guns on 31.8.1940 near Nieuwe Sluis".

at the Passage Hotel in The Hague. The following day they were driven to the Hook of Holland. A British destroyer, HMS Hereward, waited to take Queen Wilhelmina and members of Her household to England before the Germans captured her. At about noon the ship left the Hook. It was a very sad and quick departure. Rumour had it that the Germans had dropped magnetic mines in the river, knowing that a valuable prisoner was about to escape. On board HMS Hereward Haine and Kramer met Sgt Davis of No.600 Squadron and a New Zealander, Corporal Jock Barrie, who was also a crew member of the aircraft shot down by the Dutch on 28th March. Davis reported that Wells and his gunner had been killed and that he had been on the run from the Germans as well. Cpl. Barrie had been wounded and was admitted to a hospital in Rotterdam. During the bombing of the city of 14th May the poor chap was evacuated when the hospital was hit and started to burn. On board HMS Hereward the men saw little of the Royal company. They had no idea that at first the Dutch Queen insisted on going to Zeeland Province to join Her troops and continue the battle against the Germans.

This photograph was secretly taken during the war. Local villagers gathered at the grave site to bring flowers. Note the children wearing wooden clogs. A wreath hangs over the cross, with a white model aeroplane attached to it. Doing this meant a great risk, as too often the local German commander could consider it an "act of terrorism" and anti-German behaviour. It was very dangerous to show feelings of affection towards the Allies. In many cases, later in the war, people were executed at the spot.

But it was made clear to Her that this plan was impossible, as the Luftwaffe had dropped mines in the Scheldt estuary. HMS Hereward now headed for home and after an uneventful voyage she docked at Harwich at five o'clock in the afternoon. Davis and Barrie were photographed, Davis with a small bandage on the forehead. They both looked happy and quite relieved to be home. For the men of No.600 Squadron it meant freedom, for Queen Wilhelmina it was to be the beginning of a five year exile.

On 15th May the Dutch armed forces surrendered. Rotterdam was still burning and the threat of further atrocities against civilians was too much for the Commander-in-Chief of the Dutch armed forces, General Henri Winkelman. In a small school at Rijsoord, about ten miles South of Rotterdam, a very bitter Dutch general arrived. The Germans welcomed him with smart salutes and a guard of honour, General Kesselring even tried a handshake.

Winkelman, tremendously upset by what he had seen while being driven through Rotterdam, ignored the German salutes and refused to shake hands with his enemies. Little was said. General Winkelman signed the document that put an end to resistance of the Dutch army in most of The Netherlands. Winkelman insisted that the troops in Zeeland should not capitulate as they were still covering the retreat of the French. He also told the Germans that he would not order the remains of the Dutch air force or ships of the Navy to shut down their engines and wait. "I have no control", he said, "your unnecessary bombardment has cut my communications." The Germans then heard that most of the Dutch army depended on civilian telephones for communications. Then Winkelman stood up and without speaking a further word returned to his Headquarters in The Hague to announce the unconditional surrender on the wireless. Less than three months later the Germans arrested him and sent him to Poland for supporting resistance against the German authorities by signing the congratulatory register for Queen Wilhelmina's birthday in the old Royal palace in The Hague and for openly blaming the Luftwaffe for their criminal attack on Rotterdam. He was taken to a castle at Stanislau in Poland where he spent the war with captured general officers who were considered dangerous for the "peace" in their occupied countries.

The only Squadron aircraft to return to Manston was Hayes' Blenheim BQ-O. Hayes and his gunner Cpl Holmes had had a very eventful day and the return of the crew could be considered a miracle. Many years later Hayes remembered his miraculous escape from hell: "It was a beautiful May day when we approached the target. We could see the columns of smoke from fires burning in the city of Rotterdam. Further North there were fires near The Hague. We did not see any German fighters though in the distance aircraft

Laurie Isaacs, air gunner of BQ-W, the aircraft flown by Roger Moore. Isaacs and Moore were first buried "unknown". After the identification of Mike Anderson and Bert Hawkins, they too were identified and received new headstones on their graves, with their names for the first time in 41 years.

could be seen. Waalhaven drome was South of the river and high columns of smoke rose from that area. Buildings were on fire and from the cockpit I could see that there were bitter fights. Then Jimmy Wells put us into echelon to the right and led us down to attack the field. I was flying number two and followed him down. I do not remember what target Jimmy selected, but I picked a Ju52 transport and shot it up. On the way in I saw no enemy aircraft in the air. Apparently nobody else in the flight did either, as there were no warning shouts on the R/T. I made a low pass and carefully selected German tri-motors. Then I climbed away to the right to follow the CO. As I climbed I saw a Bf110 attacking one of our Blenheims. Then I saw about eight Bf110s about 800 feet above and just peeling off onto our tails. I turned as hard as I could to meet the one on my tail and he made little attempt to follow me. I then saw a Ju52 in the air and climbed to attack. When I did I saw Hugh Rowe's Blenheim go in to attack in front of me. The Blenheim was immediately set upon by a Bf110 and shot down. Immediately I was also attacked by a Bf110, which hit me several times. I do not recall what happened, for the fight was very confusing. Thanks to Holmes, who gave directions during the battle, I could keep the Germans from shooting me down.

However, I soon found that the situation was hopeless and that my only chance was to get out as soon as I could. My airplane had been hit very badly and what really worried me was the petrol leaking into the fuselage as my starboard petrol tank had been hit. I dived to ground level and tried to get home. A few moments later I suddenly realised that I was flying to the East. So I had to turn round and fly back. When I reached the Rotterdam area again I saw three He111 bombers flying low and crossing over in front of me. I attacked them, but as I saw little result and as all three were shooting at me, I broke off the attack and set course for the Belgian coast. Having trouble with the petrol feed I climbed to 15,000 feet to give myself some "gliding space". With the aircraft in a dreadful state we limped home. We were lucky enough to reached Manston and land. When we had landed at Manston we found an incendiary bullet in the tank which for some odd reason had not burned. After we touched down at Manston I reported to W/C Grice and asked him: "Who is back?" His answer was that we were the first to return. I had to tell him that we would be the only ones to return". Norman Hayes was right. BQ-O was indeed the only aircraft of "B" Flight to survive the mission. It was a terrible blow for the Squadron. For their great courage P/Os Haine, Kramer and Hayes received the DFC. Corporal Holmes was awarded the DFM. AVM Keith Park person-ally came to Manston on 2nd July 1940 to present Cpl Holmes, who

With great difficulty and skill P/O Norman Hayes (top left) managed to nurse his aircraft home to Manston. At the station he was told that he was the first to return. He could only answer: "I am the only one to return". He received the DFC from AVM Keith Park. His air gunner Cpl. Holmes (bottom right) received the DFM. Holmes can be seen behind his Vickers K-gun. He was commissioned to Pilot Officer but died in an air crash later in the war.

by that time had been promoted to Sergeant, with his medal. F/O Hayes survived the war and became the first OC 600 during the post-war years. Unfortunately Holmes was killed later in a flying accident.

BQ-N after its forced landing in the shallow waters South of Overflakkee island in the Scheldt estuary. After the Germans arrived they removed the guns and parts from the cockpit. A local teacher took his brother to the site some time later and took this photograph. The aircraft identification is still visible on the fuselage.

After Wells failed to return, the A-Flight Commander, F/L Clarke took over. Despite the loss of B-Flight, No.600 Squadron mounted a bomber escort, together with No.604 Squadron during the after-noon of 10th May as if nothing had happened during that terrible morning. They were expected to do their duty. Led by F/L Clark, six pilots, F/Os Clackson, Pritchard, Smith and Hannay, and P/O Rawlence, and their gunners, flew to Middelkerke, to Zeebrugge and to Flushing. F/L Clarke flew – like Jimmy Wells – with a navigator, Sgt Wilson. Cpl Rufus Risely accompanied them as gunner. They managed to destroy a He111. Less than a week later, on 16th May, No.600 was ordered to leave Manston and fly to Northolt to take part in the defence of London. The Squadron remained at Northolt for only two months and were back at Manston when the Battle of Britain started. From Manston the pilots carried out ferry flights to

France, taking replacement pilots for the fighter units on the journey in, and returning with vital equipment during the return flight. During the British retreat from the Dunkirk beaches the Squadron was sent in at 4000 feet to protect the soldiers trying to reach the ships and barges. However, finding themselves being shot at by the Royal Navy, which considered everything flying to be "hostile", the aircraft returned home after frantic evasive manoeuvres. On 23rd May a Blenheim of No.600 Squadron was sent to Marck airfield near Calais in France with two ground crew members on board. Their orders were to salvage a Spitfire of No.74 Squadron that stood on the airfield with a damaged radiator. They carried a spare radiator and some glycol and hoped to repair the aircraft so that it could be flown home. However, shortly after the Blenheim had taken off from Marck and the ground crew had started to work on the fighter, German troops overran the field and captured the Spitfire and two unlucky men.

With the help of Dutch soldiers P/Os Haine and Kramer managed to slip through the lines and reach The Hague. From there they returned to England on the same ship, HMS Hereward, that took the Dutch Royal Family into exile. Here is F/O Haine in happier days.

A few days after the Dutch surrender the first Germans arrived at Herkingen where the Blenheim of Haine and Kramer rested in the water. They examined the aircraft, removed the guns and some equipment. The aircraft itself stayed where it was, half submerged. They expected the tides to do their work. But BQ-N was not to disappear that easily. For many months it remained where it was, a visible sign of the help No.600 Squadron had given the Dutch at an extremely high price to the Squadron itself. One day a Dutch teacher and his cousin waded through the water to the wreckage. With his cousin on the starboard wing, he took a photograph. More than 50 years later the photograph emerged and became part of the Squadron archives.

Three weeks later No.600 Squadron flew what still is considered the first "Intruder" sortie into now occupied France, when Blenheims of the City of London Squadron flew as far as Saint Pol and Arras to find enemy aircraft. Ray Aveyard still remembers the "Intruder" sorties, because at the time it was the job of a Wireless Operator to connect up the electrical circuit of the detonator in the secret IFF-set (Identification Friend or Foe) as the last task before the aircraft took off for its mission. Connecting the fire leads to the detonator involved making sure that there was no power on the leads.

This was done by putting the leads on one's tongue. If one did not receive a mild electrical shock, it was OK to connect the leads to the detonator terminals. Failure to carry out this simple check could have caused the detonator to prematurely explode in one's face. The "Intruder" sorties were always timed for the aircraft to be over German held airfields just before dawn when German bombers were returning to their base after a raid on England. In theory it was thought that the German crews would be tired and not very vigilant as they prepared to land and would be an easy target for the RAF attackers. It was considered good policy to be back at base before the German day fighters had been scrambled for their dawn patrol! These sorties, as well as the others on 26th/27th June failed to achieve the success hoped for. In July the Blenheims returned to Manston. Soon 600 would get involved in war over Britain's territory. The Battle of France was over, the Battle of Britain about to begin.

Sgt Davies (left) safely returned from Holland on board HMS Hereward. After successfully bailing out of Wells' Blenheim, Davies was helped by the Dutch. With a slight head injury and minor burns on his hands he disembarked in Harwich. With him was Jock Barrie, a Kiwi of No.76 Squadron whose Whitley had been shot down by the Dutch on 28th March, when the Netherlands still were neutral. After his return to Manston Davies had the difficult task of informing S/L Wells' family what had happened to their son. On the same vessel Queen Wilhelmina escaped German captivity.

CHAPTER 6

THE BATTLE OF BRITAIN.
August and September 1940

Situated on the Isle of Thanet, at the south-eastern tip of Kent, Manston was first and foremost a vulnerable place. The scene in the days of May and June 1940, when the British Expeditionary Forces were desperately trying to return home and many people expected the Germans to land on the South coast within weeks, was not a happy one. Only 800 men, most of them very young and inexperienced recruits, were available to defend the aerodrome. Half of them carried some sort of a firearm. The Squadron was the only resident unit, doing night operations. During the day other squadrons would drop in to operate, but would return to their own bases for the night. The Squadron was given a short rest after the eventful beginning of the "real" war. On 3rd July the first German attack took place. Although only small bombs were dropped at Manston and no damage was done, the attack was sufficient to improve the morale and general liveliness of everybody. Regularly Blenheims were sent on patrols but no enemy aircraft were intercepted. In fact they often proved too fast for the Blenheims desperately trying to climb and catch up with the intruders. On the other side of the Channel the war was very present. When on 11th July the C/O and F/O Lawrence carried out an AI test between 2200 and 2300 hrs they had a grandstand view of the bombing of Calais.

The Blenheims flew from Rochford and Hornchurch. During one such sortie P/O Boyd spotted a He59. He attacked, and fired four bursts at the enemy, but no record could be found of the result of this attack. The German rear gunner however, returned fire and the Operations Record Book said "he was very accurate" These Heinkel aircraft were used by the Germans to locate shot down crews,

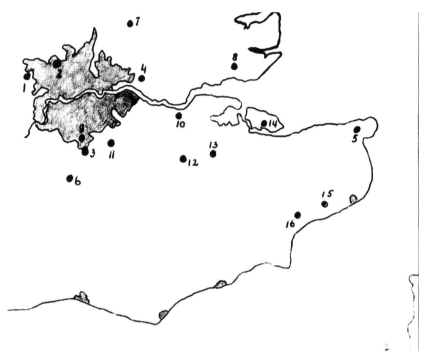

Map I.   Airfields used by No. 600 Squadron between 1925 and 1940 and other important airfields.

1. Northolt (600)	7. North Weald	12. West Malling
2. Hendon (600)	8. Rochford	13. Detling
3. Kenley	9. Croydon	14. Eastchurch
4. Hornchurch (600)	10. Gravesend	15. Hawkinge (600)
5. Manston (600)	11. Biggin Hill	16. Lympne (600)
6. Redhill (600)		

German or British, pick them up, and take them to the Continent. It was common knowledge that these aircraft, in spite of flying with civilian registration, red crosses and a white colour, often flew near convoys that were trying to sail through the Channel. It was decided that with this in mind, no immunity could be granted. On 9th July a He59 was attacked by 54 Squadron. This particular German aircraft landed on the Goodwin Sands, stranded and was towed to Deal by the Walmer lifeboat, the crew of D-ASUO were taken prisoners. On 11th July another He59 was shot down. The Germans were quite furious. That very day two more He59s were spotted and attacked by aircraft of Nos. 238 and 602 Squadrons. A third one was seen cruising in the vicinity of a British convoy off Selsey Bill. One entire

German crew of four were killed, and the crew of the He59 attacked by 238 Squadron went missing, after they baled out from too low an altitude for their parachutes to deploy.

During the Battle of Britain the role of the Squadron was changed to night-fighters. They flew constant test sorties to improve the AI device, a highly secret airborne radar set, which was supposed to pick up German aircraft so that the gun pack under the Blenheim could destroy them.

On 8th August 1940 the Squadron suffered another loss. Me109s of III/JG26 and Spitfires were fighting a fierce battle in which two Spits were lost. Two Blenheims of 600 Squadron had taken off from Manston for AI tests when the air raid siren sounded. Operations called both aircraft back and one of them landed safely. It seemed that Blenheim BQ-H did not return fast enough for it entered the area where the dog fights were taking place. The Blenheim was an easy prey for the 109s. Immediately Oberleutnant Sprick of JG26 attacked. Little is known about what happened, but a few minutes later Grice appeared over Ramsgate with both engines ablaze. The Blenheim roared over the town and crashed into the sea near Ramsgate harbour. The entire crew was killed (F/O Grice, Sgt Keast and AC1 Warren). It was obvious to the spectators that the gallant pilot had pulled his aircraft away from the town, rather than allowing it to crash into the centre. Attempts to award Grice a posthumous decoration for obviously giving his life rather than allowing his aircraft to crash into the town were not successful. The remains of Grice and Keast were recovered from the sea. F/O Grice was cremated at Charing, Kent, where his name can be found on a Memorial panel. Keast was buried in the family grave at Whitstable. The body of AC1 Warren, the radar operator, was washed up in France. He was subsequently buried at Calais. In the Operations Record Book the diarist recorded: "Civil and Naval reports at Ramsgate said that Grice pulled the aircraft out of a dive just before it would have hit a main shopping centre. He avoided the harbour and crashed into the sea, one wing first. The aircraft turned over and sank burning".

Life at Manston became virtually unbearable. The station was very vulnerable, close to the sea and often German raiders would swoop in at very low level, disappearing before the airfield defences knew what had hit them. For the ground crew the continuous attacks by the Luftwaffe meant very little rest and with many other aircraft landing at Manston, much work had to be carried out under difficult circumstances. These attacks were described by one of the Squadron members in an article in the RAFA Magazine "Air Mail" in the summer of 1990. He had arrived at Manston on July 8th. Soon afterwards Manston turned into "Hell's Corner". At that time all was normal; parades, work, eating and sleeping. On August 12th at about lunchtime the first heavy bombing attacks were carried out; about 150 bombs being dropped. There was little damage to aircraft or people. This was particularly surprising as, on "ordinary" days, when the air raid sirens sounded, it meant that German bombers were attacking ships in the Channel. Consequently the ground crew at Manston were not too much bothered by the nasty sound of the sirens and continued their work without any disturbance. Then came Wednesday August 14th. Again the Germans came at lunchtime and bombed the aerodrome. The defences of Manston consisted of a small unit of Northumberland Fusiliers, armed with four 40mm Bofors and two Lewis guns which were World War One vintage. A Royal Artillery unit with 40mm Bofors completed the AA-defence. There also was a hit on the Store hangar and one of the Squadron hangars, causing damage to three Blenheims. However the men at Manston were not completely defenceless. With the little artillery they had, they fought back.

This time the Luftwaffe paid a price. When the Messerschmitt

F/O Dennis Grice (left), Sgt Frank Keast and AC1 John Warren (right) were killed when their Blenheim was bounced by 109s. Rather than letting his aircraft fall on a shopping centre in Ramsgate, the pilot managed to fly to the harbour, where the Blenheim crashed with the loss of three lives.

Bf110s of 2./Erpr. Gr.210 swooped in, one aircraft, S9+NK, was hit by fire from a Royal Artillery 40mm Bofors gun on the airfield. The German aircraft was set on fire and crashed inside the perimeter, killing the pilot, Lieutenant Brinkmann, and his NCO gunner. During the same attack the 20mm Hispano cannon of No.600 claimed another German aircraft. This Bf110, S9+MK, collided with Brinkmann's stricken aeroplane and crashed as well. The pilot of this aircraft, Unteroffizier Steding, was killed but his gunner, Gefreiter Schenk, baled out wounded. He was taken prisoner by one of the ground staff of the Squadron, who found the bewildered German struggling about amidst falling bombs. It was the occasion when some of the ground crew of No.600 Squadron followed the German aircrew prisoner into the air raid shelter, such was the speed of the attack. Surrounded by not very friendly looking RAF men, the Luftwaffe guest prayed for the speedy arrival of the Military Police. There was one single casualty in the Squadron, the CO of Manston, S/L Clark, who got a black eye when a stone ricocheted from his Adjutant's tin hat.

Bill Sills was one of the men present who would remember those days for the rest of his life: "I was then a Flight Mechanic and was working on the port engine of one of our Blenheims. Radio-location was being fitted for the first time and all the engine leads had to be fitted with a Marconi Harness. From Bristol Aircraft Company a representative was overseeing the whole procedure. I had finished my inspection of the engine and reported to the Flight Sergeant in charge. I reported to him that as far as I was concerned, my engine could fly at any time. I merely had to put oil in the carburettor jacket and that would be that. At this juncture the Air Raid siren went and suddenly the hangar was deserted. I could not be bothered and stood on my toolbox carrying on with the oiling. Suddenly, without the slightest bit of fear, I knew I had to get out of there fast. I grabbed my tin hat and ran hell for leather to the hangar door. On my way I saw the Bristol representative moving fast at about 90 degrees to my track. There was an almighty flash and I was bowled over; the flash was between the Rep. and me. I picked myself up and saw some machine-gun bullets hitting the ground. At this I did get very scared. Beating all running records and touching the ground once in ten paces I headed for the Air Raid shelter, not knowing that my leg was dislocated. After the raid I found I could not stand up and my child-hood friend, Stan Mather, who had joined up with me, helped me.

The roll call was carried out and all were present. Stan and another airman assisted me back to the hangar. On arriving at the back of the hangar someone shouted that the Jerries were coming back. At this, the man holding me up on my right side disappeared but Stan stayed where he was. Two days later a third aircraft was damaged by shrapnel. Frightening things happened during that week. A bomb landed on the bomb dump 24 hours after it had been cleared. John Wright, one of the Squadron NCOs was caught while taking a bath. The only thing that remained for him was a hasty retreat in non-regulation dress. After this raid, damage was so terrible that the only water available had to be collected from the swimming pool.

RAF Manston under attack. This photograph was taken by a German aircraft during the attack. Bombs are exploding all over the field.

I asked Stan to remove himself, which he would not. Believe it or not, we then started a very fierce argument about leaving or staying, during which I thought I heard a whole swarm of bees buzzing around us, and then a big bang. After this all went quiet. As we looked around, tin hats were appearing out of ditches, together with some loud statements with respect to our sanity. Apparently a whole Squadron of 109s had dived down to around 200 feet and were strafing the hangar. They in turn were jumped by a number of

Hurricanes which in turn strafed them. All this happened just above our heads. Funny how bullets can sound like bees. By some miracle we were not touched and Stan helped me around to the front of the hangar, where I saw the result of the bang. It was a Me110 upside down on the ground after apparently hitting the hangar roof. Hard luck for him. My engine had indeed flown. The flash I saw was a bomb which had blown my engine clean through the roof. After a couple of days I was sent to Ramsgate Hospital where my leg was put back in joint, a service which I repaid them by kicking the surgeon who did it (on a reflex action) straight across the ward taking with him a screen which then collapsed on top of him. I knew nothing about this, but apparently it caused quite a stir in the ward. The surgeon told me about it afterwards. In 1946 I was working as an Airframe/ Engine Inspector at Northolt when the Bristol Technical manager came in the hangar. He was the chap of 1940. We looked at each other for the first time since then and said together: You're bloody dead".

With day and night-fighters using the airfield, life at Manston was hectic. During the darkness the Blenheims would fly patrols. At dawn the Hurricanes and Spitfires would land and after taking part in sorties and being refuelled and rearmed return to their home

After the attack the wreck of a Blenheim lay shattered in a demolished hangar.

stations, coming back the next morning. The Squadron armourers decided that more weapons were necessary. Anger about the German attacks and some technical skill were the foundations of two ingenious contraptions. First the "Sheep-dipper" was built, a weapon that was almost as lethal to its gunners as to the enemy, made from four Browning machine guns, rigged on a pole framework.

Cpl Cook or anyone else around, manned it as an anti-aircraft gun. Soon the second defensive contribution saw the light. It was the "Armadillo", a truck converted into a primitive armoured car by being given slab sides and a machine gun fitted amidships. Sgt Joe Smart used it to give the attacking Germans what he had, a large quantity of ascending brass. In addition three Vickers K-guns were mounted and operated separately. They were put to good use against the enemy by Cpls Hunter, De Vroome, Owen and Cox, who were soon to be known as the "Comic Corporals". Some of the officers were seen taking pot shots with .303 rifles as the 109s and 110s came in at low level for strafing attacks. But not surprisingly the primitive defence was not enough to deter the Luftwaffe and they continued their attacks. One day an aircraft was destroyed, while two were damaged. The Squadron, rather "in the way" with their now useless aircraft, did what it could to defend itself. Pilots, gunners and ground crew now occupied themselves by rearming and refuelling Spitfires and Hurricanes. It was virtually impossible for the Blenheims to get involved in combats with Me109s and Me 110s. It would have been suicide anyway. In his book "Nine Lives" Alan Deere, one of the best known fighter pilots of the Battle of Britain, remembered the dreadful circumstances at Manston, but also, unwittingly, gave air to the thought that something had gone terribly wrong at Manston and with No.600 Squadron, when he wrote: "When during the airfield bombing phase in August conditions at Manston became almost untenable, the pilots of 600 Squadron set a splendid example to the ground crews by assisting in the refuelling and re-arming of the day Squadrons. More often than not this was done under fire from the enemy and despite the fact that the 600 pilots should have been resting from the previous night's operations. It was due largely to them that we were able to continue to operate from Manston long after the airfield should have been evacuated as tactically unacceptable". No.600 Squadron received orders to leave Manston and go somewhere else. The attacks on Manston continued every other day and eventually the decision was made to send personnel of No. 600 Squadron to Hornchurch.

The sad remains of a Squadron Blenheim, destroyed during the sudden attack by the Luftwaffe on Manston.

The move was regretted by the Squadron, as, amongst others, there was a plum orchard on the other side of the service road at Manston and the vibration of the exploding bombs brought down a considerable quantity of ripe Victoria plums. The Squadron had gallantly carried out operations at night and ground services during the day. Manston now was a heap of rubble and no place at all for a night-fighter unit. Sgt Perkin, a Squadron pilot, remembered: "They gave us only about twelve days flying at O.T.U., the turnover of pupils being suddenly very rapid. The first time I fired my guns was at the enemy. At Manston we were repeatedly dive-bombed and strafed by 109s which seemed to be almost on standing patrol overhead. I still cannot understand what a Blenheim Squadron was doing there. It was hardly surprising that the airfield was then evacuated and the Squadron moved back to Hornchurch. Here we arrived in time for the first two Saturday afternoon raids. When having parked my Blenheim at Hornchurch, in a shelter bay, a stick of bombs from nine Ju88s fell across the field and destroyed my aircraft. One bomb landed about ten yards away from me". It was impossible to continue operating at Manston due to the quantity of craters and the many delayed action bombs that had been dropped. There was a problem to clear the airfield and withdraw the people not necessary for the defence, every time the siren sounded and the enemy appeared.

Manston had ceased to exist as an operational aerodrome. In his memoirs of those days Alan Deere gave credit to the airmen for a job well done. Yet in later years this particular episode in the Squadron's proud history would turn into a sad controversy, when Len Deighton, in his book "Fighter; the True Story of the Battle of Britain" quite wrongfully pictured the Squadron members as a bunch of cowards, who spent most of the time hiding from the enemy.

On arrival at Hornchurch on 24th August the Squadron had no sooner settled in, than the Luftwaffe was overhead to welcome 600 and to make known that they knew. The result of this attention was the demolition of a newly completed cookhouse and dining hall. At Hornchurch the men found themselves fully stretched mucking in with 54 and 74 Squadrons. They belted up ammunition and ignored enemy raids under the leadership of Group Captain Bouchier, who gave running commentaries on the German attacks while they took place. For night fighting the days at Hornchurch were disappointing. In fact when the Germans attacked London and the Bolingbrokes

The hardest thing was to sit and wait all night for enemy intruders to come. It meant a total change of life, day becoming the time of rest and night the time of operations. Aircrew of No.600 Squadron wait for a call to rush to their aircraft, take off and try to find a German intruder high above the skies of England.

of No.600 Squadron were to be sent up for interception, the drifting smoke from the fires from the docks was so thick that the Blenheims could not take off. Trying to operate by night from Hornchurch was very fraught as a battery of 3.7 guns were operating from the airfield perimeter. Shrapnel was flying around all the time. This caused a real danger for anyone walking out of the Dispersal Hut to assist the refuelling of the Blenheims. During the night of 28/29 August the crew of "D" was scrambled. They were told to take off as soon as possible and patrol base at Angels 17.

For the next hour they received a good number of vectors and investigated a lot of searchlight concentrations. They were sent to patrol a line across which a lot of German aircraft were making their way to targets in the Midlands. It was not long before the crew spotted exhaust flames on an aircraft close in front and above. The pilot turned and went flat out after the intruder. But they soon found that they could hardly climb any higher and that the controls were

Air gunners of 600 Squadron in leather flying clothing. Kneeling /l/r are Edwards, Risely, Eames and probably Culmer. Seated are l/r Medworth, Brown and Metcalf.

getting very sloppy. So having staggered into a line astern position at about 400 yards a long burst was given in the direction of the enemy. The German aircraft turned and dived. It was faster than the Blenheim so the crew had to let it go. A bit later, however, exhaust flames were visible below them to starboard.

Again the Blenheim dived after the German and the night-fighter got pretty close when suddenly the sky lit up and "D" was clearly visible from behind in the beams of the searchlight. Then another searchlight, coming from the front, flicked over the German and fastened on to the Blenheim. Indeed "D" was close to the opponent, so again fire was opened, just before the pilot was completely blinded by the searchlight. The pilot exhausted the remainder of his ammunition, only to see the enemy dive away and escape, much too fast for the Blenheim to catch up a third time. Soon afterwards, on 8th September, a No.600 Squadron detachment left Hornchurch for Redhill. With Blenheims IF the unit was drawn from "A" and "B" Flights to form a new Flight. Redhill, a civilian air strip, had not been occupied by other than aircraft of a Flying Club. Shelters were hastily being dug by a Canadian Construction Unit. Ray Aveyard, one of the men who was to operate the new radar, still remembers a few minor incidents: "When the Squadron first arrived at Redhill with its transport and a convoy of private cars and motor bikes, the first arrivals found the civilian flying club's petrol tanks full and not locked. Needless to say, it was just like Christmas and every privately owned vehicle was fully topped up with fuel free, until the authorities found out. Most of the ground crew were billeted in large houses or private schools about three miles from the airfield and soon thriving little businesses were set up to provide extra meals à la carte.

The intense cold during night operations made good flying clothing absolutely necessary, as two air crew members show posing in their kit.

A local traffic control was set up on the airfield using a civilian caravan and this was manned by personnel of the Wireless Section with a VHF set. One night, quite at random, a German bomb was dropped so close to the caravan that it turned over with me in it. My mates and I were fortunate enough to be able to crawl out to safety".

Soon after the Squadron arrived the first Beaufighter came. It had Hercules sleeve valved radial engines, the armament consisted of four cannons and six machine guns. But there was no ground equipment available yet to assist in servicing the aircraft, its engines or its equipment. This meant that the Beaufighter could not be used to combat the Luftwaffe intruders. Of course there also was the matter of training the crews in properly using this sophisticated piece of electronics. For the Auxiliaries it was a strange contraption and, often they were puzzled as to the function of this strange thing. In "Pilot, Diplomat and Garage Rat", S/L Pearson, OC 600 from December 1941 until May 1942, described the reaction of an airman, who had been picked to become an AI Operator. On reporting he saw a strange object on the desk and was reported to have said: "What manner of thing be that? It be a telephone I hear tell".

Soon more Beaufighters followed and by the 18th of September No.600 Squadron had six of them available. Two were flown to St. Athan to be fitted with AI. Having to train aircrew on a virtually unknown and very secret piece of equipment was not the only problem. Redhill was a very dangerous airfield for aircraft coming in to land. It was subject to fog and mist, making night operations very risky. Hence the Beau, as the aircraft was soon called, only operated by day. Yet the CO managed to shoot a Ju88 down near Bexhill, Sussex. The first operational Squadron night sortie, still on Blenheims only, under the control of Hornchurch, was made the next day, 9th September. One Blenheim was sent up to intercept German raiders. However, as radio communications between Hornchurch and the Blenheim were very bad, the sortie had to be abandoned after thirty minutes. Further flights were made on the 10th, when one of the three Blenheims despatched had to land at Biggin Hill due to raiders stalking around Redhill. The remainder of 600, under S/L D. de B. Clarke, moved to Redhill on 12th September. During that day four more Beaufighters arrived, a further delivery bringing the strength to six aircraft. Two of these flew to St. Athan in Wales to have AI radars fitted. At this time night-fighters seemed quite ineffective against the Luftwaffe. All in all it was considered a discouraging period as the Squadron was not to be allowed to do what they wanted: to hit the Germans as hard as they could.

Operational patrols were flown on most of the remaining nights of September 1940. The number of aircraft involved each night varied from two to seven. The number increased to nine during the nights of 15th/16th and 28th/29th September. The only available help apart from the crew's eyes, were searchlights. But these were only of limited value, as Dick Haine recalled when he reported about his operational sortie during the early morning hours of 15th September: "It might seem a simple matter for night-fighter crews to see bombers that had been illuminated by searchlights, but this was not the case. If the raiders came during bright moonlight nights, as on September 15th, the beams of the searchlights were not visible at heights much above 10,000 feet. If the searchlights were actually on the enemy bomber the latter could be seen some way away, but only if the fighter was beneath the bomber and the crew could see its illuminated underside. If the fighter was flying higher than the bomber, the bomber remained invisible to the fighter pilot. If there was any haze or cloud, and there were both during the early morning of the 15th, it tended to diffuse the beams so there was no clear interception to be seen, even if two or more searchlights were following the target". Another matter was the limited value of the AI radars. Below 10,000 feet the radar would be so full of clutter that nothing could be distinguished on the tube. And as the radar was intended to find low-flying He115 floatplanes carrying mines into the Thames Estuary, it was of little or no help. If a German raider was seen from below, the Blenheim's margin of performance over the intruding Germans was so small that usually the fighter could not get into an attacking position without great difficulty. By the time the Blenheim had struggled to a good position the raider had often disappeared. Every now and then a "strange" Beaufighter would operate with 600 Squadron. It was an aircraft of No.25 Squadron and the first operational sortie was made on 12th September. In the middle of the month S/L Clarke, had to say goodbye to his Squadron after stumbling into a trench, breaking several bones in his foot. It was a humiliating "crash". He went to Redhill Hospital and his place was taken by S/L B. Maxwell, from Bomber Command. Contact with raiders was very infrequent, but during the night of 15th/16th September, F/L Pritchard sighted a He111, caught in searchlights. He fired two bursts at close range and started a fire in the starboard engine of the German bomber. Pieces were seen to fall off the raider when it disappeared. Then the engagement had to be called off when the searchlights and anti-aircraft guns turned their attention to the Blenheim. The Heinkel, having been observed to be on fire, close to the water at Bexhill, probably crashed there, for wreckage was washed up some time later. A further contact was made during the night of 27th/28th September when the glow from exhausts was spotted in the Maidstone area by P/O Denby's gunner. Closing with the aircraft it was identified as a raider and Denby fired two bursts at the enemy with the forward fixed guns while his gunner gave one burst from the turret. The raider was lost when it made a steep dive near Hastings. Looking around, the crew was fortunate enough to spot the exhaust of a second raider. The aircraft was heading for France, so Denby gave chase and opened fire at short range until he had crossed the coast of occupied France. He is believed to have shot the German aircraft down. But neither Denby nor his crew members Sgts Canham and Moulton were able to prove their kill. In the latter stages of the month the Squadron achieved up to 20 hours flying time each night, in spite of the difficulties caused by heavy ground mist during "Redhill Nights".

The Squadron's first operational flight with a Beaufighter (R2076) was made on 30th September by F/O Boyd, with AC Burley as his radar operator. During the month some Blenheims were damaged when the undercarriages collapsed during rough night landings. Twice this happened during the night of 29th/30th September. Shortly after the Squadron's arrival at Redhill, radio control of the aircraft had been transferred to Kenley. Training continued throughout the month, with day and night exercises in Tiger Moths, Blenheims and Beaufighters. Experimental sorties were flown in a Douglas Boston (AW 404), a twin-engined aircraft, on loan to No.600 Squadron. This aircraft had originally been ordered by the French, but since the collapse of France it was used by the RAF. During its week's stay several daylight, local and cross country flights were made. The growing importance of the night-fighter was now being realised and during the latter part of the month the Squadron received two visits from the Commander in Chief and the AOC AVM Keith Park. It also occasioned the visit by a number of senior staff officers. During these visits the Squadron was told of the vital importance of the night-fighter. Promises were made for new equipment, aids and techniques in the near future. The Squadron had begun as a Bomber Squadron, become of Day Fighter Squadron, now it had the task of being a Night Fighter Squadron. The next month started with a flurry of activities, no less than thirteen sorties carried out on 1st/2nd October by Beaus and Blenheims. S/L Little flew three Beaufighter sorties that night. On 3rd October a Blenheim flown by P/O Hobson, took off from Redhill for an operational patrol. During his flight Hobson reported

AC2 Charles Frederick Cooper

one engine running badly, but continued to fly to his patrol line. At 0345 he reported that flying at 10,000 feet with an unserviceable engine, he wanted to come back. The weather was very poor and in heavy rain the aircraft ploughed into trees on high ground at Forest Row at a spot where the ground was 700 feet high. Blenheim "M" was destroyed and the crew, P/O Hobson, Sgt Hughes and AC Cooper, were killed. The correspondence which followed gave an idea of the shock the sad news of Cooper's death must have caused the family. In a telegram it read: "Regret to inform you your son 1003497 AC Cooper killed 3rd October. Letter follows". A few days later a second telegram informed the family: "that the

Government will send deceased home if you wish and cannot afford expense. No other travelling expenses will be allowed. Otherwise the funeral will be here and date advised later. If you wish to attend and cannot afford expenses a return railway warrant for two persons (one relative) will be issued on production of this telegram at nearest police station. Commanding Officer 600 Squadron". It was one of many sad messages S/L Maxwell had to write. AC Cooper was buried at Heath Town, Wolverhampton. His pilot P/O Hobson was laid to rest at "All Saint's" in Banstead, Surrey. Sgt Hughes was buried in the Airmen's Corner at St. Lukes, Whyteleafe.

As the weather continued to deteriorate flying was hampered, but still each night Blenheims and Beaufighters took off to do their duties. The last patrols by 600 Squadron aircraft were carried out on 9th/10th October by four Blenheims. On 11th October the Squadron received orders to move to Catterick. The main party left that evening at 1800 hours and arrived at its destination the following day. The ground crew were flown there in Bombays and Harrows.

*   *   *

Looking back over the Squadron's experiences since War was declared on the 3rd September 1939, we had taken part in the Phoney War operating from Northolt spending much time on fruitless patrols. A new Flight, 'X' Flight had been formed and sent to Manston where experimental trials on the new and secret AI radar were being carried out. This was followed by the whole Squadron moving to Manston shortly before Xmas. Although routine patrols were carried out during the very bad winter weather, much time was lost being grounded due to excessive snow. With the advent of Spring, Manston suffered many heavy day-time attacks resulting in our losing several Blenheims on the ground or in the hangars. Ground staff were kept busy rearming and refuelling day fighters which operated from Manston during the daylight hours. Many strafing attacks were made on the airfield until conditions became unbearable due to the presence of many unexploded bombs and other damage. As a result, the Squadron were evacuated from Manston to Hornchurch. However, the environment at Hornchurch was not conducive to night-fighter operations due to a Battery of heavy ack ack guns operating on the airfield perimeter. Hence a further move was made to Redhill until the whole Squadron was moved north to Catterick and other airfields for regrouping and retraining on being re-equipped with Beaufighter night fighters.

CHAPTER 7

THE BEAUFIGHTER BOYS.
September 1940 to September 1942

Then followed the move to Catterick in Yorkshire. Winter conditions were so dreadful that Squadron aircraft on standby were "night-nursed" with catalytic and convector heaters. For rations or communications the heater attendants, or Aladdin Watch, relied entirely on a tractor driver by the name of "Bluebell" Pace, who was their main link with the outer world. When reading the Operations Record Book it seemed that the perpetual bad weather completely washed out flying during the last weeks of 1940. This did not put the Squadron into inactivity. For soon personnel of No.600 were posted to three different airfields, Drem, Prestwick in Scotland and Acklington in Northumberland. For some reason it had to be done in a hurry. Only two hours after arriving at Catterick a detachment from B-Flight was formed and despatched by road to Acklington airfield, not far from Newcastle. The Dispersal Hut there was a real Canadian log cabin, but the conditions were cold and wet, as Acklington was right on the coast. The only consolation was that off duty one could go into the large mining village of Acklington itself. There were no pubs, but about fifty so-called "clubs". Service personnel automatically were made honorary members. Great times were had by all.

The first AI radars fitted to the Squadron Blenheims were the Mk.IIIs. Hanbury Brown was present when they were fitted at St.Athan. They were better than the Mks. I and II. One of the changes was to replace the wooden structure supporting the transmitter with a metal one. It had a more powerful transmitter using two air-cooled valves giving about 5 kW pulse power and a range of about 15,000 feet. Mk.IV was introduced in late 1940. It was properly engineered and, like all its predecessors, it worked on a wavelength of 1.5 metres. It had an excellent new modulator designed by the EMI company which gave a minimum range on a target of about 500 feet and a maximum of 20,000 feet. It also used vertically polarised antennae which cured the abominable troubles which the operators had with Mk.III using horizontal polarisation.

F/L Pritchard, A-Flight Commander, became Squadron Leader and took over from S/L Maxwell, who was posted to No.13 Group as the Night Controller of Operations. B-Flight returned from Drem and F/L Norman Hayes, who had survived the onslaught over Rotterdam on 10th May 1940, took over A-Flight from Pritchard. Sadly 20th December turned out to be a very bad day for the Squadron. Sgt Wilson and his Radar Operator P/O Holmes DFM took off from Catterick for a night patrol which ended in disaster. Holmes had been Norman Hayes' air gunner during the Rotterdam mission. After they returned AVM Keith Park himself had flown in to award Hayes and Holmes the DFC and DFM respectively. A very experienced operator with many hours to his credit, he and his pilot were on their way back from their sortie when suddenly R/T contact was lost. The aircraft was heard flying over base and then disappeared again. A short time later a muffled explosion was heard when they hit a hill West of Richmond. Wilson was killed instantly. Holmes survived, though very seriously injured. Holmes was rushed to hospital, but all attempts to save his life were in vain. The airman who had risen from a Corporal to Pilot Officer died at Christmas time. Celebrations therefore were marred by the loss of a brave airman. At about that time six pilots and four aircraft of B-Flight returned to Drem once again to assist in the defence against German raiders in that area.

While at Catterick 600 laid the foundation for its future successes as a night fighter unit. The Squadron diarist, with a vision for the future, wrote in the Operations Record Book: "Diaries are easy to write if the diarist leads a life of variety. If, however, he be of the hard working, steady one job type, with no variations of interest, his daily entries will consist of the same phrase: – Work as usual -. So it is with 600. Not for us at present, the thrill of the chase, the adulation of the crowds, or even photographs in the Daily Mirror. However, we have our compensations in knowing, that, by steady application to an interesting experiment, we are showing the way to more successful night fighting. Our only bugbear has been the weather. During the past month, unfortunately, we have been able to fly on only ten days; and with the best will in the world we must admit that we have hardened after putting all our theory (so ably expounded but so hardly learnt) into practical operation. But we have learnt many things beside theory.

Heinkel He111 bombers intruded to drop bombs on industrial estates.

While on paper, each day has been almost identical with lectures, exercises, lectures, exercises, we have been driven by our restless minds to experiments in instrument flying; to checking up on things we should know, to learning things we did not think were really necessary in the past. As a result, steadily and surely, we are on the way, we hope, to becoming the most knowledgeable bunch of night-fighters in the whole of Fighter Command. Those who knew no Morse, are learning Morse. Navigation is no longer a mystery to anyone; and what we can not do to cannon is not really worth doing. Our fame must be growing, for we have attached to us a pilot and operator from 25 Squadron, and we understand that further crews are due from 604, all of which (we hope) is very gratifying. We have other causes for pleasure, F/L Clackson, commander of B-Flight, has been given command of No.65 Squadron, a new twin-engine squadron forming at Catterick. One of his Flight Commanders will be P/O Dick Haine DFC. It has left us very short of pilots, of course, but the spirit of the City of London Auxiliary Squadron lives on elsewhere and that, we think, is a good thing". And so it proved to be. It was an important period in the history of No.600 Squadron as it was about to form the nucleus of what would become a deadly force in the RAF, the night-fighters. The Squadron was keen to bid farewell to the Blenheims. They were hoping to be equipped with Beaufighters only and the AI Radar Operators were close to a fully operational level. So the Squadron became non-operational for almost three months. The diarist wrote: "The sole redeeming feature about a Yorkshire February is that it has only 28 days. February 1941 may have been of great interest to the Met. Department in that it broke all records for snow, but to a Squadron engaged on intensive AI training and with all the ground work completed, a more or less permanent bad weather state became more or less tedious. There were compensations. The physical fitness and muscular development of officers and men increased as vast heaps of snow were cleared: a spot of leave was enjoyed by many; and -most important- we welcomed a new CO in the person of W/C Stainforth AFC, who could make an aeroplane do anything but talk. His great experience proved of the utmost value to us, and we looked forward to a successful summer under his leadership. He joined us on the 4th. There was no change from the daily routine of the course till the 23rd, when S/L Pritchard and three pilots were ordered to Prestwick in view of an expected Blitz on Glasgow, which by the end of the month had not matured. This left at Catterick only Squadron HQ, the lame and the weak and we said goodbye to February with relief". George Stainforth, a pilot of pre-war Schneider Trophy fame, was a character. For instance he invariably took his dog on car journeys and it was his habit, on dismounting, deliberately to leave the door open. After moving some distance from the vehicle, he would turn to the animal and say: "What about the bl—dy door?", whereupon the dog would double back and close it for its master. He also had a patent bell in his office for summoning underlings. A rope, suspended from the ceiling with a chunk of rock attached, would be swung violently against the wall and thus produced results. Numerous slightly unorthodox procedures were recounted and Stainforth obviously made quite a deep impression on his contemporaries.

In March the entire Squadron moved to Drem with a small detachment at Prestwick for the defence of Glasgow. The unit which had been based at Acklington had already returned to the main part of the Squadron. One of the Squadron members there was Bill Sills, who had been discharged from hospital after his leg injuries at Manston in August. Though his leg was in a poor state he insisted on being considered fit and swore that he was able to carry out his duties. So off he went and reached the Squadron after a long and difficult journey. But as far as he was concerned there was another snag. Being declared "Fit A1" he was expected to service the aircraft out on the airfield and often at night. He tried to overcome his leg problems by having his bicycle sent up to him from home. It had a fixed wheel so Bill pedalled with his right leg and "held" his left leg. He managed until he was posted to Catterick in the winter of 1940. He slipped in the snow and twisted his right leg under the crossbar. The early part of March was distinguished only for the continuation of the wintry weather at Catterick, Prestwick and Drem, so there was little opportunity for night operations. There was some AI practice put in by day. On 10th March the Squadron lost F/L Bobbie Braun, Adjutant and one of the oldest members of the Squadron. He was posted to No.4 ARTS in Brough. Three days later orders came to move HQ to Drem and join B-Flight the next day. A-Flight remained at Prestwick. On the morning of the move the Squadron received confirmation that P/O Gordon Denby and his radar operator P/O Gilbert Guest had made the Squadron's first certain kill. Near Glasgow they spotted a Heinkel He111 bomber. These bombers penetrated deep into the United Kingdom to drop their deadly cargo. Most surprisingly Denby and Guest flew a Blenheim, so in that respect their victory was a shining achievement. After Denby's attack the He111 went down in flames and it was not until much later, when the identity of the crew was established, that they found out that the captain of this bomber had been a Luftwaffe " ace", responsible for many of the fire raids on London, Swansea, Bristol and Plymouth. Three more Beaufighters arrived and slowly but surely the crew became operational. Unfortunately one of the Beaus was lost when Gp/Capt Rogers of 13 Group flew from Prestwick, with Sgt Lawson as his operator. The aircraft crashed into the sea, the pilot drowned, Lawson survived.

In April two new pilots arrived, P/O Ross and P/O Calvert. Ross was said to have no less than 2500 flying hours to his credit. They

brought their "own" operators with them. The Squadron flew with
19 pilots now.

The Beaufighter looked a strong aircraft. It had speed and tremendous firepower
and was expected to be an excellent night-fighter. It was flown with several different
engines, such as BQ-E, a Mk.II with Rolls Royce Merlins. This type was rather a
disappointment.

The weather was as hostile as ever. The diarist wrote: "The English
Spring may be something to write lyrics about, but the Scottish
variety seems little different from winter, with its attendant bad
weather states and for the first week of the month scarcely any flying
took place". Hayes and Stainforth had indecisive combats, making
no claims as they were unable to see the results of their attacks.
Norman Hayes clashed with a He111 during the night of 6th/7th
April. At 14,000 feet they exchanged fire, but the He111 got away.
The following night the CO fired at a Ju88 over the Pentland Hills,
flying at about 15,000 feet. But after a short burst the cannons of the
Beaufighter jammed and the German vanished into the clouds.
The enemy was claimed as a probable, but the claim was disallowed
as no wreckage was found. On 14th April Norman Hayes left for
No.68 Squadron where he continued as a Senior Flight Commander.

It meant that he would soon be in charge of his own Squadron as this was a Squadron Leader's post. After the war he returned to command No.600 Squadron when it re-formed as a Day Fighter Squadron.

On 24th April, to everyone's joy, No.600 Squadron was posted to the South again. Their new home base was to be at Colerne, a partly finished air-field near Bristol and Bath. No.600 Squadron became part of No.10 Group on the 27th. At Colerne the Squadron found "an aerodrome which seemed a mass of unfinished buildings, unfinished roads, unfinished everything, perched on a hill top 800 feet above sea level. But this does not matter as we understand the Hun comes over as in the old days at Redhill. P/O Gordon Denby received a well-deserved DFC for his brush with the He111. In the meantime the Squadron had been re-organised with S/L Pritchard as OC A-Flight and F/L Scrase as OC B-Flight. April showed more and more flying of the Beaufighters, rather than the Blenheims. It was good for morale to see the faithful but outdated Blenheim disappear from the scene.

Serviceability of the Beaus remained a problem. The teething troubles due to the change from Blenheims to Beaufighters hampered combat flying. But in the first week of May luck changed in the Squadron's favour. On 3rd May with a moon rising to its brightest quarter and the Hun coming over in some force F/O Woodward and Sgt Lipscombe brought down a Ju88 near Shepton Mallet. When congratulated with his success he said that it was all due to Lipscombe who masterly read the AI tubes and accurately directed his driver to the target. Three nights later Pritchard and Sgt Gledhill caught a He111 over Shelborne. They chased the German all the way to the French coast, in spite of the German fighting back gallantly and quite accurately, counting the holes in Pritchard's aircraft after he returned. Only the fact that the bandit kept disappearing into the clouds saved him. Returning home the CO said that "One burst put out the starboard engine and then the guns of the Beaufighter jammed. If this had not happened the Jerry would not have escape over France. The Squadron's call-sign was "Gardener", the CO being called "Head Gardener".

On 6th May the Squadron lost two aircraft. P/O Calvert while doing dusk landings in a Blenheim, was afflicted with an aircraft whose undercarriage failed to function. At a crucial moment the port engine cut out. The net result was that on landing he careered across the aerodrome, and crashed into a new Merlin Beaufighter, writing off both aircraft. The pilot and his operator Sgt MacDonald were unhurt. Compensation arrived quickly. Pritchard and Gledhill contacted a Heinkel near Colerne and destroyed it near Sherborne. On the 7th the Squadron destroyed two more He111s, one by F/O Howden and his Operator Sgt Fielding, the other by F/O Woodward and Sgt Lipscombe. Woodward and his Operator had a stern chase from Bristol to the Needles where the Heinkel blew up near Tennyson Down. Howden's Heinkel crashed near Weston-super-Mare, with its bomb load causing tremendous fireworks. The diarist said: "it made a good mess". On the 8th a Ju88 fell victim to the guns of a No.600 Beaufighter, flown by P/Os Denby DFC and Guest, the AI operator. The German escaped but was badly damaged. The next

Squadron Leader "Archie" McNeill Boyd, an RAF VR officer who flew many night operational sorties and destroyed three enemy aircraft at extremely low altitudes. For this he was awarded the DFC. On his left breast pocket he proudly displays the No. 600 Squadron badge.

night Woodward and Lipscombe were shot down by another Beaufighter. As the aircraft still was relatively unknown, some pilots took for granted that it had to be hostile. While on patrol over Plymouth they were attacked and shot down by F/O Chisholm of No.604 Squadron in a Beaufighter operating from Middle Wallop. Fortunately the No.600 crew members were able to bale out to safety and thus survived this "friendly action". Of course there were hard feelings and various methods of dealing with the "enemy" pilot were contemplated. In the Operations Record Book the diarist wrote: "Sgt Lipscombe recognised the attacker as a Beaufighter. It is a pity the 604 pilot did not do the same". But deep inside all were happy that the men had survived. The CO had a close shave over Bristol during a sortie on the 13th. His Beaufighter hit a barrage balloon cable. It said much for the wing of the aircraft, for he was able to return to base and land safely.

On 16th May, "a day and night of ups and downs" according to the diarist, the Squadron bagged a Hun, but should have had no less than three. The tragic occurrence was the experience of S/L Pritchard and Sgt Gledhill. They were put onto a "blip" South of Gloucester and followed him to five miles South of Coventry in X7544. The searchlight never illuminated the German, instead it frequently lit up the Beaufighter. This told the enemy that he was being followed, for he took the most violent evasive action, twisting, turning and climbing. Sgt Gledhill kept him in the AI screen with considerable skill and eventually a visual was obtained after a long and stern chase. Just as the pilot was positioning himself to attack, searchlights, in spite of Pritchard's appeals for them to douse, illuminated the fighter when 100 yards from the enemy. The Ju88 air gunner got a perfect target presented. He opened fire and blew in the starboard side of the cockpit, setting light to the petrol feed, causing flames to envelope the pilot. Pritchard and Sgt Gledhill baled out successfully, Pritchard suffering from burns on the face and Gledhill having a bullet in the leg. Both were taken to Warwick Hospital. Needless to say, Pritchard was in a rage when he was on the ground, and one can imagine what would have happened had he been allowed to "evaluate" the event with the searchlight personnel. F/L Boyd with F/O Glegg got a Ju88 near Honiton. It was B-Flight's first success and it was due to good co-operation between pilot and operator. At about the same time P/O Ross and Sgt Dove were gaining steadily on another bandit when the searchlights took a hand. Illuminating the Beaufighter five times blinding the pilot who could no longer keep an eye on the German who retreated in a hurry. Later Control reported that the aircraft shot down by Boyd and Clegg was responsible for the early mishap of the CO and his operator. Three days later Air Marshal Sholto Douglas visited the Station and spoke highly of 600. On 28th May a freak accident happened when F/L Howden and Sgt Fielding came in to land. The wind had changed after a very heavy thunderstorm, they were not warned of this. Howden came in from the wrong direction, landing down wind, wrecking the Beaufighter. The following day P/O Arnsby and LAC Wells crash-landed R2184.

Whilst the Squadron were at Colerne, Ray Aveyard remembers being sent to the Bristol Aviation factory at Filton, Bristol, to fit some extra radio equipment into Beaufighters which were intended to be delivered to 600 Squadron. This special radio equipment was British made and was originally designed as a landing aid for bomber aircraft. The equipment was known as the Standard Beam Approach (SBA) system. It will be remembered that for a period during the War, the German Luftwaffe were short of trained navigators and in order to make up for this deficit they devised a system of radio beams which would be transmitted from the Continent. When two beams were set up to converge over a target in Britain, all the German pilot had to do was to 'ride' one of the beams until he reached the convergence point with the second beam, then release his bombs. The German Luftwaffe knew this as the Lorenz system and the British SBA equipment could be tuned to the German beam frequency. It was the intention that the RAF's night-fighters should also be able to fly the beams and achieve interceptions. However, Ray believes that very little success was obtained as the beams did not provide information on height which would perhaps have given the night-fighter a better chance of success. The only positive information gained by the RAF was that if the Germans were planning a major night raid, the target was known to the RAF in the late afternoon or early evening on the day of the intended raid. The experiment was later dropped, but after the War ended, several of the large civilian airfields, such as Heathrow were equipped with the Standard Beam Approach system.

From Colerne A-Flight went to Fairwood Common near Swansea on 18th June and B-Flight to Predannack nine days later. They were to remain separated for about four months. First impressions of

Fairwood Common were not favourable. The runways were too short for Beaufighters. One runway was particularly undulating. At night the runways were liable to be impeded by wild ponies, sheep and cattle roaming over the Common. It was decided that landing at night was too risky. As regards the domestic side, the lack of water and light and Mess amenities was disquieting. The sea bathing on the other hand was excellent, and the messing under the supervision of a WAAF officer and staff left nothing to be desired. But operationally the field was a disaster and the Squadron was happy to return to Colerne by the end of the month.

From time to time single aircraft would land at Colerne, as night flying was more suitable from this station. At times, friends would drop in for a visit. One "old lad" of the Squadron, F/L Barnes, who was with No.600 at Manston when it suffered so terribly over Rotterdam, visited old friends during the afternoon of 5th July while on leave. John decided that it would be fun to do "a little night-fighting". It was typically John's way of spending his leave and it showed the tremendous spirit and sense of comradeship of the old guys, to return to their Squadron and "help out a little". A few days later, on 9th July, Sgts Samsom and Faircliffe intercepted a He111. Unfortunately they lost contact and the German escaped. A second Heinkel was less fortunate when F/O Woodward and AI operator Sgt Lipscombe bagged it near Abergavenny, their third. A few short bursts from below at 100 yards set the enemy aircraft on fire and it was seen going down vertically through the clouds. For his hat trick Woodward got the DFC. Three days later, however, there was sadness when the Squadron received news that P/O Schumer and Sgt Smither had lost their lives at Predannack. They were doing aerobatics during a night flying test when the aircraft got into a fatal spin. August also was bad for flying the weather was so poor that most of the time the aircraft remained on the ground. Some Army Co-op sorties were flown but a number had to be cancelled. On 14th July "Action Stations" was given at 0830 hrs. The Squadron, after a number of practices knew their allotted role and jumped to it. At 1000 hrs Station and Squadron dispersal were subjected to a determined low-flying attack by two Beaufighters, flown by S/L Scrase and F/O Denby, who, for the time being, had joined the "enemy". W/C Stain-forth, jumping into a Hurricane, drove off the "hostile" Beaus, which had however succeeded in their object of damaging and confusing the ground defences. At 1230hrs the "All Clear" was given, none of the enemy having ventured to show up in the vicinity of the Flight and HQ defences. The Squadron considered this a victory for the City of London.

Wing Commander Stainforth (OC 600) (right), was a famous pilot, who also took part in the pre-war Schneider Trophy races that ultimately gave the RAF the Spitfire.

Then came a terrible blow for the Squadron when during the night of 19th/20th July W/C Stainforth, his AI operator Sgt Lawson, and F/O Woodward, with Sgt Lipscombe carried out a sortie. After midnight the weather worsened and a landing at Colerne would be tricky due to the mist. Stainforth ordered Woodward to Middle Wallop. At 2,500 feet the Beaufighter's gyro instruments toppled and the aircraft entered a spin. Three times the pilot ordered his R/O to bale out. Then he too left the aircraft. Woodward broke a leg when he landed, but Lipscombe never got out and was killed when it crashed a few miles from Corsham. It was the end of an excellent team. During a sortie on 28th July, S/L Scrase was testing the stalling speed of the new Beaufighter. He also got into a spin from which he never recovered. His R/O Sgt Landymore managed to parachute to safety but this time the pilot was killed near Acton Turville in Gloucestershire. On 22nd August another crew lost their lives. Sgts

Martin and Smith came in to land after an operational patrol, when for no obvious reason Beaufighter R2300 crashed into the sea, a quarter of a mile from Predannack. A second Beaufighter took off for a search, but returned without further news. Early September 1941 Pritchard was promoted to Wing Commander (Flying) at 51 OTU at Cranfield, Bedfordshire. On the morning of 8th September P/O Ellis and his operator Sgt Houston destroyed a He111 over the Scillies. They came as close as 50 yards from the enemy, 100 feet below, dropped back to 150 yards and gave him a 2 seconds burst. The Heinkel went down in an almost vertical dive and exploded in mid-air. As the Squadron's last success had been two months earlier, on 9th July, this kill was received with great satisfaction. But there was little time for a party as the station was now and then subjected to "enemy attacks" to test the readiness of the defences in a real attack.

Charles Spry was an eager young NCO when he joined No.600 in September 1941. One Flight was at Colerne while the other was based at Predannack. Needless to say, Sgt Spry was deeply impressed to find out that the CO was the famous Stainforth. As a new pilot Spry was sent to Predannack to fly his first solos on the Beaufighter II. Many years later he remembered: "The Beaufighter MkII was a recipe for disaster. It swung violently on take-off and landing. As Predannack was laid across boggy heather-clad moorland a swing off the runway at speed could write off the undercarriage. Though I loved the Beau as an aircraft I did not particularly like the Merlin Beaufighters. It had the heaviest wing loading of any aircraft, yet it was very strong and extremely well-armed for its time". It had a drawback for the observer. The cannon ammunition was in round drums of about 50 rounds. These had to be changed in flight. They were heavy and difficult to handle, except in straight and level flight. A modification subsequently put the cannon ammunition in belts in boxes on the floor. This made life for the Navigator/Radar Operator a little more bearable. The drawback for the pilots was that the Beaufighter II had no undercarriage doors to the engine nacelles and one could not maintain height on one engine.

On 1st October 1941 W/C Stainford left. He was posted to command No.89 Squadron. W/C Pearson became OC600. He had been in charge of No. 54 Squadron and then did the job of Controller for No.11(F) Group during the Summer of 1940. In his book "Pilot, Diplomat and Garage Rat", he described how he was offered command of No.600 Squadron and gratefully accepted. He also made observations about great changes that had taken place in the Squadron: "Few if any of the Auxiliary aircrew personnel remained and it was equipped with Beaufighter MkII aircraft. It was stationed at Predannack, a new airfield built on moorland and bog, at The Lizard in Cornwall. The reason for this remote location was that for the air raids on Merseyside cities, those on Clydeside and Belfast, the raiders had used the Irish Sea and also St. George's Channel as the approach route, probably helped to some extent by the lights of Dublin in the neutral Irish Republic.

Beaufighter IIF BQ-H

By having a night-fighter airfield and two GCI Units within control distance of this route we might well be able to exact a toll. Also some protection could be given to such places as Port Talbot and Milford Haven. Predannack was a beautiful drome. Though it was situated in boggy country the runways were long and broad, the lighting and flying control were up to standard. The Sector Ops Room was very competent and welcomed the arrival of the Squadron, although it was still thirty miles away. The Sector Operations Room was at Portreath and the two GCI Units were at

Coverack and on St. Mary's, Isle of Scilly. Liaison and personal contact between GCI Units and night-fighter Squadrons was always encouraged and indeed transport was provided for that purpose. However, the only way to go to St. Mary's was to borrow the Miles Magister which was allocated to the Station Commander and had room for only two. No wonder the liaison with Coverack was on a much firmer basis. It was manned 100% by WAAFs, all top grade persons. Accommodation was excellent because the hotels had been closed and were now put at the disposal of the Squadron. The Pollurian Hotel was requisitioned for officers and the Poldhu and several smaller ones for aircrew NCOs. The ground crew airmen were housed in huts nearer the airfield. According to W/C Pearson there was one major snag: "The Beaufighter IIF was an unnecessary and dangerous aeroplane, and one that no one had ever asked for. It seems it was ordered because the Rolls Royce Merlin engines which supplied its power gave more at high altitude than the Hercules for which the Beaufighter was designed. It was intended to counter a high-level threat, which never materialised. The change of engines altered the centre of gravity and made the aircraft unstable on the ground at low speeds. This in turn gave it a tendency to swerve off to the right at take-off and a coarse use of rudder was needed to keep straight. A very serious defect was known as "The Shimmy". This was a violent vibration generated at the tail end of the aircraft after landing but extending to the whole fuselage. Various remedies were suggested and tried without much success. In the meantime the Engineering Officer Charles Goodacre made an internal inspection of all the tail planes and found components loose and bent. One aircraft failed to return from a patrol out at sea. The pilot had been in RT contact which ceased without explanation". Some said in those days: "The Beaufighter is a great aircraft, the Merlin is a great engine. Together they are a great disaster".

Near London, far away from Predannack, a former CO of the Squadron was also involved in a battle against the Germans. Peter Stewart, who led the Squadron before the war, ran the Air Ministry War Room, which among other things produced the Daily Summary of Operations. Peter had been appointed Assistant Director of Intelligence ADI(Photos). In his book "Most Secret War", about British scientific intelligence between 1939 and 1945, Professor R.V. Jones, now an honorary member of the Squadron Association, remembered: "I was told that he was a man who had his own way of doing things, and much would depend on whether or not we hit it off together. I therefore called on him, half expecting trouble but, as with Medhurst, we took an immediate liking to one another. Peter was a member of Lloyd's and belonged to a City insurance firm, and before the war he had joined the Auxiliary Air Force. In fact he had been Commanding Officer of No.600, the City of London Squadron; and he had an intense sense of duty and patriotism. He assured me that he wished to interpose no hindrance between me and the pilots and interpreters; in fact he immediately took me to lecture to the pilots of the Photographic Reconnaissance Unit which had just moved to Benson near Oxford".

On 10th October, when the Squadron had returned to Predannack, S/L McNeill Boyd, with F/O Clegg, shot a Heinkel into the sea off the coast near St. Ives. In November 1941 S/L "Paddy" Green DFC, a pre-war Auxiliary in No.601 Squadron, came with his R/O Sgt Reginald Gillies. Paddy had been wounded very badly over Dunkirk and, transferring to night-fighters, had crewed with Gillies at OTU. It was the beginning of a great friendship between Paddy and the Squadron, resulting in Paddy commanding No.600 for more than two years after the Squadron had moved to battlefields of North Africa and Italy. On the 27th a newcomer arrived. He was Albert Harvey, a Cornish tobacconist. Harvey joined the RAF shortly after the war broke out. No.600 Squadron was his first front-line posting. From Predannack his career as a night-fighter was to begin. Flying the black Beaufighters with their four cannons and six machine guns he stalked the skies to catch German bombers intruding the airspace where he patrolled. The Luftwaffe sent large four-engined FW200 Condors out over the Atlantic to broadcast weather forecasts to Germany. One of the tasks of No.600 at Predannack was to try and intercept these aircraft, thus robbing the Germans of valuable weather information. During one of these "milk train" runs F/L Fletcher and his R/O Sgt Grant experienced severe icing. One engine stopped and the Beaufighter had to be ditched. A search by air-sea rescue Lysanders, escorted by Spitfires of 66 Squadron failed to find the dinghy. For the crew the worst was feared. One body washed ashore much later. On 2nd December the Squadron accounted for two He111s. But four days later a pilot went missing just after he radioed having "got a Hun" during one of his milk train sorties. No further news was received and when the Beaufighter did not return a probable was claimed in the belief that both aircraft might have crashed in the course of the combat. It was suggested too that the crash had been caused by the feared "Shimmy".

S/L McNeill Boyd DFC (right) and his R/O F/L Clegg flew from Predannack to intercept German "Baedeker" raids against the cities in the Midlands.

On Christmas 1941, celebrated with the traditional waiting on the airmen by the officers, a signal announced that DFCs had been awarded to S/L McNeill Boyd and his Radar Observer F/L Clegg. The serenity of January 1942 was severely disrupted when an enemy intruder followed F/O Arnsley into Predannack and dropped three 1,000 pounders aimed at the runway while the Beaufighter came in to land. Luckily no one was hurt but some damage was caused. Two bombs fell on No.4 runway and one in a nearby field. Two Beaufighters were slightly damaged one being the aircraft that was just landing. Roofing and windowlite was blown out of several buildings in the vicinity. While during the next day the craters were filled the aircraft operated from other runways. During that same month Sgt Spry was carrying out a night flying test when the starboard engine of his Beaufighter II gave up. Being about 20 miles from base Spry thought it would be easy to reach home. It was a difficult matter

Bristol Beaufighters MK1, powered by Hercules III engines of 1425hp each. "P", "I" (X8023) and "Z" are matt black, the standard colour for night-fighters over Britain and came from the Old Mixon Shadow Factory at Weston-Super-Mare.

but with a lot of struggling and luck he reached Predannack and landed on one engine. Two weeks later the same thing happened, this time about 80 miles South of Predannack at between 10,000 and 11,000ft. Again Spry managed to return safely; he considered himself a very lucky man. During his first months with the Squadron Spry discovered other "eccentricities" of the Mk.II. No matter how the plane was trimmed, it would never fly straight and level hands off. It started with slight undulations which gradually increased like a roller coaster – the solution was for Bristol Aircraft Ltd to replace the horizontal tail plane with a dihedral plane. The Beaufighter also had an odd tail wheel shudder on landing which eventually weakened the stern frame. The solution was to replace the rear tail wheel with a ribbed tyre. The other modification was to smooth off all the rivets in the skin – it gave the Beaufighter another 5mph. Then appeared a Beaufighter fitted with a Boulton-Paul four-gun turret behind the pilot. It was never used operationally on 600 Squadron. Sgt Spry flew a sortie in the turret with W/C Pearson at the controls. Neither the pilot nor the gunner was impressed and all hoped that the idea of Beaufighters-with-turrets would be abandoned. The problem was over soon when the Squadron got new Beaufighters, with trusted radial engines.

Soon after the arrival of the new Mk.VIs to replace the ill-fated Mk.IIs, two crews from No.604 Squadron came to join the Squadron. One was a Sergeant by the name of Dunin Rzuchowski, Polish, a count by birth and a first-class pilot, with Sgt Dixon as his Observer Radar. On 1st February 1942 the first Mk.IV Beaus arrived from 19MU, St. Athan. With eight new aircraft No.600 Squadron was confident that soon they would hit the Hun again and many times – Its better performance compared to the Mk.IIF was mentioned. In the coming weeks the first operational patrols were carried out with them. Many contacts were made, but no enemy aircraft were "relieved from further flying". It was as if Lady Luck had protected No. 600 Squadron, which consisted of the following aircraft, pilots and operators:

Aircraft:	Serial:	Pilots	Operators
Beaufighter Mk.IIF	R2279	W/C Pearson	F/L Clegg
Beaufighter Mk.IIF	R2282	S/L Boyd	F/O Guest
Beaufighter Mk.IIF	R2325	S/L Kerr	F/O Baird
Beaufighter Mk.IIF	R2326	S/L Green	F/O Breedon
Beaufighter Mk.IIF	R2327	F/L Elwell	F/S Crabtree
Beaufighter Mk.IIF	R2376	F/L Denby	Sgt Burrows
Beaufighter Mk.IIF	R2396	F/L Ellis	Sgt Townend
Beaufighter Mk.IIF	R2451	P/O Drummond	Sgt Gillies
Beaufighter Mk.IIF	R2477	P/O Williams	Sgt Smith
Beaufighter Mk.IIF	T3039	P/O Harvey	Sgt Lushington
Beaufighter Mk.IIF	T3044	P/O Blevens	Sgt Farmer
Beaufighter Mk.IIF	T3146	P/O Ross	Sgt Stevens
Beaufighter Mk.IVF	X7885	P/O Duncan	Sgt Dixon
Beaufighter Mk.IVF	X7896	Sgt Smith	Sgt Webber
Beaufighter Mk.IVF	X7887	Sgt Banbury	Sgt Armstrong
Beaufighter Mk.IVF	X7888	Sgt Dunin	Sgt Georgeson
Beaufighter Mk.IVF	X7889	Sgt Spry	Sgt Coote
Beaufighter Mk.IVF	X7890	Sgt Hodgkinson	Sgt Wells
Beaufighter Mk.IVF	X7891	unknown	Sgt Graham
Beaufighter Mk.IVF	X7894	unknown	Sgt Russell

F/O Hanus, "Joe", as he was to become known, joined No.600 in March 1942. He came from Czechoslovakia and had served as a

Regular officer in the air force of his native country. When the Germans occupied it he fled to France and subsequently, after France surrendered, to England. He had an intense hate against Germans and was quite determined to pay them back for everything they had done. He proudly wore his Czech pilot's wings and at times, when upset or very emotional, would say things in his native language, no one really understanding what the hell "Joe" was talking about.

One of the other tasks to be carried out by the aircrew of the Squadron, was to escort VIP aircraft en route to the Middle East as far as the Beaufighter's endurance. Returning from such a sortie on 7th March, while they were preparing to land, Boyd and Clegg saw the navigation lights of an aircraft. Control however, insisted that no other aircraft was around. The pilot opened his throttles and climbed to investigate the matter. They saw a He115 float plane flying at cliff-top level, frantically firing cartridges into the air. Boyd and Clegg did not need much time to realise that this was their prey. They shot down the He115 and it crashed into the sea off Lizard Point, adding to the growing number of victims. It was not until they landed again that the 600 crew was told that the Germans must have been lost and were signalling that they were coming in for a landing, believing they were over France.

At the same time the Squadron had to bid farewell to now Gp/Capt "Toby" Pearson, who became Station Commander at Colerne. The diary read: "It was with great regret and a very real sense of personal loss that the Squadron said goodbye to a most popular commanding officer". S/L Green temporarily took over his duties as OC 600 until the new CO had arrived. P/O John Wright, a Squadron Auxiliary for a long time, and well-known by all as "800158 Wright, J.M.", found himself posted elsewhere too, to his dismay, as he recollected later. The man who had served the Auxiliaries with such great zeal and who had been commissioned because of his great services, was Mentioned in Despatches. But it could hardly ease the pain of having to leave his beloved Squadron. He continued to serve with similar dedication at RAF Cosford.

The new CO was a Squadron "old boy", W/C A.G. Miller, who had been in Russia and earned himself a well-deserved DFC and, as one of few RAF officers, the Order of Lenin. Miller knew the Squadron well, having been a member between 1935 and May 1940. He had served as an instructor at FIU and OC17 Squadron in the

Wing-Commander Tony Miller, who served with No.600 Squadron as an Auxiliary pilot in the thirties, came back as OC 600 after he spent some time commanding Hurricanes in the Soviet Union, where he was awarded the Order of Lenin. On his right Squadron Leader McNeill Boyd.

Battle of Britain. This period turned out to be very interesting for the ground crew of 600 Squadron, though none of the Squadron aircraft got involved in the matters at hand. His Majesty's government was aware of German rocket bases in France. Therefore Predannack became a major servicing and refuelling station for the Spitfires, Hurricanes and Westland Whirlwinds assigned to attack selected spots.

The pilots were quite unaware of the object of this campaign, yet they met many famous men who showed up at Predannack from time to time, such as "Sailor" Malan, Bob Tuck and Alan Deere. Whilst at Predannack P/O Harvey and Wicksteed teamed up as a crew in No.600 Squadron. Wicksteed, a columnist for the Daily Express, acted as Harvey's Nav/RO. On 7th June they got involved in a brush off the Atlantic coast of Cornwall. They had taken off for a convoy patrol after completing their routine cockpit drill. Dusk convoy patrols were considered dull jobs; nothing ever happened and after a long and boring stay crews would be pleased to land and catch some sleep. At about 2250 they took off and set course for the convoy they were to protect which was steaming off St. Eval. In the book "War over the West" an account was given of their sortie: "Harvey radioed that he was in position and was immediately advised that an enemy aircraft was reported to be in the area. They scanned the sea around them and within minutes had spotted the intruder skimming over the waves. It was flying so low that its slip-stream was whipping up a huge spray of water in its wake. The raider spotted Harvey's Beaufighter almost as soon as it began to dive down onto them. The Germans turned away from the convoy and the bombing run they had already embarked upon and opened up on the night-fighter with a hail of red tracer bullets streaming from the upper turret. Harvey responded with machine gun and cannon fire of his own and battle was joined with a vengeance. The intruder was identified at the time as a He111, but subsequent studies of German records have shown that it was a Junkers 88 reconnaissance aircraft, carrying a crew of four. It was no match for the lighter, faster and more manoeuvrable Beaufighter. The British pilot scored several hits before a burst of fire blew off the intruder's port engine, showering the Beaufighter with flaming debris. The German aircraft continued to fight back with a tenacity that made nonsense of its crippled status. The Junkers was still flying and kept on peppering the night-fighter with tracers. The Beaufighter was hit in its port engine. Then the starboard engine caught fire as its propellers chewed on the spitting trail of orange venom. As Harvey gave the Junkers another long burst, the German wireless operator could be heard sending out an SOS. But the pleas for assistance were silenced when the bomber crashed into the sea. The crew were Oberleutnant Baumung, pilot, Oberleutnant Klemann, navigator, Feldwebel Fug, wireless operator and Feldwebel Maier, air gunner. The bodies of two crewmen, Baumann and Fug, were found later. Having shot down the Ju88 Harvey asked his base for a fix to help him return home. His aircraft had been damaged severely and was losing altitude very quickly. By the time they realised that they would never reach home, they were too low to bale out. Wicksteed went forward to strap Harvey in his Sutton harness. He had barely returned to his own position when the Beau's port engine blew up and fell into the murky water. Having lost the engine on the port side the starboard wing dipped violently and hit the water. The Beaufighter cartwheeled into the sea. The front of the aircraft caved in on impact but somehow Harvey managed to get out. Wicksteed however was less fortunate. When the plane slipped under the waves he was trapped. At about 30 feet the remains of the Beaufighter hit the bottom of the sea. Wicksteed fought to free himself and was lucky enough to make a hole in the canopy through which he rocketed to the surface. Harvey waited for him in the dinghy and as Wicksteed's dinghy had vanished the men squeezed themselves into the one small craft. Not built for two the dinghy capsized and the men were forced to take turns in the water and in the craft. They were about seven miles off shore but Portreath's flashing beacon was visible on the horizon. After five hours, when daylight broke they could see the cliffs in the distance. Afraid of being smashed on the rocks they successfully landed at a spot between Samphire Island and Crane Island. They struggled to get the dinghy to a cove, but the high waves caught them again. Harvey was the first to reach the shore, but having lost Wicksteed when the dinghy turned over he first tried to locate his partner. It was to no avail. Harvey therefore decided to climb the cliffs and find help. He did not know that Wicksteed had landed with the dinghy and was now looking for his pilot. Wicksteed also tried to climb the cliffs but after about 100 feet he lost his grip and fell back on the beach, sustaining more bruises than he had when the Beaufighter went down. In the meantime Harvey had found a farm and woken the

Gentlemen in Blue

family living there. The family warned civilians and Royal Marines, who started an immediate search for Wicksteed. When Harvey knew that his friend had been saved he reported to his controller at the Operations Room at Portreath. He was challenged by a sentry, who allowed him in after proof of his identity. There he found the controller writing his report, saying that a convoy had safely passed. A German aircraft had been destroyed and sadly a Beaufighter had been lost as well. The next day Harvey was taken back to Predannack, from where he cycled back to his home in Falmouth to tell his wife that he was alive and well. Before the afternoon was out he was behind the counter of his shop selling fags. Harvey received an immediate DSO and Wicksteed the DFC. Wicksteed, who was a PR-man at the Air Ministry, had volunteered for aircrew duties at a very ripe age "(in his thirties)", accepting having to revert to two ranks lower to fly. The incident became the main theme in a book Wicksteed wrote later, called "Father's Heinkel".

On 19th October 1943 Harvey was summoned to Buckingham

Aircrew of No.600 Squadron in front of a black Mk1 Beaufighter at Predannack. From left to right: Sgt Scobie, P/O Duncan, Sgt Georgeson, Sgt Boyd, Sgt Peacock, F/L Clegg, P/O Craig, F/L Ellis, Sgt Webber, Sgt Clarke, P/O Yielder, S/L McNeill Boyd, W/C Miller, F/L Motion and P/O Harvey

Palace for an official presentation of the DSO by the King. In March 1946, when he was demobbed from the RAF as a Flight Lieutenant Harvey had logged 900 hours in Spitfires, Blenheims, Beaufighters and Mosquitoes. He went on to continue his business and died in 1981. His score list for the war mentioned five German aircraft and five V1 rockets. Wicksteed returned to Fleet Street and became one of the Daily Express's top journalists, entertaining the readers with his "Fun Finding Out" articles. He covered the Korean War and followed Princess Elizabeth and Prince Philip to Africa during the tour when she learned that her Father had died and she was the new Monarch. Wicksteed was only fifty when he died.

At Predannack a taste of things to come occurred when all the original members of the Squadron were asked individually if they were prepared to volunteer for duties overseas. It must be remembered that both soldiers and airmen in the Auxiliary role were recruited for home service only and could only be sent out of the country if they volunteered. This was probably altered later in the war withdrawing the option by statutory order, but in case of 600 Squadron it was great that they volunteered almost to a man to go overseas. But before this happened Paddy Green was selected to form No.125 Squadron, taking with him Gordon Denby and P/O Drummond and their two observers. In June the Squadron organised a reunion, which was held at the Pollurian Hotel. F/L Hanus, the Czech pilot of the Squadron, flew to Northolt in the Squadron's Airspeed Oxford and collected former members from Northolt, such as W/Cs Hiscox, Aste and Kellett. More about Hanus will be told in the last chapter, for he experienced harrowing adventures after the war, when he decided it was time to leave his native country Czechoslovakia.

With combats again in July the Squadron's score of enemy aircraft shot down mounted. On 7th July P/Os King and Barker destroyed a Dornier Do217. Two days later a distinguished visitor Air/Cdre HRH the Duke of Kent visited Predannack and had members of the Squadron presented to him. About three weeks later the Squadron encountered a lot of "Trade" as enemy aircraft were called. The Operations Record Book said on 27th July: "S/L Elwell with F/S Burrows from A-Flight were airborne from Predannack at 2330 hours until 0220 hrs during which time two raids were intercepted, the first at 0029 hours, raid 103, 25 miles SW of base, one He111 being damaged. The second He111, raid 122, was intercepted at 0156 hours, 50 miles SSE of base and destroyed. with the help of the full moon. Our aircraft suffered no damage. F/L Arnsby with P/O Wells of B-Flight intercepted raid 107 at 0015 hours over the Scilly Islands with the aid of a full moon and cloudless night, damaging a He111. Our aircraft received one machine-gun bullet embedded in the propeller. P/O Young and F/O Grouser and Sgt Dunin-Rzuchowski with P/O Dixon carried out convoy patrol without incident, being airborne at 2210 hours and landing at 0155 hours and 0050 hours respectively. In August the first American came to the Squadron, he was 2nd Lt Baldwin from Prestwick, posted to No.600 to see what night fighting was all about. Sadly on 22nd August two Squadron members died when Beaufighter X8006 crashed into the sea. P/O Yielder and Sgt Peacock had been on a dusk patrol and failed to return. Some days later their bodies washed ashore and were buried. During that period Sir Archibald Sinclair, Secretary of State for Air agreed to become the new Honorary Air Commodore. S/L Elwell was sent to North Coates in Lincolnshire to pick up Sir Archibald and fly him to Predannack to meet the Squadron. On 1st September 1942 the entire Squadron received orders to move by rail from Predannack to Church Fenton in Yorkshire. Three days later the CO took his aircraft to the new base. In September W/C Miller left, as he had been posted to command No. 54 OTU. His successor was W/C Watson. Under this new CO the Squadron was to prepare for a posting away from England. It was a great change, as legally no Auxiliary could be sent to fight outside the British Isles. The men of No.600 were determined to serve to the fullest. It meant that preparations for this posting were necessary. It came rather as a shock. In Yorkshire the entire Squadron got intensive field training for aircrews and ground crews alike. For the next two months No.600 Squadron would spend all its time preparing for the posting overseas. New aircraft landed, they were given very serious acceptation inspections and many modifications were carried out, mainly to ensure that the new Beaufighters would perform well in semi-tropical conditions. The aircrews flew long cross-country formation sorties over Britain to stretch the endurance of the Beau. Droning around with minimum revolutions on the engines and coarse propeller pitch with the Beaufighter shaking for five hours was not their idea of fun. The urge to see the countryside was cleverly used by making air and ground crews carry out route marches of several miles, an activity almost unheard of in flying circles. And, there was no escape, for a number of Senior NCOs held supernumerary positions in the rear and kept a sharp lookout for men who tried to break formation upon the passage of a pub. However, bad rumours had it that these SNCOs fell out during the outward trip at a place called the "Station Arms".

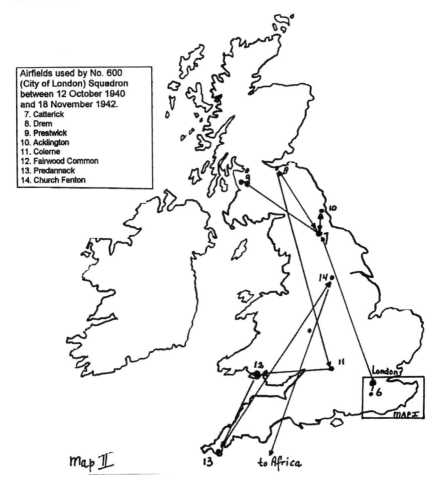

Airfields used by No. 600
(City of London) Squadron
between 12 October 1940
and 18 November 1942.
  7. Catterick
  8. Drem
  9. Prestwick
10. Acklington
11. Colerne
12. Fairwood Common
13. Predannack
14. Church Fenton

Map II. Airfields of No.600 Squadron, October 1940 – November 1942.

These SNCOs then took up the responsibility of fraternising with the natives, catching up with neat timing, as the Squadron sweated out the last stretch to camp. As a fair contribution to the day's efforts they encouraged the troops with a martial but somewhat ribald song

"There was a young lady from Hamm" translated from the King's to more basic English by Frank Yates. Rumours have it that old boys, who took part in these marches, still have not overcome the bad feelings of those days. Not all was work and there was plenty of entertainment with cinemas, dances and opportunities to see the countryside and meet the local people. "Culture" being considered a major aspect of life, a Squadron band was formed at Church Fenton, the "No.600 Squadron Dance Band". The band was first nurtured by Ron Knight, who was quite a dabster on the guitar. Frank Russell remembers how he arrived, with his violin. His previous exploits became known to Bill Cooksey and Stan Gilbert, and Frank was in. Many Squadron members claimed proficiency on various instruments. But as this turned out to be 99% goodwill and 1% ability, the band could only muster one guitar and two violins to start with. However, they managed to borrow, beg and "win" enough to start rehearsals, and soon the band consisted of the musicians Ron Knight, guitar; Taffy Baker, piano; Arthur Steward, drums; Bill Cooksey, bass; Roger Ray and "Tinhorn" Walker, trumpet; Charles Pulsford, Stan Gilbert and Frank Russell, violin; Bill Rice, piano. Church Fenton had a theatre and the band took every chance to rehearse. As the Squadron had been released from operations, they had virtually every afternoon to play. Once the Squadron band had been equipped with appropriate instruments, bought by the surrender of one day's pay by each and every Squadron member, they began to achieve something. And what the band lacked in professional skill was made up in honest endeavour. At first the tunes "Cherokee" and "Old Kent Road" were suggested and tried as signature tunes. Finally "The World is waiting for the Sunrise" was chosen for two reasons. The first reason that night-fighting was the Squadron's major occupation, the second the simple fact that they could play it. The band made its debut at a colossal "thrash" during the night before the Squadron moved off for embarkation to North Africa. Then the most frightening thing in the life of an airman happened. The whole of the Squadron was committed to a sudden Commando course. Horrified men found themselves indulging in antics which they had hitherto imagined in their innocence to be the prerogative solely of that khaki bunch, called "Army". The airmen surprised themselves by scaling 10 feet walls with no hand-holds, having carried out a long charge immediately before with fixed bayonets over rough ground. It was the last lap of a rather

frightening circuit which included swinging on the end of a slippery
rope to gather sufficient momentum to reach the opposite bank of
a stream. All this had to be done in full kit and with steel helmets
on, indeed a jolt. The Squadron also discovered that personal arms
had a purpose other than as an adjunct to guard duties, and assid-
uous practice found them adept in the use of the rifle, the revolver
and the Sten gun. However, none of these tools provided the same
excitement as the hand grenade. There was, for instance, the occasion when someone lobbed a hand grenade vertical and then had
the doubtful satisfaction of seeing it fall back into the slit trench.
Some of the Squadron are still very grateful to that Sgt who solved
the problem by giving the grenade another go. It is, however,
doubtful if that particular Sgt remembers the Squadron with very
much affection. Bad rumours had it too, that one or two airmen
"borrowed" hand grenades for a fishing trip, thus ensuring a good
catch. While many in the Squadron still wondered why they had
been made to impersonate infantrymen, big decisions had been
made between the Allied leaders. On 6th November 1942 a convoy
sailed through Gibraltar Strait and headed East. The campaign in
North-Africa looked good for the Allies. The Afrika Korps had been
defeated and withdrew to Libya. This convoy was some kind of a
mystery for the Axis military leadership. Was it heading for Sardinia,
Sicily or heading for Tripolitania to attack Rommel in the back? It
was not until the next day that the American consul-general in
Algiers informed General Juin, the Commander in Chief of the
French troops in North Africa that American forces would land that
night. Operation "Torch" was the first massive amphibian landing
by the Western allies. It was a risky operation as no one knew how
the strong Vichy forces would react. Under Eisenhower three task
forces were to land at three different places. Task Force West under
Major-General George Patton was to land in Morocco, Centre Task
Force under Major-General Fredenall West and East of Oran while
Eastern Task Force under Major-General Charles Ryder would land
between Algiers and Bougie in Algeria. On 8th November all Allied
Task Forces had landed and were on their way to occupy their objec-
tives. Four days later W/C Watson received the following message
from Sir Archibald Sinclair: "Good luck to you and 600 Squadron on
your great adventure. I shall be watching your fortunes from here
but keep in touch and let me know how you get on". On 14th
November, 1942 18 Beaufighters and their crews flew to Portreath.

They only came this time to refuel their aircraft, as they would soon find out. The pilots and O/Rs were:

Pilots	Radar Operators
W/C Watson (OC600)	P/O Lawson
S/L Elwell (Cdr A-Flight)	P/O Barker
S/L Chisholm (Cdr B-Flight)	P/O Balderstone
F/L Arnsby	P/O Wells
P/O Roberts	F/S Burrastone
P/O Bates	P/O Clark
P/O Young	P/O Ritchie
P/O Spry	P/O Armstrong
P/O Thomson	F/S White
P/O Boyd	P/O Townend
P/O Metcalf	Sgt Wingham
P/O Hilken	P/O Lushington
P/O Ross	P/O Finland
F/S Blackwell	Sgt Cadman
Sgt Shepperd	F/S Stevens
Sgt Owen	Sgt MacAllister
Sgt Wolstenholme	Sgt Clark

The presence of a strong Vichy-French, German and Italian air force made it necessary to ensure air superiority at the shortest possible notice. No. 600 Squadron was to play its part in the operation. At the same time in North Africa the French had rather quickly changed sides and joined the Allied forces. A swift move was made to attack the Germans in Tunisia. This move to North Africa was quite unexpected. Of course there had been rumours about a near departure to an undisclosed destination. The Station Dance was well under way and it was getting on for midnight, when suddenly the band stopped playing and all members of No.600 Squadron were ordered to report to the hangar at once. In the hangar they were told that the Squadron would soon be on the move. In fact the move would be so soon that they barely had time to pack and prepare. After the briefing the men were soon under way, walking in small groups along the winding country road from the drome to Church Fenton Station. None of them knew the ultimate destination but 300 men on the move at that time of the night must have caused some consternation, especially among the people living in the cottages along the road the Squadron took to reach the station. They all boarded the train for Gourock where, still in darkness, they embarked on a tender which was to take them out to a larger vessel, their home for the next week or two. The vessel was called "Orbita", a ship of 3,000 tons, originally designed as a cattle carrier, and those who know their maritime onions will appreciate that this kind of tonnage is a far cry from what we call "ocean-going vessels". The voyage of the Squadron ground staff and equipment on board SS Orbita deserves to be described in great detail. Having faithfully carried out it's new task as a night-fighter Squadron, responsible for the defence of towns being attacked at night, the Squadron had made a good contribution to the Home Defence. The scores in the United Kingdom for 600 Squadron, before leaving for the Mediterranean, were: Destroyed -17, Probables – 9, Damaged – 9.

New horizons opened for the City of London Squadron Gentlemen. The battlefields of North Africa were their next destination. Their means of transport was MV Orbita. Through some clever military thinking it had been decided that this 3,000 ton vessel could easily take 3,000 troops. With some "modifications" even 1,000 more could be transported. First, however, the entire Squadron and its equipment had to get on board. Now the Commando training showed its usefulness, for the airmen had to climb up rope ladders with kit bags and all. For sheer thrills the rope ladders were twisting and swinging in the blackness over a water of unknown depth. It was quite a relief when all men were on board, nobody missing in action. All that remained was to marvel at the ingenuity which had conceived the sleeping layout of hammock, table or deck, in this floating palace. Some of the groundcrews tried to ensure that they flew rather than sailed to North Africa, but unfortunately for them, even the adjutant F/L Dyson had to go by ship. The Orbita left the Clyde and headed South. The vessel was in the middle of a convoy of 34 ships with an escort of between 30 and 40 destroyers and corvettes, a reassuring sight. The skill with which the Royal Navy moved in and out of the convoy, constantly changing stations, dispelled any fears the men might have had for their safety in a convoy occupying so much of the Atlantic.

All the time the Aldis lamps flashed from ship to ship, the only apparent link between members of the flock as absolute radio

While sailing to Africa the "600 Squadron Band" entertained the passengers with music.

silence was observed all the time. S/L Eddie Crowder made a few notes about the Orbita which were written in one of the Association magazines: "A feature while on the Clyde was card playing, for stake money at games of Sola. The cry of Prop and Cop could be heard in the main saloon where a small section had been curtained off for religious services. The services were attended only by some Naval, Army and Air Force personnel. However, as the convoy moved off into dangerous waters the seriousness was felt by some of the card players who turned to the services, and when enemy submarines were depth-charged by protective destroyers the movement accelerated and it became virtually impossible to get into a church service. Only the iron-nerved continued with the cards. We all experienced this and the Church would undoubtedly be the first to welcome it".

The Squadron flew to Portreath and were briefed for the long flight to Gibraltar. It was to be a pilot's mission, as the R/Os temporarily lost their radar sets for security reasons. The top-secret airborne radar sets were to be flown to North Africa in a B17 Flying Fortress. The Beaufighters, however, were fully armed, just in case.

On 17th November seventeen Beaufighters took off for Gibraltar. The aircraft of Sgt Sheppard and F/S Stevens had to stay behind with magneto problems. Each aircraft was to fly individually which meant that the crews experienced a lonely trip. Officially they were to fly the long route over the sea, avoiding Spain and Portugal. Spry recalled what the briefing officer said: "If you decide to fly over Spain, make sure you stay well above 10,000ft" Spry got the message loud and clear; flying over the brightly lit towns of Franco's Spain, navigation would be much easier. The journey was long and uneventful. It was a cloudless night. After a long trip that took the aircraft wide out over the Atlantic to avoid the Bay of Biscay and thus the possible discovery by German recce planes, they all landed safely at the Rock. The only out of ordinary event was approaching the Rock. When Spry called up Gibraltar control on VHF the reply was: "Fly on course so and so, then fire the colours of the day". Spry complied: he knew the gunners at Gibraltar knew their trade and many of them belonged to the Royal Navy. After touch-down no time was lost. The aircraft were serviced and refuelled, ready to depart at first light. The next day the Beaufighters made the trip to Blida in Algeria where the aircrews were to wait for the ground-crews, who still had a long way to go. Sgt Shepperd caught up with them after having made the trip with his Operator. Blida proved to be a former French barracks, "so filthy that delousing was neces-sary", as one of the early arrivals remembers with a shiver. After landing at Blida, Spry wrote in his Flying Logbook:

Date	Aircraft	No	Pilot	Passenger	Duty	Day	Night
Nov 17	Beau IV	D	Self	P/O Armstrong	Portreath-Gibraltar	3.00	2.00
Nov 18	Beau IV	D	Self	P/O Armstrong	Gibraltar-Blida	2.30	

Having arrived in North Africa Spry had flown a total of 489hrs as a pilot, of which 127.15hrs had been carried out during night oper-ations. The aircrew were now at their destination, but the convoy still struggled South, taking the pace of the slowest participant. On the Orbita the weather turned sour and seasickness claimed the majority, underlining the overcrowding in the hold. No. 600 Squadron managed to cope and eventually a routine was established and methods devised to while away the time. Tombola schools

sprang up and amateur navigation took a firm hold, with the enthusiasts endeavouring to plot course and position with the aid of
watches, sun and stars. If not entirely accurate, at least everyone in
the Squadron came to the conclusion that the convoy was indeed
heading South. On the other hand, the more intelligent members of
the Squadron had suspected a move of such sort when they were
issued with tropical kit. The only excitement was when a Union
Castle boat, developed steering trouble. After running amok for
some time and waltzing broadside through the convoy virtually out
of control, the delinquent was slipped to make her own way, and
as the Squadron did not see her again, doubtless she made it. Typical
of the light relief which helped to make the trip tolerable was the
occasion when Cpl Bernard Ellis was in charge of the Deck Guard,
mounted by the Squadron. An incident occurred while he was
learning the ropes carrying out the daily routine of parading his
guard for the CO. Giving "Eyes Left" when the CO in fact was on
the right, was capped only by his own action in disengaging one
hand from his Sten gun and peeling off a smart salute. The CO quite
understandably took some time to recover from these novelties in
drill. The band was asked to entertain the troops – confined to mess
decks after dark – and learned to appreciate the value of a captive
audience. One night when they played "Who's sorry now" to the
troops living just above the keel, they were told off in picturesque
vernacular. Still they were well received by and large, and later, in
the transit camp in Bone, they played in total darkness for hours
to the troops, boosting morale before they moved off.

  Somewhere about midnight on the eighth or ninth day the
Squadron came within sight of the lights of Tangier, a warming experience after a period of incarceration in the Orbita. They reckoned
that they had been far out into the Atlantic before turning in towards
the Straits of Gibraltar. and had seen nothing but sea and sky the
whole time. They had also noticed that during the hours of darkness all ships changed positions and sometimes daylight found the
Orbita in the centre of the convoy, sometimes on the starboard
fringe, otherwise on the port side. It was well understood that this
was done to give all ships an equal chance to pick out the one
carrying the WAAFs. But the lights of Tangier were soon to disappear behind them, as did Gibraltar, and they were again in complete
darkness except for the flashing of signals. The convoy then sailed
into the Med, all still quiet in spite of the usual rumours of German

or Italian U-boats, which was hardly surprising as this was the third largest convoy to North Africa. Things did begin to liven up however, with depth charges being dropped from time to time. In the early hours of one morning suddenly all AA-guns opened up on one of the shadowing aircraft which ventured too close. The men had no idea if it was a friendly or an enemy aircraft, but the Navy lived according to the simple, yet lethal rule: "if it comes too close, we'll fire at it". Thereafter the convoy had escorts from shore-based Beaufighters stationed at Blida near Algiers and said to be serviced by Commandos. When the Squadron was about to land they were about to get involved in what the diarist called "a first-class MFU (Military Fudge-up)". "Authority" had contrived to land No.600 personnel at Bone and their equipment at Algiers. There was nothing else but to tackle this kind of situation with enthusiasm, and in no time at all "Authority" had decided to return the troops to Algiers to join up with the equipment, while "Authority" in Algiers, enthusiastic as well, decided to send the equipment to Bone to fetch up with the troops. In the end the problem was simply solved by the NCOs of the Squadron by taking over the equipment belonging to another Squadron. On 27th December '42 No.600 had finally arrived in Africa. All they had to do now was to disembark their equipment, and settle in to prepare for battle.

CHAPTER 8

THE CITY OF LONDON IN AFRICA.
September 1942 to January 1943

On 18th November 1942 Squadron Beaufighters took off from Gibraltar for the last leg of the journey to Algeria. They landed at Blida after a three hours flight. Once the aircraft had arrived the aircrew were accommodated in the old French barracks, twenty-two men to one room. There were only a few iron beds and the palliasses were so filthy that nobody used them. Food was good in spite of the rather unclean heating and cooking conditions. Champagne and wines were available and flowed freely helping both to accept the conditions and appreciate the safe arrival of the men of the City of London in North Africa.

The next day the CO flew to Maison Blanche to inspect the airfield. It had been severely blitzed and when he landed W/C Watson damaged his aircraft. It was found that the Squadron could not operate from this field as the damage was too extensive. Two days later they found a small drome not far from Blida and the Squadron hoped to find this one in a better state. It was found to be littered with French civil aircraft and the crews had to sleep under the wings of the Beaufighters, doing their own cooking. This was not at all the gentlemanly way to wage war. Besides, with the ground party still somewhere on the Atlantic the Squadron would have to depend on help from others to carry out sorties. Efforts were made to do something about the conditions. They were very primitive indeed. The Squadron had to live very basically. The aircrew officers were slightly better off, for they soon moved into the Girond Hotel at Blida. For the first time since arriving in Africa they had the luxury of sheets, wash basins and other amenities. The men of 608 Squadron were wonderful in giving No.600 all possible assistance.

A Cant Z506B floatplane of the Italian Air Force.

On the whole things were quiet, yet standing patrols were maintained over Algiers every night, and convoys passing through the Western Mediterranean were afforded protection. On the other hand, however, food could be much better. When P/O Bates celebrated his birthday, the only thing to dine with were tremendous omelettes, which, as some of the old chaps still remember, was novel compared to England and a much appreciated indulgence after compo rations. Yet, it was all there was.

The Squadron's operational activities in Africa started in earnest on 28th/29th November 1942, when the first Squadron pilot took off for battle. The crew was a mix, F/O Hilken, the pilot, a 600 Squadron man, while P/O Mason, the R/O was a 500 Squadron chap. The crew headed for Sardinia where the Italians had large numbers of seaplanes moored in the harbour of Cagliari. They returned after 2.15 hours and reported no less than 13 sea planes and flying boats, 3 motor vessels, 8 submarines and a submarine depot ship. The next day Hilken and Mason returned to Cagliari and wasted no time in showing that the aircraft of No.600 had arrived and meant to do business. A tri-motor Cant Z506B float plane was shot down over the harbour, having the doubtful honour of being the first of many aircraft to fall to the guns of 600 Squadron Beaufighters. The crew of the Cant were lucky. Lieutenant Brozzi, Marechallo Acton, Engineer 1st Class Bergomi, Wireless Operator 1st Class Petrella and Cadet Pintus survived the crash. The next day Hilken and Mason took off again and saw a trawler that was looking for the crew of the Cant they shot down the previous day. To their surprise they saw another Cant. Immediately Hilken and Mason made an interception. Seeing the Beaufighter coming straight at him the Italian pilot did not fight, but turned to starboard and fled into a NE direction gradually flying at sea level. Hilken got his Beaufighter into position, making the Cant formate on his starboard wing. The Italian did not open fire. Hilken hoped to force the Cant to the South, chase it to North Africa, and capture aircraft and crew. It was a wild idea. At times Hilken was flying 10 feet above the Cant and with the sun in his eyes the pilot could very well run the risk of hitting the enemy. Then suddenly Hilken noticed why the crew of the Cant had not fired at him. It carried Red Crosses and was on a humanitarian mission. Hilken turned away and left it alone.

During the first week of December W/C Watson and S/L Chisholm, one of his Flight Commanders, were posted away from the Squadron. S/L Elwell took over temporarily while F/L Arnsby and F/O Hilken became the new Flight Commanders. From 5th December the Squadron went back into the night-fighter trade. P/O Bates pranged his Beaufighter, damaging the aircraft considerably, but the crew were unhurt. The Squadron now operated from Maison Blanche. Fourteen Beaufighters, the aircrew and No.608 Squadron sent maintenance people to assist No.600 for the time being. Then, on 6th December, news came that the Squadron ground crews on board Orbita were approaching Algiers. Everyone hoped that a reunification was about to occur. Once the Orbita had docked at Algiers other ships began to leave the convoy one after the other, making for the relative safety of the harbour. Orbita, however, proceeded to Bone and the ground staff found itself alone, apart from some destroyers accompanying her. In the evening the little group moved to Bone in darkness. On board Squadron personnel were being regaled with the news that things looked a bit tricky around Bone. The aerodrome which was their future base was still being fought for and it was actually planned that the Squadron too should fight its way in. Certainly the war was still very hot, for as they approached Bone the ship could not dock as a raid was in progress. When Orbita reached her destination, fires and destruction could be seen everywhere. The men were ordered off Orbita in rather a hurry. The main party was taken to an old tobacco factory on the outskirts of town. It was here that the essential difference in the approach to basic problems as between the Regulars and the Auxiliaries was found. Contrary to the Regulars, carrying the Sherpa stuff, their own kit bags and personal effects, the Auxiliaries were recruiting the local Arabs as porters. These willing gentry were sweating it out on the four mile hike to the tobacco factory to receive the "IOUs" for services rendered, mostly signed Tom Mix, George Robey, John Bull and other colourful names. Rumour has it that one chit was signed "Stalin" and duly accepted by a deeply impressed Arab. Naturally the boys were delighted, which is more than can be said of the Paymaster's Office when the chits were submitted for payment the next day. More irregular things happened shortly after the ground party arrived in Bone. In the course of disembarking a special road trailer similar to a

Christmas 1942 at Maison Blanche, North Africa. Front row l/r: Colin Lamb, Bert Chantrey and Norman Childs. Middle row: Des Farmer, Doug Fell, McLean, unknown, Brown, Butterworth. NCOs, Bernard Wheeley. Back row: Two unknown members, Alec Hunter, F/S Opie, Sgt Yates, Ruben Spink, W/O Topping, Dev Devroome and W/O Nelson.

caravan and used as a mobile admin. office came to a sad end.

While it was being hoisted on a sling by Orbita's jib an enemy raid developed. The jib operator, very keen to survive the war, ran away for cover and the whole lot went in the drink, first bumping into the quayside on the way down with a tremendous "Doing!!" In spite of the fact that all the manuals and other technical publications were aboard this caravan the Squadron survived the crisis in style. "Owing to the equipment having parted company from the personnel, settling into Algiers was somewhat chaotic, but eventually the Squadron got going and it might well set the scene for the happy times", the diarist recorded. The former French tobacco factory was populated by some 10,000 troops and nature had ordained a generous flea population, but this was considered a minor hazard after the experiences on the Orbita. By way of morale booster Squadron Discip W/O Topper Topping mustered the Squadron orchestra which consisted of himself as conductor, Frank Russell on the fiddle, Bill Cooksey on the double bass and Ron Knight on the guitar. For their first number they struck up "Who's sorry now" and 10,000 voices gave them the answer in strictly basic English. Just prior to this someone had switched on the sole light in the factory and in the absence of any response to his request that it should be doused, Topping whipped out his revolver and shot it out.

Sadly the ground party was far from uniting with the air party. Thinking that they had seen the last of "maritime transportation" the men re-embarked on the "Llanstephan Castle" and stayed on board in the harbour. On 11th December they set sail for Algiers and from there the ground party finally made their way to Maison Blanche. At last the Squadron was together again and every man wanted to have a go at the enemy as quickly as possible. At Maison Blanche the air crews started to organise themselves. The Squadron found billets and the choice fell upon a rather second rate establishment, the Hotel de France at Maison Carrie. This hotel adjoined the village bar and the boys discovered pretty soon that there was only a flimsy wall between the respective cellars. The result, of course, was predictable: a large quantity of alcoholic beverages changed hands unofficially. The resulting stampede by a gang of merry birdmen can now be viewed with some amusement, which is more than the CO did at the time! During their stay at Maison Blanche 600 had very exciting experiences. There were German and Italian raids, but no casualties. Maison Blanche was a typical French colonial civil and military airfield. Little was left of its pre-war "grandeur". The once beautiful hangars were partly destroyed, like the other airport buildings. For this reason the CO decided that the air crews should live off the airfield and away from the target area. The only snag was that Maison Blanche stayed non-operational. It was frustrating. The Squadron temporarily returned to Blida and, with help from No.608 went operational in record time. This gave the Dance Band the opportunity to take stock and with a reasonable room in the French barracks they gave regular concerts to the troops all around. It was there that the band bought the last of their instruments, Bill Cooksey's string bass "Betsy". The way Bill got his instrument was one of the most endearing stories Squadron veterans remember. In Algiers he found one in a music shop and all would have been well if Bill had stuck to his lingual efforts which nobody could understand anyway, as Frank Russell remembered. Bill made the mistake of using his hands to outline the graceful lines of the musical instrument. This made the French music shop proprietor somewhat suspicious, as his wife was in the shop too, and extremely well-formed she was. At the same time Cooksey, whose knowledge of French was virtually nil, mouthed the odd "boom, boom", which gave the owner of the shop the idea that Bill was making rather sexual comments about his beloved wife and suggesting very intimate and direct bedroom activities. Confusion and anger took over and the owner of the music shop was close to committing first degree murder or at least some form of final bodily harm, rather than seeing great financial opportunities. Poor Bill Cooksey, who had no idea what he had done wrong, was lucky to get away intact.

During the early weeks of the Squadron's arrival only a few enemy aircraft were encountered. The first German aircraft attacked by a Squadron Beaufighter was a Heinkel 111 on 21st December 1942. Sgt Alan Owen with Victor McAllister as his operator dealt with it in true Squadron manner. But any euphoria the crew experienced evaporated when they discovered that return fire from the Heinkel had damaged the undercarriage. There was no option for Owen but to crash-land. The aircraft careered off the runway, hit a Spitfire, then a concrete mixer and a fuel tanker before being halted by a pile of stones. The Beau was written off and McAllister escaped with a badly damaged nose. By way of compensation the ground crew presented them with the clock from the rear instrument panel. It was one of the few parts of the Beaufighter that had remained intact. Christmas in North Africa was celebrated somewhat differently from the way it was at home in England. Norman Poole, who arrived shortly after Christmas 1942, remembered that the Squadron had found favour in the eyes of the locals, who were not too keen on their French masters. One of the local brothels is said to have given the Squadron a Christmas party, when everything, including food and drink, was free. Poole later admitted that he had never been able to substantiate this nor obtain a full and written account of that particular Christmas. Another important achievement of the Squadron was their securing special terms from the only brewery in the area. It meant they had an excellent supply line, but unfortunately it only lasted a few weeks before it was discovered by the NAAFI people who then took over and stopped the supply. Again the Squadron had to submit to most ungenerous rationing.

On 26th December 1942 W/C Green DFC returned and took charge of No. 600 Squadron. He was to stay for the rest of the Desert war. With him came another old Squadron member, P/O Gillies. They arrived by Flying Fortress. The new CO was a man of perfection and action. The diarist wrote: "The CO is a leader in every possible facet of the business with an unswerving determination to win the war by tomorrow or, at the very latest the day after. He despised the second rate and by his personal example inspired a standard of efficiency and devotion to duty which became the only acceptable practice in the Squadron. The weak or unwilling fell by the wayside, were posted, or just disappeared to "elsewhere". Green wanted a crack Squadron; he was willing to go the extra mile to get it; the Squadron itself did better ensuring that it happened. The Squadron duties at this time involved night patrols over Algiers to protect the incoming convoys". In spite of difficulties at times almost insurmountable, the standard set by Paddy Green was maintained. Perhaps the men of No.600 thought his orders and expectations were very severe and at times even unreasonable, but they carried them out, struggling on under exhausting and appalling con-ditions. All knew that if they did not they would be unable to carry out their duties under stress. The drome was in a deplorable condition and there seemed to be no order anywhere. It had been bombed and shelled many times. There was much activity to make the runways serviceable and operational. It was very difficult to disperse the Beaus safely, but somehow the Squadron managed to work on them and get them ready for night operations. There were aircraft landing, taking off and taxiing about all over the place with little co-ordination from Aerodrome Control at this stage. One was never really certain that one was really seeing one's own Squadron aircraft off or in and it was sometimes very annoying to run half-way across the aerodrome waving a couple of torches and avoiding being chopped into little pieces by the "fans" of a pursuing aircraft, only to find at a point of dispersal in a state of total exhaustion that this aircraft belonged to another Squadron. The ground staff chaps finally overcame the difficulty by painting a figure 6 by the side of the Squadron marking and on the nose, which helped a lot in daylight and just a little at night. This became a permanent marking for the Squadron. The aircrews flew various patrols, one being over the "Llanstephan Castle", the troopship on which the ground staff had been taken to Algiers and which was now hit by a torpedo. A few weeks later S/L Hughes arrived, a fine officer who had earned himself great credit and admiration when, during the Battle of Britain, Desmond flew the ill-fated Defiants of No. 264 Squadron. Des, as he was known by the Squadron, crewed up with P/O Laurie Dixon, who had since been commissioned, and took over B-Flight. This duo was to become one of the best crews in that theatre of war. They were to stay together until the end of hostilities. January 1943 started quietly, with a lot of showers and weather so bad that flying was a problem. On the 6th an enemy aircraft flew over the aerodrome and dropped a stick of incendiaries, anti-personnel bombs and High Explosives. One small petrol dump was set ablaze and damage was done to three Spitfires, one Hurricane and a few lorries. Five men were injured. The Bomb Disposal Officer reported that some of the unexploded bombs were of Italian make. Rumours had it that the enemy had used Hudsons they had captured earlier. P/Os Spry and Armstrong were sent up in the sky. When they got a contact on the AI they chased it immediately. But closing in for the kill they recognised it as a Flying Fortress. The Yanks, quite unaware of the fact that a lot of Mean Barrels had been aimed at their Mighty Machine, had a lucky escape and the crew never even saw the Beau.

Also in January a conference took place at Anfa near of Casablanca. Hotels and villas were requisitioned to accommodate the President of the United States, Franklin Delano Roosevelt, the British PM Sir Winston Churchill and their staffs. General Giraud, Commander in Chief of the French troops in North Africa was invited, as was General Charles de Gaulle, the Leader of the Free French. It turned out later that Churchill and Roosevelt had more problems making both French generals shake hands than setting the policy for the future of the war. Heavily guarded by American troops who had completely barb-wired the whole area the Allied leaders sat together and major decisions for the war were made. Aircrew of the Squadron were ordered to fly patrols during the conference: W/C Paddy Green with P/O Gillies, S/L Elwell with P/O Barker and P/O Crabtree with Sgt Waddell. Four more crews were detailed to follow later: P/Os Spry and Armstrong, P/O Thompson and W/O White, P/O Raybould with Sgt Mullaley and Sgts Vigar and Palfrey. It was a great honour for the Squadron. 11th January Spry and Armstrong took off. Their briefing for the 4hrs plus flight had been very scanty. Charts were much lacking, met forecast neglible. They were told to stay away from Oran. The ack-ack there was said to be plentiful, very accurate and eager to fire at anything above. The Beaufighters flew independently, not knowing wind strength or direction. The crews therefore followed the procedure of "deliberate error navigation" which took them on a course to about 70 miles North of Casablanca. Then they turned South when they saw the Moroccan coast. The Yanks however were very nervous that such a conference might attract German or Italian attention. They directed the aircraft to Medouina, a temporary landing strip with hard standings and blast proof dispersals. With their amazing ability for efficiency the Yanks had built the base in 2 or 3 days. On the other hand they expected the Germans and Italians to attack their President at any moment. Therefore four Beaufighters flew a continuous night cover. It was soon made clear that the Americans took things very seriously. The slightest sign of movement in the dark, apart from the Casbah district of course, led to considerble panic among the Yanks. But in spite of them being very trigger-happy, the detachment suffered no casualties. The main danger, however, came from another corner; the American rations. The average US Air Force meal issued to the troops completely floored the Squadron lot after the staple diet of bully and "Spratts Shapes for Pooches" invariably issued to British Forces on the move. Ice cream twice a week and other such iron rations direct from the USA made it a little difficult to convince the men of No.600 Squadron that there could not possibly be any mail from the United Kingdom for many months due to lack of shipping space.

The ground crew had left Setif before the aircrew, but when the Beau-fighters landed there was no 600 ground crew present. This was unusual for the ground crews prided themselves in being there "always". It soon turned out what the reason for their absence had been. Their pilot had taken them to Gibraltar to refuel and the men had taken the opportunity to go shopping at the Rock. They bought all kinds of luxuries that were unobtainable in North Africa. When they finally arrived and their goodies appeared from the aircraft they were happily forgiven for their late arrival. Yet it was only peanuts compared to the luxuries exposed by the cousins from the States. But honour was satisfied in due course. The Yanks were flying fighters into Casablanca, direct from HMS Eagle, and once it was known that the RAF was in residence it became the sport of the day for the Yanks to beat up the Squadron's dispersal tent and of course the RAF standard which always flew. Of course the Squadron was deeply impressed by what the "Hell's Angels" did. But it turned out to be different when it came to landing aircraft. The AAF fledglings came straight from FTS in California, with concrete runways and every other thing to help an airman make a smooth landing. However, landing on Morocco's ridge and furrow was a very different proposition. With monotonous regularity the intrepid airmen from the States bit the dust on wonderfully executed "nose-overs", "Chinese three-pointers" and other Prune-like groundabatics. The climax came when nine out of twelve were sprawled across the fairway and it was left to the old hands to recover the debris. This the Squadron did with British phlegm and remarkably little comment, in the circumstances, to the effusive thanks of the Station Commander.

With the leaders of the free world together the conference became a major event, which would turn out to be of great significance to the further direction of the war. The military conclusions were:

1. *Defeat of U-boats endangering the Allied supply lines across the Atlantic.*
2. *A decisive victory in North Africa, followed by the occupation of Sicily to shorten Allied lines of communications.*
3. *A position of Allied strength in the Mediterranean to undermine the position of the Axis in the Balkans, to force Italy to abandon its alliance with Germany and to bring Turkey with its 44 divisions army on the Allied side.*

4. *To start the largest possible air campaign against German cities.*

5. *To assemble the largest possible American force in England to prepare an invasion of Western Europe by the late spring of 1944.*

6. *To continue and expand a campaign of political and economic warfare, subversion and deception to undermine the will and ability of Germany to fight and to pin down Axis forces anywhere.*

This Allied decision was the basis for warfare in the years to come. However, the president of the United States had a surprise for the press that gathered at Casablanca. He made an announcement that had not been discus-sed during the meeting with his Allies and in a way it made the Germans aware that they would be better to fight till the end, as there was not going to be any discussion with the Allies about an honourable peace. To the PM's amazement the President proclaimed that only an unconditional surrender of Germany, Italy and Japan would be accepted.

The conditions under which the Squadron travelled to Setif could be called "rather basic". Cattle trucks were the best transport available on the Setif Express . . .

For the detachment this duty was much of a vacation though a lot of night flying was put in and sometimes the Beaufighters had to fly the day patrols as well. While the detachment patrolled the skies over Casablanca other aircraft carried on doing their duty in Algeria. But during the first week of January the Squadron went to a new station. A group of 224 men under P/O Crowder, the Ground Defence Officer, left Maison Blanche by train for Setif, with all the Squadron equipment. Despite cattle trucks or horse vans and dirty carriages all the bodies appeared to accommodate themselves to the circumstances and showed no little initiative in preparing meals and seeing to maximum comfort possible. The fine weather and magnificent scenery contributed largely to the interest of the trip. Meanwhile the remaining aircrews and personnel essential for the organisation of the new camp site at Setif went there by air with the Beaufighters and two DC3's which assisted in the move. The following day the ground crews arrived at Setif Railway Station and were conveyed to the camp by lorries. They were to live in tents at 4,000 feet on a plateau, which was quite a change from Maison Blanche. The countryside was bare, almost arid, broken by strips of trees along the streams and peopled wholly by Arabs. The mountains bounding the plateau were jagged and austere. By day it was generally clear and sunny and by night very cold. So for the time being it was farewell to the orange groves, the eucalyptus trees and, not to say, the amenities of Algiers. Setif aerodrome was an old French airfield. Being about 4,000 feet above sea level it was the highest aerodrome in Africa. A most agreeable site was allocated for the Squadron tented camp at some distance away from the drome. The camp at Setif was a good example of what was possible with imagination and a Boy Scout manual. A good tented camp with home-made heaters, improvised showers, and a football pitch soon provided the Squadron with a base in which to unify itself. The Squadron had arrived as a motley throng, consisting of very experienced Auxiliaries, a sprinkling left-over of Regulars and a large influx of bods posted in for the overseas tour.

When the detachment left Casablanca to rejoin No.600 Squadron, a deputation consisting of W/O "Twinkle" Nelson and Sgt Dev DeVroome very solemnly presented the Station Adjutant with a dustpan and a brush, advising him that the Squadron would have no further use for it and "would he please place it to our credit on the 'Lend-Lease' account?". A rather hilarious event was witnessed while in Algiers and definitely worth mentioning. One day a US Military Film Unit arrived, swinging their cameras. They made a rather upbeat bit of film about soldiers of the United States Army capturing Algiers port. Wonderful action, and great bravery was shown by the attacking Yanks. All were deeply impressed; if it had not been for the fact that the British Army had captured the very same port two weeks earlier!

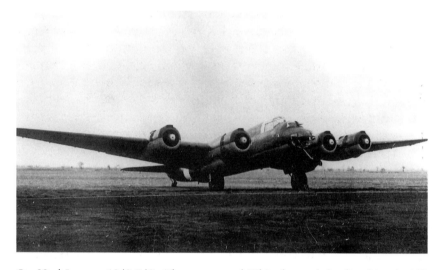

On 22nd January 1943 F/Os Thompson and White bagged the first Piaggio 108 bomber. This aircraft was the Italian equivalent of the Lancaster and the Flying Fortress. Very few came across the Beaufighters' path. The ones that did bought it.

At Setif the endless night operations, the standing patrols, and the constant guard against pilfering Arabs began to take on a pattern which unfailingly appears wherever in the world British forces take up residence. A wild knock-about inter-section soccer competition was soon under way and the partisanship was worthy of the World Cup at its best, as were the ribald comments from the fans. The "Free Welsh" contingent inevitably formed themselves into a male-voice choir and supported by other such virtuosi as Frank Yates, Jack Wain and Phil Spencer, they proceeded to entertain anyone who cared to listen, and the rest willingly. There was one good voice belonging to Jonah Jones, but obviously he was not allowed to sing as he had to conduct. What the choir lacked in professional skill it made up with honest enthusiasm and there were men who blamed this for the maladies which beset the Squadron from time to time. For a spell those who escaped the "Screamers" were afflicted with yellow jaundice and more and more resembled members of the Chinese Army. Regardless of the malady all were earnestly advised by Doc Scurlock to eat "lashings of fresh fruits" and drink "bags of hot sweet tea" as the only sure cure. However everyone seemed to recover on a diet of Meat, Vegetables and Bully, skilfully administered by the Squadron dietician Tubby Luke, who could cook anything provided it came up in a box of composite rations. More than fifty years later Laurie Dixon told how he arrived at Setif: "I remember it as a small place, built on both sides of a street – we were under canvas just to the South of it and quite near to us was No.225 Squadron camped around in a French farmhouse with the astonishing name of Mac Donald. Together we formed 125 Wing with Beaufighters MkVI. The aerodrome was about 3000 feet above sea level and I remember we had been told as part of our preparations in England that we might have to operate from an airfield at about 4000 feet! In fact the height did not bother the Beaufighters at all!!" All this aside, it did not mean that there was no action. On 22nd January 1943 F/Os Thompson and White destroyed a Piaggio 108, the Italian equivalent of the Lancaster and the B17 Flying Fortress and, as such, the only four-engined bomber ever to fly in the Italian air force. The following night, when the band was playing, the Germans decided to form a background choir by plastering the place with bombs. At that very moment Desmond Hughes and Laurie Dixon were flying. Laurie Dixon wrote about this particular event: "The idea of that evening was that anyone could put on an act, sing, recite, tell a story or whatever. Then, at the end of the evening each act would be judged on the applause it received. We got together a few prizes, a bottle or two, some cigarettes, oranges etc., etc. By around 6 pm it had got under way, when someone came in with a message for Desmond, who began to make his way out, beckoning to me to follow him. He stopped long enough to say that there was enemy air activity North of the coast and "Get your kit, quickly!" I collected my parachute harness, chute, Mae West, helmet, gloves and maps and off we went in a Bedford 15cwt truck which had come for us. We charged off to the airfield where "A" had already been warmed up for us and stormed into a clear but velvety black night sky. One thing I disliked about Setif was the loose pebbles all over the surface.

These used to fly up and rattle like bullets against the aircraft and I
felt there was always a risk of tyre damage. Our instructions were
to climb NE to Philippeville on the coast, where freighters were
unloading masses of materials for the Army and Air Force advancing
towards Tunis, 150 miles to the East. These were always lonely
moments, when one was hunting out a ruthless opponent and
looking for a fight which would be violent and probably final for
one or both of us. In this instance we were also a long, long way
from home. We crossed the coast which we felt, like bumping over
a step caused by the rising thermals. We duly made contact with the
local GCI. In forward areas such as these, they were called AMES
(Air Ministry Experimental Station) and were even carried on ships
or landing craft. Ours was stationed at Cap Serrat. This little point
on the coast was at the north end of the front, which straggled north-
south and it had a small lighthouse built on it. A famous controller,
S/L Brown, manned it and the crews who knew him always looked
forward to "Brownie" being in charge. He lost his life in September
1944, when he served as a Wing Commander on the same job during
Operation Market-Garden at Arnhem. We were vectored north-east
towards a raid which was coming from Sicily and I can remember
feeling cold, because in the hurry to take off I had no flying boots,
thick stockings or sweater. We made sure everything was ready,
radar and armament, as we were brought around onto a Westerly
course and told a "bandit" was crossing us from starboard to port
and still above. Then I had the enemy as a radar contact, crossing
fast to port and losing height rapidly. As I read out information and
instructions to Des I could feel our rapid loss of height in my ears.
It was obvious this Hun was after shipping moored off Philippeville
and needed to get lower to see them. We were all in the dark! He
was now running in diagonally towards the coast and altering course
regularly from side to side. This gave us a chance to close in and I
tried to place him above us to starboard until Des could see him. A
quiet word: "Think I've got him, have a look". At about 2 o'clock
and above us was a dark shape against the sky with two pairs of
exhausts showing like flickering white lines – a Junkers 88. As we
eased up towards it two lines of tracer flew over us from his under
gun position. These red balls seemed to accelerate as they
approached us and then finally zipped past. A bit salutary to know
that we were only seeing about one round in four of what was being
aimed at us from each gun but anyhow that gunner was very alert

and did not deserve to die. We turned to port inside his turn and hit him with a burst in the port wing root. The petrol tank there erupted in red flame and the aircraft went down like a huge torch, shedding all sorts of burning fragments. Just as suddenly all was dark again as the sea closed over our victim. All was quiet now with us for a moment, only the smell of cordite from the cannons reminding us of the noise and violence of the combat. Then a word to Control who wanted us back North in case of further trade.

We turned and climbed to about 15,000 feet patrolling an East West line. From having been white cold I found myself in a lather of sweat but soon cooled down to feel colder than ever. Another quarter of an hour and the Controller thought he had more trade. Sure enough I soon had another contact but this one was already down to 10,000 feet and jinking about like a snipe. Either he knew we were in his vicinity or else he was taking evasive action just in case. He was certainly very difficult to cope with on our radar and once or twice I almost lost him. We must by now have been over lots of shipping and any moment I expected the sky to erupt with flak. Nothing happened so somehow or other the message had got through that we were to be left to deal with this intruder. I could imagine all the itchy fingers on triggers below us and just hoped that none of them were Yanks. We finally got a visual on this bandit which proved to be another Junkers 88. Another storm of noise and cordite fumes from the cannons and this one too was well alight in the port engine and port wing root tanks.

Down he went and there was a final flash, so on this occasion the sea at least had been robbed of its victim. No return fire this time and both interceptions had taken forty five minutes from start to finish. We needed now to return to base, where we landed with no trouble around 2130 hrs. having been airborne for about three hours. A quick word and pat on the back from our ground crews and from F/S Nelson, everything had worked and they shared in our success. Then a full report to the Intelligence Officer whilst all was still fresh in our minds. Finally back to the camp site riding on the floor in the back of the 15cwt truck – very bumpy. The airmen's mess tent was still lit and somebody was singing, so we pulled back the flap, went in and dropped our kit. There was a tremendous cheer and much clapping. In a moment it was decided that we had won 1st prize and we were handed a bottle of Irish Whisky. I had never seen or heard of it before, let alone tasted it, but all that was altered before the night was out. I have never been able to face it since". Two days later an army truck came looking for the Squadron. The soldiers had found the under gun cupola and guns from the second Ju88 shot down by Hughes and Dixon, which had fallen on the beach near the soldiers. The armourers removed the Spandau machine guns and the barrels were mounted crosswise on a wooden frame. Each victory thereafter was recorded on a square white painted metal tag, which showed the date, aircraft type and names of the crew responsible. The tags were hung around the frame. Later the news came that Hughes had been awarded a Bar to his DFC whilst a well-deserved DFC was awarded to Dixon.

The AMES station needed specialist advice from the aircrew side so Des Hughes, Laurie Dixon, F/O James Ritchie, a Canadian Radar Officer were told to accompany Gp/Capt David Atcherley to Cap Serrat. This would entail a round trip of about 60 miles. The party took a Bedford 15cwt truck, a petrol generator, spares and compo rations. Dixon never forgot the contents: "COMPO BOX 2fi ˇ 2fi ˇ 1fift.,1 day's ration for 14 men in an easily divided form. Breakfast: sausage and beans. Lunch: Biscuits, jam, butter, cheese, tea. Dinner: Meat & Vegetables, pudding. Also a bar of chocolate, 6 boiled sweets, cigarettes, packets of salt, matches and toilet paper. All tins small enough to be emptied at one sitting. Heating in water, that was all that was required. As there were seven different types of boxes one had a different meal each day (in theory). Box A would contain Steak and Kidney pudding and tinned peaches, Box B might have pork stew and date pudding.

The journey took the men first back west to Souk el Arba, now quite deserted, and then north to La Calle on the coast. They then followed a very narrow and poor quality road to Tabarka. Ritchie and Dixon took turns to stand up as aircraft spotters which was just a little less uncomfortable. Along the road from Tabarka there was evidence of fighting with broken equipment, burnt out vehicles and little clusters of graves. These seemed to occur at each bend in the road in particular, indicating how the German defence had been organised. Coming up to Sedjenane, the little iron mining settlement everything was covered with a reddish, orange dust. There obviously had been quite a battle between British paratroopers and German troops with many casualties on both sides. It was the thick red dust which coated everything at Sedjenane which earned the British paras the nickname Red Devils and not as it is commonly thought the colour of their berets. The party turned off the road and travelled north across country to Cap Serrat. However this took them through No-Man's-Land, a stretch about two miles wide. It was kept well under surveillance, mined, booby-trapped and patrolled by both sides. It was a most uncomfortable drive. The men came across a foot patrol of the RAF Regiment who stopped them and warned them that the track ahead was booby-trapped. They were treating two of their own men who had been injured and carefully pointed out which direction the truck was to take. About 4pm the group approached something Laurie Dixon had read about as a boy, but never thought he would actually see – a French Foreign Legion fort with the tricolour flying over it. There it was, square in outline, with high white walls, patrolled by legionnaires in blue uniforms and with white kepis with cloth tails hanging down over the nape of the neck. It was Fort Monopole.

These men were mainly aircraft spotting and no matter how high or far away these were their sighting was announced by whistle blowing. Night was not far away so the RAF detachment decided to park just outside the walls in a small cemetery. They had a meal and

F/L "Joe" Hanus, a Regular Czech Air Force pilot, and his R/O (Radar Operator) P/O Eyles. Hanus wears the flying badge of the Czech Air Force.

as the light faded they fell asleep on the floor of the Bedford. Three of them, including stocky Ritchie were a pretty tight fit between the wheel housings. What a night it proved to be, because the French had the walls manned by armed lookouts who fired at the slightest sound or movement. Quite apart from the noise all of this shooting seemed to be just over the heads of the Squadron party and they decided the floor of the truck was too high off the ground for safety. So they took their blankets and slept on the ground between the graves. Next morning the men were cold and stiff. They went into the fort before leaving to let the French know where they were heading. What they saw inside was quite appalling. The French had an Arab prisoner whom they suspected of selling information to the Germans and they were trying to make this wretch talk. They had actually sliced his left thigh from hip to knee and they were dragging him by his feet behind a horse around the cobbled courtyard. In the end they dragged him to a sort of horse trough, pulled off his burnous and threatened to drown him. This was apparently the last straw for he began to gabble. Dixon could only guess that being plunged naked into water was against his religion but he evidently could not face it. The French certainly plummeted in the estimation of their British Allies and the group was glad to take their leave for more reasons than one. They soon reached the coast and Cap Serrat. The little white painted lighthouse on top of a small pinnacle onto which the driver took the truck was their destination. The men found an astonishing group of cut-throats in residence there, under the command of a young blonde Navy lieutenant, who was going around dressed as an Arab. He told the RAF that his men's function was to make landings and reconnaissances way ahead of the Army. The Navy lieutenant and his gang slept on iron beds in a room on the ground floor of the lighthouse and the RAF chaps shared a meal with them that night. The next morning Laurie Dixon saw the whole group of ruffians, dressed in all kinds of "uniforms" cleaning weapons. They had a variety of guns British, German, French and many of them carried knives that were sharp as a razor blade. Until this day Dixon wondered how they had come together, who paid, armed and fed them and not least how this young naval chap kept them under control. The RAF party helped with the positioning of the GCI which was to provide much needed cover of the area seaward to the Northwest and Northeast. Brownie was delighted with his new toy which looked like being very busy and told the men that the call sign was to be CLIFFTOP – not very original in the circumstances. The job finished the group made its way back to Souk-el-Khemis without further incident. Later that Spring, when the Germans tried their final push to the West, Clifftop and Brownie were strafed by the Luftwaffe. Hughes and Dixon were flying home on the deck to Setif that early morning and they could hear Brownie scream through his radio: "Come to Clifftop, come to bl—dy Clifftop". Later he told them that he was hiding under a table and that the Navy lieutenant and his gang had pushed the GCI set over the cliff into the deep. With Clifftop abandoned Brownie parted with the "naval irregulars". They finally ended up landing on Sicily and Dixon met the whole lot in a hotel in Liverpool at the end of February 1944. They never explained why they were there!

More men joined the Squadron in early 1943. One of them was earlier mentioned Norman Poole. On 5th February 1943 he and his pilot McKinnon got a Beaufighter at the Ferry training Unit at Lyneham. They lost no time in putting it through its most critical test a couple of days later. The consumption test was vitally important as it had to prove if the aircraft had the range to reach Gibraltar, their refuelling stop for North Africa. On 16th they flew to Portreath, the furthest West they could go and topped up with fuel for their long trip, as the Squadron had done in November 1942. The next morning at 0730, in darkness, they took off. The Beaufighter seemed to need every bit of runway and slipping over the cliffs they headed south over the sea. The centimetric radars had been stripped out and went to North Africa by sea rather than to risk a possible landing in not-so-neutral Portugal. Top brass decided that this was the safest thing to do – as far as the equipment was concerned. Cloud cover was complete for the first leg of the flight. This was a mixed blessing as the crews could take no drifts and had to rely on the forecast winds given to them. On the other hand it provided cloud cover should they need it whilst passing the Brest peninsula where German fighters were based and were prone to try to intercept Allied reinforcements. They saw nothing but abreast of Lisbon the cloud broke and Poole as the navigator was able to operate his drift sight and get some idea of how the wind was affecting them. Of course there was no way without a fix of determining how the wind to the North had affected the formation during the first two hours they had been flying. Not unnaturally the expanse of blue ocean began to worry the crews as they did not want to miss the gates of the

Mediterranean and run on to Africa or the South Atlantic. It called
for a gentle left hand down until they could see the coast and get a
fix on their position. In the event they were on course and had no
difficulty in reaching Gibraltar with its fascinating runway, even then
built into the harbour. It was a five-and-a-half hour flight and the
detachment of six aircraft all arrived safely with fuel to spare.
Gibraltar was an exciting place to the men. It had spirits to drink
and unrationed chocolate and white bread. Poole thought these
goodies might come from Spain by smugglers, but still it was a
welcome change from wartime Britain in February 1943. The few
days they had gave them a first experience of the Mediterranean
wines which were often not very wisely consumed.

The next leg of their flight brought them nearer the war, to Algiers,
its airfield being Maison Blanche. The six of them flew together from
Gibraltar and again the weather was bad so the crews had no fear
of enemy interception, even if they felt confident enough to tackle
a mass of six Beaufighters with their machine guns and cannons.
The worries of the new crews were more practical, like avoiding the
Atlas Mountains which spread themselves along the shores of North
Africa. Arriving at Maison Blanche the crews were told that they had
already been allocated among the RAF Squadrons there. Three crews
went to the Squadrons defending Algiers and the other three,
including McKinnon and Poole, to No.600 "City of London"
Squadron, which was operating from an advanced base, called Setif,
further along towards Tunisia. Poole felt lucky as he was to become
a part of the spearhead Squadron covering the advance into Tunisia.
The three new aircraft took off for Setif and in the prevailing weather
were grateful that the Squadron had sent one of their aircraft to lead
them in.

The route took them along the coast to a position North of Setif
and then they turned South and let down through the cloud in some
trepidation but determined not to lose their leader. They found their
new home safely enough, a rough field a few miles West of the town
of Setif. The rough field served as a reminder that they were getting
nearer the war for after landing they were marshalled into dispersed
positions before shutting down engines. Dispersal was the order of
the day for their living quarters were a tented camp some three miles
away in another rough field. They had been given a timely reminder
of the wisdom of this policy at Maison Blanche for in the days of
innocence the Beaufighters had been parked for ease of mainte-

nance in a neat row. It made life very simple for a single German fighter to run down the row of aircraft firing his cannons and destroying four or five aircraft, in one run. Then a truck took them to the dispersed campsite, its tents were of course dispersed as well. The living accommodation consisted of ridge tents with two officers to a tent but in an emergency this could be doubled to four. They slept on canvas camp beds and when the warmer weather brought flies and mosquitoes they were glad of their mosquito nets. They had marquees for messes and dining areas with mainly ridge tents for kitchens and store rooms and shelters for the ground crews maintaining the aircraft. There were a few small marquees for work areas in which the men needed the head room. Food was fairly dismal and was based on field rations so the men saw a good deal of Maconochie's meat and vegetable stew and other delights of the "haute cuisine" of wartime. The supplement they searched for from local Arab traders was the humble, but very much appreciated egg. The currency in use was the cigarette, no other payment was acceptable. There were two kinds of cigarettes in circulation, one the normal British type in rationed supply from the NAAFI and the other,

Squadron Beaufighters regularly encountered Cant Z1007 bombers.

readily available because of its poor quality, the V-Victory cigarette. Goodness knew where they came from and as a non-smoker Poole had no expertise to judge them, but everyone regarded them as the last resort. They were beyond the pale as far as the Arabs were concerned so the men used to dress them up in the NAAFI regular packs. This ploy worked for a while but it was not long before they were rumbled and eggs were in short supply again.

The days at Setif were bright and warm, but the nights were so cold that no Squadron member saw much pleasure in lifting the flaps in the morning and be momentarily blinded by the whiteness of about six inches of snow and then trudging through it to have a wash and shave and a shampoo at the toilet point some 100 yards away. Breakfast, work parade, roll-call, inspection and so on over, then down to the aerodrome to relieve the night readiness crews and get the score and hear all about it. Sgt Chantrey vividly remembered how life on Setif was and, also, how the Squadron slowly turned into a powerful fighting machine. There were memories other than those of war and violence: "I remember how, when you were facing a certain direction, one could look down the slope of the mountain and see whole Squadrons of Dakotas, flying up the valley below us to the forward areas with supplies, and in the direction where the Squadron's first detachment was soon to go".

As far as the band was concerned Setif was top of the pops, for it was there that the Army organised a garrison theatre. With the Flights both forward at Souk-el-Khemis and Sousse, the band was able to accept an invitation to be the orchestra for the week, and put on a stage show. The Squadron was split up over these satellite airstrips to spread as many night-fighters as possible over the largest possible area. With the battles moving East, the Squadron aircraft followed. Being the night-fighter umbrella of the First Army the Squadron now reached the Western edge of Tunisia. It was in the days when W/C Paul Ewell left the Squadron to command Djidelli airfield and was replaced by S/L Horne, who soon afterwards got his first Ju88, followed by the Czech Pilot F/L Hanus and P/O Eyles, who got one as well. Sgts Owen and McAllister both shot down a He111. The Luftwaffe replied by sending FW190s to North Africa to protect the bombers and other aircraft. It did not help much for the Squadron happily continued shooting down one after the other. Sgt Parkinson and F/Sgt Stevens destroyed a Ju88 off the Sardinian coast, Turnbull shot down a Cant Z1007b North of Bone. Throughout April rarely a night passed without combat. As a result aircrews were awarded decorations for their exploits over the waters between Africa and Europe. DFMs were awarded to Sgts Owen and McAllister on 29th April 1943. This made the ground crews too feel that they were really contributing to the war. Generally speaking each aircraft would have a more or less permanent ground and air crew, which soon became a real team with very great understanding between them. At the same time there was a lot of leg pulling and quite naturally keen competition between the teams and a friendly rivalry between the Flights.

As mentioned earlier, the days were long and very, very hot; the nights very cold. The speed of events began to hot up. Each day something new or encouraging, perhaps at times disappointing happened. One of the most serious problems was that almost everyone in the Squadron was suffering from Yellow Jaundice. It was noticeable enough for 600 to be called the "Free Chinese Air Force Squadron" and some of the old boys remember very few visitors. The other visible manifestation of progress of one's illness was the colour of one's urine, and since the toilets were large buckets behind a canvas screen it was customary to check on progress during rather sociable trips to the latrines. The screens were some distance down wind in accordance with the field training manual and rather than make a solitary trip it was customary to make up a small party, or at least a pair to visit the latrines. The pits were in the same area and consisted of long but stout tree trunks suspended in a tree fork at an appropriate height. It was not comfortable enough to linger, but their capacity depended on the available timber and it was normal to have three of four seaters which made them sociable occasions as well. The earth spoil from the pit was kept available and a swift kick before departure kept things in order – and the flies at bay. The Medical officer had no cure available and the illness ran its course. Crews were grounded if the "colour test" signified an acute state and this of course was reflected in a general state of debility. However the Squadron managed to keep going and the disease had run its course by the time the Battle of Tunisia was over. When Poole and "Mac" arrived the germ was obviously weakening for none of them ever got beyond a strong orangy colour and they were able to keep flying. It was quite amazing to see how the ground crews, in spite of the adverse weather situation, the filth and the constant pressure were able to have the aircraft available so quickly after landing. There could be setbacks somewhere, a technical problem which for a while defied solution, but in spite of it, or because of it, some routine was beginning to establish itself. The fighting was hard, sometimes furious and uncertain. There was a constant shortage of aircraft and rumour had it at the time that for every aircraft the RAF could put into the air, the Luftwaffe could put six. It was not surprising that the RAF were unable to quickly replace fighters that were destroyed by the enemy. Eventually a fighter aircraft pool was formed at Setif, in the main Spitfire Vs, and in addition to its normal duties, No.600 Squadron had for a time the job of maintaining this pool, at times quite large. Bert Chantrey still remembers how things went once the Squadron had settled in a bit at Setif: "With things working smoothly on the whole, we began to think it was not such a bad war after all. Perhaps we were a little too complacent for suddenly we received a jolt as the superiority of the Luftwaffe, in numbers at any rate, which had been felt in many places with such devastating results, was now somewhat nearer home after all. In spite of the RAF day fighters, aerodrome defence and the ack-ack people in general, it was inevitable that some enemy fighters and bombers got through and much damage was done. While we were operating from Setif, one of our sister Squadrons, No.225, was engaged in a life and death struggle many miles away in the forward areas around Souk-el-Arba in the desert. First Army was under tremendous pressure and engaged in heavy fighting in the plains around Bizerta and Tunis in the initial stages of driving the enemy out of North Africa. From inland to and along the coast was a vast battle area with a greatly extended front line. From the opposite direction Eighth Army was engaged in the same task and on the whole, the Germans were having a nasty time. No.225 Squadron operated Beaufighters from a hastily laid Somerfeld strip at Souk-el-Arba and no doubt made themselves a great nuisance to the enemy who had by now come to dislike the Beaufighter's four 20mm cannons and six 303 machine guns. So it was on a bright sunny afternoon at Setif the CO came down to the Flight dispersal with the grave and disquieting news that No.225 Squadron had been completely wiped out, with all its aircraft destroyed but with mercifully few casualties. The Jerries had sought revenge and decided that No.225 would not cause them any more worries".

The Squadron's duties were now suddenly extended and 600 were to take over the role of No.225 and maintain its duties in the forward areas immediately. Just as suddenly as No.225 had been removed, No.600 was to take over. W/C Green said that from this night, the Squadron would be right in it and that meant getting men and machines up to Souk-el-Arba, some 350 miles away from Setif. The CO further said that the strip there was in a very poor condition but would be repaired and operational by the time No.600 Squadron arrived. The orders were that six Beaufighters would take off to arrive at Souk-el-Arba by dusk so that the Germans could not see them, together with the ground crew to keep them flying all night with the minimum of equipment. As the risk of loss by continuous strafing and bombing was so great, the theory was the "the less you had, the less you lost". It was good reasoning, but it meant a long and dangerous spell of hard work. The CO made one concession after going over the details with Sgts Hunter and Chantrey: "He said that we had a free hand in choosing the men to take along. So we quickly made our selection and informed all concerned. There was

NCOs were the backbone of the Squadron during the African campaign.
Back row: Brown, Chantrey, Hunter, DeVroome and Nelson. Front row: Hedgecock, Farmer and Harrison, holding one of the score boards the Squadron collected in Algeria and Tunisia.

a quick check-up on tool kits and a few personal belongings, and whilst we were getting organised on the ground crew side, aircraft were being made ready and aircrew detailed and briefed. A general air of excitement prevailed all around; no doubt some who were going wished they were not, and some who were not wished they were. However, all who were detailed to go were told why and that the nature of the operation was such that we would all be only too pleased to have a break after a fortnight or so. But, alas, for some of us the break did not happen and we soldiered on to the end. I was glad about this as the initial stages were hard and hazardous and I rather felt, as did Sgt Hunter, that having had the difficult bit in the beginning it was perhaps somewhat of a reward to see the whole thing working smoothly and a little easier at the end".

At the agreed time all was ready, the roll was called, the advance party which was to fly up for the night's operation were detailed and the rest set off by road with the heavier equipment and spares. The Beaufighters took off one by one, very much overloaded with men and material and set course for Souk-el-Arba. Hunter and Chantrey would fly as passengers in BQ-B, a Beaufighter with a rather bad reputation. With four men in the aircraft, plus a lot of material and equipment necessary to run the detachment this aircraft was the last of six to take off. BQ-B was a "Jonah". There always seemed to be something wrong with her. F/L Arnsby, the pilot, his navigator Gillies and the two NCOs therefore were not entirely without concern when "B" headed into wind. Chantrey began to peer over the pilot's shoulder and to check revs, boost, temperature, air pressure, throttle positions, CSU controls and synchronisation of engine speeds. As the pilot opened up all seemed well. Hunter turned to Chantrey and said: "We're away!" The Beau roared across the aerodrome. As they bumped over the rough surface they began to hear all sorts of creaks and groans and Hunter remarked: "If we get off in one piece we will be lucky to get down whole". As the road along the aerodrome boundary drew nearer Chantrey too had serious doubts about further events. However, much to the relief of all on board and no doubt those watching on the ground, "B" began to rise and cleared the road by a few feet. Then she climbed and the pilot set course for Souk-el-Arba, about one-and-a-half hours flying time away. After a while the four men found themselves looking down on a vast expanse of wooded hills and mountains, the Atlas range which at this point were about 5000 – 7000 feet high.

The roar from the engines and other extraneous noises prevented conversation by ordinary means, but by hand movements and exaggerated facial expressions the NCOs amused themselves in a very limited range of topics mostly confined to two and four letter words. By the time they reached their destination they were able to express to each other exactly what they thought of BQ-B, the war in general and where they were going to, either whole or in many pieces! The scenery was wonderful and as they drew near their future scene of operation, they hoped it would not be spoilt by any unkind action on the part of the enemy. They kept a sharp lookout now as they approached what was a very dangerous area. The two NCOs then suddenly remembered that they had their personal belongings and tools, but no parachutes. In fact none of the ground crew did as there were not enough chutes to go round. Below them they saw a scene of destruction. There were bomb craters everywhere, there were aircraft burning and smouldering, petrol, ammunition dumps and transports ablaze. But, as the CO had promised, the runway had been repaired and after a circuit the pilot was able to pick his way through the smoke-laden air and made a good touchdown. With all

Souk-el-Khemis. Reg Gillies, Laurie Dixon and Paddy Green (with sunglasses) enjoying a well known whisky in front of one of the tents.

the aircraft on the ground the party made its way to No. 225 Squadron's Dispersal Point and Operational Area. They quickly unloaded their kit and equipment and the aircraft were refuelled and checked ready to start the first night's operations with the willing help of the remaining ground crew of No.225. The night was dark and cold, a clear sky, and the stars seemed to shine more brightly than ever. The pattern of operations was very different from the United Kingdom. Setif was the main base, but the Squadron operated their detachments where the enemy threat was manifest. One detachment was near Bone and the low level centimetric radar was useful against low flying attacks against the ports. At intervals the Beaufighters took off and landed, adding their noise to the continual rumbling of heavy gunfire in the distance. From time to time the horizon would light up as German aircraft dropped bombs on a nearby target area. It was not long before the Squadron's turn came. The Luftwaffe seemed to be all over the place, but there was at least a little consolation in that 600 Squadron was now right in the middle of it and at that particular moment was no doubt making life a little more uncertain for the enemy raiders and perhaps causing them to drop their bombs a little wide. The first night passed and the men were very busy. However, the aircrew had not made contact with the enemy. As dawn came the Beaufighters returned to home base at Setif. This kind of life was to become familiar to aircrew and ground crew. So many aircraft off to Souk-el-Arba at dusk and so many back to Setif at dawn, some showing signs of wear and tear and some signs of combat. Instructions were that when an aircraft suffered damage in combat, it was flown straight back to Setif for repair which was considered better than risking repair at Souk and a possible write-off during one of the many daytime strafing raids. These beat-ups were a regular feature taking place at precisely the same time each day at 0800, 1200 and 1800 hours. These were German standing orders so to speak. But there were other assaults at odd times, some heavy prolonged raids, others just sneak attacks, sometimes causing great damage to both aircraft and stores, at times just "hit, miss and run", but it ensured that the men on the ground kept on their toes and slit trenches were absolutely essential and happily used. Tin hats were worn to keep the sun off needless to say as there was no cover of any sort, and all the work was done in the open. Work on the aircraft was always done with one eye on the machine and one on the sky above, or better, one man would act as lookout for any trouble that might be brewing. The warning was by means of a maroon flare fired into the air, leaving a large ball of black smoke in the sky in the direction from which the attack was approaching. But soon all this was to end when the Squadron had settled in and prepared to cause a lot of problems to the enemy.

CHAPTER 9

THE BALANCE CHANGES
January to June 1943

After Souk-el-Arba the Squadron moved up to a new strip, prepared by the Army while it moved on. It was at Souk-el-Khemis, better known as Paddington, Headquarters to the famous No.152 Squadron. The Squadron knew the area as operations had been carried out on detachments. It was later used by more Squadrons, such as Nos.74, 84, 92 and 111, OC74 being none other than W/C Stainforth, once OC600. Conditions were better than at Souk-el-Arba with a good camp site in an olive grove a safe distance from the drome, ridge tents, a food store, cookhouse and the best cooks the Squadron ever had. Electricians wired the tents for light, the current for which was supplied by a little JAP motor (usually used on the starter trolleys) which they let about 4 feet into the ground to kill the noise. The camp was guarded by the RAF Regiment detach-ment who were also responsible for the aerodrome defence commanded by F/L Crowder. They did a very good job, even though once an Arab managed to get inside the compound when Chantrey had per-mission from the CO to be away from the aerodrome dispersal, and pinch Chantrey's kit and personal belongings while he was sound asleep in the tent under his mosquito net. The dispersal point was a good one at the end of the strip by the side of a single track railway line which formed a boundary of the aerodrome. There was a brick building nearby which had been the railway station and this was used as the Squadron HQ. In fact all night operations were con-ducted from there as well as housing the Flight Office, CO's office, Aircrew and Groundcrew room, Radar, RT and electricians section. The Armourers and Instrument sections were outside in a small out-building. The men were instructed never to approach the HQ building directly and never to use the same track as it would have indicated to German recce aircraft life and movement and perhaps military use when this was supposed to be a derelict area and the Squadron was supposed to be operating in great secrecy. This was because the Squadron still was the only unit to use the AI Radar overseas. Many years later Laurie Dixon recounted the days at Souk-el-Khemis. Desmond Hughes and he flew the first Beaufighter to the new strip, which was to become a forward base for No.600 Squadron. As mentioned earlier it was part of a complex of four strips, all named after London railway termini. Theirs was Paddington and there were Spitfires at Kings Cross, Euston and Waterloo. Paddington ran East-West with a disused single line railway along its Southern edge. At the Western end of the strip there was a red brick three room building, which must have been some sort of railway hall. It had no doors, only one opening in one wall and no windows. At night they used it as a crew room for wireless and telephone equipment. During the day it was such an obvious target that it was wise to avoid it. The strips were laid on level sandy ground which was covered with enormous rolls of coconut matting carpet. Pegged over this and holding it in place was wide meshed, galvanised chicken wire and the result was an adequate if temporary runway surface. There was no anti-aircraft protection of any kind and the strips were wide open to air attack. For that reason our Beaufighters arrived late from Setif, perhaps being used, and returned there early in the morning. Des and Laurie used to stay at Paddington for a few days, returning to Setif at odd intervals for a couple of days. There was a small detachment of airmen under W/O "Peggy' Neil, a splendid long service regular airman. It was a rather lonely and comfortless spot and they employed themselves in off-duty moments in some rather bizarre occupations. There were colonies of large ants and having found a nest entrance they would block it with debris – bits of stick, wire, etc. Then they intensively watched these creatures make arrangements to clean this rubbish away, some pulling, some pushing, but obviously working together. When they had succeeded the men would repeat the exercise, endeavouring to make it more difficult. Crazy? Perhaps. There were many large and odd shaped spiders and the Squadron for a short while set up a number of highly successful spider fights. Gillies, who flew with the Commanding Officer, had a champion known as the "Blackwall Bruiser". It was a normally shaped insect, but very large.

Des Hughes happened to own a somewhat oddly shaped creature about/" wide and almost 2" long. It was named the "Hughes Hacker". They kept the spiders in empty cigarette tins, feeding them sparingly with the odd fly. They were put in a canvas bath and shaken together, when they would fight to the death. "Hacker" outlasted Reg's "Bruiser" and fought one or two more fights on only seven legs and finally ended its days on six. Its very appearance frightened some of its opponents but the excitement which this daft activity caused had to be experienced to be believed."

Paddington had no happy memories for Sgt Spry. On 24th February he took off and after an uneventful flight he entered the circuit and prepared for a landing. On the final approach, about 100-150ft from the ground, he pulled up the nose to reduce speed. At once, without any warning the plane stalled. Spry opened both throttles fully; both engines responded immediately and stopped. A wing dropped and the Beaufighter crashed absolutely flat. It spun around 180º and burst into flames on the end of the landing strip. His R/O Armstrong got out before Spry and was unhurt. Spry had a head injury and was excused flying for "medical reasons". The enquiry held that the airspeed indicator was at fault, a relief to Spry who was quite upset to have pranged his Beaufighter. It was one of these unlucky things that at times happened to a well-liked aircraft. The days rolled by and the Squadron had plenty to do to replenish the stocks of petrol, oil and ammunition. Petrol bowsers were all working to the limit and were in constant need of repair and attention. Once a week as many men as could be spared would have a day out. It was the "grub run", the regular Squadron shopping expedition. The Squadron was self-supporting if not self-sufficient and the food run was about 45 miles and thus was really exciting and invigorating. They had a Thorneycroft lorry, a real Trojan, take on anything and go anywhere and could build up a top speed of 45-50 miles per hour. To get to the supply centre the Squadron had to use the only road in that part of Algeria, long and straight, out in the open with nothing but sand all round. All military supplies came by this road, so of course it received special attention from the Germans who patrolled it all day long. The RAF also had an interest in it, their job being to look after traffic using it and preventing it from being bombed by the Germans. For this trip all Squadron members took Sten guns, a lot of ammunition, a tin hat and would proceed across the sand by devious routes, eventually picking up this road which became known as "Messerschmitt Alley". The sun was blazing and for some odd reason the Squadron enjoyed tearing along this road. For a mile or two all would be well, but all eyes were wide open looking in one direction when perhaps someone spotted a speck in the distance. Soon that speck would become three, four or half a dozen and get nearer and nearer with more and more speculation. They would roar over and the Squadron would for the moment relax. The driver would have his foot down hard on the throttle and reach a speed of 50 mph on the clock. Orders were, no stopping on this road and the driver was denied the sight his passengers sometimes had of a dogfight going on right overhead as the Spitfires were driving the 109s away. The Squadron never suffered any damage or loss on these trips, but the sight of bullets hitting the sand around them, the general clatter, and when the opportunity came, a few rounds from the Sten guns was usually sufficient to make up for the lack of any other form of entertainment. It seemed only a matter of time before such an exposed and vulnerable site was attacked by the Germans. Walking anywhere near the strip in daylight made one feel like a pea on a huge drum – there was just nowhere to hide. When the attack by FW190 fighter-bombers materialised, it turned out to be a bit hilarious in a way. The Squadron had dug a trench

Beaufighters with Hercules (front) and Merlin (right) engines. The AI aerials are visible on the nose and the wing roots.

between the railway building and the railway line. The men had spent quite a lot of time on it.

They had dug it 4 feet deep so that they could stand up in it. Fortunately, when the attack developed there was no one inside. A FW190, obviously tempted by the building, missed and scored a bulls-eye on the trench. After all the work done there was just a shallow round hole. Even funnier though, the airman employed to heat the tinned food at night was having a nap inside the building. He shot out and began to run blindly East along the railway track side. He would have done better to lie down flat because, in his own words afterwards "there was a bloody great clang" and he found himself almost tripping over a 250kg bomb half buried in the sand in front of him. It took some time before he got over this.

The army were not having a good month in February 1943, for the Germans had counter-attacked at the Kasserine Pass and driven a deep wedge into the US sector. It was unfortunate for it was the first real battle experience for the Yanks and possibly they had had it too easy during the largely unopposed drive from Algiers towards Tunisia. They had met with very tough, battle hardened experienced German troops and were no match for them. The American High Command solved the dilemma in American style. Some of their generals suddenly disappeared from the battlefield to show up somewhere in the States behind desks in air-conditioned rooms. General George Patton took over and with his very personal approach made a fresh start. As for the RAF, their hold on the advanced airfields they were operating from began to look somewhat dubious, but there were experienced British regiments available to cut off the German advance. As for No.600 Squadron it meant that the tents had to be dug in a foot or two depending on how hard the ground was and this gave a degree of protection if one could work out the direction of attack and choose the appropriate side of the tent. Slit trenches were widely available if you were caught outside and the men became experts at digging them and diving into them. After one German raid they were embarrassed to see two bombs lying on the grass near the runway. They had been dropped at low level and skidded along the ground and only an expert could tell whether they were delayed time bombs or had simply had their detonator plunger bent when they hit the ground at such a flat angle. The solution was simple. Until you got an expert to look at them you built a sandbag wall around them which would minimise the damage they might do to aircraft passing that point on the runway. Meantime there remained a question mark as to who was in charge as you laid the sandbags, for the CO was looking for an officer to supervise the sandbag party. Norman Poole recalled that he pressed backward rather than forward, with a definite preference to die in the air rather than on the ground. And in the event the bombs did not go off and the crews carried on their operations, untroubled if a little anxious as they passed by the bomb enclosure.

On 12th February 1943 Desmond Hughes and Laurie Dixon shot a Cant Z1007b of No.262 Bomber Squadron IAF. Personal belongings of the pilot, Major Padovani, made this war between flying machines much more realistic.

As well as living under canvas the Squadron had one substantial building which brought them the favourable commendation of the farmer who owned the land on which the building was erected. It was a triumph of block construction, for it was made of empty four gallon petrol cans filled with earth. All the fuel came in these non-reusable cans. They had to be handed up to the man on the wing who tipped the contents into a large funnel with a chamois leather filter which fed directly into the tanks. Later on some ground trolleys with the same filters became available, equipped with a hand pump to get the fuel up to the wing instead of having to heave the can up.

It was left to the Germans and the Americans to introduce the reusable jerrycans but at least our four gallon 'blocks' made extensions possible to the flight HQ which had a number of rooms before we left the building to the farmer. The cans were green which was useful from the camouflage viewpoint because it was never attacked.

During the night of 12th February Des Hughes and Laurie Dixon went off at about 2100hrs on an offensive patrol to the North and East. They flew to the Northeast towards the French naval port of Bizerta, about fifty miles away. It was one of those velvety black nights with a great background and countless tiny stars, and in no time at all they had intercepted and identified two friendly Wellingtons. "Neither of them was taking any evasive action and they showed no signs of having seen us. I wonder if these crews ever survived the war. We were then vectored towards another bandit which proved to be more of a handful with its constant jinking and changing of height. We finally closed in on it but it was at first a bit difficult to identify and we had to be quite sure. We moved in below it and saw to our surprise that it had three engines. It was a big Italian Cant Z1007 and should have had a single fin. But this beast had twin rudders. It was Italian and as we moved in closer from astern all of our doubts were dispelled as it opened fire from a top gun position above the wing. There seemed to be two separate guns and its red tracer fairly whistled over us. He then began to dive, which put us for a short while right behind as we followed him down. We gave him a short burst aimed right through the fuselage and the effect was dramatic and horrific. The return fire ceased and I imagine the whole of the crew died in that instant. We were left looking at the sight I shall never forget. It was like looking into the firebox of a steam locomotive or down the nozzle of a blow torch. As the Cant fell out of the sky it began to shed burning pieces and red and green flares came shooting out of it. Quite a pyrotechnic display and we were reminded once again of the saying "it's them or us". We landed some three hours later and for the rest of the night sleep was hard to come by. Next morning to complete our combat report we saw our armourers, who told us that we fired 30x20mm shells per cannon, a three seconds burst!

Two or three days later some Army types came looking for Desmond and me. Apparently a fighting patrol had discovered the remains of the Cant and its crew and had sensibly collected what bits of evidence they could find for intelligence. We were shown what they had and in typical service style were required to sign certain documents, almost like confessing to a crime. There were remains of the navigator's logbook and also the wireless operator's code book, which would be useful for a while. In addition they had a two sided photograph wallet which they had found in the pilot's clothing. On one side was the photograph of a man in Italian uniform – probably the pilot. On the facing side was a photograph of a young woman – wife, girl friend or sister, who knows? Three seconds high in the blackness of a North African night sky had ended all that. Many years later I discovered the name of the Italian pilot, Major Padorani, Commander of 104 Gruppo in Sicily. It made the impersonal air war very personal indeed, but he was the enemy and this was the way to keep him from inflicting harm on the Allies. His aircraft was a modified Cant Z1007B. We had removed a very senior figure from the scene and I could well imagine the consternation this would cause to the younger airmen of his Group. In 1996 while researching Squadron kills in 1943 the author found proof of Dixon's memories when he received a letter from LtCol Giancarlo de Marchis, Chief of the Historical Department of the Italian Air Force in Rome. The pilot was Major Pietro Padorani. His fellow crew members were Cpl Di Pasquale, SgtMaj Furlanetto, W/Op Attiani, Air Gunner Panfichi and Engineer Guccione. Their aircraft was of No.262 Bomber Squadron Cant Z1007 of 104 Group.

Night readiness operations were very difficult, both for the aircrew and the ground crews. Almost everything was done in total darkness. When torches were used, they had to be kept well down and shrouded by the fingers. Because of this signals were occasionally misunderstood and could be very dangerous. The Squadron used 3000 to 5000 gallons of petrol a night and a lot of oil. All of this petrol had to be filtered by hand from 4-gallon cans and this was an all night job. When work permitted or when they were on standby the men could listen to the R/T and AI sections engaging in a running commentary with the pilots and the GCI. It was quite a thrill when an enemy aircraft was picked up and passed on to the Squadron Beaufighters on duty. Then the men waited until the R/O had picked up the "Jerry" or "Ity" on his AI screen. Then the listeners would be entertained to some choice exercises in English grammar until the pilot had visual contact. Then came the moment of attack. Sometimes the enemy did not have time to ponder what hit him, sometimes he managed to get away. No.600 Squadron also paid a price in human lives while attempting to defeat the enemy. Losses were felt very keenly and the bond between air and ground crews caused grief every time an aircrew failed to return from operations. Laurie Dixon saw this when young Peter Bates was killed after a combat with a three-engined Italian SM79. Both Peter's Beaufighter and the Italian crashed quite close to each other. The Beaufighter went deep into the ground and fuel burnt for over a day, just like one of the Squadron desert fires, but much bigger. The ground crew was shattered and a cowling from that particular SM79 was made as a Squadron score board in memory of Bates and his radar operator. The chaps of the Squadron kept an up-to-the-minute record of all the successes by painting swastikas to represent victories on an old engine cowling from one of their victims at Bone. It was permanently displayed at their railway station HQ. Often the aircrews would take a glance at it before taking off and if the pilot did not announce his intention of having a swastika added to the panel on his return he was reminded by the ground crews that paint and brush were always ready for use. Anyhow the score was always up to date by the time the victorious crew concerned returned to base and this procedure became established as an official duty. Flying could be extremely hazardous over the desert. One morning Hughes and Dixon ran into incredibly stormy weather on their flight back to Setif. They found themselves in what seemed like a vast, endless grey cavern between layers of cloud. All around them were great grey pillars of water coming down from the upper layers of cloud and seemingly suspended from them. They were spinning and snaking about like the most enormous bell ropes, a quite awesome staggering sight. What was worse, because it was affecting the men personally, was the turbulence which was quite the worst they had ever experienced. The Beaufighter was an extremely strong aircraft but now it was shaken about like a rag doll. The wing tips were clearly going up and down quite rapidly and Dixon imagined that if the wings stayed rigid they would snap off. The most frightening thing was to watch the stern frame which besides vibrating severely was showing signs of twisting. Hughes and Dixon were both relieved to emerge safely from these freak conditions.

Whilst the Squadron were in North Africa, the CO (W/C "Paddy" Green) received a communication emanating from the College of Heralds in London to say that the Squadron badge which had been

The "Crescent Moon and Sword" crest, the second given to the Squadron, was to become a source of dissatisfaction in the post-war years. The "old boys" of course insisted that the "City of London" crest with the blue eagle was theirs rather than the one with the "moon-and-paper-knife" as they called the official one, which had the same form and laurel as the crests of all the squadrons in the RAF. When reformed the Squadron took its request for the old badge to the highest person possible, the Honorary Air Commodore, who consulted S/L David Proudlove. At her request the King agreed that the Squadron should have the unique honour of having two crests, both approved by the King.

used since the early days of the Squadron's formation was not authorised by them and did not conform to the rules applicable to Royal Air Force unit badges in which the chosen Unit symbol was enclosed within a framework of laurel leaves surmounted by the Crown of King Edward. The CO let it be known that a competition would be held to choose a suitable design conforming to standard practice. Of the designs submitted, the one chosen as appropriate bearing in mind the night-fighter role of the Squadron was a Crescent Moon bisected by a sword. This design was accepted by the College of Heralds and presented to His Majesty the King, King George VI, for authorisation. This was duly given. However the pre-war Squadron members were only interested in the pre-war City badge, quite rightly as this was the crest which was painted on to their pre-war aircraft and also appeared on Squadron letterheads, ties, lapel badges and Squadron silver. With a war on their hands the Squadron were not too much worried about this change of badge. After the war, however, with the help of the Honorary Air Commodore, Queen Elizabeth, the Queen Mother, who consulted with the then CO S/L David Proudlove, His Majesty the King also authorised the City badge to the dismay of the College of Heralds and the ever-lasting gratitude of the Squadron. Thus '600' later became the only Squadron in the RAF with two official badges.

At the beginning of April a detachment of six aircraft flew down to a place called Goubrine to operate under the control of No.211 Group, Western Desert Air Force. It was to be the shortest detachment recorded in the history of the Squadron, if not in that of the RAF; two days later the six aircraft returned. On 21st April a Squadron crew took off from Maison Blanche to patrol the coast and look for enemy intruders. They were F/O Paton and his O/R F/O McAnulty. Their Composite Combat Report to 325 Wing NACAF and HQ NWAAF read:

> *"600 Sqdn 1 Beaufighter MkVII Chevron 58*
> *F/O Paton (pilot) P/O McAnulty (NR)*

A/B under C.O.L. control 896 on patrol N. of Algiers. At 0420 Chevron *58 (call sign for the aircraft, JGO)* was given a vector of 160º and told bandit in vicinity travelling N. at IAS 160. When between 100-160ft he got contact at 3fi mls which he held for 15min eventually getting a visual at 4000ft on what he first thought was another Beau. He closed to 2000' and identified it as a Ju88. E/A then opened fire. 58 formated on e/a at fiml range and then turned towards it using visual. Contact was maintained, another visual got at 5000', the bandit jinking violently at 230 ASI. 58 closed easily getting further long range burst from the enemy aircraft which he returned, observing one strike. 58 closed to 1000' firing and saw smoke coming from starboard engine of e/a. fi minute later another burst from 58 caused explosion amid-ships of e/a which heeled over to port and crashed in sea. This was at 0445hrs 100 mls. N. of Algiers. Throughout chase and combat height of both a/c 50-100 ft. Accurate return fire was experienced from e/a throughout combat of Chevron 58. Cat. AC: Claim 1 Ju88 destroyed. Weather: clear moonlight, light increasing from East during combat. Airborne Maison Blanche 0030hrs, landed Maison Blanche 0515hrs".

They successfully shot down the first enemy aircraft with the help of their brand new radar. Once Squadron Beaufighters were airborne it had mobile GCI stations to help the crews intercept their targets. One of these was quite novel as it was situated on an island behind enemy lines. It gave very useful coverage. It was on the North coast of the island and could only operate at night. During the day the operators lay covered under camouflage netting and they were never discovered. Forward cover was useful for it gave an interesting picture of the lack of enthusiasm for the war of most Italian bomber crews. They flew from Italy to attack the ports along the North African shore but when still 100 miles from their target they would turn back, drop their bombs and orbit for an appropriate time before returning to Italy. The Beaufighters had the range to attack them still so even with limited interception control some Italians were pretty unlucky. Towards the end of April, the Eighth Army were pursuing the Afrika Korps North towards Tunis, whilst the First Army were squeezing them hard from the West. Just on the Western edge of Sousse there was a dried up salt lake called Monastir. The Germans had spent a lot of time rolling it for use as an airstrip but it had fallen into the hand of the Allies on 25th April. Hughes, Dixon and another crew flew in with a tent on board their Beaufighter. They erected the tent literally in the middle of nowhere, certainly there was no vegetation, and laid down inside it awaiting developments. The first was a tickle in one of Dixon's ears, from which he extracted a fairly large caterpillar. Quite soon out of the blue a Bedford 15cwt truck drove up and a sergeant in the Royal Signals Regiment got out. In that Godforsaken place he was as smart as paint – shorts, stockings, puttees, bush shirt, and peaked cap. He gave the smartest salute Dixon had seen in years and enquired of Desmond as to their needs – a field telephone. Very soon he was back trailing a cable from a reel on the back of the truck. A field telephone was attached, the handle spun as he tested it and they were in contact with authority again. Once more the Sergeant drew an immaculate salute and disappeared again into the blue. Most impressive, as Dixon remembers.

At the end of the Tunisian campaign the Germans almost completely depended on air supply from Sicily, bottled up as they were in Northern Tunisia. Some of the No.600 Squadron crews had hair-raising experiences. A Luftwaffe air transport fleet carried reinforcements and supplies across and flying out they carried personnel not essential for the defence of this lost battlefield. The Squadron received orders to break this air bridge, preferably while the

Luftwaffe was on the way to Tunisia, rather than flying out. Monastir was a difficult place to fly from because once again the Germans had the advantage of their low level radio altimeter compared to the pressure dependent altimeters the RAF used. It gave the Germans the chance to virtually scrape the deck. As for the Squadron they had to do without any ground radar guidance. The crews were dependent on their low level search radar and the fleeting visuals on Ju52 exhausts. Once a contact had been made it almost inevitably meant a tight turn to keep the enemy aircraft in radar contact, which at this low level was extremely dangerous. Flying low over the sea at night was frightening enough when straight and level, for the sea on each side of the aircraft seemed to be rising above the plane. McKinnon was driven to the expedient of lowering his undercarriage with the thought that one would get some warning before hitting the water. It worked for him and Poole because they hit the sea on two occasions and Mac's reaction was quick enough to pull the Beaufighter up. Today Norman Poole still wonders why they flew so low, though on the other hand he realises it gave them the only prospect of a radar or visual sighting looking up with the sky as a background, as it was hopeless looking down with the dark sea as a background.

At Monastir a special Hurricane Squadron flew in. It was No.43, flying Mark IIc Hurricanes with four 20mm cannons. They had done very well in France in 1940 and during the Battle of Britain. Since then they had a very specialised and dangerous job in the desert – low level night attacks on enemy troops and armour during periods of moonlight. This sort of work, almost scraping the deck, required great courage. What was of immediate interest to Desmond and Laurie was that for the first time in months they had been stood down for the night and had offered to lay down the flare path for the Beaufighters. As there still were no Squadron ground crews they gratefully accepted the offer. When darkness came the two waited for instructions. Besides they thought it wise to see if the flare path was ready. All it was, was a long cable with lamps at intervals, just laid along the surface of the ground. At the upwind take-off end it was connected to a generator by switchgear. The men found to their horror that the lights were laid like a wiggly worm. Somehow No.43 Squadron had got their hands on a barrel of wine and they were really celebrating their night off. It left the crews in a bit of a fix but they managed to sort things out before they were asked to go on a sortie. As things turned out later they were less than an hour from a very violent, vicious and dangerous combat, but fortunately they were not to know about that until later when things had settled down again. For a brief period the two Squadron Beaufighters were the only night-fighters around. Incidentally Des Hughes and his "contingent" had no idea where the other end of the telephone line was or who was manning it. As far as Laurie Dixon could remember it ran away across the open ground in an Easterly direction. A curious rather trusting sort of situation which they just accepted. It finally did ring to order Hughes and Dixon off at 0325 with short instructions – course to steer, height to make and a code name of an AMES (GCI) and frequency to call. Off they went climbing over the battlefield into another inky black night. In no time at all Laurie Dixon had a contact on his equipment: "It was quite astonishing considering the primitive ground control arrangements. I think experience was beginning to pay off. This target, whatever it was, was well above us and jinking about all over the place as we continued to climb after it. I had quite a job holding on to my contact. Then at last we saw him, just a shade blacker than the sky around us. When Des slid in to put him above us and at 2 o'clock we recognised the shape of a Ju88. He had seen us too and turned sharply into us as he dived to port. His top gun position hosed red tracer at us and he was away. This one was not running away though, he was staying to fight and a grim dogfight in the dark resulted. We kept losing visual contact, so violent was his manoeuvring, but I managed to hold him on my equipment. He could, on such a black night, have just gone for the deck and lost us, but this joker must have had some reason for staying in the area and he was not to be easily put off.

Finally he did stick his nose down and we followed him going really fast. Just as suddenly he slowed down dramatically and pulled upwards. No doubt he was using his dive brakes. The Beaufighter did not have such equipment and still needed to lose speed rapidly to avoid overshooting him. Des' reaction was to release the undercarriage but in the general confusion and excitement he selected flaps down by mistake. The effect of the big flaps going down at that speed was quite dramatic and most alarming. Quite apart from the drag the extra lift was astonishing and the whole aircraft juddered and made the most awful noise. Everything held together and we got in a burst of fire which ended the combat. It cut the Ju88's fuselage clean in half just forward of the stern frame. I expected the forward remains to flop down but to our amazement it just stood on end and went vertically upwards, showering sparks like a rocket before finally falling over and diving headlong into the ground. To our great relief we were recalled almost at once because we had just for a time had enough. Everything was rather tense when wheels and flaps were selected but everything worked and we were safely down. What an aeroplane the Beaufighter was. Our reward was a fitful few hours sleep on the ground but we were at least still in one piece. The next day we flew to Bone to have the Beaufighter and, above all, the flaps inspected".

Many members of the Squadron still speak with great affection of the Beaufighter. At times odd manoeuvres were carried out and it complied. A story says that there was a Flight Sergeant, a most lively character from London. One day he was asked to air test Desmond Hughes' aeroplane. He took off with Dixon on board. The pilot was keen to show Laurie a thing or two. They did all the routine things and then to Dixon's astonishment – who happened to be admiring the old Roman amphitheatre at El Djem – the pilot decided to do a slow roll. The Beau's weight was over ten tons and Dixon remembered how a similar manoeuvre over Fairwood Common had ended in disaster. In the process of this the odd bits of equipment fell about besides much dust and dirt. Dixon was very cross with the pilot and thought about reporting it to Hughes. (In fact he did – after forty years) Two or three days later it was established that the aircraft had a slight twist to the wings, a legacy of the aerobatics. Hughes continued to fly the aircraft and it stayed in one piece. In the meantime a Squadron detachment went forward to join the Desert Air Force at Monastir, making the Squadron the only Air Force unit to operate on both 1st and 8th Army fronts at the same time. This unit, under Sgts DeVroome and Hedgecock pushed its own way through the Kasserine Pass, hard on the heels of the Hampshire Regiment, and the "Odds and Bods" rushed in to help the Yanks, who had found themselves in rather tricky circumstances. The Germans – and what was left of the Italians – tried to withdraw as best they could and, whether through sheer innocence or enthusiasm, our lot got through before the enemy and were forced to call on earlier commando training in self-protection. So the blisters of the year before had had a reason after all.

At Monastir No.43 Squadron had erected a mess tent, a small

marquee and No.600 Squadron were happy to share it. In the course of conversation the aircrews of the Squadron became aware of a lot of talk about "the dreaded light". Their enquiries about this light led to a most amazing story, a mystery which in fact has never been explained and which few people know about. As already explained No.43 Squadron were employed on ground attack work in clear moon periods. In the course of their work some of them had seen a bright white light in the near proximity which was not attached to anything – just a light! This light would appear in front of them or suddenly – more alarming – right behind their tails. A quick turn round and it would disappear, to re-appear out to port or starboard. With nothing but a light, range estimation was quite impossible, but they had fired an awful lot of ammunition at it with no obvious effect. They had even flown with it over the odd salt lake and seen its reflection with that of their aircraft in the water. They reckoned to have reported it to the Desert Air Force HQ and their response had been to send an eye specialist to see the pilots. One other thing, this light only ever appeared over what one could loosely call "No-Man's-Land", that area over and between the two front lines. In no time at all John Turnbull, a very sound and experienced Squadron pilot saw it with his navigator, this time on a dark but clear night. Whatever was this thing which had never caused anyone any harm, radio interference or anything?

The biggest dangers the aircrew faced were friendly fire and bad weather over the mountains. The ports had sometimes spectacular defences and as far as the people below were concerned their general attitude towards aircraft was: "No mercy, open fire with all you have, better safe than sorry". The only way crews often realised they were over shipping was the tremendous amount of pyrotechnics thrown up into the sky. There were rocket batteries and guns which often let fly so much that it would fill the whole sky. The problem for embarrassed night-fighter crews was to follow an enemy bomber approaching the target, for there was a distinct possibility that the Boys in the Beaus collected the hate meant for the Boys in the Bombers. Thanks to the initiative of the Canadian ground radar Officer the Squadron had improved blind landing equipment on their two main runways at Setif and Souk-el-Arba forward base. He had used the same technique of mounting a low powered beacon at the end of the runway and the crews were able to make an approach and let down in poor weather with the advantage in this country of having the beacon exactly where they wanted it instead of having to compromise as they did in the UK. The weather had not improved in February and March 1943 and No.600 Squadron suffered thunderstorms on the route between Setif and the forward base. It was on one of these occasions that McKinnon and Poole came as close as they wanted to being a permanent fixture of North Africa. They could not get above the clouds and had to stay in it because the mountains below made it too dangerous to try and get beneath the cloud. Their flight instruments depended on the pitot head remaining free of ice measuring relative air pressure. Unfortunately theirs iced up and McKinnon was still quite an inexperienced instrument pilot and no match for the turbulence in the thunder cloud so they lost height rapidly and the aircraft fell into a spin. Sgt Poole made the first move towards getting out of the Beaufighter which was to collect his parachute from its wall mounting and then slip it on to his harness before exiting through the escape hatch. The trouble was that the G-Force to which the aircraft was subjected to kept him stuck against the canopy and quite powerless to move let alone gather the parachute pack. It was at that point that one needed a combination of not only prayer but also luck. Poole suddenly saw the aircraft break cloud in a valley rather than on a hilltop and with about 4000 feet to play with Mac was able to recover from the spin and two shaken and very stirred airmen stayed under cloud and followed the valley to their forward base. Not that below cloud was always the safest place for unwary newcomer aircrew. Norman Poole remembered there was a particular valley coming back from the forward base which looked quite safe but the trouble was that it rose quite steadily at the mouth. Happily flying up the valley crews would suddenly face a high wall of rock. If he did not have enough power to drag the heavy Beaufighter over that enormous wall, the pilot would have to make a very, very steep turn and fly back down the valley again for another try, this time trying to get more height. McKinnon and Poole did this once. They decided that there was no need for a second time. It surely made crews very careful. Forward bases grew in number. One such strip was Dakla. The Squadron provided night cover but in general they reacted to enemy activity rather than carrying out standing patrols. One reason for this was the inadequate runway lighting. It was good enough to keep straight on take-off just using a petrol flare but landing was hazardous with no beacon either so often crews rather returned to Setif with its better night facilities. Dakla was positioned next to fairly swampy ground and the spring rains had left a lot of water about to the delight of the frog families – or so it seemed from the noise they made at night. The noise had its good points for there was never any danger of falling asleep while at readiness. The real danger was the hospitality of No.43 Squadron who had finished for the day and gathered in their mess tent. No.600 Squadron aircrew were subject to great temptation because they had to eat there.

It was a different kind of war in the African theatre in that the airfields were little more than strips which had been levelled off and covered with PSP and which had to serve as taxi-ways to return to servicing or take-off position. Often these detachments consisted of just one or two crews who handled their own affairs linked by vital telephone lines. But fortunately they had the company of day fighter squadrons so they could rely on refuelling, but little else for the night-fighter crews had nothing in common with the Spitfire people. Radar coverage was good over the sea but suffered over land because the terrain screened so much. It was not a comfortable life for the camp beds were back at Setif and there were no spares. When the crews were away from home they often slept on the floor, if they could sleep. There was no spare accommodation even at HQ in Algiers. The Beaufighters operated occasionally from there with the centimetric radar when there appeared to be an extra low level threat against the port and its shipping. Here they came across the American solution to the problem; two individual capes that buttoned together with an overlap and you slung the resultant two man tent between trees, hoping your partner was a quiet sleeper. Stones and pegs kept the edges down. Norman Poole said they were waterproof. Duty nights then were uncomfortable and so far McKinnon and Poole had not been rewarded with a kill even if they had spent a lot of time chasing the enemy – and friends of course. Such time off as they enjoyed was restricted by the lack of transport. They did occasionally get into Setif, a fair sized town with a local market but no jolly English pubs and certainly no co-operating English girls. The area produced mainly red wine, Muslim influence was very strong and the British were not popular in North Africa. They were put in the same category as the French colonial people, whom the local Arabs hated. The Mediterranean Theatre of War had its beauty too. On a glorious early morning, returning over the sea from the East Laurie Dixon watched a most amazing meteorological phenomenon take place. As he looked backwards he saw a thick, white sheet materialising out of the clear sky low over the sea. It spread like wildfire, passed underneath them and moved inland. Suddenly there was nothing to see beneath them but this brilliant white blanket. It really was breathtaking but as it was already very hot Laurie could not understand why it had formed and indeed why the sun was not burning it off. The immediate problem for Hughes of course was getting down safely through this mist which seemed to be right down to the deck. Raleigh Hilkin was on the ground with a little radio set and said he could hear the Beaufighter overhead so Hughes and Dixon orbited to think things out. There was a lot of open flat space at Monastir but Des Hughes had to aim for the "runway" which would be clear of bits and pieces. Raleigh came on the air to say that he would fire a Very Light and if the crew saw it they should try to let down from it on a compass bearing. It got quite hilarious, as well as frustrating to hear Hilken call:" Here is a red, no, a green, no a red and green", only to find the flares shooting up through the cloud behind the aircraft. Finally Dixon suggested to Hughes to fly West and creep back towards the markers with wheels and a bit of flap down. They suddenly heard Raleigh Hilken call out: "I can see your wheels, turn port!!" Apparently as they did so, their port wingtip came out of the cloud and the starboard wheel disappeared into it. Suddenly they appeared and practically on the ground which Desmond hit pretty hard. Never mind; they were down and that was the only thing that counted.

In those days the aircraft of the Squadron had been equipped with the new Mk. VIII radar and ranging far out to sea began to clobber the enemy when he tried to evacuate crack troops and equipment to Sicily in Ju52s. It was a rather lucky decision, for the Squadron Beaufighters found these aircraft an easy prey. On 30th April Sgts. Downing (pilot) and Lyons (radar operator) saw five Ju52s, filled with German soldiers. A brief but fierce encounter followed. The slow German transports were no match for the guns of the Beaufighter and the return fire from the small top positions on the trimotors hardly bothered the crew of the Beaufighter. War being horrible, especially in a case where slow transport aircraft were attacked by a heavily armed and robust fighter aircraft it all turned into carnage. All Ju52s went down into the drink and a substantial number of German soldiers were kept from joining their beleaguered comrades in Tunisia. And, more importantly, the Luftwaffe knew now that sending reinforcements to North Africa was a deadly mistake. Thus Downing and Lyons did a very good job. Of course top brass was impressed and pleased; soon afterwards "Ace" Downing was awarded both the DFM and the US Air Medal.

When Sgts Downing and Lyons shot down five Junkers Ju52 transport in one sortie the pilot got the name "Ace". This victory was later put on paper as a proud reminder of the day when "never in the field of air combat were so many Germans shot down by so few at such short notice.

Many Squadron members recalled this event when Downing died in 1996. To put things in balance W/C Green also got involved in an air battle. The rattling of cannon fire was heard on the ground and some time later the CO landed with a shattered right wing. It turned out that he had been caught and shot at by a Canadian crew in a Beaufighter of No.600's sister squadron. When they landed at Monastir the next morning they came up with a perfect reason: they had mistaken Paddy Green's aircraft for a Ju88. It said something about the level of aircraft recognition in the Squadron as well as about the offensive capabilities of the cannons of a Beaufighter.

Paddy Green took it rather cheerfully, accepted their apologies and a big bottle of whisky. As he now lives in Canada there does not seem to be any hard feelings.

No-one really liked Bone. It was considered a miserable place to be based. It had no amenities of any sort and it was quite impossible to keep clean. The only relaxation was the sea, but this left one sticky with salt; it was a mixed blessing. Just to add to the miseries there, mosquitoes abounded and were the reason why it was the worst malarial area along the whole North African seaboard. It all went back to the Romans, who had built large, fairly shallow stone pans just south of the coast which could be flooded from the sea. The hot sun evaporated the water, leaving behind the salt valuable not only for local use but also elsewhere. After over 1,600 years the pans had silted up and become marshes, an excellent breeding ground for the malaria carrying mosquito. It was the place where Laurie Dixon contracted malaria. After the sun went down sleeves had to be rolled down and fastened, shirt necks buttoned and trousers worn rather than shorts. The mosquitoes used to bite through the fabric of one's clothes, especially around the waistline and everybody had a ring of red bite marks at this level. The men were provided with a clear Vaseline-like substance with a menthol odour which was to be used as a mosquito repellant. It had to be applied to all exposed skin surfaces and believe it or not it attracted swarms of these whining biting insects. The stuff made the men absolutely filthy, as well as it did their clothes, blankets, flying clothing and anything else they touched. The men cursed the stuff and dumped it. It was at Bone that Desmond Hughes got his first malaria attack. One morning Reg Gillies and Laurie Dixon missed Des and went looking for him. They finally found him in his tent, laid on his camp bed, fully dressed in battle dress and boots, looking feverish and obviously not at all well. With the doctor the odd 100 miles away Reg and Laurie did what they could to make him comfortable. This used most of the contents of his water bottle which was all he had to drink, heavily chlorinated, warm and not very pleasant. They decided he needed something more palatable and set out to track down the local rations store. This turned out to be two or three ridge tents dug into the sand dunes and to the amazement of Gillies and Dixon it was stocked like Aladdin's cave with tinned foods. It was in the charge of an RAF sergeant they had never set their eyes on, who literally lived in the middle of this tinned paradise. The two men explained their mission, asked for pineapple chunks and received an answer from the character to the effect that he really could not do this thing. However he was willing to part with one tin. Reg and Laurie returned to Des, and spooned the pineapple into the unfortunate pilot. The next day Laurie and Reg returned to the food store with a repeated request for pineapple. The sergeant politely but firmly refused. Reg Gillies got so mad that Dixon thought he was about to shoot him. Anyhow, after the two R/Os made their point, assuring themselves that there were no witnesses of their conversation with the sergeant, they got what they needed. After a few days Des began to pull round and was able to eat normal food, corned beef and biscuits or meat and vegetables. Like all aircrew in the Squadron he was as lean as a whippet with permanent dark rings under his eyes. It was his first brush with malaria. The second was in the spring of 1944 in Britain on the Great North Road driving south to No.5 OTU which was situated just south of the Firth of Forth, when he lost consciousness and went off the road. Dixon firmly believes this happened because his friend was not treated with pineapple chunks.

The overall campaign was pressing on towards its end by now. Eighth Army, pushing on at a smart pace, surrounded a load of Afrika Korps troopers in a pocket at Enfidaville, to be given attention at a more convenient moment. Yet it was considered important that the Germans did not get too much time to rest, or even regroup. The Beaufighters of 600 Squadron were called in. It became practice to fly to the pockets and pitch out empty bottles. They would scream like the clappers on the way down and while doing no major damage it caused much fun and amusement among the flying crews. One could wonder what it did to the Germans. However, this business was frowned upon by Paddy Green, who, by the way, utilised his spare time one night taking on an Italian destroyer, the fight being declared a draw. From this moment on the main task for the Squadron was "interdiction"; no enemy aircraft would be allowed to take off or try to escape to Sicily. Beaufighters carrying Mk.IV AI radar patrolled the coast near Cap Bon, while others, with the Mark VII were sent further out to sea. This resulted in the destruction of many tri-motor Ju52s, engaged in evacuating priority cargoes from Tunisia, as well as Ju88s. With Bone as their final base in North Africa there was little activity with the end of the campaign at hand. The aircrew had other problems apart from weather in this rough and ready environment. One of the Beaufighters had lost its tail wheel on landing and it could not be replaced at the forward base. McKinnon and Poole were chosen to bring the airplane home. It was towed to the beginning of the runway with the tail supported on a makeshift trolley. Then it was positioned to one side of the runway because the runway itself was formed with American pierced steel planking which interlocked and gave a much stronger surface than the wire netting used by the British. McKinnon did not want to damage the runway by dragging the broken tail across it, so after starting up he ran up as much power as the brakes would hold and attempted a sort of jump start to get the tail in the air as quickly as possible. This, he believed, would enable him to divert to the left onto the runway for the rest of the take-off run. It did not quite work like that for they diverted left onto the runway but in fact the aircraft kept on going left across it and into the rough the other side, in fact McKinnon and Poole ended up just clearing the block-built dispersed Flight headquarters – but they made it, a shade older, very sweaty and utterly relieved that this too could be done with a Beaufighter. The landing at Setif was less dramatic but with their sledge tail they stopped fairly quickly, a new record for Beaufighters.

With ten more enemy aircraft destroyed in May morale was very high. And so after many excitements and unusual experiences and with complete victory in the North African campaign officially over on 12th May, the detachment was ordered to pack and leave Souk-el-Khemis. In a way all were sorry but the idea caught on pretty rapidly and finally the Squadron Engineer Warrant Officer arrived with details of the move. Transport was sent on its way with the equipment and personnel to Bone. Sgt Chantrey took off with F/L "Joe" Hanus and the Warrant Officer said he would follow them. They saw him taxiing along amid a cloud of sand and as Hanus and Chantrey returned in salute to the RAF (and the Arabs!) left behind they saw him on his take-off run burst a tyre. Hanus went down to investigate but all was well, only a tyre to change, so Hanus and Chantrey headed for Bone where Chantrey and his men were to resume their role for the further continuation of operations that night. No.18 Squadron had recently arrived at Bone and they were a great help in putting a large stock of petrol at No.600 Squadron's disposal. Once again No.600 was on time and completed the first night's operations as scheduled. It was a great achievement, for the strip was unknown to the Squadron and flying in at such short notice did not give much time to get fully organised. In due course the rest of the Squadron arrived from Setif and they merged to reform into a single operational unit providing regular nightly patrols and convoy protection off the African coast and out into the Mediterranean over Sicily and Southern Italy. Unfortunately in May two members of the Squadron were killed in action. On the 14th F/Os Bastow and George were on an offensive patrol around Bone for the Philippeville GCI when they were given vectors to an enemy aircraft which later was claimed as damaged. However 10 miles West of Bone the pilot again reported "trade", this time below him. As he was going down to investigate search-lights on the ground reported seeing a Ju88 and a Beaufighter. The

The 325 Wing scoreboard, as shown today at the Royal Air Force Museum, Duxford. On the right hand side the scores for No.600 Squadron.

ack-ack opened fire. What happened then remains a mystery. The Beaufighter crashed 10 miles East of Cap de Garde at 2137hrs. Both crew members died. During that month Norman Poole got news of his commission. The mail was backdated to 20th January 1943, so it had taken a while for it to reach him. He celebrated with some of his senior NCO compatriots in Setif and got splendidly drunk on Muscatel.

One of the R/Os who greatly contributed to the proud score of the Squadron was F/O Reg Gillies, who formed a perfect team with W/C Paddy Green.

So sweet and easy to drink and very hard to judge its effect. Thanks to his stalwart companions he got back to camp and he remembers swaying gently at the entrance of the Officers' Mess marquee thinking 'No, that is not for me tonight' after which he staggered off to his tent to sleep it off. It was fairly simple being commissioned in the Field. Someone gave him a few inches of P/O braid which took care of his shirts. No one aspired to anything more decorous than a bush jacket, tropical dress was unknown, the men just wore khaki battle dress and here again braid on the epaulettes was the answer. The main problem was a hat and P/O Poole managed to borrow one for the time being. He was able to buy one to replace it in wartorn Malta and return the original to his saviour. As well as khaki battle dress the men were issued with sidearms, Smith and Wesson .38 calibre revolvers. The men supposed they were intended to impress any Arabs who might collect them from the end of a parachute after bailing out. Quite frankly there was serious doubt among crews if it were better to be captured by Germans or rescued by locals. None of them had cause to use it for defence as the few Squadron casualties just disappeared, either shot down or in one case it was suspected they were blown up as the bomber they had attacked exploded in mid-air. What guns did prove was what kids some of the men were. Poole even today points a finger at some who had been known to blaze away into the sky, and even the marquee roof when it was closing time in the bar. Poole vividly remembers the effectiveness of such a request: a delayed close-down of that bar. The Squadron bar had a supply of local wine of not very good quality but also a reasonable supply of whisky and gin. Not the popular brands, as with limited shipping space and all the dangers surrounding ships at sea it would have been inappropriate to demand such luxuries. The same of course applied to English beer.

It was about the end for the Axis in North Africa and soon orders came for the Squadron to prepare for the unusual experience of leave. The aircrew were given a week off and it needed some enthusiasm to get anything out of it for there were no trains or railway warrants and no private transport. The only thing was to go where one could scrounge a lift. Poole and three mates banded together and thumbed a ride from Setif. There was plenty of military traffic and the men just hoped it was going in an interesting direction. On this basis they got to Constantine. The town's fascination was its division into two with a deep valley spanned by a single arch bridge. The temptation to the aviators was obvious – a dive from the North brought you from the high edge of the plateau under the bridge and out to lower ground. It caused a great deal of annoyance to the locals because the quiet approach turned into a deafening roar as the aircraft slipped under the bridge. McKinnon and Poole never did it but it was a tempting sight to McKinnon as he passed it every trip between the Squadron's two main bases. The four decided to enjoy the local atmosphere and managed to find beds for the night. They could not be very choosy where they slept and it was on this leave that Poole ended up sleeping in the local police station. The cell was whitewashed clean, but the beds were raised platforms without bedding. Poole had heard horrific stories of lice-ridden beds but felt comfortable enough to sleep with the local police. After Constantine they managed a lift up to Philippeville where there was an Army Base and Army Hospital. Using their leave passes they had no difficulty in getting service accommodation and meals where they were available. It was probably easier than normal at Philippeville for they were just about to emerge from a curfew due to an outbreak of typhoid in that area. The Quartet was lucky and made contact with some nurses, army girls from the Queen Alexandra's Imperial Nursing Reserve. They assured the men that the outbreak was almost over, so four airmen and four nurses went on a perfectly innocent walk along the beach. There was some wine and they made a fire on the beach for a good picnic. Poole managed to persuade one of them to walk a little further along the beach and they sat on the steps of a house, perhaps a holiday home and talked about this and that. Norman tried to advance his case a little more, but apart from feeling the texture of silk stockings and a view of those well-named "Service Issue Passion Killers" he got no other reward. He got back safely and on time from his leave and even managed to crowd in one new experience for him – a Turkish Bath, somewhat soupy water to cool off in, but he survived. At the end of the month the Squadron moved to Bone. With no transport aircraft available the Beaufighter crews packed as much as they could in the aircraft and also took stuff for members of their ground crew. There was quite a lot of room in the fuselage of a Beaufighter and they had no worries about power on take-off. They took tools, tents and spare ammunition, enough for them to operate for a short time before the three ton lorries caught up with them. The advance party of technicians had gone on ahead so the aircrew were operational again very quickly despite the move. The night of the arrival the first Beaufighter took off for a patrol.

In the late afternoon of 27th May 1943. Donald Paton, who was a pilot in the Flight of Desmond Hughes, was playing cricket at Bone. It was fairly late when the Adjutant called out: "Anyone able to scramble for an air/sea rescue Operation?" Paton replied that he was and asked his R/O McAnulty to go with him. They got themselves organised as quickly as they could and took off. The aircraft was under the control of the Regional Ground Controller who was in touch with his counterpart in Algiers. He vectored them towards the distress signal which came from a Walrus amphibian. The aircraft had been on an ASR but now the helper needed help as he himself was sinking. Paton was going to locate and mark the Walrus until a High Speed Launch from Algiers arrived at the scene to save the crew. The story of the Walrus was as follows: A USAAF Lightning P38 had been attacked by the enemy and was forced to ditch. In due course the duty Walrus arrived and the pilot of the P38 abandoned his aircraft and his dinghy. Little did he know what would follow. The Walrus, attempting to take off in a rough sea, hit a freak wave and lost one of its floats. This meant it was unable to move and it rapidly started to take in water. When Paton arrived it was already dark but his R/O and the Walrus crew managed to make contact by the use of flares, lights and rockets. The Beaufighter called the Controller and urged him to have the launch come at maximum speed. The Squadron Beau circled the Walrus for almost two hours, keeping in touch periodically with it. Then the Controller said that the launch had departed, but still had a long way to travel. Eventually the lights of the Walrus went out and the crew ceased to reply to the frantic signals from the Beaufighter. When the launch arrived, the sea was empty. It was dreadful to know that even though the Beaufighter was so close, the crew was unable to do anything for the Walrus crew and the P38 pilot.

While at Bone the Squadron was subjected to a lot of German attacks, as the enemy no longer carried out a fighting retreat. They had established themselves in Sicily and Italy but great Allied forces were massing at Bone and other bases in North Africa and part of the job of the Squadron was to protect this build-up. At the same time it was expected to prepare itself for the new mobile role during the next campaign. Desmond Hughes and Laurie Dixon were sent to Malta as a kind of pre-advanced party. Laurie still wonders what Desmond's brief was as he visited many high ranking officers. Dixon's task was quite specific. Malta had a long experience of Radar jamming by the Germans and with very limited reserves the islanders and the troops had learned to live with it. In other words, as with most other problems they had learned to help themselves. Dixon was to find out all he could about this jamming and what could be done to counter it. Dixon found the airfield in a sorry state. The surface at Luqa aerodrome where the Beaufighter had landed was a maze of patched bomb craters and it seemed as if every square yard of it had been stirred up by the Luftwaffe. As soon as Hughes landed his aircraft was led quickly into a blast pen out of the way. These were made up of a mixture of stones and four gallon petrol tins filled with rubbish all packed together with rubble. At one end of the runway was a quarry full of aircraft scrap, fuselages, wings, engines, props etc. The airfield had to be kept clear and rubbish was just dumped in the hole. Billets were well away from the airfield. Rations were much the same but much smaller in amount. There were no fat people on Malta. Dixon went to see two technical people and then went off to No.89 Squadron's radar section. It was the largest Squadron in the RAF, based in Malta, North Africa, the Nile delta and Calcutta. It had been commanded by W/C Stainforth, one time OC600, before he lost his life in North Africa. Basically what the Germans did was to transmit on the RAF wavelength and this swamped any echoes on the AI apparatus. What the Operators had to do was to de-tune and transmit on a slightly different frequency, but because the aerials were fixed in length, this resulted in a weaker signal, poorer range and operating difficulties. Malta's home-made tuning gear was made from salvaged bits and pieces, vandalised from wrecked aircraft, but it worked. They had really learned how to make do in Malta and for only one reason: the probable German invasion from the North. Desmond Hughes probably knew, but he and Laurie never raised the matter. In the event of them falling into enemy hands, what one did not know one could not divulge. After a few days they flew back to Bone where a big maintenance operation was on the way. Something was brewing.

The visit of Marshal of the Royal Air Force Viscount Trenchard on 4th June 1943 was a great honour for all in No.600. The highlight, however, was a visit by His Majesty the King to His troops in North Africa. The King flew to Algiers and finally arrived at Bone where

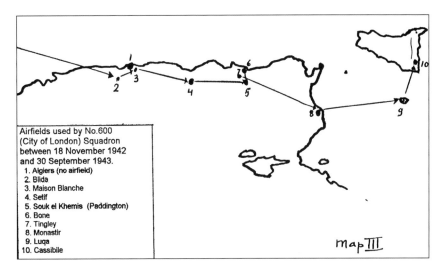

Map III.   The North African campaign.

the Squadron was based. He came along the coast in an Avro York accompanied by a flock of Spitfires. His aircraft was just parked to one side in the dunes and left quite unguarded. His Majesty having disappeared as if into thin air, Reg Gillies and Laurie Dixon wandered over to examine this big transport. It was a development of the Lancaster, same wings and engines, one extra small central tail fin and a huge whale-like fuselage. The rear door was open and steps in place, so they just walked in and looked around. It was painted lime green with comfortable seats in pairs, each pair sharing a little table. There was a little chromed button on each table and when pushed this raised a small clock from a recess in the table top. It was all pretty Spartan but the two men enjoyed browsing through the aircraft. The troops were told that the King would be driving away through the dunes on the following afternoon and anyone who felt inclined could "line the route". There was no compulsion but quite a few got as tidy and smart as possible and went there to give the Monarch a cheer. Nothing could have been more British. There was a small group of Guardsmen standing in the sand, fully equipped in battle dress and trousers in the blazing heat which did nobody any good. A sergeant was going around shining their boots front and back with a duster! Anyhow the King ploughed past in a jeep and all removed their caps and gave three cheers led most enthusiastically by one of His most loyal subjects, the Czech "Joe" Hanus. The King seemed genuinely moved by the cheers and Laurie Dixon remembers His Majesty was burnt bright red after only two days. He did not spend much time indoors.

At times the Squadron would find itself in strange situations, such as the one remembered by one of the Senior NCOs: "It was a cold and cloudy night with a strong wind blowing but we were well into our usual programme. There were three more patrols to get off and half the night readiness crews were resting, but as always with boots on and one eye open. In about an hours time I would be entitled to do the same but it was not to be that night. Our field telephone had a direct connection to the Officer on aerodrome control and we took its continual ringing in our stride during the day but somehow at night it had a different effect. Was it a scramble or warning of expected attack? After saying my usual about telephones I lifted the receiver and said "600". In reply I heard the voice of F/O Watson say: "Can you accommodate 31 Wimpeys?" Thirty-one Wimpeys on a single strip runway with no dispersal points and soft sand at the end and along the sides! I said that I could not do it but he could come along and have a look for himself. There is no need to go into details about the sort of language which followed, and with which we all are so familiar. However, this was an emergency and Watson told me that the Wimpeys had been out on a mission and owing to extremely bad weather had got lost and were running out of fuel. Bone was the only possible place to land. Before I had finished talking to him and explaining what I proposed to do as ideas came to mind we could hear the hum of approaching aircraft. Obviously the only course was for Watson to control their landings according to their fuel reserves, warn them of conditions and tell them to keep a lookout for our torch signals. So I hung up with more than a twitch, and bundled all available ground crews into a truck to cope with the situation. We decided to get as many to land and park at the end of the runway as possible provided we ourselves could get there first. The idea was to get them on the area of sand on the other side of which the Americans were making a perimeter track. As the truck sped along the runway keeping well to the side I followed on my bike. However we were well and truly beaten by the first Wellington bomber flashing by, followed by the second and the third. By the time we reached them the three had come to a halt about fifty yards from the end of the runway with engines ticking over. I contacted the pilot of the foremost and it was agreed that he should open engines to practically full boost and attempt to skim over the stretch of sand, but about twenty yards off the runway he got bogged down. This was better than nothing and when the second and third kite did the same at least the runway was free. Still they came in and by the time a couple of dozen had landed and been stacked in threes across the end of the runway or pushed off the sides into the sand, things were getting a bit dodgey. If only we could have turned them on to a small track leading off the main strip all would have been well. It was impossible but somehow the whole bunch got down safely and we had to turn our thoughts to getting our own patrols in the air. I reckoned that by keeping the brakes on, putting his throttle levers through the gate to 2950 revs with 9lb boost, and then releasing the brakes he would just about clear that conglomeration of Wellingtons by a few feet. However, as I was pondering this there was a terrific roar and a "BQ" Beaufighter was off on time with a few feet in hand. And so we carried on shifting the Wimpeys, now using the sides of the runway and bogging some of the aircraft down left wing low etc. All were eventually shifted off the runway and after leaving a guard on them we settled down to the rest of the night's programme. It was a relief to call Control and report all down safely and no damage or injuries. As dawn approached a spectacle met our gaze! A flock of 31 Wimpeys are a fair crowd and looked at in the cold light of day our previous night's episode assumed its true perspective. Many seemed to have sunk deeper into the sand and I began to wonder what sort of rollicking I would get for putting them there. But the difficulties were recognised by all concerned and eventually "600" had them all on the runway and airborne the next day. I lost my bike which had been dumped in the sand beside the runway and became buried in the stuff blown up by the Wimpeys. F/O Watson got a special congratulation from Group Command for getting the visitors all down safely and for keeping the runway fully operational. We had a well earned breakfast and rested content with the idea that come what may No.600 Squadron would cope". At last there was a chance for a good swim and a lot of sunbathing. The weather was gorgeous after a rather indifferent winter. A lot of the men drank more than they should have done normally but for some reason there seemed to be a sudden and never-ending supply of gin. So much so that some chaps decided to use it in their paraffin lamps – less for reading books than to play cards. And, it smelled so much better than paraffin. The sunbathing had its perils, however, as one poor soul was to demonstrate. He was quietly lying on his back and had dozed off when unfortunately an earth mover extending the taxi way went straight over him without seeing the poor chap. What a way to end the war in a foreign country. The Squadron also lost a chap, who went swimming from the beach and was carried out. In fact due to the "advanced" way of cooking a few of the cooks also ended up with health problems. The method was to fill a four gallon square can, not to be confused with a "Jerrycan", with petrol and cook on the resultant flame. The trouble was that on initial ignition it paid to stand well back or one could get enveloped in flames – a lot of cooks did. The Squadron was still in tents of course, this time dug in a bit more as the enemy was rather close by. It also meant the loss of a few tents. Paddy Green was not at all pleased. He had other thoughts when mentioning "crashed in flames".

A few days later the Squadron gathered its prodigals and moved to the South. The ground crews went to Sousse for a short breather, and to prepare for their next station of war, Malta. Dixon's last task at Bone was compass swinging. After all the work done on the aircraft it was necessary to check the magnetic compasses. This was a slow and laborious job, with the aircraft moved around by hand to point to various bearings, whilst corrections were made to the compass readings. In the end the crews had a compass card which showed the necessary corrections for each compass reading. It was a very serious task which was carried out very carefully indeed. Once more – in Shakespeare's words – the Squadron "stood like greyhounds in the slips". During the last days at Bone, Laurie Dixon received a letter from the Inland Revenue Department in England. Apparently over a period of about a year they had over-collected more than £60 income tax from him. If he wanted the money refunded he had to make a claim for it, which of course he did. The money was duly paid; it seemed a bit unfair to charge someone, sitting in a tent in North Africa, for roads, street lighting, police and what have you, far away in Blighty . . .

Some of the old faces disappeared as the Squadron was streamlined for its forthcoming role as a highly mobile unit. North Africa had now been cleared of both the Germans and the Italians and it was time to chase the enemy off the Continent of Southern Europe. Laurie Dixon left with one big question, to which he will probably

On 26th April 1943 Roberts and Thompson destroyed a Savoia Marchetti SM84 near Monastir. This three-engined bomber served with the Allies after the Italians surrendered.

never get an answer: "On the top-most ridge of the Djebel Zagouhan, a ridge of mountains across the Southern neck of the Cape Bon peninsula I saw the weirdest sight of my time with the RAF. A tri-motor Junkers Ju52 was sitting astride the ridge as if a giant had planted it. How it had got there was a mystery to all. An amusing sight it was. I cannot think that a German pilot with unearthly skill had landed it there and we were sure nothing would have been left of it if someone had force-landed the aircraft at that spot. I have wondered what happened to it since". A "new" war was waiting for the men of the City of London Squadron. Next stop would be the brave little island of Malta. Having been a thorn in the flesh of both the Italians and the Germans numerous attacks had been carried out to break the island and the people who lived on it. Virtually each and every building had been hit. The harbour was full of wrecks and vessels that had barely made it through constant attacks by U-boats. The airfields should have been declared un-serviceable a long time ago, but still aircraft took off from them to encounter the enemy. Day and night bombs came down and in spite of the gallantry of the RAF personnel and the islanders it had been turned into a heap of rubble. But now the island was to become the stepping stone in the move North. And, it was expected, the next

Conditions in Sicily were somewhat basic, and with the Germans still around the need for helmets to be at hand was obvious. Five members of the Squadron seated in front of their "residence". Smoking his pipe is Tom Lloyd, Radar Operator of "Ace" Downing. Tom was killed off Anzio.

step would be Italy. At last the battle would be fought on the enemy's ground. In support of the invasion of French North Africa, No.600 Squadron had first been under Eastern Air Command and then under north-west African Coastal Air Force. Being one of the three night-fighter Beaufighter squadrons it had fought as a self-contained unit, complete with their own cooks and butchers, equipment and postal clerks and therefore could move around at will. As a highly versatile unit it had worked for both the First and Eighth Armies until the Germans had been driven to Cape Bon in Tunisia. It was entitled to rest for a while at the battered and mosquito-ridden airfield at Bone. The Squadron had successfully completed its task in Africa with a most impressive number of enemy aircraft on its account: 38 destroyed, 5 damaged. The "score-list" for the North African campaign, today still on display at the Imperial War Museum in Duxford, speaks for itself:

29 Nov 42	Cant Z506B	NE. of Nagalite	F/O Hilken – P/O Mason
21 Dec 42	Heinkel 111	NE. of Algiers	Sgt Owen – Sgt McAllister
22 Dec 42	Junkers 88	N. of Cap Sigh	F/O Ross – P/O Finlay

22 Jan 43	Piaggio 108	N. of Philippeville	F/O Thompson – W/O White
23 Jan 43	Junkers 88	N. of Philippeville	S/L Hughes – F/O Dixon
23 Jan 43	Junkers 88	N. of Philippeville	S/L Hughes – F/O Dixon
27 Jan 43	Heinkel 111	NNW. of Philippeville	Sgt. Owen – Sgt McAllister
12 Feb 43	Cant Z1007	E. of Cap Serratt	S/L Hughes – F/O Dixon
12 Feb 43	Cant Z1007	N. of Cap Negroe	F/L Arnsby – P/O Gillies
21 Feb 43	Cant Z1007	N. of Cap Serratt	F/L Arnsby – F/O Lawson
21 Feb 43	Savoia SM84	E. of Bone	P/O Simpson – Sgt Gillies
28 Feb 43	Cant Z1007	N. of Bone	Sgt Harrop – Sgt Redmond
01 Mar 43	Piaggio 108	NE. of Bone	Sgt Owen – Sgt McAllister
23 Mar 43	Piaggio 108	N. of Cap Takouch	F/S Vigar – Sgt Dalfrey
04 Apr 43	Junkers 88	N. of Bone	F/L Hanus – P/O Eyles
07 Apr 43	Junkers 88	NE. of Algiers Bay	S/L Horne – F/L Brown
18 Apr 43	Junkers 88	N. of Algiers Bay	F/O Mellersh – P/O Stanley
18 Apr 43	Junkers 88	N. of Algiers Bay	F/O Mellersh – P/O Stanley
21 Apr 43	Junkers 88	N. of Bone	F/L Hanus – P/O Eyles
21 Apr 43	Junkers 88	N. of Algiers Bay	F/O Paton – P/O McAnulty
21 Apr 43	Junkers 88	East coast of Sardina	Sgt Perkinson – F/S Stephens
23 Apr 43	Cant Z1007	N. of Cap Serratt	F/O Turnbull – Sgt Fowler

23 Apr 43	Junkers 88	NE. of Mateur	F/O Bastow – P/O George
24 Apr 43	Junkers 88	NW of Pont du Fahs	F/L Hanus – P/O Thompson
26 Apr 43	Savoia SM84	N. of Monastir	F/O Roberts – P/O Thompson
26 Apr 43	Cant Z1007	NW. of Sousse	F/O Roberts – P/O Thompson
26 Apr 43	Junkers 88	E. of Tunis	S/L Hughes – F/O Dixon
30 Apr 43	Junkers 52	S. of Cagliari	F/S Downing – Sgt Lyons
30 Apr 43	Junkers 52	S. of Cagliari	F/S Downing – Sgt Lyons
30 Apr 43	Junkers 52	S. of Cagliari	F/S Downing – Sgt Lyons
30 Apr 43	Junkers 52	S. of Cagliari	F/S Downing – Sgt Lyons
30 Apr 43	Junkers 52	S. of Cagliari	F/S Downing – Sgt Lyons
07 May 43	Savoia SM79	10 mls S. Aegodeon	Sgt Hutton – Sgt Carlan
08 May 43	Junkers 52	Menzil – Memine	F/O Mellersh – P/O Armstrong
09 May 43	Junkers 52	E. of Cap Bon	F/S Downing – Sgt Lyons
11 May 43	Heinkel 111	SE of Tunis	S/L Horne – F/L Browne
24 May 43	Heinkel 111	E. of Bone	F/O Newhouse – P/O Tate
25 May 43	Heinkel 111	NE of Cap Rosa	S/L Horne – F/L Browne

The late Desmond Hughes remembered how at about this time Paddy Green knew for a fact that only one of the three Beaufighter squadrons were to go across the Med, to the Desert Air Force, to fight on Sicily and in Italy itself. He decided to make sure that No.600 Squadron was not going to stay behind to protect cities in liberated North Africa. Sensing that the Air Staff at Algiers were unlikely to part with their best Squadron, he called for his first class Engineer

Officer Clennett for a talk behind closed doors. Then suddenly things changed. Clennett sent in aircraft serviceability returns which reflected neither the true situation nor much credit on the Squadron. No.600 was apparently a sloppy and useless heap. And, what Paddy Green had foreseen happened: after a few weeks news came that the motley lot of 600 had been nominated to join the DAF.

The score since the beginning of the war had risen remarkably: Destroyed – 55; Probables – 9; Damaged -14.

CHAPTER 10

MALTA AND SICILY.
June to September 1943

On 12th June 1943, No.600 Squadron received orders to prepare for Malta. A total transformation of the Squadron took place. New ground crews arrived. Only a few pre-war Auxiliaries remained. But they worked flat out. New Beaus with sand-coloured camouflage flowed from storage depots and were given strict acceptance checks and thorough air tests. The old battle-scarred grey-green aircraft were polished up and flown away. There was a deadline to be met at Malta and with the help of "Chiefy" Nelson and his gang the Squadron made it. On 23rd June the ground crews left. They embarked on open LSTs, perched on top of their equipment. After 24 hours on the Mediterranean they arrived, unshaven and scruffy, in the Grand Harbour of Valetta. The men of the ground party were met by a tiny, but fierce looking Warrant Officer, backed up by two Corporal SP's in immaculate khaki. He made it quite clear that the first impression was not at all of the highest order.

In fact he considered this scruffy RAuxAF troop a bit of a shower. Since it was not the done thing, at this time, to tell anyone in Malta "to get some in", the only thing the ground crews could do was mutter in their beards and wait for another day. Whether the natural resentment at this affront triggered off an extra determination, or whether the toughening experiences in North Africa had tuned 600 up for bigger things, the sheer guts graft and achievement of the next few weeks caused this same W/O by the name of "Shorthouse" Stone to admit that this was the very finest Squadron he had ever seen anywhere. Twenty Beaufighters set course for Luqa, quite a powerful and experienced reinforcement for that island. They flew over Malta to let their presence be known. The Squadron settled into Luqa, a badly damaged airfield. From 25th June No.600 "City of London" Squadron effectively joined the Desert Air Force. The Squadron was to operate immediately. The crews found working conditions on the ground "rather basic" to put it mildly. Their operations room was about 12 feet square. The outside entrance was an opening in a wall and the passage leading in was indirect like a maze to minimise blast effect. There was no seating of any sort. The men just sat on the concrete floor, which was thickly covered with cement dust. Lack of creature comforts made impossible any chance of relaxation. The aircrew were billeted in a building on the sea front at Sliema Creek and travelled to and from the aerodrome in a ramshackle little bus driven by a Maltese. His driving was quite terrifying and once when asked which side of the road he drove on he happily replied: "Whatever side is clear". One or two things made an immediate impact on the aircrew. First there was the glare which was quite uncomfortable and second the number of priests the Squadron saw about the place. It gave an idea of constant availability of clerical support which some men found frightening. Also very interesting was to watch the Maltese stone masons at work as they cut the local stone and shaped it into building blocks. They sat on the ground and shaped the soft, honey coloured blocks of stone into cubes. When first cut, the stone was soft and easy to shape. But on exposure to the air the stone rapidly hardened. Most of the buildings were erected quite without mortar. The living conditions were tough. Food was often literally putrid and the heat intense. Blankets were spread on rock, and to the sick and weary the word "rest" became a thing remembered, rather than enjoyed. As a result of the Axis siege of the island petrol was strictly rationed to two gallons per vehicle per day. Consequently every move and every effort was made on sore, hot feet. To add to these difficulties, the Squadron was beset by the trials of a local malady, known as "Malta Dog". It was a cross between dysentery and sandfly fever. But such was the importance of the coming battle that only those unable to stand on their feet were classed as sick, and the rest were M&D (Medicine and Duty) – with fingers crossed in hope – and a cork. The men of 600 could not care less. They built blast pens of soft yellow stone and rubble-filled petrol cans for each individual aircraft. The officers were billeted in the Meadowbank Hotel in Sliema, a happy change after the tented camps of North-Africa. The only snag was that the mattresses were lousy with bed bugs. The joy of having proper beds soon disappeared and after a few days the men returned to the old camp beds. At least the bugs did not find canvas very appetising and soon the bumps subsided. Another Malta novelty was white women. Many of the younger ones looked quite beautiful, but they were strictly off limits to the Protestants. The story went that you had to be a good Catholic and meet "Mamma" before any progress could be made.

Warrant Officer Yorke and some of his armourers working on the Beaufighter guns.

Food and drink were plentiful and the fare and service at the Union Club was very good. But who would not appreciate any luxury after Soya links and Meat & Vegetables? The Squadron had about 36 hours to familiarise themselves with Malta. They had to learn the system of both airfield and airborne control. The whole island was absolutely crammed with aircraft, ready for the invasion of Sicily which was by now an open secret although it was not discussed at all in public. Besides the Squadron itself there were Wellingtons, large numbers of Spitfires, Blenheims, Hurricanes, Mosquitoes and the odd Swordfish. Starting up prior to take-off was carefully controlled and during daylight there was a constant but moving queue of aircraft. Overheating was the major problem and the Spitfires and Mosquitoes in particular could not afford to hang about in the extreme heat. If they did their radiator temperatures went quickly off the clock, puffs of glycol vapour could be seen from vents and they had to be switched off, towed away and left to cool off which took a long time. The Squadron was lucky in that they had more leeway in this respect but it was dreadfully hot in the aircraft when still on the deck. The bare metal of the Beau was too hot to touch with any comfort.

Across the waters was Sicily. It was the doorway to the Italian mainland and one did not need to be the greatest strategist to know that this was the place the Allies would land sooner or later. Italy was the country of Il Duce, Benito Mussolini, who had declared war on France when it was on its knees and who joined the Germans at the end of the Battle of Britain when he believed that the invasion of England would take place in a matter of days. But when his pilots found out that the RAF was rather keen to have a go at them, the Italian air force had made a hurried retreat to Belgium and then home to Italy. It was the country of the friendly soldiers, surrendering happily in North Africa, hoping for a safe job in a British Army kitchen, thus ensuring their new friends from England of better cooked, well-seasoned meals. Many wondered how they would fight with the Allies about to invade their homeland. The invasion of Italy marked the start of the most intensive period in the Squadron's life. No.600 Squadron was to provide the air umbrella for the whole island of Sicily at night, supported by one flight from each of Nos. 108 and 256 Squadrons. By day the enemy was loath to show himself, and concentrated his attacks on the nights, which placed a considerable responsibility on the night-fighters and also robbed the ground crews from badly needed sleep.

As mentioned earlier the Squadron was based at Luqa. Norman Poole saw that it was possible in those days to taxi from one airfield to another. Once No.600 Squadron arrived they tucked themselves away in a blast proof shelter. All were impressed by the size of Malta. Doing circuits it seemed the aircrews were flying over the sea most of the time. The whole of the southern end of Malta, the widest bit, seemed to be a huge airfield. The shelter gave an idea how the people had survived. It was coupled to excellent deep shelters cut out of the rock and between the two features they provided a degree of confidence they had not experienced anywhere else. The Gentlemen in Blue felt happy at Luqa. HQ was set up in a hut at the end of one of the two runways. The Maintenance Echelon found a place at Takali aerodrome. "Dev" mentioned these men with affection and admiration: "Without the spur and satisfaction of the Flight Erks when the tally of victories began to rise, and without the added pride of adorning their own "bag of nails" with another swastika, these blokes worked like Trojans. The Squadron flew 1000 operational hours in one month, plus a fair whack of day flying, on escort of Air/ Sea rescue searches, and with inspections occurring every 30 hours they were numerous. Ben Opie, who met an untimely end at Naples a few months later, was in charge, ably assisted by Sgts MacLean and Wheeley. The quality of their performance was due in no small measure, to a strong nucleus of Auxiliaries and pre-war Volunteer Reserves, and an unashamed name-dropping of some of the chaps involved will support this modest praise in the memories of those who recall them. It was reputed that the only heat treatment ever used in a workshop was to expose metals to the blistering wit of Wilf Hall, while in friendly badinage with Joe Farley and Charley Delavigne. Such redoubtable men as Bill Cooksey, Peter Potter, "Chippy" Chapman, Bob Hills, George Nunn, Mickey Noakes and Jack Wayne toiled through the heat, and the gutretching sickness that beset them, to produce the kites on time or before". When 600 returned to Malta for Summer Camp in 1956 a Squadron badge was erected, carved from a block of sandstone and not a little of the reputation the Squadron still enjoys stems from those previous residents, and their efforts. On 14th May 1995 the stone was deposited in the Church of Saint Bartholomew the Great in London.

Finding Malta in the dark was not too easy. It was of course very small and the people down there were experts in black-out matters. There was a very dim flarepath which was quickly dowsed after aircraft landed. A little truck then materialised in front of the aircraft The only light it carried was a very small notice right under the vehicle which said 'Follow Me' and that was it. Quite difficult for vehicle and aircraft and at times they were very, very close to the large whirling props of the Beaufighter. There was a very amusing perk when one night Des Hughes and Laurie Dixon operated at night. It was the opportunity to "purchase" a small paper cup of Horlick's, the "RAF Life Savers". Whenever a crew returned hot, tired and dirty from a sortie over a pitch black Med it was marvellous to taste that warm drink. Another thing typical of Malta was the fact

Wing Commander "Paddy" Green and his aircrew. From left to right "Ace" Downing (pilot), Cyril Fowler (R/O) and his pilot John Turnbull (RCAF), Reg Gillies (R/O) and his pilot W/C Paddy Green, Desmond Hughes (pilot) and his O/R Laurie Dixon, Vernon McAllister (R/O) and his skipper Ginger Owen and Harry "Bugs" Newton (pilot-RNZAF). Kneeling are Frank Thompson (R/O) and John Parkinson (pilot).

that one could buy big bottles of Brylcreem hair dressing for 5 shillings.

Realising how near Malta was to utter starvation, the fact that some essential supplies could hardly reach the island and the fact that many lives were lost trying to supply the island, it was amazing to see the large stocks of Brylcreem, available all over the island. The members of 600 soon found out that they had no spending money in Malta. In North Africa they had managed on their overseas pay and allowances paid by the Accounts Officer. Malta, it transpired, was "Home Service". This meant that the men had to use "Bank of England currency as if in Britain. The only problem was that there was no way of getting one's hand on it. Some in the Squadron managed to get a small amount of cash from a ramshackle branch of Lloyds Bank by writing a cheque for £5. Lloyds kept the original cheque and two copies were sent to England, one by airmail and one by surface mail. At least for the immediate moment some were sleeping in a real building and in a real bed. There were even washing and laundry facilities. They felt much better now that there was a regular shower and a clean shirt. On the other hand the men got a bit of a shock when one morning they were woken up by a chatting group of Maltese cleaning ladies, who were happily

A Coles crane is used for an open air engine change of one of the Squadron Beaus.

sweeping the room. All the chaps were naked without the usual mosquito netting. There was a blond Australian navigator who was very much under the weather with a feverish condition. His chums wrapped him up well before leaving him to go on night state and next morning they found him quite out with a very high temperature. During the night he had got one foot stuck under the low rail at the foot of the bed and tossing and turning in his fever he had actually broken his ankle.

The medics took him away with what was obviously a bad attack of malaria. Roaming round to the south of Luqa during the first few days there Reg Gillies and Laurie Dixon happened on something quite fascinating. It was a very large wooden shed with big doors, painted green which housed of all things a German Heinkel 115 floatplane. It was complete with German camouflage and markings. Reg and Laurie were quite puzzled by the sight of this aircraft which was in mint condition and looked as if it could be flown away at any moment. More amazing was the fact that there was no guard to be seen anywhere. It was not until after the war that Dixon heard that this aircraft was used by the RAF in the Med. In 1996 he was told that this particular aircraft was one of three Norwegian Naval He115s which, after Norway fell, had been flown by their crews to Sollum Voe on the Shetlands, had been handed over to the RAF and after being overhauled at RAF Helensburgh, were put into service for SOE missions.

One of the first visitors was AM Sir Keith Park in his red MG sports car. Laurie Dixon never forgot this particular visit. He remembered: "A tall thin figure came into the little building where we were. It was Keith Park, who had commanded No.11 Group Fighter Command during the Battle of Britain. He was in charge of the landings being mounted against Sicily. He quietly insisted that we all stayed put and then turned to Desmond. 'How has it been, Desmond?' I was struck immediately by two things. First his addressing of Desmond in front of junior officers by his Christian name. This was against all custom and tradition but this marvellous man lost nothing by his approach that morning. On any other occasion he would be strictly formal and we knew that. But now he felt the need to get close to this particular Flight Commander. Second he had done his homework with regard to Desmond whom he remembered from 1940. Des had been a pilot on No.264 Squadron Defiants, one of the worst and bloodiest jobs during the Battle of Britain. It was a nice touch from a man carrying such a load of responsibility at that moment". Considering the pounding Luqa had received the airfield was in a reasonably good condition. The only problem was that the runway ended in a quarry. It helped young pilots to execute perfect take-offs. The Fighter Controllers knew their trade and had the confidence of the crews. The Flights were amalgamated for servicing and operations as far as aircraft were concerned, as practically everything not on inspection was needed each night, but personnel were divided into "A" and "B" Flights for night Ops, working alternate nights. These had no slouches among them. With bods such as Dennis, Cowell, Hayhoe, Renton, Williams and Spencer, Sgts Bert Chantrey and Dev Devroome had little to worry about in A Flight. The same could be said of men like Arthur Butterworth, Dai Williams, Bill Stapleton, Nobby Cockerton, Moggy Cooke, Lofty Hutchinson and Ted Pellet who served and sweated under Sgts Fred Mayne and "Barty" Bartholomew in B Flight. The day always started early before the heat came on, and the Squadron marched up from its camp among the ruins of Luqa village, because of the petrol shortage mentioned earlier. The last lap to the runway was uphill, and each morning the weary night crews would see the column march over the brow to the tune of "There was a young lady from Hamm", sung by Frank Yates and Rube Spink at the rear. Automatically there was an "Eyes Left" to the nearest Beaufighter, to see if the protecting fabric had been blasted off the gun ports, and this meant the Squadron had been in business during the previous night. At the head of the column, as always, was W/O Topping, whose broad red face has been described as everything down to a well-smacked backside. In sighting range, his eyebrows would shoot up in anxious question, and the crew to be relieved would signify the night's bag with the appropriate number of fingers. Some may have lingered on two fingers a little overlong, but as the importance of the night's success was realised, so "Toppers" face would develop a ruddy beam from ear to ear, like the rising sun and the step would pick up, as if the Central Band had struck up with the "March Past". There was pride in everyone, pride in the achievements, pride in the comradeship that charged each one, consciously or otherwise with the determination that his day or night shift would be worthy of the one just done. Then began the great trek down to dispersal to get the line ready for the night. Instrument bashers hauled their trolley with its quarter of a ton of oxygen cylinders. The plumbers humped garlands of ammunition. The lilywhites carried gash sets on their backs like papooses, and the workhorses of every unit, the fitters and riggers, humped everything else but the kitchen sink. According to "Dev" DeVroome's memories "the Exodus from Egypt had nothing on this". Times was precious, as by early afternoon the aircraft were literally too hot to handle. The more fortunate, with serviceable kites, mucked in with those with snags, regardless of trade. The less fortunate worked on through the heat but the line never once went short, and so, with the dusk the game was on. Patrols were mounted throughout the night, one aircraft relieving another, and for the Erks, refuel, re-arm and push kites was the order for the next twelve hours. This smooth co-operation allowed the Squadron to operate as clockwork. Scarcely a night went by without the CO and his operator F/O Gillies being in the lead. If not in the air W/C Green would direct operations from his beautiful operational caravan, converted from a

Sgt Owen (pilot) and Sgt McAllister (R/O) were both awarded the DFM. Together they shot down seven enemy aircraft.

kitchen trailer, complete with VHF, aerodrome control, etc. and manned, seemingly at all times, by the CO's "shadow", "Club-foot" Coggins. Unflappable, immune to wrath, sarcasm or epithet, LAC Coggins performed a perfect "Brad" to the CO's "Harry Lime". The tasks of the Squadron were manifold. W/C Green took Generals Montgomery and Browning over to Kairouan, Tunisia, and back. At the same time the nightly skies over Malta had to be made safe from German and Italian intruders. With an actual strength of twenty Beaufighters twelve operational and one spare were the minimum requirements every night. Inspections piled up on each other rapidly, but were ably kept under control by the chaps of the Maintenance Echelon, farmed out to Takali which had one hangar still standing. Everything else was coped with by the two Flights at Luqa, who worked 24 hours on and off alternately, with the "walking sick" making up a day shift. The aircraft were dispersed in bays round a perimeter track some two miles long, running through the ruins of Luqa village, and were never allowed out in the open, except to taxi and fly. This led to much pushing and shoving by all hands. The day started at 0600 hrs in the morning with a thorough search of every inch of runway for splinters and fragments left over from the shells fired or bombs dropped by Royal Navy, Royal Artillery, Malta Artillery, Luftwaffe and Italian Air Force during the night before. The effort was made to save tyres which were in very short supply.

The Squadron kept up their patrols to defend the Island during the few days they had there before the invasion of Sicily and generally enjoyed life. They swam from the rocky beach in front of the hotel and they even went to the pictures on a few occasions. There was some risk of picking up the bugs while in the cinema, as there was no air conditioning, just a hole in the ceiling. In June the Squadron covered the successful rescue from the sea of Sgt Edwards of No.723 Squadron. In July many enemy aircraft were shot to pieces, burning on the ground after having been surprised by No.600 Squadron Beaus. Without the constant loyalty of the ground crews it would have been impossible to maintain the high score and the morale that was so typical for the Squadron. Snags were worked out and cured by the light of the dimmest torches, and by hook, crook, and sweat, the line remained complete. Crews which had started out down at dispersal for the first night flying tests frequently stayed there for the whole night, without a break for food, going from job to job, to return only when the Squadron was relieved by day fighters. It is rare for ground crews to be genuinely complimented, but in a diary kept in the orderly room, the CO recorded the following: "To them, much of the credit is due for the kills made". From W/C Green this was praise indeed. "From the strong and the weak, the fit and the sick, there was a selfless and unswerving devotion to duty, to the point of fatigue, and beyond". Mention should be made also of the very few moments when Squadron members off-duty would hike themselves to Valetta to join the social whirl of "The Gut". In common with everything else, there was a shortage of money in Malta. The currency was made up with over-printed shilling notes, squares of Lino representing pennies, postage stamps, and if these were inadequate, cards printed "I.O.U 1/6d Joe's Bar". After a night of living it up on a rather odd brew, labelled "Port & Lemon" or "Near Beer", and consorting with the local wenchery, whose conversation seemed limited to such profound statements as "Up Your Pipe Jack" and "My Old Gum Boots", one could finish up with a fair start for the bathroom floor back in "Blighty", and a nap hand of cards well worth every cent of ten bob, if it were possible to remember where the hell they came from in the first place. Nevertheless, they made the Squadron right welcome, especially the watch repairers in Kingsway who, inundated with watches to be cleaned of the sands of Africa discretely closed down for two days prior to the Sicily D-Day and no doubt flogged the spoils to the Squadron's successors once No. 600 had moved to Sicily.

A very strange incident happened one night just before the landings took place. One of the Squadron aircraft in the vicinity of the island in the night reported by radio "the aircraft terribly hot". This puzzled all on the ground not least Paddy Green, the CO, who got quite ruffled. The message was repeated with a request for advice. Before this could be considered a further transmission advised that they would have to return to base much to the annoyance of one or two people. When the aircraft did finally land it was actually very, hot indeed despite having been in its own slipstream at about 10,000ft. It was a long time cooling down but the technicians never found any answer to this one. It became an aeroplane which nobody wanted to fly in – all very mysterious, as Laurie Dixon remembered. Whilst waiting for the invasion of Sicily during the first nights at Malta no contact was made with the enemy, but when the invasion of Sicily began on 9th and 10th July, things began to warm up.

After another victory Reg Gillies paints a small new swastika on the nose of the Beaufighter. W/C Green watches with pleasure

Towards the end of the first week of the Squadron's arrival in Malta 51st Highland Division appeared off the coast in landing craft. They were to be part of the assault landing on the east coast of Sicily, just south of Syracuse. They had a miserable time at sea because just before the landings the Mediterranean had its worst storm for fifty years. Code name of the Sicily landing was "Husky" and it was the biggest operation in terms of men put ashore at once since the beginning of the war. The seaborne landing was to be preceded by an airborne assault of British and American paratroops and glider borne troops and their equipment. These were flown from Sousse in Tunisia by American Dakotas (or C47s as the Yanks called them). The gliders were pulled by American and RAF aircraft. Almost all of the aircrew in the airborne assault were without operational experience and this coupled with the bad weather and heavy concentrations of light flak almost ruined the whole airborne operation. It was only saved by the improvisation and great courage of the paratroopers who managed to get ashore and form a bridgehead. The American drop arranged for Gela on the south coast went down all over the countryside. The British para-drop on the east around Syracuse also had mixed fortunes. The paras who took and held the bridge just outside Syracuse did tremendously well and Parmasole bridge is on their battle honours. Their glider train had less good fortune and hundreds of heavily armed and laden men were put down in the sea to drown without a chance. Many of these men were of the Staffordshire Regiment. Not only did their tugs have to face the coastal flak but the ships of the Navy put up a quite indiscriminate flak barrage. They did not wait to identify especially in the dark. It was an often heard complaint of aircrew; the Navy seemed to fire at anything over their heads, friend or foe. Unfortunately this serious problem was never resolved during the entire war. The Royal Navy did not seem to understand air power, but they were obviously aware of their vulnerability to it. They operated a group of ships along the east coast of Sicily bombarding at night. This group, known as H – Force, consisted of the 16 inch gun battleships Nelson and Warspite along with a Fleet carrier and all of the ships, destroyers, etc. necessary to screen and protect them. One day Laurie Dixon watched this force coming into Grand Harbour after such a sortie. The carrier was tipped to one side to lift an enormous torpedo hole clear of the water line. It was a tremendous hole caused by a torpedo from an Italian SM79 aircraft which had got inside the screen. In the confusion that followed one of the destroyers had fired inwards with the result that one had its front turret and bridge blown away. The Luftwaffe showed up and had the bad luck of running straight into the Gentlemen in Blue from the City of London. After the GCIs got ashore and deployed, they did it with incredible speed, and after this the Squadron inflicted heavy casualties on the Germans and Italians. Poole and McKinnon were the first ones up on 9th July at 2035hrs. Initially they could not see much of the invasion fleet because they were looking from a relatively light position whereas the fleet down below was in the dark. Not for long though for the guns started to fire furiously when Poole and Mac were still nowhere near the Sicilian coast. Aircraft recognition was not the strongest skill of the naval gunners and one can see they have an argument once you find yourself on a vulnerable ship. But sadly the tremendous wall of fire sent up had a rather bad effect on the pilots towing the gliders. They were mainly transport crew and they were not used to anti-aircraft fire. Therefore it was not surprising that many of them decided they were close enough to the enemy coast to release their gliders. A considerable number of these flew into the water and those that made the coast ended up on unwelcoming rocks and beaches. It was fortunate that quite a lot came down in an area defended by the Italians, who no longer had much of a stomach for fighting. There were few German troops in that area and it certainly saved many lives. Nevertheless all was chaos, for a number of transport pilots unwilling to dump the glider aircraft in what they knew to be the sea, returned to Malta with their glider in tow and released them in the circuit before landing themselves. McKinnon and Poole, also on the way back, had to find a way to evade all these flying objects. Fortunately there was a strict radio silence observed, for if they had asked for permission to land they certainly should have been orbiting until out of fuel. Now they just joined the melee and hoped for the best. On the third day of the Invasion McKinnon and Poole struck lucky. They were patrolling at about 2300hrs at about 10,000ft when they got a radar contact and turned on it. They closed in using their own radar. In this case they carried the older Mk.IV metric radar, which meant they were limited in range to their height. They closed in and got a visual on a Do217. Now it was up to Mac. The noise of the cannons going off was really astounding, as was the smell of cordite. They hit him and he started a slow descent with an engine on fire. The German rear gunner with great heroism was firing away at the Beau hoping to level the score but despite his valiant efforts the burning aircraft got nearer and nearer to the water and finally plunged in which put the fire out. McKinnon and Poole of course were overjoyed to finally strike one and decided they had been operationally bored rather than tired. They had another exciting chase with a Ju88 after this but unfortunately they could not bring it to combat. As their aircraft had suffered a bit itself and the crew had sustained some minor injuries they decided to go home. However, with the radio out and the flaps stuck they had to land rather fast hoping for a very long runway. They stopped just before the end of it and got out with the feeling of having become aces. During the night of 12th/13th July six enemy aircraft were destroyed, Paddy Green and Reg Gillies accounting for two, as did F/Os Mellersh and Armstrong. Des Hughes and Laurie Dixon got involved in a sharp little raid on the port of Syracuse. As ever the Navy hosed light flak all over the sky. Quite suddenly a Heinkel 111 lifted up beneath them and appeared very close on the starboard side. He was too close for comfort. Hughes dropped back and when the Heinkel turned away to starboard Hughes' guns finished him off over Syracuse. The bomber went down like a torch and exploded when it hit the ground. P/O McKinnon got one as well. The combat report of the CO read: "Took off in V8700 at 2040hrs. Landed at 2240. Patrolled from Luqa. After various vectors we had head-on contact with a bandit flying East. We obtained a visual contact at 2,000 feet but lost it, but we maintained AI contact. We regained visual contact at 1,000 feet and identified the bandit as a Ju88. I opened a two second burst from 150 yards. The enemy aircraft was hit in the fuselage and the cockpit caught fire. The enemy aircraft exploded when it hit the sea 5 miles North of Augusta at 2200 hrs. We then commenced a freelance search and obtained another contact. It turned out to be a Mosquito which shot down a Ju88 about 50 yards ahead of us. We then caught up with a He111. It also exploded after a two seconds burst". Paddy Green reported having seen a Mosquito flying in front of him. During several encounters crews reported to have seen Mozzies. Soon they began to doubt the identifications, for further on in the Operations Record Book they mentioned the possibility of these aircraft being Me210s, aircraft with a similar silhouette and task. In the sky at night one not only needed good equipment but also a watchful eye and the ability for a very quick identification of aircraft.

McKinnon and Poole had a frustrating encounter with Mosquitos at about the same time. A few nights later they saw the whole thing from the opposition's point of view. They were returning to Malta after a late night sortie taking off at 0230. It was around 0500 when while returning Poole got a contact behind the Beaufighter. This was possible because the radar had a "backbeam" arising from the forward transmission. It was a weaker signal and it did not have the range of the forward beam, but at least it told you there was someone behind them. They dived and turned and threw him off. Shortly after he was back again. They escaped again and then began an interesting struggle to keep him from getting in a firing position. By now Poole knew what it was; for there was only one unit of fighters that could perform like this and this was a half squadron of Mosquito night-fighters who had flown out to Malta for the invasion. The CO of that unit was flying that night. McKinnon and Poole kept evading because they did not want to make up his score sheet. There must have been a lot of swearing and sweating inside the Beaufighter that night.

Malta was a crucial base for the invasion. It was some 60 miles away from Sicily and a wasp nest of aircraft. It was the unbelievable home of no less than 37 squadrons. Not all were full squadrons, but most were and even on the five airfields careful flight discipline was necessary. There still were enemy raids on Malta from time to time. These happened mainly at night which gave the Squadron the chance of inspecting those deep air raid shelters. But they were light raids and by day they were mainly high altitude reconnaissance sorties. The men of No.600 Squadron had a different pattern of life from most of the other Malta squadrons, as these were mostly involved with daylight operations.

A man and his melons; W/O Fred Topping seems to enjoy a new supply of fresh juice.

The crews of the Wellington bombers were of course operating by night and so was 600's sister night-fighter squadron. These crews would return in the morning and roll into their camp beds. In noisy Malta it was difficult to sleep well but the night-fighters tried to do

their best in the morning. The afternoon was always interrupted by
air tests. They were short ones and lasted only about one hour and
a half but the crews wanted to be sure that everything worked when
at nightfall they were preparing for duty. It was during one of these
quiet mornings that McKinnon and Poole found their favourite wait-
ress enjoying herself with the barman; hopefully they both were
good Catholics.

One night Brigadier Bowen of the Airborne Forces accompanied
Paddy Green as a third crew member. He wanted to reconnoitre his
troop operations south of Catania. The paratrooper had no idea
what he was going to see on that sortie. Standing on the escape
hatch behind Green the Brigadier suddenly caught the glimpse of
an enemy aircraft. Fearing that Paddy had not seen it Bowen started
to pound Green on the back and the head, meanwhile pointing to
the enemy. Paddy of course got the shock of a lifetime when he
was concentrating on the information given to him by Reg Gillies.
Fortunately after the inevitable chase the He111 was shot down with
the Brigadier in a ringside seat. After he landed the parachutist
declared it "the most thrilling night I have had since the war began".
In 1st Airborne Division he had seen quite a few, but this was the
top. Paddy Green walked away with a strange sensation in his upper
body; the Brigadier certainly had a hard punch. He should have
been with the CO during the night of 14th/15th July when Green
and Gillies shot down no less than four aircraft, damaging a fifth
one. Des Hughes and Laurie Dixon also got involved with an aircraft. It turned out to be a very alert Wellington. A chase to catch a
German flare dropper proved unsuccessful. Each time, after dropping his flares, this aircraft went for the deck and his trail could be
seen by the tracer following it from the naval ships. Hughes and
Dixon knew that following the enemy could mean suicide, with the
Navy's ideas of anti-aircraft defence. Then they were vectored to
another bogey. When they closed in for the kill they suddenly recognised it as an Albermarle which apparently was on its way home
after towing a glider to its destination. Hughes turned away, the
crew of the Albermarle never noticed them. F/O Turnbull and Sgt
Fowler got three Ju88s and F/O Roberts with Sgt Burraston took
care of number eight. But this was by no means the end of that
story. During the night of 16th/17th July six enemy aircraft were put
out of action. Near disaster happened during that night when
Newton and Ross identified an aircraft as a Do217. They went after

the bandit, and then opened fire. The shells hit the fuselage and set
fire to one of the engines. Another kill? No, suddenly Newton
realised that there were no swastikas but white stars on the wings
of the "enemy". Instead of hitting a Do-217 they had almost shot
down a B25. The American managed to struggle home on a wing
and a prayer. Newton and Ross were shocked; it proved once again
that identification was of great importance during nightly encounters. For McKinnon and Poole the night of 17th/ 18th July proved
to be very successful. They patrolled down the East coast of Sicily
with Mount Etna as a landmark for holding position. They had
ground control interception control because by now the mobile
stations had gone ashore and were able to give the crews radar
cover. Allied troops attacked Catania and the artillery barrage could
be seen as glowing shells showed up in the night sky. The enemy
attacked Allied positions around Catania. Then Poole picked up an
Italian Cant Z1007bis. It was making its run on the target. Poole was
not pleased for the Italian was heading straight for the central target
area where the ack-ack fire was at its fiercest. Poole tucked his head
in the radar visor and hoped for the best. Once again the throaty
rattle of 20mm cannons supplemented the six machine guns. Poole
feared they would be in the middle of the target area, but no, the
sensible Italian had changed course away from the guns and was
creeping round the Northern edge. It did not do him any good for
soon the aircraft was burning fiercely and plunging steeply down –
difficult to say if anyone got out. On the same sortie they were given
a contact on a stranger and after radar chase they found a bomber.
They still had plenty of ammunition and a short burst left him burning and spiralling down from about 10,000ft. McKinnon and Poole
were pleased with their work. The next night the Beaufighters took
to the air again, a further five enemy aircraft were disposed of. The
Germans tried to retaliate by sending their Ju88s on a raid, which
did the Squadron no lasting harm. To counter future surprises, however, more night-fighters were detailed to patrol. The raid was
regarded a bloody cheek by all, and added great stimulation to the
rush for volunteers for the crossing to Sicily, for which the Squadron
had been alerted. The continuous operating at night under great
stress began to take its toll. At times Laurie Dixon and Desmond
Hughes flew three sorties per night which was utterly draining On
18th July they took off early, at 2230hrs. It turned out to be a night
packed with action and a sortie of 3fi hours. They were inland over

the Catania Plain and this time were harried by what were probably German night-fighters. Although their Mk.IV AI was designed to look forward and either side it did receive echoes from astern. These were much weaker than normal but with experience could be readily interpreted for what they were. By this time Dixon certainly had no difficulty recognising the difference between the echo from behind or that of faulty equipment (the code words for the latter were "Bent Weapon"). The possibility of being chased added to the stress of chasing and at times aircrews felt absolutely exhausted.

There was really nothing in the way of relaxation in Malta. However some of the crews were free to wander about in the afternoon, preferring to do their air testing after tea time before operation during the night. It was amazing what a help and relaxation these little breaks were. The men used to cross Sliema Creek on ancient steam driven ferry boats. They had a round vertical boiler in the centre of the boat which glowed red hot in spots around the firebox. The whole thing wheezed and shuddered and both looked and sounded as if it might blow up at any moment. An old man playing a fiddle sat in the stern during the crossing – perhaps to take the men's minds off the boiler. If they stayed on the base aircrew would often sit in the hole, the control centre cut deep in the rock. During the previous evening a Wellington bomber had put out of action the German VHF radio centre at Taormina on the road from Catania to Messina. All German fighter operations were controlled from this centre and until repairs were effected they were reduced to the much less efficient W.T. It was being intercepted by Allied Signals personnel in the hole. The gen they got from the Germans was then going through the Duty Controller who sent it to a Spitfire Wing doing a sweep over Sicily. This Wing was being led by "Cocky" Dundas, who was a well-known Battle of Britain pilot. He and Paddy Green were close friends. While sweeping over Sicily Cocky was simply told where the German Controller had directed his fighters to. Cocky must have had a whale of a time and the Germans must have been terrified to be bounced all the time.

Flying night operations was not at all an easy turkey shoot. Often dull hours were spent flying in the designated sector, guided by a ground station. More than often blips on the AI suddenly disappeared when enemy aircraft hit the deck and flew so low that they could not be chased. At times Wellingtons, Hudsons, Hurricanes and

Spitfires would light up the screens. And it was all thanks to expert knowledge of both pilot and Radar Operator of silhouettes that "friendly" aircraft escaped the guns of the Beaufighters, often quite unaware that a No.600 Squadron Beaufighter had crept in for the kill.

On the other hand nights passed without "anything to report", meaning that the skies remained empty and the enemy firmly on the ground, well aware of the "Whispering Death" high up in the air. Twenty-five bombers were destroyed during the first week, with Paddy Green and Reg Gillies accounting for seven and John Turnbull RCAF and Sgt Fowler notching up six. Desmond Hughes and Laurie Dixon got two. The morale of the Squadron was top and there even was inter-Flight rivalry to get the best time of the night for patrols. The Squadron was continuing its successes from Malta and they were on their way to shooting down a hundred enemy aircraft in the Mediterranean theatre. The Commander in Chief Sir Hugh Pugh Lloyd came round to congratulate them in their crew room which was a pretty unusual event. Poole had only seen the Duke of Kent and the AOC 11 Group at the commissioning interview – the most senior officers he came across were the Squadron Commanders. Pugh Lloyd came across as an understanding man who gave them credit for all they had achieved. It was a curious business the Squadron was in. Almost everything depended on their individual efforts. The same was true of the ground crews who kept them flying. It was their individual consciences that made them work so well. They worked the longest hours when they were needed and the planes had an amazingly high rate of serviceability.

While the battle on Sicily raged with Generals Patton and Montgomery trying to push each other out of the limelight and the front pages of the papers, preparations for the move of the Squadron to Sicily were made. They received a 24 hour warning to cross, as soon as a suitable strip was available. Sgt Kenneth Batchelor and his drivers Roger Ray, Jim Parks, Ron Pavitt and Reg Spooner were busy waterproofing the MT for a beach landing, while W/O Neill organised the essential stores and spares with Cpl George Redding. An exercise was set up in a deep tunnel, carved some fifty feet down in solid rock, and while it was strictly out of bounds in view of a store of HE shells and torpedoes that the Navy was saving for a rainy day, it became a regular calling spot for most, because of the coolness and relief from the heat. This caused much pithy comment from the

Sgt MacLean (left) and F/L Clennett, the Engineering Officer of 600 Squadron. While in North Africa Clennett and W/C Green agreed that poor serviceability reports might help the Squadron to be kicked out, direction Malta. They were proven right . . .

ebullient Redding, and is believed to be the original source of his phrase which remained a Squadron catchphrase and greeting for the rest of the war – namely "Ardships you b——ds, you don't know what they are". In spite of the interruptions the job was done, and on July 21st the honour of going first fell to A Flight. With a Sten gun, a tool kit and a couple of blankets they took off in Hudsons. They landed on a strip of dirt, thereafter known as Cassibile Airport. It was close to Catania where Brigadier Bowen's Airborne Division had made a heroic stand against a much stronger enemy. The Sappers made a magnificent airstrip, long and smooth, cut clean through orange groves and almond plantations. The Allied troops on the ground were making progress but the German opposition was very strong and although the Allies had overrun the West end of the island and the capital Palermo it was hard fighting on the Eastern end. The Squadron moved its patrolling areas inland to intercept bombers attacking the ground troops but there were fewer of them and the Squadron was considered hostile with ground fire aimed at them whenever they flew over Allied positions. McKinnon and Poole had a few chases after bombers but the Italian aircraft had dropped out of the battle and the German bombers were wise enough to make life difficult by continuous weaving and diving for home after they had released their bombs. This reduced the Beaufighter R/Os detection range and it was not considered wise to risk the centimetric radar over enemy territory. They had some ground radar supporting the efforts but the problem was accuracy of target height-finding since it was largely guess work and frequently left them too far above the target. The pilots would approach from above keeping the target within range but throttling back to lose height and stay above and behind. It was very difficult and did not have any success. For the time being B Flight continued to mount patrols from Malta, while A Flight humped up enough petrol and ammo from the landing beaches to start operations. B Flight soon followed and landed at Red Beach, amongst the wrecks of gliders which had barely made it. On 26th July the whole Squadron moved to Cassibile. US Engineers had torn a runway out of the orchards through the local vineyards and almond trees and laid pierced steel planking for the Beaufighters to take off on. Dusty, as it was high summer but it worked and the Yanks deserved great credit for their speed. Cassibile was their home for the next two months. It was self-contained and well-controlled. Bays were cut into the orange groves and the slog became a little easier, as they virtually lived with the aircraft. They were back in tents again dispersed about a mile from the runway. The abundance of grapes was obvious though again the men had to live on service rations that were distinctly boring. It was "back to Field -Technique of living". They had their own enamelled plates and "irons" on which they collected their food. This was usually meat and veg stew and after eating their ration there was the gauntlet of washing up water to be faced. This consisted of two huge vats of boiling water. They were kept boiling by pressure stoves underneath and the system was to dip your plate – or plates and irons into the first vat, this was the rough vat and if you waved them around you got rid of most of the remaining food. Rumours had it that after half an hour this had turned into the soup for the next day. The next vat was the cleaner tub and gave a finished hot plate that would dry off without much difficulty. You could be sure that no bacteria would survive this treatment, indeed it was difficult to emerge unscathed yourself. Norman Poole still believes that it was this early exposure to hot dishes that accounts for his resistance to heat and accounts for a reputation of asbestos fingers!

The Squadron were wiser in their tent dispersals these days and did not present neat rows to any passing strafing fighter. They dug slit trenches for air raid shelters and dived into them without much ceremony if they felt threatened. The occasional enemy fighter-bomber came over and one provided one of these comic moments of the war. Night flying meant that the Squadron did rest up during the day if they had been on duty. The warmth of Sicily often made men move their beds out of the tents to catch any available breeze. One of the Warrant Officer R/Os was indulging in this fashion when a Bf110 suddenly whistled over the camp firing bursts from his nose guns. W/O Burraston woke up at this, leapt out of bed stark naked, adopting the crouched position and holding his steel helmet above his head to cover it. The trouble, however, was that he was facing the wrong way with his bottom to the enemy. Roars of laughter rang out after the fighter had gone by and was not likely to risk another run. The second snag was that the field was close to Syracuse where Allied ships anchored. During dusk patrols each and every gun in that area seemed to be firing at the Beaufighters while the pilots were gaining height after take-off. The Squadron protested again and again but with the same regularity the Navy swore that they were under attack from Ju88s.

It was not until Hilken's Beaufighter returned with a 20mm Oerlikon shell embedded in his wing and after W/C Green and S/L Hughes dropped the shell on the desk of "the Sailor in Command" that the Navy reluctantly accepted the validity of aircraft recognition. They tried to make up by serving pink gin and, more importantly, a hot shower. There Des Hughes was very surprised to find out that the shell had come from the guns of a former cross-channel ferry on

A devoted echelon was the backbone of the ground organisation. Here they pose in front of one of the Beaufighters. The radar equipment is clearly visible on the wing and the nose, while the guns can be seen under the nose. This photograph apparently escaped the censor, as normally the secret AI would be "removed". The men on this photograph are: back row, l. to r.: Hooper, Lewis, Hughes, Cpl Brett and Cpl Hall. middle row , standing l/r: Cpl Hills, unknown, Twells, Cpl Bear, Stokes, Sgt Twitchet, Cpl Noakes, Farley, unknown, Flintoff, unknown, Wyles, Baker, Swabey and Cpl. Richardson. Seated, l/r are Cpl Haresign, Perry, Owens, Morgan, Cpl Williams, Sgt Wheeley, W/O Opie, F/L Clennett, Sgt Maclean, Cpl Wayne, Cpl Nunn, Horner, Stephenson, Curry and Ellis. On the ground f.l.t.r. are Watkins, unknown, Smith, Cpl Daniels, Cpl Cowan, Cooksey, Cpl Chapman, Cpl Taylor, Rosson, Winter and North.

which he had travelled many times before the war from Belfast to Liverpool and back. At Cassibile it would be so hot that ground crews had to be very careful not to touch the aircraft while working in shorts only. The Medical Officer Peter Scurlock warned the men that these burns, and the cuts, were very difficult to heal. The strip being within easy reach of the sea, most of the off duty hours were spent in the drink in the nude. This of course was no golden beach of the Mediterranean Cruise brochure, but a rocky shore, still strewn with the smashed wrecks of gliders of the airborne attack. Many of the gliders had been cast off, in an off-shore wind, by their American tug pilots, and had barely made it. Several never did. In spite of this the troops had got themselves ashore and with the Para Battalion, had captured the vital bridge at Catania, and held it, until the main force had fought its way forward to join them. This was the crux of the whole campaign, and on which its success depended. The chaps with the seaborne troops from North Africa, were those the Squadron had protected. The glider wrecks served as a constant reminder that this was no sojourn in the sun. The bush vines with their black grapes coming to a sweet ripeness saved the Squadron from the dullness of Maconochie's meat and veg. Probably they ate too many but did not suffer unduly. Norman Poole was a victim of the vines though for on one occasion he bent down rather too quickly to pick a bunch and impaled his eye on a stalk that was poking up with a small cross section that he did not see. It was very painful and left him with an entirely red eye. It even frightened off beggar children when he closed his good eye and left his awful red one peering out. He could have worn a patch over it, but needing two eyes for their radar – and looking for the opposition – it would have looked as if he was malingering, which never happened on the Squadron for it would have meant someone else would have to do his share. It was in Sicily also that the Squadron had its first experience with Italian ice cream. They had some time off and borrowed one of the Squadron lorries and went to the nearest town of Noto. All medical advice would have warned them off such a project but the ice cream was delicious and had no side effects. They had another excursion into the local economy as Americans would call it – Marsala. It came about because one of the navigators, earlier in his career had trained for the holy orders in the Catholic church and had made good contacts with the local monastery. The quantity of communion wine he could get hold of was not unlimited so it was not on general release but fortunately he and Norman Poole were good friends, making it possible for Norman to take advantage of it; it certainly made life on Sicily a bit better.

At Cassibile No.600 Squadron was to work with the newly formed 415th Night Fighter Squadron of the USAAF, one of the first units to fly the Beau. The Yanks expected a lot from the Beaufighter and with typical American zeal began to prepare for action. McKinnon and Poole went to see them to exchange gossip and were delighted to find an American friend who had enlisted in the RAF and trained with them. His name was Littlejohn and he was quite a character. In fact he was laid up with stomach trouble when the Squadron visited, as were most of his squadron. According to memories of former members the American night-fighter planes were not much of a success. They hardly succeeded in getting the Yanks off the deck after dark, and their ground crew found the Beaufighter much too complex. But the Americans had marvellous tools and extremely good equipment, and following a local lend-lease agreement, the Squadron used this stuff in good stead for the remainder of the war. Much valuable enemy equipment had been captured at this time. The hurry with which they seemed to have withdrawn helped 600 improve its equipment in a considerable manner. It included a brand new aerodrome lighting set from the Italians and an ingenious refuelling unit which had been the proud property of the Germans. The booty also consisted of a fully equipped German ambulance. Night flying facilities were much improved with the Cooking Trailer converted to a mobile Ops Room where invaluable LAC Coggings ruled as a king. It was equipped with eight channel VHF speakers, remote control flarepath, flood and funnel lights, even with the Squadron's own "private" telephone exchange. Thus with this and the mobile aerodrome lighting equipment, the Squadron was ready to take over any landing strip and start night flying immediately. It stood the men of No.600 Squadron in good stead for the remainder of their very mobile war. Once in they settled down to the task again but in slightly easier conditions. Beds were made of petrol cans and straw, under sunroofs of ground sheets and bivouacs. They were essential, as the Squadron had been neatly placed between two AA barrages. And as what goes up must come down, there was plenty of it at times. The German night attacks continued to be heavy. The peak came in the night of a savage Luftwaffe raid on Lentini, home of No.244 Wing, DAF which included No. 601 Squadron. Almost completely surrounded by grass and corn it was very vulnerable to fire, and most of it was set off by incendiaries. Ringed with fire the Spitfire Squadrons were trapped like rabbits in a harvest, but much of the final weight of this attack was fought off by the counter-blast of the Squadron aircrew. No.600 Squadron shot down five enemy raiders and damaged a sixth, enough to dampen the enthusiasm of the enemy crews. Three of these aircraft were destroyed by Hughes and Dixon within 31 minutes. Although a number of Spitfires were damaged at Lentini, casualties were few. The enemy continued its attacks on Allied airfields. The Squadron experienced a number of daylight strafings, intended to blow up the petrol dump, thus trying to rob them of its "blood". Fortunately the dump was not hit. The consequences would have been horrible. Two Squadron aircraft were now diverted from operations over Sicily to help protect the brave island. Once the enemy realised that his attacks with formations of Ju88s and He111s were too costly he began to send single Ju87 Stuka dive bombers. These were difficult aircraft to catch as they were so slow that it took considerable skill of the pilot to stay on top of them. Also the dive bombers were able to aim much better than the conventional bombers in their vertical approach to the target. The Ju87s operated alone. One Stuka would fly around within spitting distance of the strip, in the hope that the inevitable landing lights had to be used. This gave the Squadron the feeling of being the victim in that horrible dream, when caught naked in someone else's drawing room, and was very exhausting on the short hairs at the nape of the neck. With a low stalling speed, and high manoeuvrability these were hard to nail. But it could be done, as was demonstrated by S/L Hughes and F/O Dixon, who put one down off Syracuse. Thus the lessons were soon learned and the Stukas too bit the dust. The dive bombers also attracted much attention from two AA barrages, whose fire seemed to be centred over the Squadron ammunition dump. Nobody was very keen on this, especially the CO. Having acidly asked Frankie Yates if he was losing his nerve, when he found him building a shelter out of rock, in which to sleep, he forthwith instructed W/O Topping to have one built for him as well, for his limited sleeping hours. To recruit volunteer labour for this task was impossible, so Topping nailed four unfortunate bods for not having had a proper hair cut. Consequently they got an extra duty, exactly: to build a shelter of rock for the Boss. Yet it should be said that the ground crews did exceptionally well in keeping sufficient aircraft flying. Out of an establishment of sixteen aircraft and an actual strength of twenty, a minimum of twelve were needed every night, so the ground types were hard put to finish servicing one aircraft before another was due for inspection. Furthermore the aircraft were too hot to touch in the afternoon so that work had to be carried out in the mornings and evenings, and also the strength of the ground staff was much depleted by that dreaded "Malta Dog", which continued to harass the men. During the night of 11th August the Luftwaffe tried one of its attacks, this time mainly with incendiaries against the airfield of Gerbini, near Catania. Hughes and Dixon happened to be on patrol that night. Ably guided by GCI they got three Ju88s. When they followed the fourth one into the Allied AA zone Hughes had to make a quick retreat for he was getting all the shells that were intended for the enemy. W/C Green got another Ju88, Johnny Turnbull got two and Mellersh got one as well. Nights with No.600 Squadron in the sky proved costly for the Luftwaffe. P/O Thompson was awarded a DFC, while Desmond Hughes received a Bar to his DFC. AVM Harry Broadhurst flew in to present F/L Hanus with a DFC and AM Coningham went on Ops with the CO

Open all day; a Squadron Beaufighter gets a major overhaul.

to see for himself why "600" was such a successful bunch. Luckily for the Air Marshal no enemy aircraft ventured up that night.

When the Squadron was made responsible for the night safety of the whole island of Sicily it had to split up into detachments again. Though some problems of servicing and administration occurred, the men pressed on as usual, with Downing and Lyons shooting down a pair of Ju88s. The 99th and 100th confirmed kills were registered by DFMs to both F/S Downing and Lyons, crowning their achievements. The occasion called for a group photograph and fortunately no one interfered, otherwise there would have been a mad scramble for the nearest slit trench. Though some die-hards compared the summer days of 1940, this period of Malta and Sicily, with its great obligations and duty, must rank as the most concentrated and intensive of the war. Poole had an interesting experience while flying with Togs Mellersh whose R/O was sick. They were patrolling off the East coast and there they had a useful landmark in the shape of Mount Etna rumbling away. It had become more active recently and the story was that someone had dropped bombs in the crater to stir things up a bit. However that may be, it could be seen from many miles away and it was a useful station keeper. On this occasion they were directed to a bandit and they found themselves well above him. They again had to use the "high/low" technique of interception. It required a series of S turns to lose height without gaining too much speed and overshooting the customer. They got a visual on a Ju88 having dropped below it to get an easier visual contrast against the sky. Togs opened up and the formidable armament blew it to pieces at short range. It was not a nice sight and Mellersh was close enough to collect a number of fragments in the engine nacelles, fortunately without doing any serious damage.

At about this time, far away from Italy, a former Auxiliary of No.600 Squadron who joined in 1934 as "800.360 AC Riseley, Rufus", now a pilot and a Flying Officer, had quite different problems to cope with. With his crew he had taken part in a raid against the railway repair yard at Valenciennes. His aircraft had been shot up very badly, some of his crew members were wounded and there was little or no chance that he would make it home. He therefore decided to force-land in a field. At broad daylight he put his bomber down. He then turned his RAF tunic inside out and set off to find friendly people to help his crew. After arranging for the care of his

companions, he struck out to make his way back to England. Risely
would have been passed along the Escape line organised by the
French, had he not heard the unlikely tale of a Gestapo official
named Weiler, who seemed to be willing to change sides and help
the Allies. Taking a serious risk Risely met the German through the
Resistance and accompanied by Weiler in his official car he toured
the area along the coast where German installations were plentiful.
All the information was passed on to England. Then rumours were
heard of highly secret activities near Saint Pol. Dressed as a labourer
Riseley and two Frenchmen managed to infiltrate and found the new
launching ramps for the German V1s. Once this intelligence reached
England Riseley was taken out of France in a fishing boat, his secrets
stuffed in a French loaf of bread. Another former No.600 Squadron
member had given an essential contribution to the war against the
Nazis.

Over and over again the tremendous value of skilled technical
echelons was obvious. The CO fully trusted the skill and devotion
of the ground crews to the aircraft and the crews flying it had the
highest opinion about the men who were sweating during the day
and shivering during the night to keep the Beaufighters ready for
action. A typical event happened when a Beaufighter had developed
hydraulic trouble. Laurie Williams and another mechanic had
worked into the night exchanging the master control valve. They
were well satisfied, but as the CO was off for the night, they had
wrapped it up for an air test in daylight. In the small hours, the
Engineer Officer F/L Clennet, called them out to verify it was serviceable and would fly. During the night, HMS battleship Warspite was
hit off Stromboli, and we were ordered to provide cover until dawn,
while she made it back to port. The CO nominated himself for the
task and while lesser men would have shunned "F", pending a
daylight air test, the boss took it straight off, and maintained a patrol
until daylight, without question or fuss. It typified No.600 Squadron,
the leadership and example of the Commanding Officer on one
hand, and the trust in the standard of the individuals he commanded
on the other. How the Squadron fulfilled their duty can best be
judged from their records. In thirty-one nights between 10th July and
10th August 1943 No.600 Squadron flew no less than 1000 operational hours, destroying more than forty enemy aircraft. Many
German aircraft had fallen for the Beaufighters of the Gentlemen in
Blue. But as "machine was fighting machine" the crews seldom saw

anything of the results of their nightly endeavours. It was a rare occasion, therefore, when on 15th August a bewildered German Sergeant was marched into the mess by the Squadron Intelligence Officer. The poor chap was a Flight Engineer, now a POW, and a crewmember of the Ju88 which Mellersh and Poole had bagged on 10th August. He said he had been saved by a Motor Torpedo Boat after floating in the Med in his Mae West for 32 hours. He had been supported by it to a large degree but the raw bruising on his arms where his life jacket ended showed that the chap had done an awful lot of swimming to stay alive. The crews expected more resentment about the fate of his fellow crew members but after he had explained their system it was easier to understand. It seemed they did not allow crews to stay together but mixed them – perhaps as a way of checking up on their performance? He said that he had over 90 missions to his credit and had been crewed with inexperienced crew members. He also said that he warned his pilot that something was on their tail.

It cannot be denied that there was some kind of longing for London. For this reason City street names were used. Here Paddy Green pays a visit to a tenant at "Old Street".

The German pilot replied: "What do you say?" and took no evasive action at all. The only reply for this Luftwaffe engineer was a quick departure by parachute. Since the Intelligence Officer had briefed the 600 crews to maintain a friendly atmosphere because they were anxious to find out how much coverage the German rear warning radar gave, the discussion got the aircrew to gossip about this and that. It made the German feel at ease and as he was regularly provided with a drink. In the Operations Record Book the diarist noted: "After that the chap became rather talkative." With the Intelligence Officer as interpreter they casually walked the prisoner to one of the Beaufighters and then took him for lunch. During this lunch they got the answer to their question – 30 degrees. It helped the Squadron and many others because while adopting the high/low approach technique it meant staying outside the 30 degree cone until as late as possible, hoping to get a visual on the target and spending the minimum time in the cone before firing. They parted friends and they even got him to sign McKinnon and Poole's logbooks, something of a rarity to have such confirmation of a success. At this time the Jerry still felt sure that Germany would win the war. The chaps of 600 politely disagreed, but let him have that small satisfaction. The only Squadron member with a totally different idea of entertaining the German was the Czech Joe Hanus, who was quite willing to make the prisoner pay for what had happened to his country in 1938 and who had to be restrained and kept from rushing into the mess and shooting the German prisoner on the spot. Paddy Green had Hanus marched out and gave strict orders for him to stay at least 500 yards from the mess.

Life was not only fun. On 17th August a horrified Squadron watched helplessly when a No.23 Squadron Mosquito crashed at Cassibile. It was not possible to save the crew. They both perished in the flames, a grim reminder of what war was like. During the night of 29th/30th August the Luftwaffe tried a last attack against Sicily. About 60 bombers came over, He111s, Ju88s and Ju87s. At first the Squadron was caught napping for they were used to higher speeds and they overshot their customers by tens of miles an hour. The Ju87s were cruising below the stalling speed of the Beaufighter, so apart from frightening Germans the Beaufighters at such critical slow speeds could do almost nothing although the pilots blasted their guns away hoping for a lucky hit. The Squadron watched from the

ground how five Ju87s were shot down by ack-ack before the rest
turned tail and rushed back to the mainland. As August 1943 moved
on, the ground battle reached its conclusion. The capture of Palermo
was matched by the squeezing out of the enemy towards the Straits
of Messina and ultimately into the toe of Italy. Diplomatic activity
had been intense and resulted in Italy suing for peace and leaving
the Germans to fight on their own – which effectively they had been
doing for some time as the Italians had no real enthusiasm for
warfare. As for the Squadron the Italian capitulation was fascinating
for they flew the first night patrol over the Salerno beaches on 3rd
September 1943. They took off from base at 2320hrs and were over
the target area just after midnight. It was an extraordinary scene for
Mac and Poole for the lights were on in Italy, something wartime
flyers had never experienced before, because the blackout was very
effective in England and indeed in the Mediterranean battle areas
the Squadron had flown over. There was no enemy air activity in
the area and the Germans were too busy filling the gap the Italian
cease-fire had opened. When McKinnon and Poole returned to
Cassibile in the early hours of the morning they were met by a deputation of the press who wanted to know what was happening in
Italy. They were first back and duly reported: The lights are on. Now
preparations were made for the move for which the Squadron had
already been warned, to join the invasion of the Italian mainland at
Salerno.

The Battle Honour on the Standard – Sicily 1943 – was hard fought
for and fairly won by all. And, the whole Squadron shared the pride.
It had been a campaign of great achievement and very little losses.
When the Sicily brush was over, the Squadron score for that part
of the campaign was: Destroyed – 42; Probably destroyed -1;
Damaged – 3. The total score for the war had risen to: Destroyed –
100; Probables – 10; Damaged – 17.

The Merchant Taylors Company presented pewter tankards to the Squadron. The Rt.Hon. Sir Archibald Sinclair, BT, KT,CMG, Secretary of State for Air and the Honorary Air Commodore of the Squadron, received the tankards on behalf of the Squadron.

CHAPTER 11

GOING NORTH THROUGH ITALY.
September 1943 to August 1945

The Allied advance onto the Italian mainland had been anticipated for some time. Three separate landings had been planned. The first, "Baytown", on 3rd September, under command of General Montgomery, intended to land troops in the area of Reggio di Calabria. After secret negotiations Italy surrendered on 3rd September and while the invasion fleet headed for the beaches the troops were told that from now on the Italians were Allies. It looked as if the operation to liberate Italy would be a piece of cake. Things turned out to be quite different. Stiff German opposition and mistakes within the Allied command, made it a costly and hard fought campaign. German troops under Luftmarshall Albert Kesselring occupied Rome and disarmed the Italians. Five days later No.600 Squadron began to cover the Salerno invasion beaches, over 200 miles away. The Squadron's job for the early days of September was to provide air cover for the invasion fleet at night. This involved patrols of over four hours. There was no ground radar to guide the crews so they acted independently using their own limited radar cover. At least the crews knew where the fleet was and if the enemy was going to do them any harm they would have to fly over them so the Beaufighter crews had some idea of the combat area. Of course these days one would expect to be able to talk to the ships and get battle information from them where possible but naturally they preserved radio silence and took a suspicious view. This meant that – as usual – the Navy would happily release as much ack-ack as possible and direct it at the Beaufighters. Being used to this the crews kept away from the Navy as far as possible. The Squadron shot down three enemy bombers during the first night and then exacted a steady toll thereafter. The patrols were full of interest as the crews could see battles raging below. Exciting interceptions of enemy aircraft were made, often resulting in a magnificent display of fireworks right over the ground crews' heads. There had been the sight of concentrated fireworks from the warships lying off Syracuse harbour and land-based AA guns as the Beaufighters took off or returned after a long and tiring patrol. The fighting at Salerno was probably more fierce and lethal than they had ever witnessed. Squadron achievements both in the sky and on the ground were marvellous, from the aircrew who shot down four enemy aircraft in one sortie, to the ground crew who changed a main wheel in seven minutes during the same night. Two more landings followed a week later. "Slapstick" and "Avalanche", on 9th September, took strong forces to Torente and the Gulf of Gaeta, north of Naples. During the week separating the invasion of Italy across the Messina Straits by 8th Army, and that of 5th Army at Salerno, no air opposition at night was encountered. It was a long way from Cassibile to the Bay of Salerno and the crews could only stay on station for about two hours. On 8th September 600 Squadron started operations from Milazzo on the Northern coast of Sicily. It was about 30 minutes by air from Cassibile and the crews used it to check the aircraft and their radars before they moved to their war zone. Milazzo airfield was exciting, a strip cut through the olive groves, the runway pierced steel planking and as there was no room for dispersal as the sea was on one side and the hills on the other the Squadron only had the side of the runway to park the aircraft. They all prayed for no tyre burst on landing! Flying conditions too were hazardous. Being on the coast Milazzo often disappeared under a very low cloud base. Electrical power depended on auxiliary petrol-driven generators which were unreliable enough to cause 600 to provide a permanent standby facility – a can of sand filled with petrol at the end of the runway. Any trouble with the lights and the runway controller torched off the petrol flare to give the aircrews something to aim at on take-off. The use of spaced out paraffin flares was ruled out as it did reveal the airfield and it was not possible to switch the paraffin flare path on and off. Fortunately by this time the Squadron consisted of experienced pilots who had flown in this theatre for quite some time.

Their task, however, was to be over soon, as the war moved further north on the Italian mainland. On 11th September Salerno was occupied after bitter fighting. One day later SS-Colonel Skorzeny liberated Mussolini, a prisoner of his own people, from the Spa Hotel in Gran Sasso, where a small group of Carabinieri were supposed to guard him. Once "free", or rather under German control the Duce declared the "Republic of Salo". From that moment the former ally became a puppet of Hitler. Retreating Germans set fire to the town of Naples and it was not until the end of the month that the Allies broke through the German lines north-east of that town. In fact it took more than three weeks before the Italian mainland was considered safe enough for No.600 to leave Sicily and head for a new base. At the same time the aircrews kept on knocking German aircraft out of the sky.

It was a particularly beautiful part of Sicily as the hills behind the airfield rose gradually towards Etna and the colours, particularly in the evening, were an artists dream. No wonder they flocked to that part of the world. The Squadron had other visual treats in that part of the world because the island volcano of Stromboli lay on the route to Salerno. It was a useful landmark. At Milazzo Poole came across the less inviting side of war when having a walk round the airfield before he went on night readiness having flown from Cassibile

After the surrender many aircraft of the Italian air force and navy landed on Allied fields, as had been agreed in the Armistice. It was hoped to keep as many aircraft as possible out of the hands of the Germans. Some Italian aircraft fought alongside the Allies in the Balkan Air Force. Here a SM79 bomber is being investigated by Allied soldiers, while No.600 Beaufighter "Z" stands near.

earlier that day. He was stopped by an Italian girl with a baby who claimed she had no milk for her child. This was understandable as the country was in chaos and all administration had broken down. She made it plain that she was offering herself for some milk for her baby. In retrospect Group Captain Poole wonders if she may have been earning a living this way, but in those days the young man felt sorry for this young and very pretty girl. He confessed he did not have any milk and that he could not solve the baby's problem. However, he had some chocolate from his flying rations and handed it all over to her hoping she might be able to swap the chocolate for something more useful for her baby. The incident gave Norman Poole an insight on what happened to Italian society when the system of order broke down and he thanked God it had not happened in Britain.

Meanwhile things at Salerno were not easy. The troops were ashore but instead of being welcomed by cheering Italians they were bitterly opposed by the Germans who had taken over completely. The fleet was anchored in the Bay of Naples and were being attacked by what little remained of the Luftwaffe in Italy. The Squadron carried out its protective role and added one enemy aircraft to their tally. They now had mobile radar stations ashore and these helped to locate the targets, although in some cases the Beaufighter crews spent a lot of time intercepting friendly aircraft. The system of Identification Friend or Foe (IFF) was not totally reliable and often Allied aircraft did not switch the IFF on thinking it might indicate their position to the enemy. Another problem was the sudden participation of former Italian Air Force aircraft now on the Allied side. As another part of the IAF had stuck to their old masters from Berlin the problem of knowing who was who really became a serious one. The Navy did its best to protect the ground troops ashore by shelling the Italian countryside. It was quite fascinating to see the huge shells, probably 15", curving high in the air and then plunging down on enemy targets. The crews could see them because they glowed red hot as they flew through the air. The men in the Beaufighters did not know whether it was their speed of flight or the initial push from the gun barrel. They only felt grateful to see where they went and made sure to stay away.

It was during the days of the introduction of deadly German FX1400 gliding bombs that a lot of trouble occurred. On 11th September one of these horrors, launched by a Do217 bomber flying at about 18000ft, landed on the American cruiser Savannah, which had to be withdrawn from action. Little did the Germans know that the Allied Commander in Chief General Mark Clark and his staff were on board Ancon, a few hundred yards from Savannah. Escorted by four destroyers Savannah limped to Malta. It caught the eye of the press and the RAF PR people understood the value of mentioning the Squadron in their press releases, such as that of 13th September 1943, which read: "RAF night-fighters continued their vigilant patrols over Allied shipping in the Gulf of Salerno on the night of September 11th/12th destroying two Ju88s. Both were shot down in sight of our forces. These victories were scored by the same crew that shot down a Junkers Ju88 the previous night, and this latest success maintained the Squadron's average of two destroyed per night for four consecutive nights. The pilot, F/O Paton, of Oxford and his observer P/O J.W. McAnulty, 26 Montague Road, London, E8, had now four victories to their credit. "The Jerries were after shipping in the Bay of Salerno", said Paton. "I only saw three or four flares at the time and no bombs dropped, so their effort couldn't have been very determined. The first one we chased for about ten minutes. He weaved

B-Flight ground crew working on one of the cannons of a Beaufighter. Note the AI aerial on the nose and the aerial on the starboard wing root.

about trying to evade us, but the first burst set the port engine on fire. I saw three of the crew bale out. The Ju88 then burst into flames and hit the ground about three miles inland. The other one was intercepted outside the flares. He saw us, but not quick enough. A short burst resulted in the Ju88 exploding in the air. I think the starboard wing fell off as it spun down very quickly into the sea, where it burnt for about 30 minutes".

At the same time General Montgomery's Eighth Army was to land at Taranto on the heel of Italy. After a delay of some hours during which final orders were received and given the Squadron ground party was safely on board a US Navy landing craft. Soon the men were on their way accompanied by an armada under Navy escort. This was the ground staff's fourth move across the water and the shortest one. They had been among the first in the North African landings and at the end of that campaign had migrated to Malta. Re-arming, re-equipping and getting themselves in trim for the final fling at the mainland of Italy they had really softened up the island they were now leaving behind. While confined to the restricted space afforded on these landing craft there was nothing much one could do other than look back on their travels and stopping places prior to the new adventure and whatever was now in store. The ground party was confident of success. Crossing the Messina Straits was pleasant with a calm sea and for most of the time no interference from the enemy who seemed to have called a halt to allow the Squadron to rest a bit. The pilots and radar operators had already patrolled the area which No.600 Squadron would soon occupy, in particular that of Monte Corvino airfield. It had been bombed and strafed mercilessly in an effort to keep German aircraft on the deck and destroy them. After each patrol crews had returned with encouraging news of their encounters, but they had also been told about the strong coastal defences which the Royal Navy was already in the process of softening up. In spite of the knowledge that the landing area was overlooked by a range from which German observation posts had a commanding view, the Squadron expected to get in fairly comfortably under the additional protection of a concentrated umbrella of RAF Spitfires. Under the very noses of the enemy the Allied forces landed at the shallow beaches at points between Sorrento and Salerno.

It was decided that a Squadron advance party should be included with the invading army troops. F/L Raleigh Hilken was chosen to head this contingent of 10 vehicles with 52 airmen who were fully armed with sten gten guns and ammunition as well as carrying the tools of their trade. The intention was for them to fight their way forward to the airfield of Monte Corvino, muster petrol and ammunition and prepare the airfield to receive the Squadron's Beaufighters. The time scale was for them to reach the airfield at D+2. However, there was very strong opposition from the German forces. First of all the British army Sappers had to clear mines, booby traps and other obstacles on the beach and lay out well defined landing strips, colour-coded to facilitate landing organisation. All this was done under heavy fire from the Germany artillery located on the hills outside Salerno from which the landing beaches could be observed. According to Chantrey, the ground party landed at Blue Beach, though DeVroome said it was Red Beach not far from Sorrento. Men and vehicles proceeded at speed up the beach, taking such cover as they could among the shrubbery and other vegetation, whilst the Navy and the Army were winkling out the remaining opposition including the airfield which was to become the Squadron's base until the enemy had been driven up the road that led to Naples. It was a great feeling to land on the Italian mainland.

There was the sight of many ships disgorging thousands of troops and equipment and no-one taking much notice of the few enemy aircraft which got through or the odd shell lobbed by the coastal defences occasionally hitting a ship with little damage or loss of life. Very slowly the Advance Party pushed its way up the road in the direction of Monte Corvino, but progress was at a snail's pace due to the opposition of the Germans making counter-attacks preceded by heavy gunfire.

Luftmarshall Kesselring had put a lot of 88s in the hills and these guns caused the Allies great problems. The deadly rocket launchers, or "Minnies", were so accurate that according to "Dev" Devroome "they could pop a mortar bomb in your mess tin without touching the sides". The Squadron ground party pushed on and all went well until they came to a standstill. In fact many other units had not yet moved from the beaches. The Germans seemed to muster more opposition and skirmishes between the two forces were going on all around. This meant that the ground party was unable to occupy the airfield and prepare it for use by the Beaufighters. No less than three times the aerodrome changed hands – the first time just in time to see enemy tanks approaching from the other side, and the second

Seated on the tailplane of a Messerschmitt Bf110 from left to right W/C Paddy Green DSO, DFC, P/O Watson, F/O Armstrong, F/O Paton and F/O McAnulty.

time occupying front row seats in an irrigation ditch immediately below the release point of some P38 Lightnings which were low level skip bombing enemy occupied buildings on the drome. For a while things became so bad that the advance party and air force personnel were put directly under army command. So now the almost forgotten skills learned at the period of commando training at Church Fenton came to good use. Frankly, with some trepidation the men were face to face with reality and after the initial shock which all airmen experience when suddenly turned into foot-soldiers, they convinced themselves that with Stens and extra ammunition they were able to add something to the records. After heavy and costly fighting the field was finally taken on D+8 and the Squadron was in business. One of the tasks of the Squadron aircraft was to escort HMS Warspite from the battle zone after the battleship had also been hit by a gliding bomb, this time dropped by a FW190. A Beaufighter of 600 provided top cover while Warspite sailed south, away from the battle. In appreciation the Navy never fired a shot at the Squadron aircraft.

It took the Allies some time to gain a reasonable size bridgehead to allow airfields to be bulldozed out of the flat plain inland from the Bay of Salerno. They were helped by the 8th Army advancing from the Straits of Messina. No.600 Squadron, with its advance party in the middle of the fighting, received a bit of disturbing news when it became known that instead of essential equipment the Squadron Band's instruments had been taken ashore. Of course these were not calculated to frighten the enemy, though some former members claim that the sound made by some of the members of the band could very well make the Germans believe that a deadly and sophisticated weapon was being used against them. It was another reason to give full support to the ground staff fighting as infantry at the landing sites. The route to Salerno was marked by the perpetual beacon of Stromboli volcano and often as the Beaus arrived on the beachhead they were greeted by the shells of American AA-guns. During D-Day itself they found at least some customers. During the first night at Salerno things were a bit livelier. Owing to R/T failure on the GCI/LST "Flame-tree", the Beaus freelanced over the beach-head, and obtained contacts on a number of aircraft. These were mainly friendly, but three of them were not. They were Ju88s and soon the Luftwaffe was to know what it was to meet "600" again. The Ju88s were shot down, the first by F/L Turnbull and his Nav/RO Fowler, the other two by "Ace" Downing and Lyons. This third Ju88 had the questionable honour of being the 100th enemy aircraft destroyed.

During the operations R/Os experienced some difficulty with the sets, and it was soon established that this was due to the first positive dropping of "Window" by enemy rather than Allied aircraft. An AI transponder beacon was set up on the beachhead, and by the time the main Squadron party arrived on 26th September 1943, no less than twelve Ju88s, three He111s and one Do 217 had been shot down: two by Turnbull, three by Downing, four by Newhouse, three by Paton and one each by Bates, Harrup, Young and Joe Hanus, the Czech. In this they were assisted by their R/Os Fowler, McAnulty, Tate, Lyons, Palfrey, Redmond, Finlay and Armstrong. No.600 Squadron lost one aircraft. Fortunately the crew were saved. Hughes remembered vividly how he arrived at Monte Corvino, being the first Beaufighter pilot to make a voluntary landing on the mainland of Europe. Raleigh Hilken welcomed him. He told Desmond about the days when Tiger tanks made nightly forays into the Allied lines.

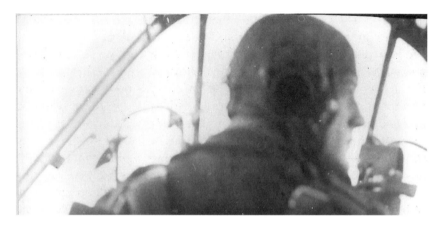

Standing behind his pilot Norman Poole took this photograph of McKinnon, who is scanning the skies for "customers".

The main Squadron party received their orders to move from Cassibile on the afternoon of the 29th September 1943. They were to move off at dawn on the following day. They had done this kind of drill before but it remained a sizeable task with 16 aircraft and 350 men, all their equipment plus the odd pieces of equipment previously used by the opposition. It called for a sustained effort working right through the night, aircraft to be serviced and kept fully operational and all transport to be checked and loaded. However, all was ready on time. The ground party set off for Catania on the north-east coast of Sicily where they embarked with their equipment and vehicles for the voyage to the Italian mainland. The actual destination on the mainland was not disclosed. The other troops landed with the Squadron were mainly Americans as it was their operation.

The Squadron was told that the Bay of Salerno was their objective and that they were one of the ten RAF Squadrons and some British Army units which were to be attached to the US Fifth Army with Royal Navy support to add a little backbone to the effort.

Once the airfield of Monte Corvino was firmly in the hands of the Allied forces, the Squadron prepared it for action. A camp was quickly set up. It was not an ideal place but the orange trees gave some cover, though the tomato plants beneath them were a real problem. In the end it was decided that the only course was to lay ground sheets on top of the plants, pitch the bivvies and crawl in for a little rest. The airfield itself was in a very poor state. The nearness of war was very evident. It was full of bomb craters and shell holes, quickly filled in. In fact it was the first time the Squadron saw the casualties of war. Soldiers lying where they fell, in most cases the shallow grave that had been their slit trench of protection Over the next days the area would be organised by burial parties but for the moment they were marked by a cross and the occasional identity disk over the cross. There was still fierce fighting going on and the first night enemy infantry patrols penetrated as far as the edge of the airfield before being repelled. The Sappers came to clear the mines while the Squadron ground crews began to make paths and roads and set up the larger tents for stores, messing and administration. During the lull in the battle W/O Topping and Sgt Spink organised a first class camp, and everyone was in the lap of luxury. Tent lines were built in the orange groves. In the end all was so well organised that the Company of Sign Writers under Cpl Redding – known as the City Sign Ltd – had all the tracks and paths signposted with names of London City roads and streets. Bed boards were found for everyone. "Banjo fires" and other rather ominous heating appliances were built by local initiative and the electricians even managed to install a lighting system in every tent. The airfield was ready and safe to be used and soon after the aircraft arrived they resumed their patrols for British 8th and American 5th Army. Then the weather deteriorated and soon the rain and mud made the field virtually unserviceable. Sunny Italy turned out to be a very muddy place. The pierced steel planking which the Americans had introduced served the Squadron well. The slipstream of aircraft would easily and quickly erode the ground, usually rolled earth, but with this invention the pilots could easily taxi to the points of their take off. Yet the Squadron ground crew had to work very hard to keep up the high standard of efficiency. In spite of the aircraft sometimes sinking to their engine nacelles in the mud, patrols were maintained over Naples from Monte Corvino and over Brindisi by a unit at Bari, led by W/O Nelson. As a stop gap Sgts Chantrey and Devroome took a group to Gando, continuing the operations by night. However, for a month there was no enemy opposition, until the Luftwaffe tried its luck on 24th October. Watson and Paton both got a Ju88.

When things quietened down a bit the men explored the local area and found that Monte Corvino was only a small village in the hills behind the bay of Salerno. The nearest town was Batapaglia and it had suffered intense bombing on the theory it was a communications centre and in fact the North-South railway line did run through the town. The Squadron turned devastation to their advantage by collecting the railway station restaurant bar and transporting it to the Officers' Mess marquee where it added a distinct touch of class to the canvas of the Gentlemen in Blue. It should be pointed out here that the Town Marshal had given written permission to save the bar from possible destruction by German aircraft or other vicious means. Besides all agreed that it would take a while before a regular train service would start again. The Italian population were slowly drifting back and showing all the signs of a defeated and downcast nation. They had not wanted to go to war and current events confirmed their forebodings. Their sudden status as "Co-Belligerents" gave them some respect but all they really wanted was for the war to come to an end, for there were real problems. First and foremost it was almost impossible to get food. Norman Poole once entered a house in the town of Salerno and found the people sitting around their evening meal – chestnuts. Poole was looking for material to improve the appearance of the mess marquee tent and the trail led to this address. The man in the house took Poole to a clothing factory which still had some stock. If paid for by some tins of canned food anything was available in those days. One of the more enterprising New Zealand pilots obtained a beautiful BMW bike for himself this way, driving it with all the Wehrmacht signs and plates on it. A new thing in the life of the Squadron was silence. There was a lull in the battle and the noise of barrages had ceased after the capture of Naples and the Germans' further retreat to the North. Somewhat further was a hill with a Monastery on it, called Monte Cassino; it looked a nice place to visit in the near future.

On 30th September Des Hughes flew his last operational sortie with the Squadron. Then he suddenly succumbed to a two-prong attack by malaria and jaundice. He was rapidly moved through Base Sick Quarters, the former Married Quarters of the Italian Air Force, and then was taken to the Army General Hospital in Salerno. He was very ill with a temperature of over 106 degrees. After he was considered well enough to be transported Hughes was taken to one of the luxury hotels of Sorrento for convalescence. The Italian cooks worked miracles from Army rations and there were glorious wines and liqueurs which had previously been hidden from the Germans. Life was quite wonderful. Having flown continuously since the days

of the Defiants of No.264 Squadron in June 1940, He was declared
tour-expired and sent home for Christmas 1943. Des, who was to
end his career as Commandant, RAF College Cranwell, wrote about
his time in 600 Squadron: "I took with me, needless to say, endur-
ing impressions of my nine months with the "Gallant 600". The
inspiring leadership of Paddy Green. The trust and tolerance of my
navigator Laurie Dixon as fatigue and approaching illness shortened
my temper. The skill and devotion of the ground crew. The high
level of experience of the aircrews which took a considerable load
off the Flight Commanders' backs. Warrant Officer Neill, our chief
armourer, with his revolver slung low on his hip "High Noon" style.
Ritchie, our Canadian radar officer and gin rummy ace, who flew
very successful operational sorties as a navigator, though not
officially aircrew, and won a DFC. The skilful and sensitive Doc
Scurlock who, unlike me, knew at a glance that the victims of a
crash at Bone who were showing signs of life were past his help,
and that those apparently dead would survive. The NCO crew who
survived a night crash landing in a forest near Cassibile with just
cuts and a badly sprained ankle between them. The Czech pilot, Joe
Hanus, who wept with frustration when he obtained a visual on a
Ju88 in the moonlight but could not catch it. The mystery of the
phantom light which we and No.73 Squadron encountered on the
enemy side of the lines, looking like a red-hot exhaust but producing no echo on radar AI or CGI. And, most of all, the 100 plus enemy
aircraft destroyed for the loss of just one pilot and two navigators
killed. After so long it is not easy to pick any one incident for
detailed account. Rather is it better to set out one or two lasting
impressions which jump readily to the memory. 600 Squadron operated in conditions varying from the snow of Setif and the mud of
Souk-el-Khemis to the searing heat of Sicily and the thunderstorms
of Italy. One remembers with affection the model tented camp at
Setif, the station dispersal at Souk-el-Khemis, the mosquito and fly
plague at Bone, the stone buildings and petrol can blast bays of
Malta, the vineyard in Sicily and the orange grove at Salerno. On
the flying side there were grim early days at Maison Blanche, when
the aircraft flown out from the United Kingdom without their AI
radar equipment and useless as night-fighters, suffered damage and
destruction whilst groundborne during enemy night raids. One
remembers the period when we reckoned we were just keeping
pace with the enemy production of Piaggio 108 four-engined

bombers, and Ace Downing's dawn action in which he shot five Ju52's into the sea – and had his own aircraft damaged by a type who hung out of a window firing a tommygun. Then followed extremely well-planned enemy attacks on Bone, which were difficult to combat, and then that fantastic first week of the assault on Sicily, when the Squadron "notched" 25 kills, seven by the CO W/C Green and his navigator F/L Gillies (including four in one sortie), and six by F/L Turnbull and F/S Fowler – nor will one ever forget the cheers of the ground crews when Turnbull got a perfect "flamer" right over the camp at Cassibile. Outstanding was the GCI control by S/L Brown and others, such as that which presented myself and Laurie Dixon with three Ju88s during a night attack with incendiaries on the day fighter airfield near Catania, and F/Ls Newhouse and Tate with a similar bag over the Salerno beaches. *But most of all, perhaps, one remembers the terrific morale and devotion to duty of the ground crews, and their amazing powers of improvisation under working conditions which were at times quite appalling. The spoils of war were there for the taking but, without their untiring efforts, the story of 600's Mediterranean journey would have been quite different".*

Desmond Hughes went, and took his R/O Laurie Dixon with him. They stayed together and joined No.604 Squadron continuing to shoot down German aircraft, the last one, a Junkers 88, in January 1945 over Barendrecht, home town of the author of this book.

General Mark Clark's 5th Army were in the battle and the Squadron did not waste time in forging good relations with the Yanks. The Squadron had a great bargaining valuable -whisky- and the Americans had delicious canned food. The Squadron got an enormous quantity of tinned pineapples, peaches and so on for just a couple of bottles of whisky and all parties were perfectly happy. Norman Poole said the chaps of 600 made the conversion to Italian wines much easier than the Americans so the British could afford to sacrifice their spirits. They had an efficient and enthusiastic team of wine samplers to keep the mess stocks high and one memorable triumph was a white wine they found at Amalfi. Perhaps the chaps had been ill-served in the past with some of the wines, but this particular wine become known as the "600-non-hangover" wine. Poole does not remember the name but once 600 established contact with this godly wine they drank nothing else. The Americans provided other benefits too as one of the Squadron aircrew was to find out after bailing out from the Beau and landing south of Salerno. He was taken to an American field hospital for a check-up and kept in for the night. A feature of the US Army was that they allowed female nurses much nearer the battle area. It worked to the advantage and pleasant surprise of this member. After lights out, when the ward was sound asleep, one of the American nurses invited herself into his bed on the reasoning that he was the only patient fit enough for her. Apparently he was!!

The Squadron kept up the night patrols while the army was bringing the port of Naples into service again. Ground radar stations had been established on the Island of Ischia and it helped the Squadron efforts tremendously. The Allied progress across the whole width of Italy had increased the defensive duties and they not only defended their Naples area but also operated small detachments across Italy to Bari and Brindisi. They were not always successful as the bombing of an ammunition supply ship in the harbour of Bari by the Germans proved. They also defended the central area of Foggia where a large number of bomber squadrons were based. Foggia Main, which the Squadron used, was home of some SAAF Mitchell bomber squadrons. It was also home to South African Brandy which the chaps of the Squadron thought was very acceptable and quite available. One of the main reasons why there was a decrease of activity was the weather. Winter was approaching again and the change of the season was very dramatic in Italy with a lot of thunderstorms and turbulence. This particularly hampered the Luftwaffe as they did not have the same sophisticated radar support and still needed good visibility for accurate bombing.

By the end of 1943 a spectacular event took place at Monte Corvino. The day was chilly and damp, the blazing Italian summer was forgotten. No.600 were beginning to settle down to what turned out to be a miserably wet winter, which sometimes was very cold indeed. The craters that had been filled up after the airfield had been captured now turned into soft mud puddles and the men had to work very hard to de-bog the aircraft. The Germans lent a helping hand. After they vacated the field they had been forced to leave a lot of equipment behind. Huge inflatable rubber bags came in very useful for getting aircraft of the Squadron out of its "swamp predicament". The general idea was to clear the ground under the wings as near to the undercarriage as possible. Then the bags were pushed under and inflated, a very tedious job as the only things available were bicycle pumps. However the men succeeded eventually in getting a compressor from somewhere and as the bag was filled with air raising the Beau inch by inch the ground under the undercarriage would be filled with hard core and if they were lucky the aircraft would be pushed or pulled to firmer ground. A German aircraft, the Me410, was successful at night. The Luftwaffe used very clever tactics to operate this new aircraft. It would fly with an older type, that looked almost the same, the Me210. The Me210 would act as a decoy and get itself picked up on the radar of the pursuing Beaufighter. As soon as the chase was on, the Me410 with its greater speed would close up on the rear of the Beaufighter, which could not scan backwards. The rest was relatively easy. A completely surprised Beaufighter crew would fail to return from operations, not knowing what had hit them. That particular day all hands were busy about the place after the night's operation, preparing for the next night's shift. This consisted of forward area patrols and "rhubarbs". Daily inspections were carried out, oil filters dropped for the never ending search for white metal. Petrol filters were cleaned and lighters topped up. It was all part of the normal service given by a top rate firm. Riggers were busy pulling ailerons, elevators and rudders upwards, downwards and sideways as appropriate. Here and there one who had just tested the tyre pressures in the manner of the expert, but without perhaps the same precision, could be seen limping around. There was the all-pervading hum and buzz of aircraft running up and taking off and most of the ground crews could identify in flight by sound and so it was realised that there was a stranger about. Sgt Chantrey told this amazing story: "It turned out to be an Me410 flying low with its German markings clearly visible. I stood there in amazement for a second or two, pointing it out to my nearby colleagues. Then I proceeded at the double to the nearest American airfield defence AA unit. They had not spotted it. Anyhow, by then it had gone off and could not easily be seen, but it began to turn towards the airfield once again. I thought: "This is it. He has done a dummy run and now for our chips".

I asked the Americans why they did not fire. The German aircraft was getting dangerously near again. The Yank simply answered that he had had no orders to fire. Whereupon I remarked that as he probably would get in first, why wait for the order to fire, and jokingly

A brand new Me410 night-fighter, a brilliant prize that landed at Monte Corvino.

said: "Have a go, Joe". A second later they did and all the guns on airfield defence opened up simultaneously. What a wonderful sight it was. The sky was full of exploding shells and tracer. The German in an attempt to survive, fired all the cartridges he had, hoping that amongst the lot would be the correct ones for that time of the day. While this went on and nobody scored, the Me410 reached the airfield boundary, and went into a very steep dive towards the runway down-wind. It was now clear beyond doubt that the pilot was making a desperate effort to land in one piece, which he did successfully, and sped at some knots towards our end of the runway. Before coming to a halt the German turned the aircraft completely round and faced the direction of his approach. The firing had now ceased, our own aircraft which had been flying in the vicinity of the airfield had moved off to a safer distance to allow the Americans to enjoy themselves for a while. Then all was silent. Looking across the airfield in the direction of the hangars of No.600 Squadron Care and Maintenance Flights, I spotted a 15cwt truck bouncing over the rough and muddy ground towards the runway. It seems it was not clear if the German pilot had turned to take off again, so the truck was driven to within 30 yards or so in his path to prevent this. An officer and a sergeant jumped off the truck brandishing their revolvers in a very menacing manner at the enemy crew of two. They managed to make them understand that it would be very much appreciated if the engines could be cut, please. The Germans complied and stood up in the cockpit with arms upraised through the top hatch. Eventually they climbed down complete with shaving kit, a small camera and pictures of their girlfriends. One may wonder if this landing may have been planned some time before." So there it was, an almost brand new Me410, a present from Adolf to the RAF, its logbook suggesting that it had been flown straight to Monte Corvino after reception by the German Squadron that operated from a base somewhere in central Italy. Not a single operational sortie to its credit. What a gift! There was a rush from all units to have a look at close quarters and all daily inspections at 600 Squadron were held up and 700's were late being signed up that day. Some of the ground crews got pretty worried about their serviceability state. In a effort to round up his ground crews and to have a crafty look himself, Chantrey was soon lost in the thick of a vast crowd of airmen and soldiers milling round the machine and, incidentally, preventing the runway from being used. Chantrey was ordered by a senior officer to muster the men and "push the bl——dy thing off the runway". It turned out to be quite a difficult job in the mud and rough ground. So ended the story of the capture of an Me410, a type of aircraft responsible for shooting down a considerable number of Beaufighters.

At Monte Corvino the Squadron allowed itself some valuable additions to the MT park. They obtained BMW motorcycles for personal use and pleasure, as well as two Opel trucks, a very ingenious oil bowser and a sophisticated delivery pump system much appreciated by the fitters and put to constant use after careful examination and preparation for the rest of the Italian campaign. At one corner of the airfield was the Graveyard. It was a place where many enemy fighters had found a resting place and often the more technical members of the Squadron were seen searching through the rubble, coming up with all kinds of refinements to existing tools. The aircrew kept themselves busy flying for 8th and 5th Armies and later when the front moved forward engaged in sorties to defend Naples and the great aerodromes established at Foggia and Bari, where they destroyed a number of Ju88s. The terrible winter conditions turned some men into inventors. They experimented with all kinds of devices to keep themselves warm in the night. The most effective method was to cut a hole in a 5 or 10 gallon oil drum and burn oil or dirty used petrol soaked rags using shell cases which were about 12" long, a number of which were joined together and put over the bung hole and extended up to the top of the tent and through the end flaps. It was a very effective solution, but at the same time it was lethal. The improvised flue pipe would soon get red hot and it was not uncommon to see the tent fabric alight. The CO put a stop to it before too much damage was done. The Squadron then resorted to a more technical system using the small aircraft oxygen bottles removed from German aircraft in the graveyard and some of their own aircraft and small bore copper tubing and a jet made out of domed nuts with a small hole in the top through which the atomised fuel passed. This lot when assembled gave the Squadron members a form of pressure stove and on the whole it worked well and, according to the assurances of the inventors, was not too dangerous. It was the second time the Squadron celebrated Christmas far from home. The NAAFI did not let the men down and Christmas was celebrated in relative luxury. The weather was very bad and for days there was no flying at all. The Squadron had dinner with roast turkey and Christmas pudding. Orange branches took the place of the traditional holly. Owing to a large number of Scots on the unit, the ritual of Hogmanay was observed and the Squadron also received a message from its Honorary Air Commodore Sir Archibald Sinclair, Secretary of State for Air, offering his congratulations for the victories secured in 1943. About the same time Italy had officially become an ally. From 8th December Italian troops fought alongside the Allies and their air force joined as well. Many of the Duce's former "Three Million Shining Bayonets" now attacked Germans. The first action was at the front with American 5th Army.

At this time the renowned "Hurricane Club" was founded. It had no connection with any other enterprise of the same name, and let its exploits not besmirch the revered memory of the old thoroughbred. In the camp, "lights out" was at 2200 hrs. So the Sergeants' Mess won itself a hurricane lamp. One member was duty "Aladdin" on the mess roster each week, and at 2159hrs stood ready. At "lights out" the lamp was duly lit, all initiated members chanting "Jesus bids us shine with a pure, pure light", accompanied on the piano, swiped from the Batapaglia railway station sidings. The Squadron was now responsible for the night-fighter cover of the beachhead just established some 30 miles south of Rome at Anzio. The airstrip was about 200 miles back, near Naples, and while there was an emergency airstrip on the beachhead itself it had no night flying facilities, so in case of trouble the pilot had at least to fly for half an hour to get home. By the way, when Vesuvius erupted a few weeks later it made a fine visual homing beacon, visible from the patrol line, and this was a great help if one was flying on one engine.

A lonely killer; a Squadron Beaufighter on its way to its prey.

With the capture of Naples a new prospect opened up for enterprising Squadron members. A recce party driving up had discovered the possibility for renting furnished accommodation quite cheaply. At that early stage landlords were quite grateful to have anyone who paid a rent. The Officers' Mess took on a villa as a R&R (Rest and Recreation) Home. The problem of transport was always there but the CO lent his car from time to time and there were flight trucks which could drop parties off and collect them later for it was only an hour away. Naples was quite a thrill after all the tented experiences far from any built up area. Of course the city was not looking at its best but then Naples always had and has good looks problems depending on the surrounding bay and Mount Vesuvius nearby. The people were in poor straits, but happy to see the back of the Germans. And, Naples was and is always well provided with "hostesses" who were able to do a quick conversion course from German to English language. Norman Poole remembered: "On my first visit, with the CO in our small party, I suppose there were six of us and in the evening a couple of girls joined us. This was quite a novel event and we were happy to share our wine with them and help them to improve their English and abandon their German which was much better but distinctly out of date – we hoped. We shared our rations with them, eating in the flat as no cosy restaurant was open yet. It got late enough to think of bed and the electric supply was quite unreliable and tended to reduce volts as the evening wore on. The general view was that I was the youngest – still only nineteen – I ought to entertain the youngest girl and the older girl was allocated to the oldest of our navigators. Come to think of it he was not even in his thirties. When we moved into the bedroom I had been allocated she unbuttoned her dress and stepped out of it to reveal a complicated arrangement of underwear. Complicated, for she had a one piece foundation garment with suspenders holding up silk stockings. I suppose these rarities must have been supplied by the previous invaders. Certainly my rather limited experience was confined to passion killer WAAF knickers and lisle stockings. No wonder American forces with their access to nylon stockings overcame our girls' better judgement. The bed was single size and although she could not have been any older than me she was rather experienced and it was a while since I had had any intimate contact. Poole was aware of the possibility of picking up an infection and was prepared for the eventuality. He must have been a disappointment for the wine and the energy expended left him sound asleep and unresponsive to her middle of the night attempts to arouse him. In the morning, before she left, she showed Poole her family photographs. "I think they were calculated to increase her reward – and they did – but I was not proud of myself even though my reputation on the Squadron advanced considerably" remembered Norman Poole. They were one of the first new visitors of Pompeii after the landings. Here again there were few of the Squadron able to explore and they were relieved to see that no significant damage had been done to this great monument of history. And as they were an all male group, the guides had no qualms about opening the doors on the walls covering the most erotic paintings which revealed the pleasure seeking atmosphere which must have prevailed there so many centuries ago. Poole had to admit that he did not understand each painting shown to him.

Flying became intense and in September and October McKinnon and Poole flew 30 and 25 sorties respectively. On 5th November there was a notable Guy Fawkes night when the Squadron was defending Naples against an enemy attack when Poole got a good solid contact to port. They turned into that direction and then Poole picked up a second contact, still at port. It did not take long before "Mac" said: "You know I think we are orbiting the same spot". And so it was. The Beaufighter was flying against "window", the strips of metallised paper which gave the same response to a radar set as a real aircraft. Shortly after this event Poole had an unplanned rest from flying due to a burst eardrum. It was a slit perforation acquired through flying with a cold and diving steeply after a target. It was a fairly straightforward healing problem and needed nothing other than Mother Nature to effect a cure. The doctor's daily medical examinations were optimistic and he reported a gradual closing of the slit. It kept Norman Poole on the ground for about a month and although it gave him the opportunity to explore more of the local area, including the namesake village of Monte Corvino, Poole was glad to be declared fit once more. It was halfway through December and the Squadron were making an effort to mark Christmas as something special. New Zealand pilot Harry Newton had been a farmer before joining and he was responsible for getting together the principal appropriate ingredients, two pigs and two turkeys. There were no such goodies on the West coast where most of the fighting had taken place but the situation was better on the East side where the Squadron were doing regular detachments. Harry had scouted about and after obtaining his livestock on one of the detachments he had decided that they were fit for flying duties. So he personally flew them to Monte Corvino. No doubt their first operation was to be their last, though all four had a contented few weeks in pens that had been constructed under Harry's supervision. It was also under Harry's dedicated leadership that the butchering of the quartet took place. What a Christmas feast though for the contrast between rations and Christmas food was almost too much for the men's constitutions. They had traded spirits for tinned fruit with the Americans again. The handicapped Squadron cooks had done absolute miracles to create pudding as well. The Squadron however was well placed for wines and this helped everything to go with a swing. There was no Santa Claus, but the crews at readiness were stood down as the Opposition was probably celebrating Weihnachten on the other side of the fence. McKinnon and Poole did readiness over the New Year but that was the last operational sortie they made for in January they were declared "Tour Expired" and sent home.

Early January 1944, patrols were flown from Gaudo and Lago, for the defence of forward positions of 5th Army. Intruder patrols were carried out in the Rimini/Bologna area from Tortorella. On the ground 5th Army was about to finish its successful operations against the Germans by capturing Monte Trocchio, the last objective before Cassino. On the 22nd an American surprise landing at Anzio gave them a bridgehead south of Rome. During the last week of January 1944 the Squadron aircrew were busy again. They were directed by a GCI (Ground Controlled Interception) station, observing on its cathode ray tube the behaviour of both friendly fighter and "bandit". At Anzio the Controllers lived in dugouts under shell fire all day long, then operated their radar at night from a converted TLC (Tank Landing Craft) which sailed at dusk and worked a mile or two off shore to obtain an unobstructed coverage of the area. On at least one occasion this vessel was torpedoed by German E-Boats so all in all the radar direction officers had their hands full. In addition to the problems of operations, the Squadron aircrew, in common with so many of the forces in Italy that winter, suffered extensively from jaundice, which depleted the numbers of crews available for flying duties. Soon the Squadron found itself short of trained navigators, who also operated the Beaufighter's airborne radar. The consequence was that all R/Os were obliged to make extra sorties. Peter Montgomery vividly remembered that his own navigator had to fly night-after-night without a break during his convalescence from jaundice, with any pilot who was short of a radar operator. During the icy weather of January and February the living conditions in the tents had left much to be desired and these factors tended to reduce the standard of efficiency of all concerned. In spite of this many German aircraft fell to the massive weaponry of the Beaufighters. On the 24th F/L Turnbull and P/O Fowler caught a Ju88 at 1915hrs. The aircraft crashed about 10 miles from the town of Circeo. The next day S/L Horne and F/S Cadman bagged two Junkers Ju88. One aircraft was shot down about 10 miles North of Anzio at 0155hrs, the next one fell West of Anzio, some 10 minutes later. At about 0530hrs W/C Paddy Green and F/L Gillies shot down a Ju88 which crashed about 10 miles North of Rome. One day later F/O "Ace" Downing and P/O Lyons had another very successful day. At 1750 hrs they clobbered a four-engined, two-propeller He177, getting a second one only six minutes later at 1756 hrs. Both aircraft crashed near Circeo, a familiar place for victims of the Squadron. They finished their sortie by catching a Ju88 at 1920 hrs, approx. 30 miles south of Anzio. Sadly their luck ran out less than a week later, when this crew were patrolling the beachhead and their Beaufighter developed engine trouble. They both bailed out and landed in the sea, to be picked up by a High Speed Launch. Downing was uninjured but, unfortunately Lyons died en route to Ischia. He and Downing had 12 victories to their credit. Later news was received that they both had been awarded the DFC. On the 29th F/L Hilken and his Canadian Nav/RO F/O Ritchie took off for a sortie in the Anzio area. At about 1750 they spotted four Dornier Do217s. Hilken immediately pursued the enemy and at 1805 hrs the first Do217 went down north of Anzio. Not yet satisfied the crew attacked a second Do217, which was seen to crash at 1810, about two miles north of the mouth of the Tiber River. At about the same time, another 600 crew ran into serious trouble. At 1802 F/O Ditzel, Operator of F/O Adams, reported that they were about to attack an enemy aircraft. The Germans fought back, for thirteen minutes later a Mayday call was heard. The crew then flew about 15 miles NW of Anzio. Forty minutes later they were heard again. "Going to pancake on the beach". Then there was silence. The next day a Beau took off to try and find the missing crew. The search for this crew was in vain. On 1st June the Squadron Operations Record Book reported the two men "missing, presumed killed". In balance, the day after the disappearance of these men W/O Harrop and F/S Redmond shot down a Do217 26 miles SSW of Anzio at 1046 hrs while F/S Bamford and Sgt Battersby damaged a Ju88 40 miles north of Rome at 2107 hrs. It showed that air warfare was a costly business. Until this time, through a variety of causes, chief of which were good luck, experienced crews, and the large number of flying hours carried out by the aircrew of the Squadron, there had only been two crews lost for 101 aircraft destroyed. However, after the first few weeks of the landings at Anzio several aircraft and crews were lost, as it seemed that not only were the new crews rather inexperienced in comparison with their predecessors, but also the run of good luck seemed to have evaporated and from 101 aircraft destroyed for 2 crews lost a further 6 were lost for only 20 enemy aircraft destroyed. During February only two aircraft were shot down by City of London Beaufighters. On the 4th an enemy offensive against the Anzio bridgehead started, and it was only with the greatest difficulty that they were repelled. The beachhead was a dangerous place, for RAF, USAAF and Luftwaffe alike. Allied flak had priority, so if a contact with a "customer" was made the choice was either to break off the chase before leaving enemy territory or pursue it through "friendly" flak. Frankly, Peter Montgomery said "I found our anti-aircraft fire much less accurate than the German and usually carried on with the chase." The ever improving radar sets were a great asset in this continuous battle. In fact they were the most recent arrivals bringing out the centimetric radars by February 1944 and by wartime standards the men were experienced night-fighter crews who had operated in the European Theatre of Operations for some time. However, some of the confined runways with obstructions lined up alongside would have been ruled out in the UK. The weather under which the crews operated was another risk factor of some significance, but they were fortunate with their radar beacons to home in on and the additional good fortune that most of the airfields were near enough to the sea to make a low level approach possible.

When patrolling over the Hun there was considerable interference on the radar, especially during turns, when the screen became blotted out by "chaff or window and the solution to this was only to be found when the Squadron converted to centimetric radar from the metric type in use at that time. The patrol height was usually 20,000 feet and the cockpit heater warmed only the left foot so that if one wore flying boots one felt nothing. However, if not, one's left leg was scorched. It was found that by flying with one hand on the "spectacles" one could warm the other on the hot pipe that passed behind the pilot's seat. A change of hand every few minutes kept the feeling in all fingers. On the 6th F/L Hilken and F/O Ritchie got a Do217 at 0405 in the morning. It crashed 30 miles north of Rome. A few days later Allied bombers started their first operations against Cassino and the German positions at Anzio. On the 15th W/Os Kerr and Wheeler caught a Do217 north of the Tiber mouth.

During eight successive nights Squadron Beaufighters shot down ten Stukas. These German dive bombers were trying to bomb and strafe Allied troops in the battle area of the Gothic Line. S/L Burke AFC (left) and his R/O F/L Healy had a narrow escape during one of their low level sorties against the Stukas. Thinking that he was following a friendly aircraft it was not until he was 200 feet behind it that Burke realised that he was on top of a Stuka (with a rear gun). He immediately opened fire literally carving the Stuka to pieces. The Ju87 exploded in mid-air and its flames struck the Beaufighter. When Burke and Healy landed their ground crew told them that the fabric of the tailplane of their Beaufighter had burned away . . .

It was 1820 hours when the enemy crashed. It was the day of the heaviest attacks by bombers and artillery against the Monte Cassino monastery. The Allies were convinced that the Germans had changed this place into a massive fortress. It was not until the end of the battle that they found the Germans had not, until the Allied attacks started. At this stage of the war, many of the experienced and successful crews were running out of operational time, and in spite of "operational extensions" and some other clever schemes, organised by Paddy Green, they were told to go. In February 1944 W/C Green was promoted to Gp/Capt. He was posted and became OC No.1 Mobile Ops Room, DAF. He left just before the Germans started another desperate attack against Anzio. Green left after a remarkable service. His duties in the RAF started in March 1937, when he joined No.601 Squadron. In October 1939 he, with Roger Bushel and Jack Monroe had formed No.92 Squadron, flying Hinds. In June 1941 he went to Tactics Branch HQ RAF. In November he returned to No.600 as A-Flight Commander. Six months later Paddy Green commanded No.125 Squadron to return to 600 at Maison Blanche in December 1942. For more than a year Paddy inspired the men to great achievements. His further career showed his abilities for leadership. In November 1944 he was given command of No.232 Wing and in January 1946 Group Captain Green was in charge of Operations at Central Fighter Establishment. When he left the RAF in August 1947 he returned to South Africa to go into the mining business. His place was taken by S/L Styles DFC, an "old boy" who had served with the Squadron in the Thirties. A different type from Green he successfully led the Squadron during the move to the North of Italy.

On the 29th February, Peter Montgomery had a memorable experience when he flew a mission north of Anzio. He and Sgt Robertson took off for a sortie North of Anzio. Montgomery has never forgotten what happened during this very strange sortie. After taking off about 2100 hrs, they reached Anzio and were patrolling near the beachhead when the GCI station reported unidentified aircraft to the north east and vectored them towards these aircraft. This course took Montgomery and Robertson deep into enemy territory and after 15 minutes or so it was apparent that they were right on the edge of the radar control area, for the radio instructions became fainter all the time and their own radar was subjected to intensive German jamming. The type of radar then fitted to Beaufighters had a backward looking capability, so when the operator reported a "back-blip" Montgomery knew that there was an aircraft on his tail. He started a hard turn to starboard, but the pursuer remained behind them slowly closing the range, and although Peter increased speed and tightened the turn, the German continued to hang on. Finally the Beaufighter gave Montgomery all she had but he could neither shake off the opponent nor win the winding match to get on the enemy's tail, so putting the aircraft into an all-out dive Montgomery headed for the hills below. Fortunately a brilliant moon enabled Peter to hedge-hop back to Anzio and his pursuer seemed to have no relish for a night contour chase through hills and valleys. Returning to the beachhead Peter and Jim resumed their patrol but a few minutes later they were again directed to the north-east.

This time, however, when they got nearly 20 miles from the GCI station Peter declined to go further and told the Controller that he intended to go back on patrol. This was agreed and no sooner was Montgomery in position than a bomber stream came down the coast towards Anzio. The Controller quickly vectored the Beaufighter to intercept and then Jim Robertson reported that he was in contact with a target which was soon silhouetted above them against the stars and identified as a Ju88 bomber. Montgomery dropped back and climbed to bring the enemy in the gun sight and was about to open fire when Peter suddenly realised that he was aiming directly at the bombs hanging exposed between the engines, from a range which seemed unhealthily close. Deeming discretion to be the better part of valour Peter opened the range another 50 yards, aimed at the port engine and reached for the gun button. As he did so he felt something catch momentarily on his flying gauntlet, but the noise of the fire from his four 20 mm cannons and six machine guns dismissed the incident from Peter's mind while his attention was riveted on the Junkers, now illuminated by the explosions of the

W/C L.H. Styles succeeded W/C Paddy Green as OC600 in March 1944. In the early thirties Styles had already served in No.600 as a young Auxiliary pilot and a keen rugby player for the Squadron team.

cannon shells. As anticipated, the Junkers' reaction was to peel off to the left thus dragging his fuselage, cockpit and other engine through the gunfire, and Montgomery dived to the left in pursuit, shouting to Jim to hold the contact on the radar.

But there was no reply and soon Peter lost sight of the enemy. Pulling out of the dive at approximately 350 mph Peter called Jim repeatedly without reply, but as the ears recovered from their temporary deafness caused by the firing of the cannon, Peter realised that the radio was dead. Instinctively he checked his headset to find that the helmet lead plug had been pulled about a quarter of an inch out of its socket, thus breaking the electrical contact and thus explaining the tug on Peter's gauntlet when he opened fire. Ramming the plug home Montgomery called Robertson again but although the radio was now "live" he still got no reply, so he shone his torch into the back of the aircraft only to find it deserted. The rear cockpit was some 12 feet from the pilot and it seemed probable that Jim might be lying under his seat, possibly injured, unknown to his skipper by some return fire during combat. Since Peter could not achieve anything without an operator, he informed the Controller that he was returning to base. When Peter approached the airfield he arranged by radio for an ambulance to stand by, but as soon as he had stopped the engines he was told that both Jim and his parachute were gone. Further examination revealed that he had fused the detonators in the interception and identification radar sets, so that these would be destroyed instead of falling into enemy hands if the aircraft crashed in hostile territory. Then he had jumped, presumably under the impression that Montgomery was dead or unconscious; and since the aircraft was descending rapidly without much height in hand, Peter could scarcely quarrel with his decision. It turned out that this was exactly the way of things, and when Jim's parachute opened his flying boots fell off. As he hung below his canopy he saw an aircraft crash below him in a burst of fire. This he assumed to be the Beaufighter, but it was the Ju88. Robertson landed in his socks and started to walk towards Anzio. It looked a 10 miles walk and he was confident he could cover the distance in a short time. But he had not gone far when he stumbled and fell into a trench. In the trench was a German soldier, who seemed just as surprised as Jim. Unfortunately Jerry had the advantage of holding a rifle and Robertson was a POW. For two days he was closely interrogated by German field security police who viewed him with some suspicion since there was no crashed British aircraft to substantiate his story. Besides the Germans were a suspicious crowd and they thought this was another strange story from another funny Englishman. However they eventually decided that it was true and sent him to the North. Robertson ended up in Stalag Luft III, better known as Sagan, from where the Great Escape had taken place. He spent over a year in captivity and was forced to take part in the horrible marches westwards from East Prussia to escape liberation by the Soviets.

No.600 Squadron Sergeants' Mess, Marcianese, 1944. Standing l. to r.: Ruben Spinks, Roy Atkinson, Bert Chantrey, Norman Childs, Frank Yates, Dev DeVroome. Seated l. to. r. Colin Lamb, Fred Topping, W/C Styles (OC), Ken Maclean, Bernard Wheeley. Kneeling left Fred Maine and Bart Bartholomew. The score-board is the one presented to Hughes and Dixon in North Africa.

Montgomery crewed up with another operator and continued to make life difficult for the Luftwaffe. Two hours after this incident S/L Bailey and F/O Williams shot down another Ju88. It crashed twenty miles North of Rome. By this time many of the experienced crews had left. Their replacements were rather green and therefore a Training Flight was set up under S/L Horne, who earned himself the distinction of being awarded both the DFC and AFC with the Squadron. The Training Flight operated mainly from Foggia and brought the new crews up to the demanding standard of the CO and the task in hand. The remainder of the year was largely non-operational owing to poor weather conditions, except for two raids on Naples. Yet there always was the possibility of a serious mishap. One such incident could have caused a catastrophe had it not been for the skill of S/L Horne. The occasion followed a major overhaul and engine change of one of the Beaufighters. The machine was taken out on the drome and the usual ground tests were carried out. Then all appropriate sections of Form 700 were signed and countersigned and the aircraft handed over to Horne for air testing. He took off in his usual confident style and to the assembled onlookers, some of whom had spent so much time adjusting oil pressures, temperature control flaps, synchronising engine speeds and throttle control linkages and settings, boost pressures and propeller Constant Speed units, all seemed as usual to be going well. It was not long however, before S/L Horne realised something was amiss as both engines suddenly cut. With nothing on the clock he headed straight back to the aerodrome and with great skill brought the Beaufighter in to a perfect touch down although at about twice the usual landing speed. It was S/L Horne's last exploit in No.600 Squadron, for "Higher Powers" had plans for him and some others. S/L Horne, F/L Turnbull and P/O Fowler were all posted back to Tunis and it was difficult to replace them. During March only one Ju88 was bagged. On the 17th W/C Styles and F/O Ritchie shot down a Ju88 over the Anzio area during a short brush at 2050 hrs. Over the beachhead there was still some hunting to be done and, altogether, 32 enemy aircraft went down before 5th Army made contact from the south. It should not be forgotten, however, that with the Italians "out" German resistance stiffened. Intensive use of "German" Window and AI jamming made interception very difficult. Things did not improve either for the reason that both the Germans and the Allies were throwing up a tremendous amount of ack-ack whenever Beaufighters ventured over the front.

With the Squadron's arrival in the Naples area, the war effort going well and Spring 1944 in the offing, the men of No. 600 Squadron felt entitled to a little light diversion. A suitable outlet appeared to be a boxing tournament. This was right up W/O Topping's alley, he having done a bit of boxing in his service days in the Army. This was evident by a generously spread nose, and so the organisation of the match fell promptly into his able lap. Since

it was to be an inter-Service affair it became necessary to find without delay a suitable bod to represent No.600 Squadron. In no time
at all Fred had found a "volunteer" in LAC Ted Pellett who had done
some club boxing. Topping put Pellett into training. For six weeks
Ted was excused from all night readiness duties and carefully nurtured on a special diet of steak – not the nutmeg or Soya bean
variety, but genuine goat from the local free-range herds. Sparring
partners like "Wog" Ellis, "Rube" Spink, "Tubby" Dean and other
more or less willing helpers from HQ Flight prepared Ted for the
fray, and hopes were high of triumph for the scientific boxing as
taught by Topping over the roughhouse style of the licentious sol-
diery who had been very adequately spied upon as to merit and
ability. It was crystal clear: Thanks to LAC Pellett and his very able
trainer No. 600 Squadron was bound to become the prime boxing
squadron of the whole of Italy. The great day dawned and the off-
duty troops went in force to the venue – a disused theatre in Naples
with the ring erected on the stage. Bout 1 featured Ted, clad in
immaculate white strip "donated" by the US Army PX with a pale
blue sash round his middle indicating the Service he so proudly represented and for which he was about to gain a great and memorable
victory. On reflection this would have been too "chic" in view of
the company he was keeping in the ring at this particular moment,
his opponent being a matelot who in appearance resembled a beer
barrel mounted on billiard table legs. Whatever poor Pellett might
have been thinking the Squadron supporters were not in the least
daunted and wagers were struck with all and sundry. Some were
sure that after Ted's certain victory they would collect large sums of
money, allowing them a bright and financially sound future once
home in Blighty. The gong sounded and out of the corner came
600's hope just as was expected of him. A quick touch of the gloves
and out came the classic straight left, the left jab and even the left
hook off the jab, this last subsequently copied by one Henry Cooper
which indicated the sheer poetry of the move Topping had taught
Pellett. Sparkling footwork from Ted and again the classic left, pink-
ing the matelot with consummate ease and bringing no real reaction
from him. It seemed the Navy had found their master. For about
twenty-five seconds Ted Pellett was the master in the classic
Queensbury mould. Then, alas, things went rather awry. It would
seem that the Navy had spent his youth on a fairground and completed his education in the boxing booth. He had obviously never

learned the finer arts of self-defence thereby not realising that he was way behind on points and definitely outclassed. In fact he had the temerity to step forward and catch Pellett with what could only be described as a right bash in the chops – no skill, no science, but to be just, not a little power. Down went Ted, square on his "unkers", gently easing back to full length on the floor. With his belly full of goat-steak and the warm atmosphere in the theatre this was quite understandable, and there he remained until the Squadron had finished doling out vast quantities of 100 lire notes to the winning punters, hard hearted to a man refusing any discount on the Squadron's plea that the better man had lost. Twenty-five seconds of glory and a five minute kip in His Majesty's time was a poor return for six weeks of special training. After all steak was scarce, after this goats were even more scarce, and more to the point so were lires for a month or two. Of course the fight was lost in training – everybody knows that a hungry fighter is a potential winner. A much slimmer Ted Pellett was later re-mustered as centre-forward of the Squadron soccer team and remained so for the duration. After all there must be some justice, even in War. As if the Hun was not a sufficient enemy to contend with, nature decided to play its part. On 21st March Vesuvius began erupting, and both Vesuvius and Pompeii aerodromes were threatened with extinction. The aircraft moved to Marcianese, while the Squadron and other units went to Pomigliano at an hour's notice and stood by on readiness there. At the same time, on 27th March no less than three German counter-attacks against Anzio were stopped. A few days later, however, the Americans were forced to withdraw about two miles. German attacks continued through April and May, when British forces too were forced to withdraw.

In the late spring and early summer the front was pushed forward very fast and in quick succession a number of moves were made. First to la Banca, then Voltone and on to Follonica.

It did not keep aircrews from a good hunt. On 28th April F/O Branch and F/S Balchin got another He177 about 55 miles NW of Anzio. The month of May also saw the Squadron being equipped with Mark VIII AI, which, when the Nav/ROs had become fully accustomed, proved to be much better for intercepting through 'Window'. While the new radars were installed, the last Allied attack against Monte Cassino took place. The exceptional bravery of the Polish 2nd Army Corps under General Anders finally broke the

(Above) The Beaufighters were replaced by Mosquitoes in December 1944. Instead of BQ the Squadron identification was now "6" as can be seen on this Mossie at Cesenatico. The latest AI was mounted in the cockpit, next to the pilot's seat. This meant that pilot and R/O flew "side by side" (below).

Germans. On 14th May F/Os Rees and Bartlett destroyed a Ju88 10 miles NW of the Tiber Estuary. By the end of the month the Allies were a little less than 15 miles south of Rome. On 2nd June Rees and Bartlett got a Fiat CR42 over Lake Vico, the only one of that variety that fell to the guns of 600 Squadron. It was so slow that the Beau had to lower its wheels and put on 30 degrees of flap to avoid over-shooting. During the same night S/L Bailey and F/S Wint shot down two more enemy aircraft, a Ju87 Stuka North of Celle Fasiole at 2340hrs and a Me110 over the Tiber Valley North of Rome about fifty minutes later.

The Allied invasion of France caused great disappointment for 600 Squadron. Having been present at the landings in Sicily and at both landings in Italy they all expected to be invited to take part in this event as well. They knew that 12th Tactical Air Command had, indeed, asked for No.600 Squadron, but HQ Desert Air Force refused to let No.600 go. And, there was no Paddy Green around who, with his numerous contacts could have worked out the "Malta-trick" for a second time. After the link up, the front moved forward so rapidly that the Squadron was hard pressed to keep up. On 13th June No.600 moved to La-blanca airfield at Nettuno and six days later to Voltona landing ground near Tarquinia. This was conveniently situated near Rome, and daily trips for NCOs and airmen were immediately laid on. The officers were fortunate in that two rooms at the Albergo Regina Carlton were permanently reserved and nearly all of them spent a 48 hour pass there before the Squadron moved again. This was not long in forthcoming, for on 5th July they set off full of expec-tations to Follonica, a seaside resort opposite the Isle of Elba. Their hopes were fully realised, for not only was there a good aerodrome, but also a superb beach densely populated with bright-eyed Italian signoritas in the most fetching bathing costumes, which left little to the imagination of the gallant gentlemen of 600. It allowed many of the officers to reach an admirable standard in the Italian language, of which the words "amore mia", "molto bene" and "que bella" were often used phrases. The fact that a large German battle group was being encircled by the Americans, between Grosseto and Follonica, did not seem to bother the Squadron very much. At Follonica the GCI was in a beautiful villa with a remarkable vista, quite the kind of housing for such a renowned Squadron. The owner was still in residence and had three beautiful daughters. One of the men recalled how suddenly many aircrews visited the villa after they discovered a keen interest in the workings of a GCI station. Interest in diminishing the Luft-waffe continued as well. The Operations Record Book for June/July showed the following scores:

04 Jun F/S Cole – Sgt Odd	0320hrs	Ju 88 near Biglio
04 Jun F/S Cole – Sgt Odd	0335hrs	Ju88 NW Frosinone
02 Jul W/O Ewing – F/S Chenery	2242hrs	Ju88 NE Lake Trasimeno
06 Jul S/L Baily – F/S Wint	time unknown	Ju88 area not known
07 Jul F/O Jeffrey – F/O Brewer	0210hrs	Ju87 Position R6315
10 Jul S/L Bailey – Sgt Wint	0115hrs	Ju87 nr Lake Trasimeno
27 Jul F/S Waitman – F/S Goss	2245hrs	Ju87 near Volterra
29 Jul F/L Thompson – F/O Beaumont	2343hrs	Ju87 Position R5083

By mid-July all Germans had been driven out of Toscane. US 5th Army liberated Livorno while the Poles took Ancona on the Adriatic coast. Despite the speed of the German Army's retreat, the Luftwaffe kept up its activities. Consequently the Squadron continued to shoot them down. Although they worked very hard, the men of 600 managed to enjoy life, for in addition to the swimming aforementioned and the serious attempts to learn the language of the new ally, there was international cricket and volleyball, and a cinema show at least four times a week. The idyllic life in Bella Italia was too good to last, and another move was carried out, this time to Rosignano. This place had a highly moral effect, as everyone kept to the straight and narrow paths in order to avoid the mines so thickly sown around by the opposition. Nevertheless, a volleyball court was quickly marked out, and the enthusiastic cricket captain lost no time in securing the services of a bulldozer to clear a space for a cricket pitch. Bathing was suspended until the beach was cleared of mines. Throughout all these not one night's operations was missed and the destruction of enemy aircraft over 5th Army forward positions continued with great zeal. It was evident that the Ger-mans no longer used Ju88s extensively, and were relying more and more on the Ju87. These aircraft were particularly suitable for ground attacks on moonlit nights. Soon the problem of overshooting these aircraft was overcome and a large number went down in flames. With patrols continuing and fewer enemy aircraft venturing into 600's pastures, Allied aircraft flying around over Italy could be in for a nasty surprise. While a Squadron Beaufighter was on patrol from Follonica on 27th July a very curious and mortally dangerous incident happened. F/S Waitman had an enemy Stuka in his sights and was about to attack the dive bomber over Volterra. When he pressed the firing button he suddenly saw a Baltimore medium bomber of No. 13 Squadron fly through his sights. The devastating salvos of cannons and guns of the Beaufighter hit both enemy and friendly aircraft. The Ju87 was seen to crash in flames; the Baltimore pilot was able to make base where he did a wheels-up landing. After landing both pilot and Nav/RO showed a keen interest to meet the Baltimore pilot in private.

By early August British troops crossed the Arno and entered Florence. On 25th August 1944 8th Army started its assault on Rimini and 600 Squadron said goodbye to 5th Army to move to Falconara. For the first month on the new front there were a fair amount of victims available, mainly Ju87s that were attacking troop positions and trying to destroy viaducts and bridges at night to slow down the Allied push. While most of the Squadron were at Falconara supporting the attack on the Gothic Line, a few aircraft were left at Rosignano. One of the German answers to the assault was the extensive deployment of Ju87 Stukas. The Squadron was only too pleased to help and by the first week of September 1944 ten had been destroyed and two damaged. Shortly after this the weather deteriorated considerably and many nights passed with aircraft on readiness only. On one of these nights, when the aerodrome was unserviceable, Rimini airfield was attacked by Stukas and casualties were inflicted. Therefore it was decided to form a detachment at Lesi airfield, which had a concrete runway. In October, due to a flooded aerodrome, No.232 Wing were unable to carry out intruder operations from Lake Commacchio to Grado, and so 600 Squadron was again asked to assist. Crews welcomed this request and soon German night activity was practically negligible; being confined to high and low recces, which were too fast for the Squadron Beaufighters. These intruders, despite adverse weather, provided creditable results. Another feature of operations at Falconara was the number of Air Search and Rescue (ASR) trips. Altogether 21 trips were made , totalling 55 hours and 15 minutes, and resulting in the rescue of no less than 25 survivors. Highlight of October was the return (on a stolen motorbike) of Hill and Chenerey, who had been missing in action after a mishap. Another source of great pleasure was the fact that the pilot of the Stuka, shot down by S/L Archer and F/L Barrington, was captured and turned out to be a veteran Stuka pilot with no less than 300 missions to his credit.

The Squadron went to Cesenatico, a fine station with much more room and comfort compared to Falconara, which would be remembered for mud and cramped dispersals. The new base was north of Rimini, situated on the seaward side of the road to the north of the town and was constructed of the usual PSP (Perforated Steel Plate). The area itself was very sandy and also running parallel to it was a secondary unmetalled landing strip, as an emergency runway for aircraft in trouble. This was an ideal location for such a strip, being on a direct route to Foggia, in the south, where the main bomber force was stationed. From there the bombers flew sorties against targets in NE Europe. At this time in the war air activity in that area was very heavy, especially in support of the ground forces.

It was the beginning of the last wartime period, the new CO being W/C Drummond, who succeeded Styles upon his posting home. Drummond, like many Commanding Officers, had served in the Squadron earlier. During the last five months of 1944 the Squadron suffered no losses. On the ground all went well. British troops crossed the Rubicon River on 26th September. And while in Holland the last British paratroopers returned after the failure of Market-Garden at Arnhem, it seemed as if the final thrust through Northern Italy would be easy. The Squadron increased its number of shot down enemy aircraft. August to December 1944 turned out to be very rewarding Ju87 period for them, as the Operations Record Book showed:

01 Aug F/L Thompson – F/O Beaumont	2113hrs	Ju87 NNE of Arezzo
02 Aug W/O Crooks – Sgt Charles	0300hrs	Ju87 NE of Pisa
02 Aug P/O Jefferson – P/O Spencer	2235hrs	Ju87 SW of Arezzo
03 Aug F/O MacDonald – Sgt Towell	2245hrs	Ju87 E of Arezzo

27 Aug F/L Thompson – F/O Beaumont	2210hrs	Ju87 Florence area
29 Aug W/C Styles – F/O Wilmer	2115hrs	Ju87 SE of Florence
03 Sep P/O Judd – F/O Brewer	time unknown	Ju87 Rimini area
03 Sep P/O Judd – F/O Brewer	time unknown	Ju87 Rimini area
04 Sep S/L Burke – F/L Whealey	time unknown	Ju87 SW of Rimini
04 Sep F/S Cole – F/S Odd	0305hrs	Ju87 WSW of Rimini
05 Sep F/L Davidson – P/O Talford	0415hrs	Ju87 SW Rimini (dam.)
10 Sep F/L Thompson – F/O Beaumont	0315hrs	Ju87 SW of Rimini
04 Oct W/C Styles – F/O Wilmer	2020hrs	Ju87 SE of Cesena
28 Nov S/L Archer – F/L Barrington	time unknown	Ju87 Forli-Faenze area
01 Dec W/O Bait – F/S Lothian	1715hrs	Ju87 Forli area
23 Dec F/L Rees – F/O Beaumont	2110hrs	Ju87 NW of Forli
23 Dec F/L Rees – F/O Beaumont	2120hrs	Ju87 NE of Forli (dam)

In December 1944 the last move before the end of hostilities was made. Shortly after Christmas some pilots were sent to Foggia to convert to the "Wooden Wonder", the Mosquito 19 night-fighter. Navigators left for Pomigliano to train on the new Mk.X AI Meanwhile patrols over the enemy lines continued as usual, and the year closed with the destruction of two Ju87s and the damaging of a third one in a sortie by F/L Rees and F/O Beaumont. During the winter, enemy air activity was almost non-existent. His aircraft came over the forward 8th Army positions only three times in January, resulting in the loss of two Ju87s. February 1945 had the poor claim of being the first month the Squadron shot no enemy aircraft down at all. That month George Curtiss joined the Squadron. The recent arrival of Mosquitoes asked for additional carpenters on the strength. He found an airfield as busy as a beehive. The Squadron had to share the aerodrome with a couple of other Squadrons and nationalities. Australians with Baltimores, Americans and South

Africans and not forgetting the odd Savoia Marchetti tri-motor bomber of that part of the Italian air force now fighting on the Allied side. These aircraft were used to supply Italian partisans in the Italian mountains and Tito's forces in Yugoslavia. There had been days when No.600 Squadron would finish off these types of aeroplanes, rather than escort them or fly alongside. Living and domestic quarters were in the town, south of the canal, making do in the war-damaged buildings, which was the accepted thing in the Desert Air Force in Italy. On the drome it was sand with everything, Curtiss' diary recorded a few occasions when work came to a stop as high winds created dust storms. The engine fitters' most treasured possession was a magnet with which to grovel in the sand to find nuts and bolts. In general, for the ground crew, life could be rather routine, but there was always the sense of expectancy. Such as when a Baltimore of an Australian Squadron yawed on take-off, and just cleared, by the narrowest of margins, the marquee which served as the Carpenters shop. Or when a Baltimore made an emergency landing in the early hours of the morning, after a brilliant exchange of Verey Lights with the control tower. When the men rushed over to push it clear of the runway they found the underbelly of the aircraft dripping with the blood of the observer. March proved to be another blank month, and only three times did enemy aircraft come near. S/L Hammond was successful in shooting down a FW190 – it was the last victory the Squadron could claim. During March the enemy proved consistent; no aircraft dared enter the skies which belonged to the night-fighters of "The City of London". The boredom was somewhat lessened by the area night cover patrols over Udine and Gorizia. They were laid on to parallel the operations of No.100 Group of Bomber Command, because of the number of losses sustained by Bostons of No.232 Wing. Some of the aircraft reported seeing single-engined fighters at night, and it was supposed that these might come from the Udine area. It was obvious that the enemy was running out of bait. On the other hand it gave No. 600 Squadron a good opportunity to gain experience on the Mosquito. Two Mozzies a night were sent up to the Udine region to keep a watch on the airfields, and although the flarepath of one of them was seen lit up on one occasion, no enemy aircraft were observed. Although such trips proved fruitless from the Squadron's point of view, Boston losses declined sharply.

The Hun stayed away until the middle of April when at last light

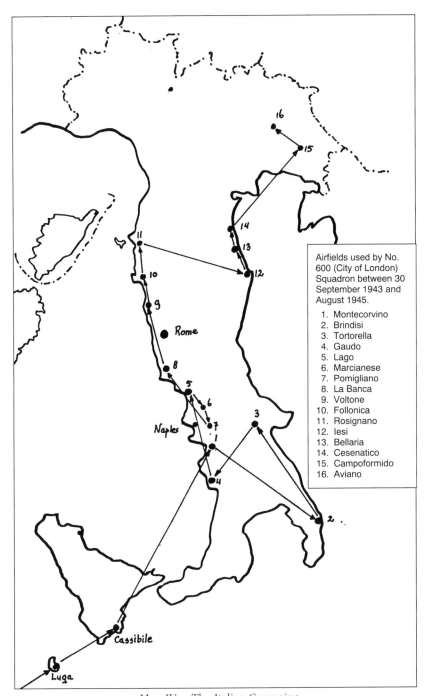

Airfields used by No. 600 (City of London) Squadron between 30 September 1943 and August 1945.

1. Montecorvino
2. Brindisi
3. Tortorella
4. Gaudo
5. Lago
6. Marcianese
7. Pomigliano
8. La Banca
9. Voltone
10. Follonica
11. Rosignano
12. Iesi
13. Bellaria
14. Cesenatico
15. Campoformido
16. Aviano

Rome

Naples

Cassibile

Luqa

Map IV.   The Italian Campaign

on the 13th two FW190s, flying in formation were intercepted by the dusk patrol. One of the enemy aircraft was shot down, and the other damaged. These were the last successes enjoyed by the Squadron, as after the breakthrough at Argenta no more enemy aircraft came over at night.

The Poles had liberated Bologna and Ferrara had fallen after British forces had broken heavy German defence. On 25th April US 5th Army entered Parma and Mantua. The same day a most memorable event occurred at about 10 in the morning at Cesenatico. George Curtiss etched this event in his memory: "That morning a B25 Mitchell of the American Air Force approached the field. It had run into trouble during a sortie in the north. We were alerted as usual to such events by the frantic exchange of Verey Lights between the aircraft and flying control. The Mitchell put up a "red", indicating it required permission for an immediate emergency landing. These were answered by Flying Control by similar colour in an attempt to make the pilot use the secondary landing strip. The Yank aborted the first attempt, then came around low, and despite more "reds" came in to land, no undercarriage visible, straight down the main runway, and in a series of crashes and sparks, and grinding metal ploughed to a stop at the far end of the drome. There were two crash tenders on duty, one RAF, one American. Both tore down the drome in the wake of the bomber, but the American arrived first, stalling his engine as he stopped. The bomber crew had already abandoned their aircraft, running for their lives, desperately shouting there was a bomb on board. Thus the RAF tender kept going, and in a very tight about turn raced back as far as possible. Then the whole thing erupted as the bomb exploded, taking the American tender and its driver with it. It certainly was a case of "hitting the deck" for everyone. The debris flew far. I believe that in that moment the Squadron had more aircraft rendered u/s than in any other single incident during the war. Thankfully there were no casualties on the Squadron. All other plans were set aside and everyone was mustered to A-Flight dispersal which was nearest to the blast, and tidying up began. I, and another carpenter were allocated Mosquito "X", which had received damage to the underside of the port main plane, caused by flying metal, which had cut a very deep and jagged cut to the bottom spar member, outboard of the engine. Obviously this really required the facilities of a base Maintenance Unit to fully repair, but after consultation with our Engineering Officer F/L Boult, it was decided to carry out a patch up job, so as to fly the aircraft to Brindisi, where No. 8 ARD (Aircraft Repair Depot) was situated. This was typical of the conditions we were accustomed to in that theatre of war, very much a make do and mend situation, "forget the book and keep 'em flying" was the unwritten motto. Also the big war effort seemed to be concentrated on NW Europe, and this left the ground crews in Italy to use their own ingenuity and skill to overcome the shortages. The Squadron ground crews were absolute masters of improvisation. So, instead of returning to the domestic site for meals, the cooks would bring the food to us on site, and everyone worked till dark, with an early start in the morning in an effort to regain full Squadron strength as quickly as possible. The aircraft had been towed to a dispersal bay, just off the runway. We had found the necessary materials to do a patch up job, so as far as we were concerned all was well. Other teams of men were of course carrying out various repairs to aircraft at dispersals all over the drome. There was, however, more excitement to come the following afternoon as once more there was an exchange of Very Lights between Flying Control and this time with a Spitfire, which eventually flew out over the sea, and we were treated to a wonderful display of aerobatics as the pilot tried to dispatch a bomb which refused to leave the aircraft. After quite a long time – his fuel must

Ground crew in front of a Squadron Mosquito, Cesenatico 1944.

have been low – and no success, he came in to land, once more using the main runway and not the emergency strip. Then, as he put his undercarriage down, off dropped the bomb to explode among the salvage area just off the opposite end of the runway to where the Mitchell had ended up. The Spitfire landed safe and well. I for one hit the deck as soon as I saw the flash before the sound of the explosion reached me. A few days later a pilot arrived from the Maintenance Unit and with fingers crossed I watched him take off in "my" Mossie. With no hesitation, he went straight for Brindisi where he landed safely.

By coincidence, in October that year (1945) I was posted to that same Aircraft Repair Depot. It was under South African Air Force command. I found out that my repairs on "X" had come in for a certain amount of criticism and that I should have refused to carry it out. On the other hand they admitted that it had been successful, that the kite had arrived safely and that, in the comfort of a proper hangar, it had been restored to A1 serviceability. I remembered the words of Air/Cdre Harry Broadhurst, when he gave the Repair and Salvage Unit I then served with a pep talk prior to the invasion of Italy, saying – Your supply lines will be stretched to the limit, so improvisation is the order of the day. If you haven't got it, you make it, you acquire it, you improvise. And that was exactly what we did".

Then came the end of the war. It was hard for the men, as two days earlier, on May 5th, a Squadron Mosquito caught fire on take-off, causing the death of the crew. The carpenters had to make two more coffins. There were celebrations, but as everyone knew that the war was coming to an end, when it really happened it was a kind of anti-climax. The Squadron stood down from operations on 9th May 1945; the war was over. The diarist of those days had other things to worry about: how to get sufficient equipment to add golf to the long list of Squadron sports activities. One club and two balls were hardly enough to allow the Squadron great scores in this field of conflict. Seven days after VE-Day No.600 Squadron moved to a new airfield, Campoformido, near Udine. The base had been on the Squadrons hitlist, now it became its home. The aircrew practised formation flying for the big DAF fly-past that was to take place on 28th May. Four days earlier a well-deserved MBE was awarded to W/O Nelson, the Squadron Engineering Officer. Some crews made sight-seeing tours in the area and it looked as if No.600 Squadron embarked on a long-delayed holiday. With the cessation of hostilities it was essential for the military to establish itself in the area around Trieste, and to the Austrian border as soon as possible. Tito, the Yugoslav partisan leader had claimed Trieste for his victorious republic and the Allies believed he had received enough. The move to Campoformido was completed on 29th June 1945. It was certainly a change to be near a town not touched by the ravages of war. The cinema had a revolving roof, closed during the show but opened to reveal the stars during an interval. However there was still work to do, but the urgency was not so great and liberty trips to Venice and Grado were arranged for the men. At this stage the Squadron had been continually in action since landing in North Africa in November 1942. There had been no real leave and the majority of the ground crew had been abroad for nearly three years, mainly living in tents or bomb damaged houses. The procedure was for everyone to have eight days off in rotation. It was therefore natural that the men's thoughts now turned to organising some form of break from the general routine. All units of the Desert Air Force, of which No.600 Squadron still was a part, were encouraged to make their own arrangements for local rest camps. Hotels were taken over, even in some cases retaining the original staff. No.600 of course were quick off the mark on this venture and a recce party soon located a small Albergo on the shore of Lago di Alesso. It required a certain refurbishment before they could use it, so a working party was detailed. George Curtiss was included as the carpenter as were two local Italian painters collected en route.

The men erected tents for sleeping accommodation, and George's task was to erect a bar, complete with shelves, which, from a miraculous but unknown source were soon filled with a full selection of wines and liqueurs. The lads nicknamed the beer "Onion beer" which was self-explanatory. The camp kitchen was also constructed using the, by this time, well tried and tested method of Diesel fired ovens made from 50 gallon oil drums. Very effective but smelly and really frightening when in full operation. The lake was a big attraction to the Squadron. Nestled among surrounding mountains it was a picture of tranquillity and beauty. The Albergo had its own landing stage, dilapidated but serviceable, complete with two rather dodgy looking row-boats These were soon put to good use, and swimming became the No.1 sport. The small town of Alesso was about 15 minutes walk away at one end of the lake, a typical mountain place, with the central walled fountain in the middle of the square, and a stream which flowed alongside the main street with the big stones where the local women did their laundry. The apparent owner of the Albergo was not overjoyed to see the Gentlemen in Blue, until he realised they were friendly and that he was getting his place refurbished. Curtiss made friends with Olivo, the local carpenter, who had some interest in the Albergo, as he owned the boats. One particular evening he was very mysterious and asked George and another chap of the Squadron to slip away with him quietly in one of the boats. He rowed them to a remote part of the lake where he dived into the water and disappeared, briefly coming up for air at intervals. Then the reason became obvious, as, from the depths there appeared a lovely rowing boat, in perfect condition which, as he later explained he had sunk there during the war to hide it from the Tedeschi.

In fact there were two such boats, which Olivo kindly put at No.600 Squadron's disposal. Curtiss' mind boggled as to what other treasures were hidden in that lake, but he never asked. Later the Squadron engineers, with two oil drums and odds and ends made a lovely diving platform which the Squadron anchored in the lake. One annoyance was the local fishermen who discovered the easiest way to fish was to toss hand grenades into the water and just collect the stunned fish from the surface. As former partisans they still had

Cesenatico, May 1945. VE-Day; a last photograph in front of the Mosquito.

a fair selection of weapons, but this habit was very unpleasant if one was swimming under water. Also they were surprised at the lack of buoyancy in the water, having been used to swimming in the Mediterranean. It had been a real partisan area during the war. The road past the camp to the north alongside the lake, with the mountain cliff on one side and a sheer drop to the lake on the other, had been partly blown away, leaving a very treacherous passage, just the width of a three ton lorry. No Squadron personnel were allowed on the transport while the driver negotiated this stretch of road.

The Squadron, with the help of their friend Olivo, engaged two local girls as waitresses. They were typical of the local girls who had only been accustomed to the hard work on the land, that to have such a job looked like heaven to them. It was from these girls that the Squadron learnt of the dreaded Cossacks, or "Cossaki" as they called them. These Russian collaborators had been stationed here and their cruelty seemed to have been worse than that of their masters. It appeared that the Germans were tolerated in the area but the very mention of the Cossacks really did upset the people. In fact the men of the Squadron could not understand the situation as they believed that the Russians were Allies and friends. It was not until much later that they did learn facts relative to these Cossacks. One by-product of this was the fact that the retreating Cossacks had commandeered all the horses and mules, which were later rounded up in Austria and the Royal Veterinary Corps had the job of returning these animals to their rightful owners. The route they used passed the 600 Camp and often they stopped for a cup of char. It was also obvious that not all the horses ever reached their real destination, as although each man started off with eight animals, numbers were very depleted by the time they reached Alesso. In fact No.600 Squadron acquired or rather borrowed a few for the lads to ride, which meant the establishment of a new RAF trade had to be invented, that of "AC/Stable Lad", a very popular job among many ground crew. As a change to the usual menu Olivo recommended the local women be invited to supply the Squadron with pasta. A lady arrived with all her equipment, the Squadron supplied the necessary ingredients and soon she had a clothes line full of pasta drying in the sun. Certainly a sight very few of 600 had ever seen before. Yes, the pasta harvest in Alesso was quite good that year.

The rest camp continued until the end of July when the Squadron "campers" returned to Aviano to be told that the Squadron was breaking up, and much to the disgust of the original Auxiliary men, were posted to other units, not being sent home as some had expected. Campoformido was the place where the Squadron lost a great deal of its pride. First they were reduced to a "number only organisation", thus becoming a unit without a purpose. The last flights were made by W/C Drummond, F/Ls Clark and Taylor and P/O Leech. They took up visitors from the Honourable Artillery Company, their friends from Finsbury Barracks, for a Cook's tour of the area. Subsequently the pilots flew away to hand their Mosquitoes to No.256 Squadron. Farewell parties were held during the night of 17th August 1945. It ended with a hilarious Chance Light lit midnight volleyball game, at a normal sporting hour for No.600. W/C Drummond left to take over No.114 Squadron. Funds were distributed, tents were struck and, except as a number, one of the greatest night-fighter Squadrons ceased to exist on 21st August, VJ-Day. Aircrew returned from POW camps. One of them, F/L Wilmer, told his friends that his interrogator apparently had the greatest respect for the Squadron for, after being shot down and captured, he was brought in front of this German, who asked very interested: "And where is No. 600 Squadron nowadays?"

The war was over, No.600 Squadron had fought in the entire conflict. It had cashed and paid, paid dearly in good friends and respected comrades. The diarist made the final account for the war:

Enemy Aircraft
Destroyed	165
Probably destroyed	13
Damaged	34

Enemy Railways
Destroyed	3 steam locomotives
	1 electric locomotive
	20 trains
Damaged	10 trains

Motor Transport
Destroyed	16
Damaged	15

<u>Enemy Shipping</u>

Destroyed   1 "I" boat
Damaged   1 "I" boat
                        6 barges

Such was the war story of No.600 (City of London) Squadron, Auxiliary Air Force, the Gentlemen in Blue.

CHAPTER 12

AUXILIARIES IN PEACE.
August 1945 to March 1957

The disbanding of the Squadron was a bitter anti-climax. Having been the highest scoring night-fighter Squadron of the RAF with a service of thirty-two years, it seemed, all had come to an end. The Regulars were posted to other units and some of the Auxiliaries became Regulars. The majority returned home to England and the Dominions to find a place in civvy street.

The first officers after the reformation of No.600 Squadron. Standing from left to right: Gerrard Pete, Jack Atkinson, Robert Beeching, John Wright and Alan Chisholm-Will. Seated from left to right are David Proudlove, Norman Hayes (OC600) and "Togs" Mellersh.

Within a year everything changed. In July 1946, the Squadron was reformed as a day fighter unit under S/L Norman Hayes DFC. During the war he had risen to the rank of Wing Commander. To become OC600, the Squadron in which he had experienced the frightening start of the war over the skies of Holland in May 1940, Norman reverted to the rank of Squadron Leader. Sir Archibald Sinclair continued as the Honorary Air Commodore and Town HQ remained at Finsbury Barracks. Hendon however was unsuitable for modern fighters, so Biggin Hill was chosen to accommodate the Squadron. Two Regular officers were posted to assist in the build-up. They were F/L "Togs" Mellersh DFC (Adjutant), who was in the Squadron during the campaign in Africa and Italy, and F/L Atkinson (Assistant Adjutant). Other officers were Gerrard Pete, David Proudlove, Robert Beeching, Alan Chisholm-Will and John Wright. A party of fourteen Regular airmen arrived on the 14th followed by two Harvards on the 17th. These two-seaters would serve as training aircraft. The composition of the reborn 600 Squadron was 3 Flights, of which one was a Training Flight with two Harvards and four Spitfire XIVs. The two Operational Flights of nine Spitfires XXIs or XXIIs were led by an two Auxiliary Commandants. The cadre establishment was thirty-nine Regular and hundred-thirteen Auxiliary airmen. On 1st July the first Regular airman arrived. He was Cpl Haywood (Signals). On 19th August the Squadron received its parachutes. Recruiting for Auxiliary personnel began in November 1946. On 20th March 1947 Spitfire XXI, LA330, arrived as the first operational aircraft. Within ten days the second landed. The first post-war Camp was held at Tangmere in 1947 with Spitfires, while the following year Camp was at Thorney Island in June 1948, where S/L Proudlove took over from S/L Hayes. S/L Proudlove went into active service from his university Air Squadron in May 1940. During the war he flew with No.91 Squadron and held other operational and staff appointments, being twice Mentioned in Despatches. In addition to the maintenance of a fully operational fighter Squadron, Proudlove saw as his main immediate tasks, one, to resolve the question of an Honorary Air Commodore who was at that time Sir Archibald Sinclair (later Lord Truro), Minister for Air in the wartime Government and, two, to ensure the recognition of the pre-war badge. After the war Sir Archibald had moved to his estate at Thurso in Scotland and had intimated to Proudlove that he felt it would be appropriate to have an Honorary Air Commodore who could provide more readily available assistance than he could. He agreed that Proudlove should pursue the question of a new appointment. Through his family connections Proudlove had access to the Queen, and additionally Gp/Capt Peter Townsend, Equerry to the King, was a great friend. Following lunch with Townsend a meeting was arranged at Windsor Castle with the King, the Queen, Peter Townsend and David Proudlove. At this meeting the King said that as 600 was the Senior Auxiliary Fighter Squadron He, the King, should be the Honorary Air Commodore. Townsend quickly pointed out that as Monarch He was already Honorary Air Commodore in Chief. At this moment the Queen grasped the nettle and said: "Oh, then there is nothing whatever to stop me being Honorary Air Commodore", and so with a glass of champagne and much jollity the matter was settled. An immediate announcement could not be made because it was necessary for Proudlove to fly to Scotland and acquaint Sinclair (now Lord Thurso) with the situation. For various reasons this could not be accomplished for about two months and in the meantime the change was to be kept a dead secret. This secrecy led to the Squadron officers adopting a new procedure for any after dinner toast to the Honorary Air Commodore. The officers whispered from one to another around the table "Honorary Air Commodore" before the PMC rose to give the toast "Gentlemen, The Queen". This was the origin of a custom which remained throughout the active life of the Squadron.

On 16th December 1947 HM the King granted the title "Royal Auxiliary Air Force". It was a great reward for the Gentlemen in Blue to have this prefix to their Air Force. Since the reformation of the Squadron the aircraft no longer had the "BQ" registration. From now on the fuselage would show the Reserve Command "RAG" code to indicate that this was No.600 Squadron. The City of London crest proudly depicted on the port side of the nose. That year the first large social function was held by the officers at Finsbury Barracks with some of the Squadron trophies on show. In February 1949 a Squadron Annual Dinner was held, at Finsbury Barracks. In the news media it said: "600 (City of London) Fighter Squadron give a party". No less than eleven photographs showed happily smiling officers and glamorous ladies enjoying a cool drink and good company. The Gentlemen in Blue were back in business. To celebrate a "Grand Dance" was held on 11th March with tickets costing 2/6. Those were the days!

The 1949 Annual Camp was at Biggin Hill. The diarist recorded a new demand on the pilots: "Instrument flying; one of the curious evolutions required of us in order to produce an All Weather Air Force". During Camp the pilots were photographed between their Spitfires and their Austin Sevens. Someone noted that S/L Proudlove was pictured in uniform, flat on the ground amidst his fellow-officers "still wearing his tennis socks."

Another event in the Squadron's Association with the City of London was St. George's Day on 23rd April 1949. Exactly at the same moment when the Lord Mayor, Sir George Aylwen, was inspecting the Squadron at Armoury House, aircraft roared over in salute. The papers wrote: "Many a Londoner must have been puzzled by the sight of nine Tiger Moths circling for half an hour over the City's centre last Saturday afternoon. Familiar as the veteran trainers are, they have seldom previously appeared in formation over the capital. At Finsbury Barracks that afternoon the Territorial and Auxiliary Forces Association had arranged a parade of auxiliary and reserve forces as part of St. George's Day and to publicise local recruiting. Among the "troops" present were contingents representing the

Four Squadron Spitfires in close formation during the 1948 Camp at Thorney Island.

Territorial Army, the Navy, Marine and RAF Volunteer Reserve and the pre-service units.

"The Central Band of the RAF provided part of the music for the parade, which was commanded by Major General Whittaker, and inspected by the Lord Mayor, Sir George Aylwen and Sheriffs of the City of London. To conclude the parade there was to be a formation fly-past by aircraft of the Royal Auxiliary Air Force and the RAFVR. The Volunteer Reserve was represented by nine Tiger Moths of No.17 Reserve Flying School, based at Hornchurch. Flying in three-flights-in-vic formation the trainers orbited at 80ft south of the Thames, waiting for the nine Spitfire 21s and 22s of No.600 (City of London) Squadron which were to precede them. From the front cockpit of the aircraft flown by F/O Bunting the writer had ample time to consider the balanced dignity of the city below with palace and power station alike sharing the relaxation of the warm weekend sun. Such day dreams, however, were suddenly shattered by the arrival from the south (appearing almost supersonic from a Tiger Moth) of the nine Squadron Spitfires, led by F/L Meadows DFC. As the fighters passed a few hundred feet above us, their Griffon engines drowned the crackle of the Gypsy Majors with an almost contemptuous roar". It certainly made people aware that 600 Squadron was very much alive indeed. No effort was spared to interest people in the possibility of joining. An extensive advertising program was carried out in May 1949 with the net result of two applicants. With an almost bitter sense of humour the diarist wrote: "The first had not flown before, but as a variety comedian specialised in standing on his head, and considered that with this experience he would train as a pilot with very little difficulty. The second had an excellent war record, with a number of enemy planes to his credit. He had also been an A2 Flying Instructor. Unfortunately however all with the Luftwaffe. The Squadron did not give up it's quest for men. It came with a quiz for groundcrew recruits, inviting applicants to use their spare time profitably. It read as follows:

Q. What is the Royal Auxiliary Air Force?
A.   It is the front line of fighter aircraft
Q. What is 600 Squadron?
A.   It is the Senior squadron in the Royal Auxiliary Air Force. Its present role is as a fighter squadron for the defence of Great

Britain. (Some further facts about its history are given at the back of this pamphlet).

Q. **Where is it located?**

A. At Biggin Hill aerodrome. Town Headquarters are at Finsbury Barracks.

Q. **What trades are wanted?**

A. There are vacancies in most ground trades, especially in the engine, airframe, wireless, electrical and instrument trades.

Q. **Where and when does training take place?**

A. At weekends at Biggin Hill and one night each week at Finsbury Barracks. In addition the Squadron moves to an operational station for two weeks continuous training each summer.

Q. **How much training is required a year?**

A. 15 days continuous training (at summer camp). 30 hours non-continuous training. 15 weekends at Biggin Hill. On completion of the above, auxiliaries are entitled to a bounty of £9 per annum free of tax; if a further 60 hours non-continuous training is carried out a supplementary bounty of £3 is payable.

Q. **What about pay?**

A. Auxiliaries are paid for training as follows: 1. For a period of 8 hours, one full day's pay in their rank and trade; rations are issued and meals provided free. 2. For periods of less than 8 hrs, a subsistence allowance of 9d. an hour is paid. 3. For summer camp, full pay and allowances of the rank and trade. 4. Bounty is paid as outlined above.

Q. **Are there any allowances for travelling expenses?**

A. Yes. Mileage allowance of 1fid. a mile is paid for travelling from home to place of duty by public transport. Those who have cars or motorcycles can also draw petrol coupons to cover their mileage, and allowance of up to 3d. a mile.

Q. **Is previous service essential?**

A. No, but there is a great need of trained men. If your civilian trade is of a technical nature it may be easy to train you to the required standard.

Q. **What ranks are granted?**

A. Every airman, whatever rank he may have held before, is enlisted as an Aircraftman second class (AC2). Those who held higher ranks are quickly reclassified to leading

Aircraftman (LAC). Promotion to NCO rank is by selection.

Q. Who may enlist?

A. Men between the ages of 18 and 38.

Q. How long is the engagement for?

A. Four years. Re-engagements are allowed for periods up to a further four years.

Q. HOW DO I JOIN?

A. Come to Biggin Hill any weekend, or to Finsbury Barracks, City Road, on any Monday evening, or write to: The Officer Commanding, No.600 Squadron Royal Auxiliary Air Force, RAF Station Biggin Hill, Westerham, Kent.

Operation FOIL took place in June 1949. It was a very important Air Defence exercise in which nearly all the squadrons of the Royal Auxiliary Air Force took part. This participation was limited to the weekends only. The men worked very hard and the standards set were a source of surprise to umpires and reporters alike.

Spitfire RAG-J, ZA328, flying over the beautiful Kent countryside, 1949. Note the "City of London" badge below the cowlings.

The exercise was followed by an invitation to take part in the D-Day celebrations held in Cherbourg between the 4th and 6th of June that year. The French hosts had chosen the dates for a rally to commemorate that it was five years ago that the huge Allied Armada had crossed the Channel and driven out the Germans. The occasion was the first post-war revival of the annual air rally attended by officers from all over France. Six Spitfire XXIIs and two Ansons with groundcrew flew from Biggin Hill to Maupertus, Cherbourg in the early morning hours of June 4th. In the afternoon the French Minister for Air inspected the Squadron. David Proudlove presented a letter from the Lord Mayor of London to the Maire of Cherbourg. A superb show of air drill by Squadron pilots left a deep impression with the French. On landing the pilots were piled into a jeep for a triumphal ride in front of a cheering crowd. The pilots were David Proudlove, Jack Meadows, George Webster, Keith Haselwood, Tim Clutterbuck and Sgt Cables. After the show the men were entertained by the French. It was the most exhausting part of the commemoration. A municipal reception in the Town Hall was followed by a banquet at the sixteenth century Chateau de Tourlaville, where they were welcomed by the Minister for Air. S/L Proudlove to the delight of all the hosts replied in French. Then followed a grand ball. On the Sunday the President of the French Air Reserve and S/L Proudlove laid wreaths on the Cherbourg war memorial. After an excellent lunch at Barfleur the party toured the battlegrounds and took part in a ceremony at Sainte Mère Église, the first town liberated by the Allied troops in 1944. On the Monday No.600 returned to Biggin Hill via Rouen where the Spitfires took part in a second display. When the Squadron returned they were very enthusiastic about the hospitality of the French. The diary gave a vivid account of the ground duties carried out: fine menus, wine labels and the proud remark that the Squadron had set a new French record for the number of "Trou Normand" consumed during one meal. (Few people know that the Trou Normand is the art of drinking Calvados from a chamber pot).

Social life played an important role in the life of Auxiliary squadrons. In June 1949, during summer camp at Thorney Island, the Squadron held a Guest Night and entertained Air Marshal Sir Alan Lees, AOC-in-C Reserve Command. But it was not just all play. "Flight" magazine wrote in admiration that the "near perfect station-keeping of these Spitfires is an indication of the results of many hours' weekend and annual training by squadrons of the Royal Auxiliary Air Force". They published a photograph of No.600 Squadron during a sortie at the fortnight's camp at Thorney Island. A few weeks later, in July, great men came to spend an evening with No.600. Field Marshal Sir William and Lady Slim, Air Chief Marshal Sir John Slessor, and Air Marshal Sir Basil and Lady Embry were among the guests at a cocktail party given by the COs and Officers of Nos.600 and 615 Squadrons at Biggin Hill on 16th July. Lord Huntingfield, the Hon. Air Commodore of No.21 Squadron of the Royal Australian Air Force was present to represent the members of this Reserve unit from so far away.

Cherbourg, D-Day 1949. Some of the 600 Squadron officers who took part in the fly-past, the celebrations, dinners and other functions. From left to right George Webster, Sgt. Cables, Keith Haselwood and Tim Clutterbuck. S/L Hughes (right) seems somewhat apprehensive.

If any announcement caused great pride and joy it must have been what was written in the second supplement to the London Gazette of Friday 29th July. It was a deep wish and maybe some thought it was too much. But to the great delight and pride of each individual squadron member it said:

Air Ministry, 2nd August, 1949

With the King's approval, Her Majesty the Queen has graciously consented to become Honorary Air Commodore of No.600 (City of London) Squadron, Royal Auxiliary Air Force, and No.2600 (City of London) Light Anti-Aircraft Squadron, Royal Auxiliary Air Force Regiment, 22nd July 1949.

It was a great honour indeed. Squadron officers met at the Antelope Bar to have an informal celebration of the news that the Queen had accepted her appointment. On the occasion of Her Majesty's birthday on the 4th of August the Squadron sent a telegram to which She replied: "My sincere thanks to all ranks for their loyal message of birthday greetings which I have received with much pleasure".

September saw another commemoration of the Battle of Britain. More than 200 aircraft took part in the fly-past. A single Hurricane, the last (sic!) remaining serviceable aircraft of this type, flown by Air Vice-Marshal Vincent, himself a Battle of Britain pilot, opened the fly-past. There were six groups of aircraft. The first group consisted of 24 Lancasters and 30 Lincolns, The second group was a formation of 10 Washingtons and 5 Hastings transport aircraft. In the third group 30 Mosquitoes brought back proud memories of the Pathfinders, the night-fighters, the strike aircraft and the civilian Mossies. In group 4, 18 Spitfires -some of 600 Squadron- were followed by Hornets, Sea Hornets and Sea Furies. Fighter Command represented itself in group 5 with no less than 42 Meteors. The last group consisted of 18 Vampires and 24 Meteors. It was one of many moving events with strong links to the Squadron's own past.

In October the 10th Annual Dinner was again at Finsbury Barracks, followed by the highlight of the year, when on the 29th the new Honorary Air Commodore, Her Majesty Queen Elizabeth for the first time visited the Squadron at Biggin Hill. As admission to the enclosures was by tickets only there was no undue crowding and ATC cadets lined the route from the guardroom to the place where the parade was to take place. Then the Squadron marched out, led by the combined Bands of Nos.2 and 4 Areas RAF. The time was 1430hrs. Five minutes later the officers marched on. At the parade ground twelve Spitfires had been lined up in two Flights of

Her Majesty the Queen inspecting No.600 Squadron at Biggin Hill, the first time after becoming Honorary Air Commodore. From l.t.r: Jack Meadows, Fred Doherty, Her Majesty, David Proudlove, P/O North.

six each. In front of each aircraft stood the pilot with two airmen. At 1500hrs Her Majesty arrived and She was officially welcomed by the Lord-Lieutenant of Kent, Lord Cornwallis, after which she was met by the CO, S/L David Proudlove. Then the Queen was introduced to the VIPs, being Lord Limerick, Air Marshal Porter. Air/Cdre Ackerman and the Squadron Adjutant F/L Sammy Osborne. Then Her Majesty's Standard was flown.

In what "Flight" called perfect English weather, Her Majesty the Queen reviewed Her Squadron, of which she had recently become the Honorary Air Commodore. The Squadron's Spitfires were lined up facing the traffic control tower, which had been transformed into a royal dais and was decorated with chrysanthemums. All Squadron aircraft were resplendent in their new coats of aluminium dope, with burnished engine cowling and red painted spinners. Each aircraft bore the Squadron's pre-war badge, which incorporated that of the City of London. The Queen, inspecting Squadron personnel and aircraft, walked the whole length of the line-up and stopped a number of times to talk with the pilots and ground crews.

After the inspection the Queen addressed the Squadron: "I think that all of us who lived in London during the war have a very special feeling towards the Squadrons who defended us, and a great pride in their exploits. We must always be grateful to those who served in the Squadron as peacetime volunteers before the war, for by that service they laid the foundations on which later triumphs were based. I am indeed pleased that all of you on parade today also believe in giving voluntary service to your country, for it helps to consolidate the victory we won in war and is a bulwark against the threat to peace. I am glad to be at Biggin Hill. The finger of history has written many pages of gallantry here and in the skies above our heads".

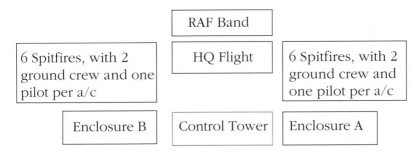

The Queen also mentioned how proud she was to be appointed Honorary Air Commodore of the senior Squadron of the Royal Auxiliary Air Force. She called it a personal link between herself and the Auxiliaries, and she continued: "My first words to you as your Honorary Air Commodore are to pay tribute to the achievements of this splendid Squadron. You have a great tradition now, linking you to that ancient city whose name you bear and in whose defence so many of your comrades fought and fell I am sure from what I have seen today that it is in good hands". At the close of the speech the Queen received three cheers and, as Jamie Morrison, one of the members present, said, there was a scramble take-off of every available serviceable aircraft and then the Squadron flew a perfect display. "Flight" said in its article: "It was a joy to watch the precision with which the pilots mounted their aircraft together, started the engines and, turning right, taxied to the end of the runway to take off in flights of three. No squadron, could have improved upon their performance. Squadron Vic was formed immediately after take-off and in this and other formations the Spitfires were flown low across the airfield in front of the dais. The final run-in was "flights in line astern, in echelon to starboard", from which each machine in succession peeled off to port and landed from the turn. It was a most effective manoeuvre carried out with perfect timing. The officer in charge of the parade and fly-past was F/L J.P. Meadows". At the close of the flying programme the Queen took tea with the officers and their ladies, and later joined a number of guests who were gathered in another anteroom. The majority of the visitors were ex-members of the Squadron and officers of No.615, who shared Biggin Hill with 600 Squadron.

Queen Elizabeth with the officers of No.600 Squadron after the inspection. Standing l/r: F/O John Cormack, F/O Peter Lovegrove, F/O Mike Oliver, F/O Tim Clutterbuck DFC, F/L "Doc" Pattrick, F/O Glen Williams and F/L Robert Beeching. Seated l/r: F/O Keith Haselwood, F/L Sam Osborne DFC, S/L David Proudlove, Her Majesty the Queen, F/L Jack Meadows DFC, F/L Morris Maxwell and F/L John Wright MBE.

Escorted by David Proudlove, who made the introductions, Her Majesty chatted with many of the guests, having a special word for S/L Hayes, who commanded the Squadron before S/L Proudlove took over. On 25th November She came to THQ and for the first time Her Majesty was noticed wearing the "unofficial" Squadron badge comprising the arms of the City of London with a scroll. This badge was made of rubies and diamonds, set in platinum and had been presented at Buckingham Palace earlier in the day by S/L

Proudlove as a gift from the Squadron. *(Her Majesty has on every subsequent visit to the Squadron, and later to the Association worn the City of London shield badge).* The Queen as Honorary Air Commodore was for the first time photographed seated between the officers of a very proud Squadron.

In 1949 all Royal Auxiliary Air Force fighter squadrons were transferred from Reserve to Fighter Command. It was a recognition of the proficiency of the squadrons, fully able to serve and if necessary to fight alongside the Regulars as they had done during the war. From now on Fighter Command would be responsible for training, operations, and administration. Reserve Command was to remain responsible for recruiting, service conditions and all dealings with Territorial and Auxiliary Forces Associations. Squadrons were to remain at their present airfields, and existing local associations and links with cities and counties would remain the same. Biggin Hill and North Weald returned to the bosom of Fighter Command, unlike most of the other reserve airfields. It brought the Squadron into the spotlight once again. Flight Magazine of 3rd November published an eight pages article about what John Yoxall called "The Queen's Squadron". He reported how 600 Squadron was formed and what gallant actions they had carried out during the war. Soon afterwards the first reactions appeared in the press. P.L. Burke wrote that he had detected errors in the story of Yoxall. No.25 Squadron had not been mentioned as having been equipped with Blenheims like No.600. He was upset by the fact that No.600 was given the honour of having been the first Squadron equipped with radar-Blenheims. "No.25 was first!!" He also remarked that not the entire Squadron, but just A-Flight had moved from one Italian airfield to the other in 1944. Someone else disputed the fact that 600 was the first Auxiliary Squadron. A former navigator (Mason of No.500 Squadron) wrote that although technically not a Squadron member, he and a No.600 Squadron pilot (Raleigh Hilken)had shot down the first Italian aircraft, albeit in a Beaufighter "on loan" from No.500 Squadron.

On 8th June 1950 Proudlove led a section of 4 Spitfire 22s over Paris as a further celebration of D-Day. This flight was recognised in a limited edition of Royal Doulton plates. Two days later the Squadron abandoned propellers and went "jet". Between 10th and 24th June they were the first Auxiliary Squadron to be equipped with twin-engined Gloster Meteor jets. It happened during the Annual

Camp for the Squadron's Silver Jubilee at Thorney Island. Eleven
Meteor IVs, two Meteor VIIs and the two Harvards, forming a
Training Flight of six (two Meteor IVs, two Meteor VIIs and the two
Harvards) and A and B-Flights of in total nine Meteor IVs. A and B-
Flights carried out tactical and gunnery exercises, utilising the rather
poor weather on certain days to practise snake climbs through
cloud, and cloud formation flying. Both air-to-air and air-to-ground
firing was carried out, firing 5,000 20mm rounds. During night flying
exercises the A-Flight Meteors operated between 20,000 and 40,000
feet, while five pilots from B-Flight converted to the new Meteor jets.
Four accidents occurred that week. Twice it was a pilot error (One
pilot undershot the runway and broke his undercarriage, the other
pilot retracted his wheels too soon, causing the Meteor to slide and
damage its belly). Twice the undercarriage proved too weak to stand
the landings made by the pilots. The Squadron was learning jet
flying the hard way. But nevertheless the media were impressed by
the civilians who spent so much time and devotion in the Forces.
The newspapers reported:

Tools and jets at Thorney replace Pens and Desks

Sun-tanned, a 29-year old Treasury clerk adjusted his new blue forage
cap as he stood beside a jet fighter at Thorney Island yesterday, and
said: "It's good to smell aircraft again". "We can leave our wives
beside the sea, too", he added. The Squadron, who were celebrating
their silver jubilee that year, were the top-scoring night-fighter
Squadron in the RAF during World War II. Said the CO, S/L D.
Proudlove : "What we have done before, we can do again. We are
not right up to strength, but we should have no difficulty in making
up the establishment in an emergency".

The Squadron's love for fun was a known fact too. The Gents in
Blue were never without an idea for a good joke. After working
hours the men would get together in their "field headquarters",
"Advanced Landing Ground" or whatever they called the pub where
the hospitality of the landlord, the price of the beer and the
endurance of the staff was beyond the limits of civvy street. The
Squadron were always keen to let the landlord know whether his
handling of the catering of "600" had been to everyone's liking.
    To show their appreciation for the hospitality given by the

proprietors of the "Ship & Bell", Horndean, they wrote a handsome and most impressive letter of recommendation, which said:

To whom it may concern:
Greetings.
We, the Auxiliary Officers of 600 City of London Squadron.

By this deed of gift hereby give back to the regular patrons of the hostelry known as the Barge & Clanger (or Fishticket & Tram-pleasure or Ship & Bell) all that peace & quiet and all those seats at the bar which they have been accustomed to enjoy: and to Judy we hereby give freedom from Meadows: and to all and sundry others who may read this notice we hereby recommend the aforementioned hostelry as a good place for serious drinking. We hereby give notice that the above gifts and freedoms are not rights in perpetuity and that we intend to return and revoke the same at the earliest possible moment. As witness the signature of the aforementioned officers of 600 City of London Squadron Royal Auxiliary Air Force

Keith Haselwood and his Cooper Trophy Team in front of his winning Meteor.

Apart from a great sense of humour and a continuous need to have fun, the Squadron seriously carried out its duties when expected to do so. This showed in July when F/O Haselwood won the Cooper Trophy, the annual high speed race for Auxiliary flyers at a speed of 511mph. The Evening News of 7th July wrote:

London Businessman Wins Race At RAF Display
A 'Week-End' Pilot, he flies at 511 mph.

Spectators saw a thrilling finish to the Royal Auxiliary Air Force annual high-speed race for "week-end" flyers at the first post-war display at Farnborough today. Flying a Meteor IV jet fighter, Flying Officer K.N. Haselwood managed to get his nose in front to gain first place with a speed of 511 mph. Haselwood, aged 31, a City business man, lives at Blake Lane, New Malden, Surrey and flies with 600 (City of London) Squadron.

Flight Magazine reported about this victory:

The Cooper Trophy Race –

"With a handicap of 5min 13sec F/O Haselwood (No.600 Squadron – Meteor 4) had just become airborne as the slower entries completed their first lap. Cornering technique was, as always, varied, but the finish was excellent. The Spitfires appeared first over the trees with the Vampires overhauling them rapidly, and then the Meteor came as if from nowhere to shriek over the line one second ahead of F/O Smith (501,Vampire 1), who was followed into third place by F/L Storrar (603, Spitfire 22). The winner's speed was 511 mph, and the Cooper Trophy thus passes from No.502 (Ulster) Squadron to No.600 (City of London) Squadron".

However, soon the papers would be less complimentary when 600 Squadron jets took the expression "on the deck" a bit too realistic. The Evening Standard wondered who the culprits were when its reporter wrote the headline:

"4 Jets roar over City at '0' feet.

Four RAF Meteor jet fighters roared at nought feet over rooftops of the City and Central London this afternoon. The Air Ministry said inquiries were being made to find out what the aircraft were doing over London.

The Squadron diarist's comment was: *"Whose City is it anyway?*

On 26th July 1950 Her Majesty the Queen came to the Priory Church of Saint Bartholomew the Great to unveil a memorial stone in the Lady Chapel. The chapel was dedicated to those who lost their lives whilst serving with No.600 Squadron in war and peace. This Jubilee Service during the Squadron's twenty-fifth Anniversary drew much attention of the press. "Flight" showed a drawing of the chapel and reported at length how S/L Proudlove accompanied Her Majesty into the church and during the service that followed. The Lord Mayor and Lady Mayoress were there and a contingent of French Air Force officers joined the Auxiliaries during this important event. The following day the Private Secretary to the Queen wrote to David Proudlove saying how greatly Her Majesty had been impressed by the Service. "It was clear that all those responsible for it had taken the utmost pains, with the result that it was in every way a worthy and memorable tribute to the Squadron's Jubilee".

Long before the war the Squadron had received a badge consisting of the City of London crest surmounted by Air Force eagle and with the words "City of London Squadron" underneath. This badge, approved by the Lord Mayor of London, was never registered with the College of Heralds. During the war in common with all Auxiliary Squadrons the personnel changed dramatically and by the time 600 was a night-fighter squadron in the Desert there were no more Auxiliary pilots flying with the unit. Paddy Green, the Commanding Officer, understandably wanted 600 to have a real identity and an appropriate one for a night-fighter Squadron. Hence the design of a crescent moon dissected with a sword was approved by the Chester Herald and the original signed by HM the King. When the Squadron was reformed all pre-war members and the new Squadron members wanted the pre-war badge to be re-substituted. After protracted and fruitless negotiations with the Chester Herald, S/L Proudlove decided that he would ask for help from the Honorary Air Commodore who immediately expressed the view that the Squadron should have its pre-war badge back. The King intimated that he was prepared to cancel his signature on the war time badge and would sign the pre-war version.

However, he was advised by the College of Heralds that under no circumstances could a Monarch cancel his very own signature,

The two badges, above, the 1927, unauthorised but "right" one, below, the authorised but "wrong" one. Subsequently both badges have been approved.

and also that the pre-war badge was "heraldically impure"! Finally a compromise was reached whereby the Monarch agreed to sign the pre-war badge and that this one would be considered, henceforth, to be the badge of the Squadron: the use of the war time badge would be discontinued. As a result of this the Squadron became unique in having two signed Squadron badges. It was great news and the press jumped on it. The headline in the Evening Standard said: **"The Queen settles a five year battle over this"**, and showed a small finger pointing at a picture of the beloved "Dust-Cart Crest". The article read: The Queen chose the "dust-cart" badge last night and settled a five-year-old battle over the Royal Auxiliary Air Force City of London 600 Squadron's two crests, the "dust-cart" versus the "moon and paper knife". The Queen, Honorary Air Commodore of the Squadron, joined officers at dinner at Finsbury Barracks for the first time. On her black net gown spangled with gold sequins, she wore a diamond and ruby crest, the Squadron's gift – the crest they have always claimed as their own. "We have had this crest since the Squadron was formed more than 20 years ago", said F/L Haslewood, second in command. "It is the air force eagle over the arms of the City of London – we call it the "dust-cart" crest. During the war the squadron – the nightfighters – wore an Air Ministry crest of St. Paul's dagger across a crescent moon – the "moon-and-paper knife" crest. Afterwards it was this crest that the Royal College of Arms registered. "All our trophies have the old crest", said F/L Haselwood, "so we simply refused to admit that the new one existed. When the Queen became Honorary Air Commodore the old crest was readopted. Last night they asked her to make it the official one. The Queen agreed. Query – how does this affect the Battle of Britain window in Westminster Abbey, which now carries the moon and dagger?. The answer to the question was simple: In May 1951 S/L Meadows was informed that the "City" badge would replace the "Moon and Paper Knife" badge in the Battle of Britain window in Westminster Abbey.

With his appointment as Civil Adviser to the United Kingdom High Commission in India and Pakistan S/L Proudlove had, necessarily and with great regret, to retire as Officer Commanding No.600 Squadron. They were years he would always treasure He was succeeded by S/L Jack Meadows. In December Meadows accepted the Cooper Trophy during a presentation by ACM Sir Ralph Cochrane and AM Sir Basil Embry.

Biggin Hill: Sgt Dennis Overton and Cpl Eric Salisbury at work on the engine of a No. 600. Squadron Gloster Meteor.

On 16th April 1951 the Squadron members received calling-up papers for three months' training which would enable the Auxiliary Squadrons to share primary responsibility for Britain's Air Defence in the event of an emergency. All members enjoyed this call-up and the Squadron was at top-line efficiency. High ranking visitors like the Secretary of State for Air, Mr. Henderson came to see how the Auxiliaries did. The Meteors, proudly showing the old red-and-white shark teeth on the fuselage, flew like a charm when Henderson scrambled the Meteors by firing a green Verey light from flying control. The exercise started at Biggin Hill.

The second month was spent at Acklington on air-firing practice to return to the home base during the last month. All the Auxiliary Squadrons were called up, apart from No.600, there were Nos. 501, 502, 601, 604, 605, 608, 609, 613, 614, 615 and 616 with Meteors and Nos. 500, 504, 610 and 611 with Vampires. Nos. 603, 607 and 612 flew with Spitfires. Before 600 left there were good wishes from their Honorary Air Commodore and from Denys Lawson, the Lord Mayor of London. Sir John Slessor, the CAS and Mr. Henderson both congratulated the Squadron on a splendid turnout. But the exercise was to be very costly. On 18th June three RAF jets crashed within minutes of each other near Farnborough. A woman was injured and an ambulance overturned whilst being driven to the site of the accidents.

Three pilots lost their lives. Two of them were 600 Squadron members. The first was F/O Philip Sandeman, the second was Sgt Clarkson. According to investigations one aircraft had hit the other while turning in the Biggin Hill circuit. The pilots were too low to bale out. Meteors did not have ejector seats in those days. One aircraft crashed in the garden of a bungalow while the owner was

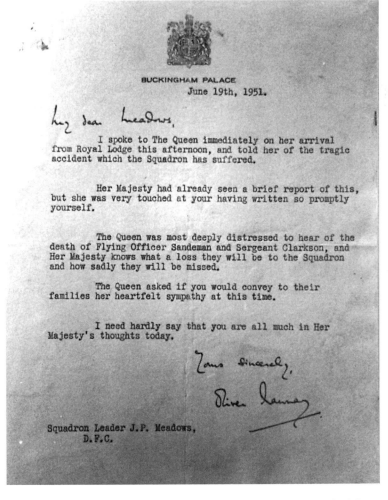

BUCKINGHAM PALACE
June 19th, 1951.

My dear Meadows,

       I spoke to The Queen immediately on her arrival from Royal Lodge this afternoon, and told her of the tragic accident which the Squadron has suffered.

       Her Majesty had already seen a brief report of this, but she was very touched at your having written so promptly yourself.

       The Queen was most deeply distressed to hear of the death of Flying Officer Sandeman and Sergeant Clarkson, and Her Majesty knows what a loss they will be to the Squadron and how sadly they will be missed.

       The Queen asked if you would convey to their families her heartfelt sympathy at this time.

       I need hardly say that you are all much in Her Majesty's thoughts today.

Yours sincerely,

Oliver Dawnay

Squadron Leader J.P. Meadows,
     D.F.C.

After the death of Sandeman and Clarkson a newspaper article described the crash, while the Honorary Air Commodore wrote letters of comfort to the relatives and to the CO.

Plane Hits Garden as Man Cuts Grass

THREE JETS CRASH IN TEN MINUTES

By Daily Mail Reporter

ON A HILLSIDE.—*All that is l₁ of a Meteor jet lies scattered abc the garden of Mr. Frank Bule bungalow. He was cutting gra there when it crashed after a m air collision with another jet. Br pilots were killed. Mr. Bu went to hospital with shock.*

cutting the grass. One aircraft crashed into a house, setting it on fire and injuring Mrs. Beatrix Harvey. The pilot of this aircraft was F/L MacDonald, an RAF officer. Almost immediately HM the Queen had a letter written to the Squadron. Her Private Secretary said: "I spoke to the Queen immediately on her arrival from Royal Lodge this afternoon and told her of the tragic loss which the Squadron has suffered. Her Majesty had already seen a brief report of this, but she was very touched at your having written so promptly yourself. The Queen was most deeply distressed to hear of the death of F/O Sandeman and Sgt Clarkson, and Her Majesty knows what a loss they will be to the Squadron and how sadly they will be missed. The Queen asked if you would convey to their families her heartfelt sympathy at this time. I need hardly say that you are all much in Her Majesty's thoughts today".

In his Will, Phillip Sandeman declared that almost all he had was for the wife of John Hawkesworth, the film producer. Their son was Sandeman's god-child. Meadows was approached by Mrs. Hawkesworth, who said she wanted part of the money to be used for the benefit of the Squadron. S/L Meadows consulted Peter Stewart, the "eminence grise" of the Squadron. It was decided that the money was to become the start of a trust fund. Solicitor Lindsay Hancock was to take care of legal matters and the trust was set up with Jack Meadows, Peter Stewart and a third member (Ralph Hiscox, David Clark or Norman Hayes) as the trustees. In essence the fund was to be for the welfare of any member or past member, welfare being deliberately an all-embracing term. The founding contribution of Mrs. Hawkesworth of between £500 and £1000 was quite large in those days. Other contributions from a variety of sources, inside and outside the Squadron, added to that amount. When Jack Meadows left for South Africa he was succeeded as a trustee by S/L John Cormack. After the Squadron disbanded the responsibility of appointing trustees moved from the Hon. Air Commodore to the President of the Squadron Association. In 1966 Jack Meadows returned to Britain and again became a trustee, with John Wright and Norman Wheeler.

In 1952 the whole nation was shocked when King George VI died. The funeral of King George VI, however, was to become one of the proudest duties of the Squadron. Jack Meadows has those days etched in his memory: "When the Squadron assembled at its Town HQ, next to the Honourable Artillery Company in Finsbury Barracks, on the evening after the King's death in 1952, we remembered that 600, 601 and 604, the then Hendon Squadrons, had been part of the forces lining the streets of London at King George V's funeral. Apart from a small cadre of Regulars we were all civilians, "weekend flyers". 600 flew its Meteors at weekends from Biggin Hill, trained at THQ on weekday evenings. As part of Fighter Command, the front line defence of the country, we prided ourselves that we flew as much as our brother regular Squadrons, and that some of ours were even better at the job than they were. That particular evening normal training was promptly replaced by practising the little known funeral drills; reversing arms, resting on arms reversed, changing reversed arms on the slow march. At Biggin Hill on Saturday I was shown a surprise signal from Air Ministry; no street lining for the Royal Auxiliary Air Force this time. Instead 600 and 603 the two Squadrons then with Royal Honorary Air Commodores – the former Queen and the new Queen respectively – were to provide a detachment of sixty men to march in the procession itself. We quickly obtained our share of keen volunteers ready to desert their paid employment for four days and accept this honour. On arrival at Uxbridge on Monday they drew rifles and bayonets while I reported to the Group Captain commanding. "Bad luck for you, old boy; I know your chaps cannot possibly be trained in time in all these strange drills; I have had the Regulars, two Squadrons each of 120 men, drilling away here since last Thursday, but you have only got two days now. It is impossible for you to be good enough in such a short time, so I am going to hide your chaps down the middle of the six-abreast column where they won't show". He meant it kindly and expected me to be grateful. I politely pointed out that my orders were to command the separate detachment of the Royal Auxiliary Air Force, that we were perfectly capable of giving a good show, that if necessary Air Ministry and the Inspector of the Royal Auxiliary Air Force would confirm this. "No good, old boy; I have already told Air Ministry the problem and they have agreed my plan, given me full authority. We have got lots of experience of these things, we know what we are talking about". I continued to protest. Finally he said: "Right, just to satisfy you, you can train separately and be an independent unit at the dress rehearsal on Wednesday afternoon. If you are bloody good then you can stay that way, otherwise – and that is what is bound to happen – your chaps will be hidden up between the Regulars, OK?" There was no choice but to accept, with as much grace as possible. "You can have any help you want", he said. I asked for the loan of two drill Sergeants to help our own Senior NCOs. With No.603 Squadron's Commanding officer, the second in command, Meadows went to explain to our combined troops what had happened – he had served a while with 603 and found some old friends from earlier Turnhouse days. There was no doubt of the view of both Squadrons. The Uxbridge Drill Sergeants arrived, already knowing the position and entered into the challenge with great heart. In miserable weather until eleven p.m. and again all next day and evening and the following morning the chaps drilled. In the rain and the dark they used open-sided draughty tin sheds with just enough dim electric light to enable us to keep at it. The dress rehearsal was at 2 p.m. on Wednesday. As the junior branch of the junior service the Auxiliaries would be right in the start of the parade, only the Central Band of the RAF ahead. In that order they slow-marched round and round the square with arms reversed, halted, did arms drill, repeated the march.

No.600 and No.603 Squadrons' contingent during the slow march, arms down, at the Funeral of HM King George VI.

After another half hour of this came a halt, the parade was stood at ease and the order came: "Fall out, Squadron Commanders". The three CO's marched to the Group Captain. He called for the Uxbridge Station Warrant Officer, always the most feared person of the Air Force, a magnificent figure of a man with an enormous voice and a long service career devoted to the finest points of ceremonial drill. "Well, Mister, what is the verdict, which was the best of the three Squadrons?" "No doubt about it, Sir, the Auxiliaries were the best." The Group Captain grinned at Meadows: "You win, well done." That night Jack went round the barrack blocks to congratulate the chaps again as they polished boots and brass and blancoed webbing. Next morning they marched to Uxbridge tube station and were on a special train by 6 am. Detraining at Trafalgar Square they marched halfway up the Mall to the head of the procession which wound back through Admiralty Arch down Whitehall to Westminster Abbey and had its tail somewhere down Victoria Street. There was then more than one hour's further wait before at last the Auxiliaries set off at the slow-march, Mendelssohn's "Dead March in Saul" echoing and re-echoing; up St. James's Street, down Piccadilly, through the Park, Marble Arch, Edgware Road, to Paddington Station where the coffin of our late Monarch would go by train to Windsor. Despite changing arms frequently they were after all this slow-marching a pretty stiff bunch of chaps by the time, in Paddington Station, their part in the proceedings was completed and they could break into a quick march, slope arms and move away. Worse was the demand from the bladders which had not been relieved since the men left Uxbridge five hours before. One or two men could not wait for their arrival at tents in Hyde Park with latrines and lunch, and were allowed to fall out and knock frantically on doors in Sussex Gardens, begging for relief. Jack Meadows then lived just across the Park. It was an anti-climax to have to go back by RAF bus to Uxbridge to collect civilian clothes and cars. Meanwhile the men were proud indeed of having done some small thing to honour their dead King and Honorary Air Commodore-in-Chief, and to have supported their Honorary Air Commodore in Her sorrow".

The June 1952 Annual Camp took the Squadron to Celle in Germany. Flying over that part of the Continent was quite pleasant, especially since the Squadron was allowed so many sorties. Soon after their return they experienced another historic occasion when

Biggin Hill, 1952. The Meteor Two-seater, John Wright in the cockpit. From left to right: George Long, Harry Lindup, three unknown airmen, Strudwick, unknown, Roy Monday, Dennis Overton, Rogers, Bill Harris, Dennis Nicholas, George Hodgkins, Stotesbury, Ron Benn, two unknown members, Champion, unknown, Devroome, and kneeling Frank Cook. The men on the wing are Joe Keyte and an unknown member.

Her Majesty as Honorary Air Commodore of No.600 Squadron and Sir Winston Churchill, as the same for No.615, arrived to inspect both Squadrons at Biggin Hill. Both COs, S/L Meadows for No.600 and the famous test pilot S/L Neville Duke for No.615, reported to Her Majesty. The parade was unfortunately in the hangar as the weather was very poor. The fly-past and the march-past had to be cancelled. The inspection was very thorough and the Queen often stopped to chat with Squadron members. Other high dignitaries present were the Lord-Lieutenant of Kent, Lord Cornwallis, AM Sir Basil Embry, AOC-in-C Fighter Command, AVM The Earl of Bandon, AOC 11 Group, Air/Cdre Morris, Sector Commander and W/C Pitt-Brown, RAF Biggin Hill Station Commander,. After the inspection officers of both Squadrons were photographed in front of the Mess with the Honorary Air Commodores. The 600 Squadron officers were:

S/L Meadows DFC	F/L Cormack	F/L Hawker DFC
F/L Warburton	F/L Lloyd-Davis DFC	F/L Bond
F/L Symonds	F/L Oliver	F/L Clutterbuck DFC
F/L Maxwell	F/L Moody	F/L Williams
F/L Wright MBE	F/O Reckitt	F/O Burvill
F/O Taylor	P/O Robarts-Arnold	P/O Miles
P/O Bridge	P/O Hale	P/O Muntz
P/O Holt	O/C Cunningham	O/C Crewsdon

"A good landing is a landing you walk away from", P/O Percy Prune used to say during the Second World War. When Meteor WE153 crash-landed on 12th September 1952 the pilot walked away from it in spite of the aircraft being badly damaged.

This "challenge" could not remain unanswered by No.615 Squadron. The next evening, during drinks at the King's Arms Hotel in Westerham, OC615, Neville Duke – the famous test pilot – sent a hand-written message to Jack Meadows:

To Six Nil Nil

We did not stop and buy one.
We would not even try one.
(but they did inspect your aircraft, crafty schemes.)
But we'll see you in the papers ,
With all the Sunday morning rapers
And at least you will be worldly, so it seems
Oh, you airmen of the Queen,
though your feathers oft you preen
You haven't even dispossessed a duke
With your clamour ever ready
Schweppersvescent, though more heady
Is enough to make a real squadron PUKE.

Two Honorary Air Commodores and their Officers at Biggin Hill in November 1952, during the visit to Nos.600 and 615 Squadrons. Back row, left to right F/Os Taylor and Burvill, P/Os Hale, Miles and Muntz. Third row l/r: P/Os Holt and Robarts-Arnold, F/O Reckitt, F/Ls Williams, Clutterbuck DFC and Moody. Second row l/r: O/C Crewsdon, P/O Bridge, F/Ls Oliver, Symonds, Maxwell and Wright MBE. Front row l/r: F/Ls Warburton, Lloyd-Davis DFC, Bond, Cormack and Hawker, S/L Meadows DFC (OC600), Her Majesty, Air/Cdre Sir Winston Churchill and S/L Sowrey (OC615). All other officers belong to No.615 Squadron.

F/O Colin Muntz who was sadly killed on 25th April 1953.

On 1st January 1953 the London Gazette announced the immediate award of the AFC to S/L Meadows. It was the first time this award went to a Squadron pilot. On 1st June another AFC was awarded to F/L R.T. Williams. It was the second AFC for No.600 Squadron in six months. The wonderful news of this award was soon to be overshadowed, when on 25th April F/O Colin Muntz was killed in an unfortunate flying accident. Immediately the

Queen Mother through her Private Secretary wrote to Muntz' mother: "I have been asked by Queen Elizabeth the Queen Mother as Honorary Air Commodore of No.600 "City of London" Squadron, to write and tell you how shocked and grieved Her Majesty was to hear of the tragic accident which occurred last Saturday in which your son lost his life. In your overwhelming loss I am to send you a message of Queen Elizabeth's deepest sympathy". Three weeks after the death of Colin Muntz No.600 Squadron assembled on the lawn of Buckingham Palace for the most important event in its history.

It was to be the first Auxiliary Squadron to receive a Standard. The Queen Mother had invited many important guests for this grand occasion, the Secretary of State for Air Lord de l'Isle and Dudley, AM Sir Dermot Boyle, C-in-C Fighter Command, AVM The Earl of Bandon, AOC11 Group, AVM Yool, Director of Auxiliaries, Reserves and Air Cadets, and AVM Constantine, AOC Fighter Command. In attendance was Gp/Capt Townsend, Equerry to HM. No.600 Squadron, over 100 strong, commanded by the S/L Jack Meadows, was inspected by the Queen.

The standard then was uncased and consecrated by the vicar of Saint Bartholomew's the Great, the Rev. Dr. Wallbank, Honorary Chaplain, in whose parish No. 600 Squadron had its HQ. "The Aeroplane" of 29th May reported how the Queen Mother had received the standard from the Inspector of the RAuxAF, Gp/Capt Birkin and then presented it to F/O Taylor, the standard bearer. The battle honours were impressive and covered virtually each and every battlefield where the Squadron had fought so gallantly (in the mid-nineties two more battle honours were given, Mareth Line and Gustav Line, Italy):

Home Defence 1940-1942
Battle of Britain 1940
North Africa 1942-1943
Sicily 1943
Salerno
Anzio
France and Low Countries 1940
Italy 1943-1945
Nettuno

In her speech the Queen referred to the Squadron having been the longest serving Auxiliary Squadron, and how it had fought in many different places to defend the country and defeat the enemy. She called the Standard "a symbol of trust, a shrine of the Squadron's traditions and a reminder of the devotion and sacrifices of the predecessors, and would be an inspiration to them all". In his reply S/L Meadows said how much the Squadron realised that it had been the King's wish that the ceremony should take place at Buckingham Palace. After parading for the Queen Mother the Squadron marched to Wellington Barracks.

On 18th May Meadows wrote to the Squadron how pleased he was by the Squadron's turn out. "I want to thank you all, Regular and Auxiliary, and to congratulate you at the same time for the very great success you made on Saturday of the Standard presentation at Buckingham Palace. The hard work and extra training put in by all those concerned was a great credit to them and was reflected without doubt in the magnificent bearing of the Parade. The arms drill was worthy of note, and the pride which we all felt at marching through the crowds in London with our Standard was fully justified. At the same time I like to thank all those who put in work on the less exciting but no less vital preparations and arrangements without which the Parade could not have been a success. The spectators seemed universal in their praise, the former members of the Squadron happy that the Squadron continues from strength to strength. As I told you at the end of the Parade the Honorary Air Commodore specially asked me to let you know how magnificently she thought you carried out the ceremony. Once again thank you all for making possible a really memorable day in the history of the Squadron. Now we must get back to our operational flying responsibilities and in preparing for camp".

There was little or nothing in the press about the great event. The only thing was a small article in which it was reported that the drum major lost his stick when he threw it up. Another remark was overheard by the diarist and put down for posterity. It happened when the Squadron marched through the Electricians Gate. A voice from the crowd was heard to say "Elsie, just look at all those medals for valour". Chests were puffed out even further. The reply was devastating: "Yes, maybe for valour but certainly not for good conduct".

On 29th May Squadron officers attended the Coronation Ball at

F/O Taylor kneels to receive the new Standard from Her Majesty Queen Elizabeth, Honorary Air Commodore.

the Savoy Hotel. The Queen Mother attended as well and of course the press was keen on reporting about it. The grapes appeared to be very sour for No.601 Squadron. They sent a telegram to Meadows: *"Regret to see CO hit News of the World again. From 601- the oldest auxiliary squadron"*.

On 13th June, for the second time since the war, the Squadron went abroad for its annual camp. They spent a fortnight with 2ndTAF. They moved to Oldenburg in Germany, taking all personnel and equipment. A small advance party travelling by road was followed by the Meteors, 10 Mk8s and 2 Mk7s. A Valetta transport aircraft of No.622 Squadron carried part of the ground crew and the remainder of the aircrew. The main party followed by rail. On the first day in camp all the pilots made "sector recce flights" in order to familiarise themselves with the local area. These proved to be an introduction to violent thunderstorms typical of the area that time of the year. A landing in heavy rain on the exceptionally smooth, water-covered runway, without Ground Control Approach, proved an adventure on first experience. Oldenburg was situated near the centre of the north German plain. Formally it was a grass-surfaced training airfield of the Luftwaffe, and after the surrender had become a British camp. It was turned into a fighter airfield, the necessary runways and buildings having been constructed a year earlier in a remarkably short time by German contractors. The station offered first class operational facilities and living conditions in the style typical for the pre-war Luftwaffe.

The fate of every aircraft: the scrap-heap. Here Meteor F8 WK 951 "Y" at RAF Kirkbridge minus its wings.

Thorough ground reconnaissances were carried out as well. In the Squadron scrapbook we still find evidence of the latter: Menus and bills from the "Graf Anton Günther", "Güldenhaus", "Weingut Bodenheim" and other German bars and restaurants, even official Bundesbahn toilet paper illustrated the report on this camp. At the same time, however, much hard work was done. For the period of the camp the Squadron was divided into two Flights run on a competitive basis for a cup. Both flew together when larger formations were required, but otherwise there was little contact between the Flights. The programme started with met briefing at 0630hrs, the first pilots being airborne at 0700hrs. One-hour sorties were flown, with 45 min turn round time, until 1500hrs. Serviceability of the aircraft was excellent, a great credit to the groundcrews, who worked very hard. The tempo of flying increased as the groundcrews got into their stride, to a pitch where the aircraft were regularly being refuelled in 2-3 minutes. By the end of the week the official flying target for the whole camp had been comfortably reached, despite the fact that one day had been spent in 35min. air-to-ground firing sorties only, and that one morning eight aircraft were diverted to Jever, 24 miles to the north, due to low cloud and mist. The first week ended with a memorable dining-in night. During the second week an extremely full routine of work began to tell on aircrew and groundcrew alike, and it became generally recognised that the most precious commodity on the Station was not the Deutschmark but sleep. The schedule was fully maintained with another day's air-to-ground firing and a full programme of war practices, instrument flying, high-level formations and drill. Six new White Jet Instrument Ratings were obtained, and a series of re-ratings begun. At this point the persistently damp weather began to have its effect on the aircraft. Minor electrical unserviceability became frequent and extremely moist air also caused very heavy misting of hoods during and after descents from high level. A combination of such factors, with cunim and low stratus, had to be allowed for in many of the final sorties of the fortnight. However, the enthusiasm of all Squadron members and particularly of the groundcrew emerged very clearly. The unit worked hard to produce a flying achievement of between 430 and 440 hours spread over more than 600 sorties. One aircraft remained unserviceable for over 24 hours. It was with great regret that the Squadron left Oldenburg and armed with a substantial amount of bottles and cigarettes, according to good

Squadron practice, the Gentlemen in Blue returned home, to their civilian occupations.

The Coronation Review at RAF Odiham on 15th July 1953 allowed the people of Britain to see the strength of the RAF and RAuxAF. The ceremony was the largest one the country had seen since the end of the war. Six bands were on parade. Twelve Squadrons formed up in Review Order, there was a static parade, and hundreds of thousands of people came to Odiham to witness the unique proceedings. Hundreds of aircraft took part in a majestic fly-past consisting of 46 different groups. Virtually every aircraft in use with the RAF was shown, as were the latest experimental machines, still "property" of the Ministry of Supply. The public which had come in many tens of thousands saw a fleet of aircraft roaring over and on static display. There were 16 Chipmunks and 12 Prentices of Home Command. Flying Training Command was represented by 12 Chipmunks, 12 Harvards, 24 Oxfords, 24 Ansons, 12 Balliols, 12 Meteor 7s, 12 Vampire 5s and 6 Varsities. Transport Command showed 6 Valettas and 3 Hastings aircraft. Coastal Command partici-pated with 3 Sunderlands, 5 Neptunes and 9 Shackletons. They saw and heard 24 Canberras, 9 Lincolns and 12 Washingtons of Bomber Command. Fighter Command flew with 12 Vampire NF 10s, 18 Meteor NF11s, 24 Meteor 8s, 8 Swift F1s and a Sycamore. The 2nd Tactical Air Force sent a large contingent, 24 Venoms and 24 Sabres. The Commonwealth air forces had a proud representation of 12 Vampire 5s (Royal Australian Air Force) and 36 Sabres (Royal Canadian Air Force). The Ministry of Supply showed the latest and most advanced aircraft the RAF was to fly in the future, the Swift F4, Victor, Vulcan, Javelin and Hawker Hunter.

On 4th October 1953 Jack Meadows left the Squadron and handed command to S/L John Cormack. In his farewell message to the Squadron Jack Meadows said that he wanted to thank everybody for the magnificent support they had given him personally and for their devotion to the Squadron with everything it stood for. A busy time started for Cormack, for in October the Queen Mother was granted the freedom of the City of London. One of his first duties was to escort the Queen Mother during the inspection of the Guard of Honour at Guildhall.

It was appropriate for the Squadron to be the Guard of Honour for their Honorary Air Commodore. The Lord Mayor gave special permission to the Squadron to parade the Standard in the City on

Three Meteors of No.600 Squadron, recognisable by the red and white triangles on the fuselage, in a tight formation. The aircraft are "W", "Z" and "U".

the occasion. In November the Squadron marched in the Lord Mayor's Show in pouring rain and very chilly weather. They had their fourteenth Annual Dinner at Finsbury Barracks with almost 175 members present.

The Squadron was still based at Biggin Hill and in January 1954 the Squadron diarist recorded "the Arctic Circle slipped so far out of place that it was just about centred on Biggin Hill". There were more frostbite fingers and more streaming noses on that weekend in January than the aerodrome had known for a very long time. The New Zealanders came to Biggin Hill on 31st January and watched S/L Scannel doing his hair raising aerobatics between the snowstorms. Again the diarist made a remark, saying that "they may have been All-Black when they came, but they were All-Blue when they left". The Kiwi connection resulted in HRH The Duke of Edinburgh and Queen Elizabeth, the Queen Mother agreeing with the Governor General of New Zealand that 600 Squadron should be associated with No.1 Auckland (T) Squadron RNZAF, to foster an even closer relationship between both countries, by exchanging news and views and by extending hospitality to Squadron members visiting each other's country. In exactly the same way "600" was linked with No.21 (City of Melbourne) Squadron of the Citizens' Air Force, the Aussie equivalent for the Auxiliary Air Force. The name CAF was better than RAAAF, all involved agreed. In the New Year's Honours list for 1954 John Cormack was awarded the AFC.

Sadly the Squadron lost a pilot that month, when F/O Mike Bridge was killed in a flying accident with his Gloster Meteor. The diarist wrote: "In his fifteen months with the Squadron Mike became so much part of it that the gap which he leaves will be impossible to fill. At RAE Farnborough he had his own laboratory for meteorology research and designed airborne equipment which is still in use. After his National Service he went to Oxford where he read Theoretical Physics and joined the Air Squadron. On going down from University he was employed on research of missiles with the De Havilland Company. We have lost an outstanding pilot, a brilliant scholar with a very promising career ahead, and a companion who was always cheerful, helpful and able at anything to which he set his hand".

The interest shown in the Squadron and the Association by HM Queen Elizabeth the Queen Mother was absolutely marvellous through all the years. On 24th February 1954 she honoured her Officers by dining with them at the mess at Finsbury Barracks. At 2000hrs a Squadron Guard of Honour welcomed the Queen Mother and returned to bid Her farewell shortly after midnight. It was the first of many occasions when the Honorary Air Commodore joined

The ever-present danger of flying jet aircraft could lead to tragic losses. F/O Mike Bridge served with No. 600 Squadron for about fifteen months and was killed during one such sortie.

Her men. In May the Squadron held the annual church parade at St. Bartholomew the Great in Smithfield. Then came the Summer: and what a glorious summer it was. The whole Squadron returned to Malta for the first time since the war, for its Annual Camp. On

Saturday 29th May the Gloster Meteors of No.600 Squadron took off from Biggin Hill for Istres near Marseilles, their final destination being RAF Takali on Malta. When the aircraft approached Istres the CO received an invitation by radio from the RAF controller to land and crack a bottle of champagne with a Colonel of the French Air Force. Those were the days; 600 landed to find an old friend waiting for them at Istres. He was Colonel-Aviateur Astier de Vilatte, the President of the Association Nationale des Officiers de Réserve de l'Armée de l'Air. After a brief party the Squadron took off again and on arrival at Takali were greeted in the traditional Australian manner by members of No.78 Fighter Wing of the RAAF with bottles of iced lager. The remainder of the Squadron set off from Biggin Hill later on Saturday morning in chartered Vikings and Dakotas to fly to Nice and then on to Luqa. All arrived on Malta safely, but one Dakota full of Auxiliaries had the misfortune (?) to spend one night in Nice. Life could be very tough for a weekend airman.

One of the Auxiliaries who took part in this exercise was the present Association Welfare Officer "Jamie" Morrison BEM, who remembered he was the first and only black volunteer who joined the Squadron. During the war he served for some time on the vitally important Takoradi Route. This route was not made known to the public. When the Mediterranean supply route to North Africa and Egypt was closed by enemy action, it became very difficult and took a long time to send supplies round the Cape via the Red Sea to Egypt and to reinforce the Middle East Forces. There existed the staging posts of weekly passenger and mail service set up by Imperial Airways from Takoradi in the then Gold Coast, now Ghana, to Khartoum. The staging posts were equipped by the RAF and brought up to standard to take any of the wartime aircraft. The planes were packed in crates. Each crate contained a complete aeroplane. The crates were loaded on ships and sent to Takoradi, where all aircraft were assembled and flown via Lagos, Kano, Maidugure to Genana and Khartoum and finally to Abu Sueir in Egypt. From there the RAF units in the Middle East Command were reinforced. Jamie Morrison would never forget the vast amount of equipment that passed through at such a tremendous speed. After the war Morrison continued his service with the RAF Reserve and trained with several regular Squadrons. Whenever he trained with a regular Squadron, they completed some forms and sent them to his unit. This went on for about two years till after a pay parade, the pay officer saw Jamie and said that he did not see Morrison on the pay parade. Jamie answered that he never attended the pay parade as there was no money ever paid to him. The officer got a bit upset and said: "I have seen you work bl—dy hard for the past two years, why have you not been paid?" Morrison answered that he did not know. The officer shook his head and walked away. Some time later Jamie was called to the Adjutant's Office. The Adjutant informed Morrison that a rather strange mistake had been made. There was no way he would get a refund of the money that should have been paid, but, if Morrison wanted, there was another solution. Rather than stay in the RAF Volunteer Reserve, he could join the Auxiliary Air Force. There was a vacancy in No.600 Squadron and would Morrison like to fill it. Jamie said yes, so he was given forms to fill in and return to the Adjutant.

No.600 Squadron Auxiliaries. Back row 7th from the right is John "Jamie" Morrison, now the Squadron Association Welfare Officer.

So now AC Jamie Morrison was a full member of No.600 (City of London) Squadron. Malta was one of his first Annual Camps. In the consistently good weather a heavy programme of flying, bathing, air firing and snorkelling was undertaken, with intervals for recces on this interesting island with which the Squadron shared many wartime memories from the days of the Beaufighters. During the fortnight 150,000 gallons of fuel were used and the armament section achieved a stoppage rate of less than 1 per 4,000 rounds fired. During the time in Malta Jamie Morrison used to sit in the shade whenever there was a break. The white members of the Squadron of course went sunbathing each time they could. Jamie would never forget their amazement to see a Negro obviously trying to stay out of the burning sun. After trying unsuccessfully to get Jamie to sit in the sun – Jamie had told them that his tan had reached a point of saturation, so he would leave them as much tan as possible – some of the Auxiliaries started a competition to find the person whose tan would get as near as possible to Jamie's. Many people sat in the sun for such a long time that some of them had to be treated for sunburn and sunstroke. The Medical Officer got so annoyed that he got all the men on parade and ordered that anyone who came to see him to be treated for sunburn or sunstroke would be put on charge for self inflicted wounds. That put an end to the competition. The Squadron entertained their hosts at Malta. The Malta Sunday Times of 6th June 1954 said:

Cocktails at Takali

No.600 City of London Squadron Royal Auxiliary Air Force, who, like many Squadrons, are doing their fortnight's annual training in Malta, gave a cocktail party in the Officers' Mess, Takali, on Wednesday evening. An abundance of flowers relieved the habitual harshness of the building. Over the fireplace in the Mess hung the Squadron Standard, which was presented by the Queen Mother last May. It bears the Squadron's arms and battle honours. The guests were greeted by Squadron Leader Cormack, the CO of the Squadron, and Mrs. Cormack. Judging by the lateness of the hour when the party finally broke up, it was a very successful event, except in the opinion of "Marcus", the mastiff who belongs to the station. Marcus had a very sore paw and not feeling like a party he took a dim view of the proceedings. H.E. Sir Gerald and Lady Creasy attended, and others among the 80 guests were Air Marshal and Mrs. Reynolds, Group Captain and Mrs. Eaton and Officers representing Air HQ Malta, HMS Falcon, and other service establishments, who were accompanied by their wives. During this Summer Camp F/L Frank Moody, a long serving Squadron member, was honoured with the MBE on completing 30 years of service with the RAF. Frank retired from the RAF and promptly joined the Squadron as an Auxiliary, which allowed him to call himself "F/L Frank Moody MBE, RAF (Retd) Royal Auxiliary Air Force", a rare distinction. Remembering his days with the Squadron Mr. John "Jamie" Morrison recalled: "I got on very well with the members of the Squadron and later joined the Association which has become a part of my life. When the Welfare Officer of the Association passed away I was elected to take his place and I still perform this duty with the greatest pleasure. It is typical of the Squadron and its Association that Welfare matters have always been important. It also seems to me I am one of only a few black Auxiliaries." The exercise over the Squadron returned to England in York aircraft in a seven hours flight home. The Meteors first flew to Tunis en route for Istres and Biggin Hill. The usual bad weather greeted them at home and the aircraft were diverted to Stanstead, Bovingdon and Blackbushe.

September 1954 proved to be a very interesting month for 600. First and foremost there was the sailing trip made by F/Ls Linford and Harrington and F/Os Peattie and Simpson. The men had chartered the yacht "Osterling" from Guernsey and were on their way to England. Their destination was the Empire Restaurant in London for the Annual Dinner, where Jos Linford was to address the guests. However, what was expected to be a very pleasant trip turned into an adventure. It all started with a telegram Jos Linford sent to F/L Norman at Biggin Hill, saying: "Delayed by gales in St. Peter Port, Joskin". Then a second telegram came, telling Norman "Suffered mishap, please substitute for speech, Joskin". Peter Norman did substitute and told the guests of a foolproof method of unofficially extending one's leave. "Charter Osterling", Peter said in his speech, "and either become becalmed or bewildered". Then suddenly the press smelled hot news and once again 600 Squadron hit the pages!! The Bournemouth Daily Echo of 11th September reported in an article with no less than four photographs: Steamer rescues four from yacht in gale. The article described how four young RAF officers barely survived the ordeal of a horrifying gale. The Echo Staff Reporter really gave his article all the suspense he had:

Transferred to Swanage Lifeboat

Four young RAF officers were rescued from heavy seas off St. Albans Head yesterday afternoon when their 30 square metre class racing yacht Osterling got into difficulties. They were picked up by the Greek steamer Eptanissos, and the yacht taken in tow. In Poole Bay, about two miles off Bournemouth Pier the men and the boat were transferred to the Swanage lifeboat. As the lifeboat arrived at the Swanage slipway hundreds of holidaymakers cheered loudly. The officers were F/Ls P.J. Harrington of Bassingbourne, and R.J. Linford, F/O T. Simpson and F/O R.C. Peattie from Biggin Hill. F/L Linford told me: "We had been to Guernsey and left at midnight after a fair weather report". He smiled at this. "The weather wasn't so fair, however, and we got into trouble off St. Alban's Head. Then the Greek steamer came along. They were grand to us. They could hardly speak any English but they dried our clothes and gave us eggs and bacon and rum. The yacht, hired from the Royal Air Force Yacht Club, was sailed from Chichester. They were returning to Chichester when they got into difficulties. A lifeboat officer told me last night the Osterling was hardly damaged. The lifeboat crew were at their posts some time before the message from the Greek steamer was received. They were there for an exercise, and the lifeboat was afloat within three minutes. The sea was very rough with a full south-westerly gale blowing. At times watchers from the land saw the lifeboat stand almost on end as she battled through the raging seas. Even in the calm Swanage Bay wind and tide made the conditions far from ideal. The lifeboat had some difficulty in reaching the slipway and her rudder was damaged, but not sufficiently to keep her out of service. From Bournemouth beach at about 4pm, the Greek steamer could just be seen through the driving rain. When the RAF officers had changed into dry clothes they left by road for Bournemouth. The other members of the Squadron were hardly impressed by the adventures of their fellow members. In the diary, next to a picture of Linford with a boy scout's cap on, one had written: "Linford gets on board for half price?"

In September 1954 John Wright, celebrated the fact that he had served for no less than 25 years. In 1951 he received Royal recognition, when awarded the MBE. In May 1954 he was given a second clasp to his Air Efficiency Award. John marked his Silver jubilee by presenting a ceremonial sword to the Squadron. His career had been remarkable. He joined the Squadron in 1929 as AC2 Carpenter/Rigger. At the outbreak of the war he was a Flight Sergeant/Metal Rigger. He served with 600 Squadron until 1942 when he was discharged from the AuxAF on being granted a commission in the RAFVR (T) Branch. After the Royal Auxiliary Air Force was re-established John immediately returned to No. 600 Squadron and became the Engineer Officer.

On 23rd April 1955 the Queen Mother honoured the Squadron with a visit. She arrived at Biggin Hill by helicopter, a novelty, for it was the first time that the Queen Mother had made a Flight in a helicopter. The press reported quite extensively about her flight. F/L Jos Linford presented her with a single red rose as it was St. George's Day and as a token of the Squadron's affection. It was much appreciated by Her Majesty. It was the same routine with the inspection parade, drinks and warm word for the men of her own Squadron. The officers serving in the Squadron at this time were:

S/L Cormack AFC (OC600)	F/L Warburton	F/O d'Arcy
F/L Linford	F/L Clark	P/O Hawkes
F/L Williams AFC	F/L Horrell	P/O Burman
F/L Maxwell	F/O Burvill	P/O Peattie
F/L Moody MBE	F/O Snook	P/O Stewart
F/L Reckitt	F/O Simpson	P/O Starr
F/L Furse	F/O Robarts-Arnold	P/O Russell
F/L Oliver	F/O Miles	P/O Bishop
F/L Wright MBE	F/O Lambert	

Other events in 1955 included a weekend with the French Air Force at Biarritz in May. "La Nouvelle Gazette de Biarritz" wrote almost half a page about the air rally and the various nationalities taking part. From what the Squadron diarist wrote there was little flying, yet a lot of entertaining going on.

In June the London Gazette said that the Queen had been "graciously pleased, on the occasion of Her Birthday, to give orders for the publication of the names of the undermentioned personnel who have been commended: The Queen's Commendation for Valuable Service in the Air". F/L Mike Oliver was the first member of No.600 Squadron to receive this award. The Church Parade that year was memorable too. The diarist expressed his admiration for one very brave man, when he wrote: "Marching through the City in the July heat wave was Jeremy Snook, our Standard bearer, soaked with his own perspiration and almost collapsing with exhaustion afterwards. How he managed to keep going is anybody's guess . . . ."

For the Annual Camp of 1955 the Squadron moved from Biggin Hill to Wunsdorf in Germany. Situated north-west of Hanover, not far from Steinhuder Lake and slightly north of the central hills of

West Germany, it had been a Luftwaffe airfield during the war. It was apparently a round of hard work interspersed with even harder social activities and was voted a great success. In September that year the Squadron was able to return the hospitality to the French officers who had been host on the Squadron's visit to Biarritz. Eleven French air force officers came to join the Squadron during the Battle of Britain Air Display on the weekend of 17th/ 18th September. They flew in Vampire jets. Sadly one of the French pilots, Captain Flandin, son of a former French Premier, was killed a few days later back in France. Also in September a major RAF exercise took place, "BEWARE". It was an air defence exercise and the three major components were early warning, the destruction of enemy bombers and the deterrent effect of the two earlier points. It was very much like the Blitz, fifteen years earlier. "Flight" of September 1955 explained why this exercise was so important and why participation of Auxiliary Squadrons was essential. In the exercise Royal Observer Corps and Civil Defence units were to play an important part. An attacking air force had been formed out of aircraft from Bomber Command (not the Vulcans, it was stressed), 7th and 49th USAF Air Divisions, 2nd and 4th ATAF, French Fighter Command, NATO Mediterranean Commands, even the Fleet Air Arm and RAF Flying Training Command. There would be attacks by aircraft of the air forces of the USA, France, Belgium and the Netherlands, even Italian aircraft were to be expected. And no less than 90% of these aircraft would be jets. Britain was to expect Thunderjets, Thunderstreaks, B45s and B47s. Defending forces would be RAF and USAF squadrons, flying Javelins, F86 Sabres, Sea Venoms, Meteors and, for the first time, a large number of the new Hawker Hunters. Radar was to play an essential role, for, as the enemy could very well try to carry out a nuclear attack, the attackers would have to be spotted early to enable the interceptors to get them at least 30 miles from the British coast. Basically no-one should have to worry, for "Flight" said, "B45s, B47s and similar types are now easy meat for Hunters". However, due to the limited endurance of the Hunter at low level, this part of the war was to be played by the Auxiliaries in the Meteors. Again the Squadron enjoyed itself tremendously, especially since it operated from Biggin Hill, home turf. Yet, there was little time for entertainment and everyone worked extremely hard to maintain maximum serviceability.

Gloster Meteor "W" of No.600 makes a low pass by the lighthouse at Beachy Head.

In 1956 the Father of the RAF, MRAF The Viscount Trenchard died after a long life of service to his country. The Squadron was present at the service in Westminster Abbey. The 1956 Annual Camp took the Squadron again to Takali. During Camp two Squadron Meteors collided, fortunately without loss of life. On 4th October that year F/S Bryan (Royal Auxiliary Air Force) and F/S Horning (RAF) were awarded the BEM. AVM Bowling CBE, AOC No.11 Group, came to Finsbury Barracks to present the awards. The year ended with a dinner at the Merchant Taylors' Hall on the 6th. The Honorary Air Commodore joined the Squadron as did Sir Cullum Welch, Lord Mayor and MRAF Lord Tedder, a great honour indeed. Then, by the end of the year, bad rumours were heard. On December 13th the Evening News said: "Week-end fliers may be stood down in new cuts". The Daily Express cried out: "Stand up for the Empire's interests – or fall". The Evening Standard reported: "Week-end jets silenced?". The Squadron received and sent many Christmas cards, but wondered what was going to happen to them. On 1st January F/L Bergh, of Dutch origin, was awarded the AFC. On 11th January 1957, the axe came down and it came down very hard indeed. "The week-end fliers are disbanded", said the Daily Express. The Times reported: "Reserve Air Units Disbanding". The Defence correspondent wrote: "The decision to disband the week-end flyers of the RAF and the Navy, which was foreshadowed last week, has been taken partly on operational but mainly on economical grounds. The costs of these two part-time air forces, direct and indirect, must be at least £6,500,000 a year, and a considerable numbers of Regulars are required for maintenance, administrative and instructional duties. The disbandment will be unpopular in several quarters, with the flyers themselves, who naturally believe they can fly modern aircraft effectively, and with others who feel that the decision cut across the voluntary spirit. On the other hand all admit that economies have to be made, and part-time flying can never be an economic undertaking".

Five alternatives were now open to members of disbanded squadrons. One was to transfer to one of the retained fighter control or radar reporting units, subject to suitability and certain other conditions. A second alternative was to transfer to the RAFVR for service in Reserve Flights. For officers suitable to be earmarked for special war appointments, there would also be a number of vacancies in the Royal Auxiliary Air Force general list. The fourth course was to transfer to the Royal Auxiliary Air Force Reserve, an inactive reserve with no training liability and normally no bounty. Finally members of disbanded units might sever their connection with the RAF altogether. Few understood why £6,500,000 and 17,000,000 gallons of fuel were sufficient to put an end to their highest aim: the Squadrons. Immediately the Auxiliaries mobilised the media. A protest statement in the press was made by four Commanding Officers of Auxiliary Squadrons. One of them was S/L Cormack. The statement said: "This decision is against the national interest. Past performance has shown that the auxiliary fighter squadrons can do the job which at present is done by the regular squadrons. While there is a requirement in Fighter Command for day fighter squadrons this can to a great extent and more economically be efficiently carried out by auxiliary squadrons. The country is throwing away an organisation whose worth is far greater than its face value, employing people whose time is spent working five days a week in civilian life and two days in the service of the Crown. There is no doubt that the Royal Air Force is short of pilots and disbanding the auxiliary fighter squadrons means that the country will lose over 300 fully trained fighter pilots. In addition it means the loss of more than 2,000 trained groundcrew.

The statement was issued by:

Sqdn. Ldrs J.M.Cormack – 600 (City of London)
P.R.Edelston – 601 (County of London)
T.C.Turnbull – 604 (County of Middlesex)
R.A.Eeles – 615 (County of Surrey)

It was not all Cormack wanted to do. The following day the news-papers informed their readers of a plan to prevent disbandment. Cormack suggested that the auxiliaries should be attached to the regular squadrons, use their aircraft and equipment during the quiet time of the week for the Regulars, the weekend. Auxiliaries would not mind travelling to the station, even if it had to be at their own expenses as long as their units stayed alive. The Government Air Committee agreed to discuss the proposal. "It's madness to scrap the week-end flyers", wrote Neville Duke DSO, OBE, DFC and Bars, AFC in the Evening Standard of 18th January. As former OC 615 Squadron and the Chief test pilot of Hawker Aircraft Ltd, his was a voice people could be expected to listen to. But to no avail. It seemed the government wanted to rid itself of all volunteer units. The Royal Auxiliary Air Force Regiments too were to be disbanded. People started writing letters to their Newspapers. J.M. Birkin, a retired Squadron Commander and Inspector of the Royal Auxiliary Air Force, wrote that is was nonsense to say that the Auxiliaries could not handle fast jets, such as the Hawker Hunter. The Auxiliaries themselves, John Cormack in front, left nothing untried. They went to speak with the Air Committees of both the Conservative and Labour parties. Other members of the Squadron wrote to their MPs. Harold Macmillan got a very angry letter and so did Mr. Donald Summer, MP for Orpington. It would, however be wrong to think that the entire nation opposed the disbandment of the Royal Auxiliary Air Force. Mr. Goodwin from Orpington, clearly not a friend of the Squadron, wrote in the West Kent Mercury: "What an immense boon petrol shortage is proving to those of us unfortunate enough to live within close range of Biggin Hill. At last, we shall be able to enjoy a really peaceful weekend. I am sure our Monday labours will benefit tremendously. Even when the petrol shortage is over, the Auxiliary Air Force must remain disbanded, for they serve no purpose at all in their rooftop manoeuvres. As the Prime Minister himself points out, the aeroplane is now an obsolete weapon, and all our future efforts must be concentrated upon atomic missiles. We have already wasted millions of pounds in financing these weekend playboys; the money must be diverted at once into more realistic channels". Of course the editor received an immediate reply, saying:

1.) It is quite untrue to say that the aeroplane is now an obsolete weapon. The fighter aircraft will probably become obsolete in five to ten years time, but until we have in quantity production an efficient ground-to-air guided missile, the fighter will remain our only defence against the high altitude bomber.

2.) What Mr. Goodwin describes as rooftop manoeuvres of the Auxiliary Air Force, have a very definite purpose. The aircraft with which the Auxiliary Squadrons have been equipped up to now were partly for the purpose of dealing with the low-level attack. It was therefore necessary from time to time that exercises should take place at low level. Low flying on other than such an exercise is strictly prohibited, and a breach of low flying discipline results in severe action. I fear that Mr. Goodwin's concern for his quiet weekends has led him into making statements about the Auxiliary pilots which are totally untrue. I am not and never have been a pilot, and therefore may perhaps be allowed to defend the Auxiliary pilots from the charges of being "play boys". These young men work at their desks or other labours during the week, and I can assure Mr. Goodwin that flying a modern jet at low height is not like joy riding. The competence of these pilots more than measures up to the average regular pilot, and to my mind it is ridiculous to throw away the accumulated experience of these men and of the squadrons of which they form part. This is not to say that I disagree with Mr. Goodwin's desire for economies. Economies properly applied are absolutely essential. The proposal that the Auxiliary squadrons should at weekends fly the regular squadron's aircraft would secure this purpose. Please do not think that I or any of the Auxiliaries that I know are unsympathetic with the residents of Biggin Hill and the area surrounding. Unfortunately so long as we have to maintain a fighter defence force – and I believe it must be for some years yet – this inconvenience will, I am afraid, continue at least five days a week". Much has changed since those words were written. Biggin Hill was closed down and today's RAF front line aeroplane, the Tornado, seems to make a louder engine sound and consumes a bit more fuel. But who can look into the future?

The end was near for the Royal Auxiliary Air Force. With the belief that the days of the "manned" aircraft were numbered and an even firmer belief in missiles and rockets few could be convinced that pilots were an outdated kind of species. The decision had been made and there was no way the government was to revoke it. On Thursday 7th February, a meeting of the Air Council was held in the Air Council Room of the Air Ministry. Present were George Ward MP, (Secretary of State for Air), Charles Orr-Ewing MP (under-secretary for Air), ACM Sir Dermot Boyle (CAS), AM Sir John Whitley (Air Member for Personnel), ACM Sir Donald Hardman, Sir Maurice Dean, ACM Sir Ronald Ivelaw-Chapman and AM Tuttle. Also in attendance were the Deputy under-secretary of State Sir Folliott Sandford, Mr. Kent and AVM Harvey. Several points were on the agenda. For the Royal Auxiliary Air Force "Item II(b)" was the most important and highly feared: "Disbandment of the Royal Auxiliary Air Force". In the minutes of this meeting we read how the fate of the Royal Auxiliary Air Force was sealed: "The Secretary of State said he thought the Council should go out of their way to make one special gesture on taking leave of the Royal Auxiliary Air Force. The proposal was that the council should give a dinner in the House of Commons on Saturday, 16th March, to the Commanding Officers of the 47 Squadrons or units and to the senior Auxiliary Officer in each flying squadron, where these were commanded by regular officers. The hosts, in addition to the Air Council, would include the Commanders-in-Chief of Fighter and Home Commands, DARAC and the Inspector of the Royal Auxiliary Air Force. It would be best, he thought, not to attempt to link the RNVR flying squadrons with this function. The Chief of the Air Staff thought that operational group commanders in Fighter Command should be invited; it was not, however, necessary to invite group commanders from Home Command. The under-secretary said that Treasury approval for the dinner would be necessary. The Secretary of State informed the meeting that consideration had been given to other possible measures. A march past was not favoured and he agreed on reflection that this idea should be dropped. A suggestion that the FCUs being retained might adopt the Unit numbers of the flying squadrons had been favourably received both by AMP and C-in-C, Fighter Command. Sir Folliott remarked that the question of a Royal Message remained. It had been suggested that the Queen might be asked to receive the squadron commanders of the squadrons which had been formed before the 1939-45 war. George Ward said that he was not in favour of selecting certain squadron commanders for a signal honour of this kind; it would, he thought, lead to difficulties particularly as some of the squadron officers would be regular officers. Sir Folliott wondered whether it could be arranged for all the officers invited to the dinner to be received at Buckingham Palace the day before, on Friday, 15th March, by the Duke of Edinburgh, who could be asked to hand them a message from the Queen. Such a gesture would, he thought, be highly appreciated. Finally the Council came to the following conclusion: A dinner should be held in the House of Commons on 16th March, the Under-Secretary of State for Air Sir Charles Orr-Ewing would seek approval and Air Marshal Sir John Whitley would sound out the Palace regarding a Message from the Queen.

Maybe Punch best understood what the Gentlemen in Blue felt like, when a poem was published in the issue of 30th January 1957, illustrated by a drawing of three pilots walking away from their Meteors. One of the Meteors carried the shark-teeth markings of No.600 "City of London" Squadron:

> When we could serve by flying
> we gave up our time and flew;
> But now, it appears, our country
> has nothing for us to do.
> No doubt the boffins have got it taped;
> but we'd like to make it clear -
> If ever they find anything else for us,
> they will always find us here.

It was a very nice tribute, as was the article in the "Illustrated", with a photograph showing eight Auxiliary Meteors in an immaculate formation over Malta. The headline simply said: **THANKS.**

The protests had been to no avail and the final salute and disbandment parade of No.600 "City of London" Squadron in March was taken by the Hon. Air Commodore herself. The City Corporation gave a reception in the Guildhall and the Standard was formally laid up in the Lady Chapel of St. Bartholomew the Great. Of course the

Queen Mother attended both functions, close to her Gentlemen in Blue, which said more than a long speech. It was a statement, understood by all the members of the Squadron. The days of a magnificent and loyal fighting unit, No.600 "City of London" Squadron, Royal Auxiliary Air Force, might have been over. But, the memory of the Squadron was as alive as ever.

The saddest moment in the History of No.600 "City of London" Squadron, Royal Auxiliary Air Force. The Standard is laid up in the Lady Chapel of Saint Bartholomew the Great. One of the members present remembered: "I shed tears twice in my life. The second time was when our Standard was laid up and our wings were finally clipped".

For in its place came the No. 600 "City of London" Squadron Association. Lord Tedder, one of the men who led the RAF through six hard years of sacrifice and valour, made the strongest statement about the disbandment of the Auxiliaries, when he spoke in the House of Lords on Thursday 9th May 1957. It was a heart-warming speech, bitter as it may have been.

He said: *"The almost brutal way which the auxiliary squadrons had the hangar doors banged in their faces without a word of warning, explanation or apology, was not a happy example of the way to treat one of the most purely voluntary and most active organisations in the country. It was a supreme example of what not to do and how not to handle men."*

These words must have cut deep into the hearts of the Gentlemen in Blue.

CHAPTER 13

UMBRELLAS AND BOWLER HATS; THE ASSOCIATION.
October 1953 to the present day

After cessation of hostilities in 1945, some Squadron ex-members met occasionally at irregular intervals. They decided to approach a prominent former member, Peter Stewart, who had been OC600 before the war to discuss the possibility of the formation of an Association for present and ex-members. He gathered men around him and the group set to work.

Association members together. L.t.r.: Kelly, Wheeler, Hadland, Beer, Nicholson, Butterworth, Dobson, Stewart and Edwards.

The Squadron Association was formally constituted in October 1953. A fortnight earlier circulars had been posted to no less than 343 ex-known members. Peter Stewart, who had been asked to be the first chairman, said that a quarterly magazine for members should be possible. It was to keep the present and past members together. Members would be all presently serving in No.600 Squadron as well as past members who paid their subscriptions. Also welcome were members whose addresses were not known but who should report to the secretary indicating their interest in joining. The first action of the Association on 2nd October was to send a telegram to the Honorary Air Commodore saying "The Association for present and past members of Your Squadron was formally constituted by a General Meeting this evening. All members of the Association at home and overseas have the honour to discharge their first duty and salute their Air Commodore with loyal greetings. The first and unanimous resolution of the meeting is to re-affirm our fealty to Your Majesty and earnestly we pray you may long be our example and our incentive in all our endeavours in the service of our beloved Sovereign". The same evening the Queen Mother replied through Her Private Secretary. "Her Majesty has bidden me tell you how glad she is that the Association is to be formed and to send her best wishes to all its members". Several suggestions were made and approved during the meeting. Minimum subscription was to be 2s.6d annually, while life membership was available at £5.5s.0d. There was to be an Association tie, showing narrow stripes of red and white "sharks' teeth" from left to right on a pale blue background. The stripe was the fighter Squadron marking allotted to the Squadron before the war, the background being the colour similar to that of the RFC. The Association badge proposed design was the original Squadron badge, the City shield, the RAF eagle and scroll surrounded by a pale blue circle bearing the words 'City of London Squadron Association' all surmounted by the royal crown. The Committee did not lose any time in organising functions. They suggested that a reunion should be arranged before Christmas 1953, a dinner at Town HQ at a maximum of 15s. per head. After the formation of the Association new members applied from everywhere, such as Aden, Iraq, the Persian Gulf, Germany, Australia, Canada, the United States, Northern Rhodesia, and the Philippines. On 10th February 1954 no less than 397 members had joined. In Wales five ex-members formed their own branch. Some had reached high ranks in the RAF, like Air Chief Marshal Lord Elworthy, (1935), Gp/Cpt Radford (1937-38) and Gp/Cpt Colbeck-Welch (1938-1939) were some of them.

The interest shown in the Association by the Queen Mother was a great morale boost through all the years. At many occasions the Queen Mother would meet her Squadron. On 24th February 1954 she honoured her Officers by dining with them at the mess at Finsbury Barracks. At 2000hrs a Squadron Guard of Honour welcomed her and returned to bid her farewell shortly after midnight. It was the first of many events when the Honorary Air Commodore joined her men. Much credit for the formation of the Association was due to the first Committee. They were Messrs Stewart (Chairman), Owen (Secretary), Cowan (Treasurer), Yates, Wheeler, Pritchard and Wright (Serving member). Thanks to hard work the membership of the Association grew to no less than 455 in September 1954. It should be mentioned here that John Wright was a man with a remarkable career in the Auxiliary Air Force. He had joined the Squadron in 1929 as AC2 Carpenter/Rigger and worked on virtually each aircraft that flew for the Squadron. In 1939 he was a F/S Metal Rigger and stayed with 600 until March 1942 when he was discharged from the Royal Auxiliary Air Force on appointment to a commission in the RAFVR Technical Branch. Having served in the UK and South East Asia until the end of the war, he returned to No.600 in 1947 as an Engineering Officer. John was exemplary for all Squadron members who served faithfully and loyally for so many years and stayed in the Association with the same dedication and enthusiasm as during their active service. Much of the Association news dealt with the Squadron, links with No.1 (Auckland (T)) Squadron from New Zealand and with No.21 (City of Melbourne) Squadron from Australia, the presentation of a No.138 Squadron badge were just a few of the events mentioned in the first newsletter. Under the letterhead "The Latest Hawker Project" the newsletter mentioned the christening of Antonia Jane, daughter to F/L and Mrs. Hawker. F/L Attrill lectured on the Squadron's future camp at Malta, a place with memories for those who had been there during the campaign in 1943. Regular RAF personnel joined the Association. A very sad occasion was the death of F/O Bridge, killed in a flying accident on 13 February, mentioned in an earlier chapter. There was a very strong feeling of friendship; when a pilot of the City of Melbourne squadron was killed, the Association decided that part of the money raised during the April reunion should be sent to his widow. Often Association members visited the Squadron at Biggin Hill. The first Reunion was on 30th April 1954. No less than 128 members were present, among them was Hugh Rowe, who remarked that he had met people whom he had not seen since he took off for Rotterdam on that fateful 10th of May 1940. There was an excellent buffet and, according to good Association rules, "a well-stocked" bar. The magazine started with good material which became a continuous part of all future magazines and newsletters: a section about welfare and whereabouts of past and present members. It also was the earliest start of an attempt to write the Squadron history, with stories about past members, such as F/L Henderson, the first medical and indeed auxiliary officer. W/C Blackwood, a well-known publisher, remarked: "I hope that one day the history of the Squadron will be written. If that day comes I hope my firm may be given the opportunity of printing and publishing it". It was to take 42 years before his hopes were fulfilled. The magazine always contained news of the Squadron. The Annual Church Parade, the Annual Camp, postings to and from the Squadron of Regular personnel, as well as news about "Relations and Friends" such as 2600 Squadron Royal Auxiliary Air Force, Nos.601 and 615 Squadrons, about Hendon, the Aussies and the Kiwis. Each year whilst the Squadron was still actively flying, invitations were given to past members to visit Biggin Hill and attend all Squadron functions such as the Annual Church Parade. This went on until in 1957 when the Squadron was disbanded and the virtual responsibility to maintain the link between the men who served with the City of London Squadron and to continue to guard the traditions and reputation of the Squadron fell on the Association. Annually the Association took part in the Lord Mayor's Show and during the Commemoration of Armistice Day in St. Paul's Cathedral there always was a Squadron contingent present with the Standard.

After the Squadron was disbanded members continued to use "The Castle", opposite Farringdon Tube Station as Headquarters. George Blackman, who once had been Steward at THQ Finsbury Barracks, was the licensee. The Castle was a unique pub, a typical 600 hang-out. It was the only public house in the City of London with a pawnbroker's licence, dating from the days of King Charles I. Members would meet on the first Thursday of the month and enjoy their beers and bangers. There they told tales about the glorious days of the Harts, the Blenheims and the Beaufighters. In one of the magazines John Wright told a story worth remembering here. He had come across the following entry in an aviation journal: *"Registrations cancelled: G-AEWU Aeronca 100 (c/n AB116) dismantled as spares for G-AETG"*. The Aeronca given to the Squadron by Lord Carlow in 1939 had re-appeared. The aircraft had been stored when war broke out and when it was obvious that little or no Aeronca flying would be possible it was "parked" in the barn of a friendly farmer in Luton and suitably wrapped and inhibited against corrosion G-AEWU was laid up for the duration of the war. In the summer of 1946, when the Squadron was reformed at Biggin Hill with Harvard trainers the Aeronca was brought out of storage and a start was made on restoring it to service. However, the task soon proved to be beyond the Station facilities and ultimately it had to be sold in 1947. But the Association did not want to give up flying. On 1st March 1958 the 600 (City of London) Flying Group took to the air in a Prentice and a Tiger Moth (G-AOES). The Flying Group grew and flourished in a manner which must have astonished its most ardent supporters. The Group regarded their aircraft with as much affection as the Squadron did with its Meteors. Funnily enough the Tiger Moth was slightly faster than the 1925 DH9A. Soon the Group had about 120 members and became the fifth largest group in annual flying time. The numbers of hours (well over 600) were quite amazing, as were the visits during the summer of 1960, when the Group flew the Prentice to Rotterdam, Lyon, Avignon, Le Touquet, Deauville, Bordeaux, Le Mans, Paris, Marseilles, Nice, Cannes, Calais, Rennes, Luxembourg, San Sebastian, Madrid, Seville, Malaga, Geneva, Brussels, Ostend, Florence, Rimini, the Scilly Isles, Tangier and Faro. The cost was £6 per hour for the Prentice and £2 per hour for the Tiger Moth. First the Group flew from Biggin Hill, but soon moved to Croydon. When the latter closed they returned to Biggin Hill where the members built their very own clubroom. The house-warming party was a memorable affair lasting the night through, the pace being set by a raffle for which the chairman donated a goat's head. The "lucky" winner had to get home by bus, which required some pretty deft emergency drill. Several members learned to fly and took their licences thanks to the Chief Flying Instructors Miles and Rutter.

It was possible for members to get their PPL (Private Pilot's Licence) for as little as £100. One of the pupil-pilots, Arthur Crisp, remembered: "I started flying with the Group on its formation and hope to have accumulated sufficient hours by early spring to obtain my licence, getting a lot of fun in the process. A high standard of instruction is set by John Miles and Ken Rutter, very important as the better the instructor the fewer hours to solo standard. A few

600 Flying Group Tiger Moth G-AOES, with red-white Sharks' teeth on the fuselage.

words about the actual instruction on the Group's red Tiger Moth bearing Squadron markings which to a novice appears to be something of a paper and string effort engendering misgivings about its airworthiness as he straps himself in the tiny cockpit. After the usual preliminaries there is a roar from the Gypsy Queen engine and you are surprised that the whole thing has not burst into flames. But you are reassured by the nonchalant attitude of the instructor and almost immediately you are trundling off to the end of the runway to begin the first lesson. Satisfied at last that the aeroplane will not fall to pieces you settle down to the rudiments of straight and level flying, descents and gliding descents, turns and gliding turns. About the time you feel that you are the cat's whiskers a rude awakening occurs as the instructor starts you on circuits. First landings and take-offs reveal too many fingers, too many feet, too few eyes, too little time, but as the weeks pass progress is achieved and your solo looms nearer. At this stage you begin to tell yourself with each trip that you are really not ready, hope it won't be today. The evening I went solo was calm and clear and with many other planes in the circuit I was sure that this was not the day for me, but after we had landed and taken our place in the queue I saw the instructors straps flung back over his shoulders and realised this was it. He whacked me over the head and said "once round the circuit and pick me up here" and from then on I forgot my anxiety as I was so completely occupied. Next thing I was at 700 feet over the circuit with the moment arriving when I should have to land on my own. Oddly enough it went off like clockwork and almost before I realised it I was on the ground again. The excitement on realising that you have flown solo successfully is tremendous and so, picking up the instructor you taxi back to dispersal and find yourself in the bar celebrating with the rest of the members present". This of course did not mean that all flying went like clockwork. On the evening of 26th June 1960 a gust lifted a wing as the Tiger Moth was landing, resulting in a cartwheel onto the nose. Happily the pilot was uninjured, but the aircraft sustained serious damage and needed extensive repairs. The Prentice made its first overseas trip of the year with three members of No.21 Squadron from Australia on board.

On 22nd October 1960 a commemorative plaque was unveiled at Biggin Hill. That it had to take place in the old home of No.615 Squadron and not in 600's own was a quirk of fate but at least it was the next best thing. The ceremony was performed by AM Lees, Deputy Chief of Air Staff. On the plaque was recorded the enemy aircraft destroyed, probably destroyed and damaged by the Squadron. The Annual Dinner of the Officers' Dining Club was a great opportunity for members to meet. On 29th November 1960, the Queen Mother attended and was presented with a silver model of the Meteor as a memento of her eight years as Honorary Air Commodore. The Annual Dinner of 10th March 1961 saw no less than 70 members attending. Some of them were very new, others like Peter Stewart looked back over 34 years since joining the Squadron. The Association now counted 473 members. With Peter Stewart, Arthur Wesley, F/L Dobson, Ken Battrick and six Committee members the Association remained as strong and active as ever. One of the activities was the Car Rally. Ray Aveyard wrote about this event in the Winter 61/62 Magazine that the rally was held on Sunday 22nd October 1961, but possibly due to the shocking weather in the morning only five members turned up. To cut a long story short all five members received their prizes and it was hoped that more competitors would show up the next time. On 8th April 1962 another rally was organised. This time 9 members and 18 passengers took part. Frank Yates won, closely followed by Arthur Butterworth. One chap, who shall not be mentioned, got so terribly lost that he retired early. The Flying Group faced problems when in 1962 the Prentice had to be put out of commission due to the Certificate of Airworthiness expiring. With a dwindling membership the board was faced with the difficult question if they would be able to keep the Prentice or not. A happier occasion was the 1962 Annual Dinner. New members joined, one of them being W/C Styles, ex-OC 600 in the Mediterranean Campaign and also a Squadron member in 1930, but then as an AC Plonk.

An interesting character and former No.600 Squadron member was Captain John Crewdson, about whom an article was written in the winter 62/63 issue of the Association magazine. He belonged to an organisation called Film Aviation Services. He advised and flew in many films and one of the best known was "Lawrence of Arabia". The film called for action sequences in the Middle East during the First World War and while property masters could produce uniforms and dress of the period without turning a hair, flying replicas of WW1 aeroplanes were something else. The Crewdson organisation took this in its stride and the three German aircraft in the picture, a Fokker DVII and two Rumpler CIVs were products of his workshops after having entered the front door as Tiger Moths. Another example of Crewdson's determination was shown when he got himself involved in the film "The War Lover". He found three B17 Flying Fortresses at a scrap yard in Arizona where they had been standing for ten years. The aircraft were reconditioned and with a limited certificate of airworthiness flown across the Atlantic to Bovington airfield, the location of the film. The entire flying programme for the picture was undertaken by Crewdson involving formation flying over England, maintenance of the aircraft, briefing of Directors and actors and even simulating the shooting down of one of the Forts.

On 25th May 1968 Peter Stewart died suddenly. It was a great loss to the Association and all who knew him. A memorial service to Peter was held in St. Bartholomew the Great on 25th June and the church was absolutely packed. In the Squadron Magazine a fitting tribute to Peter said that the Association had "lost a true friend and comrade to all". Prof. R.V. Jones, with whom Peter had worked so closely during the war, gave the Address in which he remembered how Peter and he had first met and how keen Peter had been to ensure that none of his brilliant reconnaissance pilots were wasted on senseless sorties. At the same time, Jones said, Peter's father S/L "Pop" Stewart, now a junior officer to his own son, had unofficially passed the photographs of Peenemünde missile launching base to Professor Jones. The best example of Peter Stewart's sense of duty was given when R.V. Jones told the congregation what Peter had done after his brother died leaving a struggling preparatory school – Shirley House – and three sons. First he improved the school, then he rescued it from difficulties with his own money and then he took the opportunity to sell the existing site to the substantial benefit of his three nephews. He bought Beechwood House, an early 18th century mansion near Hemel Hempstead with the same benefit and set about reconditioning it as a new home for the school. He gave up his own post in London and tackled it with his own hands aided by a few tradesmen. In 1963 a tornado struck Beechwood, severely damaging the building. Yet in September it was ready to receive the pupils. Such a man was Peter Stewart. Many members attended the service. Among them were Sir Charles and Lady Elworthy, Group Captains Beer, Healy and Hiscox, Wing Commanders Wetton, Hayes, Kerr and Nicholson and about sixty past and present members of No.600 Squadron. Gp/Cpt Ralph Hiscox OBE, one of his contemporaries, read the lesson. Many members wrote about their memories of Peter Stewart. G.de H. Vaizey, who had served between 1925 and 1929 recalled how he and Peter had flown Mono Avros as members of the "plus four/ grey flannel" coterie. He said: "Peter was a neat and skilful pilot. I never had a moment's anxiety when I was leading the Squadron and Peter's wing was close to mine". Gilbert Beer remembered how during the summer camp at Sutton Bridge Peter Stewart went to an immense amount of trouble to extricate Beer from a not particularly creditable escapade in which he had become involved in a Public House at Hunstanton. On Beer's behalf Peter went to see the landlord and spoke with such devastating charm that far from having to return the ashtray Beer had removed, they both were stood a considerable quantity of drink at the bar. Gilbert Beer also recalled another amusing story which showed the kind of gentleman Peter was. Whenever Beer went to London during the war he did his drinking in a fairly innocuous semi-nightspot called the Liaison Club in the Princess Arcade, Piccadilly. On one particular evening Peter Stewart walked in, accompanied by an elderly Flight Lieutenant whose features were vaguely familiar to Beer. The din at the bar and the activities of a frenzied pianist drowned Peter's attempt at introductions, but in a quieter moment when the human pianola had left in search of subsistence, Beer asked the Flight Lieutenant if they had, in fact, met previously. After all was not Beer a Squadron Leader and did he not, therefore, know a large number of Flight Lieutenants. He answered that they might have met in 1935 or 1936. Beer then asked where it might have been. The Flight Lieutenant said that it was during a 600 Squadron Dance, when prior to taking his departure Beer rather foolishly came to the bar carrying a silk hat, in which he had the impertinence to put a quantity of bitter beer. Suddenly Beer realised that he was talking to Peter Stewart's father and hurried to apologise. But "Pops" Stewart replied: "Forget about the hat, my boy, I mean Sir. It was a damned silly hat and a damned good party". The sudden loss of this prominent member was keenly felt, but there was no reason for the Association not to continue. Peter's place as Chairman was taken by John Wright. Having been so very long with the Squadron John knew virtually every member.

"Yes Mr. Aveyard, I wear my Squadron Badge". Her Majesty with Ray Aveyard. Dennis and Mrs. Overton watch the conversation.

One of the Association activities was a visit to Manston in April 1971. The group visited Manston Parish Church arriving in good time for the morning service. They then went to the Sergeants' Mess where Master Navigator Pierce, the Mess president welcomed them. W/C Scott, the Station Commander joined the members of the Association for drinks and accepted a 600 Squadron plaque from John Wright MBE. After lunch the former tenants visited the airfield, the air traffic control and the fire fighting display put on by the RAF Fire Fighting School. In the Control Tower they were given a lecture on the Manston area. It differed a lot from the old days. Aircraft of the Red Arrows who happened to be at Manston did an air display. Ray Aveyard remembered how the aircraft did a low-level run aiming directly at the tower and passing very close on either side of the tower below the viewing level of the visitors. During the tour of the airfield it turned out that the old 600 hangar at dispersal still existed. Members who were at Manston in 1940 had no difficulty in picking out where the "Sheep-dipper" was operated from in August 1940. The old Station headquarters were still in the same place on the main road. It was a memorable visit for all.

Annually the Association took part in the parade of the City of London Federation of Old Comrades Associations. One such parade was in May 1971 and "Dev" wrote about it: "Following a short march from Lothbury to the Royal Exchange Standards were paraded and wreaths laid at the memorial in tribute. Our contingent was commanded by Chairman John Wright, and the wreath laid by Ken Battrick, other members being Titch Cardew, Arthur Wesley, Maurice Rosin, Bert Chantrey, Bill Peters, John Rosbrook, who acted as Marshal, and Dev DeVroome as Standard Bearer. Unfortunately 601 Squadron could only muster four bods and as a "special concession" were allowed to march with us.

Following a good and tidy march to the Artillery Ground at a nice middle-aged pace set by the excellent Band of the Honourable Artillery Company we marched past the Inspecting Officer, Field Marshal Sir Gerald Templar KG, Lord Lieutenant of the County of London, who subsequently inspected the parade. In deference to the age of some of the older soldiers, the parade with the exception of the Standards fell out for the Service, given this year by the Bishop of Dover, the Right Reverend A.P. Tremlett, who did not mince his words on the subject of service given and the price paid for the peace and liberty we enjoy. At the conclusion the assembly was addressed by the Field Marshal – still a fire burner in spite of his years – who urged all and sundry in stentorian tones to spread the spirit of voluntary service among the younger generation. After the formalities we adjourned to the historic Suttling Room of the HAC for refreshments and here we were joined by the Field Marshal who commanded a Corps of the 5th Army which included the 47th (Bow Bells) and 56th (Black Cat) Territorial Divisions together with the 6th Army Division whose tie he sported on that day, a familiar to those who served with the Squadron in Italy. He knew 600 and 601 Squadrons well from those days and when in conversation he learned that not only were we representatives thereof but that some were serving with the Squadrons in those days. He exclaimed: "Two bloody fine Squadrons, who knew how to get on with it without taking too much notice of Command. I'll salute you!" and proceeded to do so in the middle of the bar to the amazement of all present and the special delight of our chaps. Such tributes do not come easily from such men and all those who were unable to be present can take a little glow of pride by proxy. It started with the news item that No.21 (City of Melbourne) (Auxiliary) Squadron CAF was presented with the Standard in September 1970 by their Honorary Air Commodore, Governor of Victoria, Sir Rohan Delacombe. Some time later John Wright realised that the 600 Squadron sword was hanging in his wardrobe, having been returned to the Association in 1957. John thought it to be a good idea to present the sword to their friends down under. A note to OC21, S/L Tom Wright received immediate acceptance and an additional inscription was agreed. Then how to deliver it? During a chat with OC Flying Wing RAF Manby, W/C Peter Norman, it was suggested that it might be worth asking for passage in an RAF aircraft. Norman made the application and with a little encouragement by AM Sir Dennis "Splinters" Smallwood, a great post-war friend of the Squadron, a return trip to Singapore was authorised while the RAAF agreed to continue the trip onwards. On Saturday 13th May 1972 John reported to RAF Brize Norton. The next day at 0700hrs a VC10 of No.10 Squadron took off to arrive at Tengah/Singapore 20 hours later. From here he was driven to the Merlin Hotel where he was made welcome by S/L Collings (introduced by Josh Linford). After some days there a Hercules of 37 Squadron RAAF took off, carrying eleven passengers, each one clutching a box of rations. It looked like old-fashioned flying. After 7 hours of noisy flying they arrived at Darwin. A Lieutenant of the Singapore Armed Forces invited John to join him for a tour of the town and then for a meal with an uncle. The next morning the Hercules took off again and after 17 hours they landed at RAAF Richmond. After a giant tea John was taken by another Hercules to Laverton where Tom Wright welcomed him. As the Ministry of Defence had agreed to "remuster" John for the duration of his visit, F/L Wright Royal Auxiliary Air Force enjoyed all the pleasure of military life once again. At an early-hour call on the Base Commander, Gp/Capt Newham, John was pleased to hear that Newham remembered the 600 Annual Camp at Takali in 1956, when he served in 78 Wing RAAF. The Aussies went to the limits to please their British guest. They virtually dragged John from the Aircraft Research and Development Unit to the Radio School, then to No.1 Aircraft Depot, followed by a visit to the rehearsal room of the Central Band of the RAAF who played the RAF March Past for John's pleasure. After lunch John was driven to the birthplace of the RAAF at Point Cook, then to the RAAF Museum, where he almost lost his brass "A's". The next stop was at the Aero medical Centre. During five days John Wright was entertained at such speed and with such hospitality that at times he wondered if he would be able to survive the friendship showered on him. Then came the big day. Leaving at 0700hrs (!) to see 21 Squadron at work during one of the training weekends it was decided that the presentation should be at 0900hrs to ensure no loss of training time for the bods. The Base Commander made a speech, John said a few words. He especially conveyed the greetings of Gp/Capt Peter Vanneck, the Inspector of the Royal Auxiliary Air Force, whose father, Lord Huntingfield as Governor of Victoria and Honorary Air Commodore of No.21 Squadron, had arranged the bond with 600's Honorary Air Commodore Lord Lloyd of Dolobran in 1938. He then handed the sword to S/L Tom Wright, who read a message of greetings from the Queen Mother. A lot of presentations took place, one of the most generous gifts being a handsome cheque from the members of No.21 Squadron for the Restoration Fund of St. Bartholomew the Great. At 1400hrs that afternoon John again boarded a C130 Hercules, destination Singapore, where John to his surprise was taken over the Island in a Whirlwind of No.103 Squadron RAF. He arrived again at Brize Norton on 1ˢᵗ June, after 24,000 miles, 3 marvellous weeks and less a sword. It had been worthwhile.

On 14th November 1972 the Queen Mother visited the Association at a reception at Armoury House. For the reception the Honourable Artillery Company kindly allowed the Association to use the impressive and historic Long Room. More than 70 members with their ladies and other guests assembled to receive the Honorary Air Commodore. After a word of welcome by Association President Jack Meadows and John Wright as Chairman, the Queen Mother, her Private Secretary Sir Martin Gilliat (himself a former lodger of the infamous and "escape- proof" Colditz POW Camp during the Second World War) and Lady in Waiting Mrs. Campbell Preston met the guests. Typically the Queen Mother requested informality to be the keynote of the whole evening. She was splendid and tireless in her tour round the gathering having a kind word for everyone She met. Another honoured guest was Mr. Guest from the USA. He was the son of "Freddie" Guest, the Squadron's first Commanding Officer and later the first Air Minister. Two officers from No.21 Squadron, RAAF, were present as well.

The 50th Anniversary of the Royal Auxiliary Air Force must have been a bitter-sweet event for the Gentlemen in Blue. With only three Royal Auxiliary Air Force units still in service, comprising three Maritime Headquarters units, i.e. No.1 (County of Hertford), No.2 (City of Edinburgh) and No.3 (County of Devon), the majority of attending people were former Auxiliaries, many of whom served many years ago. The occasion was honoured by the presence of the Queen Mother and HRH Princess Alice, Duchess of Gloucester. Westminster Abbey was packed on Sunday, 27th October 1975. After a fanfare of trumpets the Ensign of the RAF was carried to the High Altar by F/L Paris, Royal Auxiliary Air Force, escorted by two Auxiliary Sergeants. The National Anthem was sung and the Dean standing at the High Altar paid special tribute for the service of the Royal Auxiliary Air Force during the past 50 years, especially giving thanks for those Auxiliaries who helped to preserve freedom during the Second World War. Great men like Max Aitken read or spoke. It was a grand occasion for all.

For the last twenty years the Association had managed to stay together and though the number of members decreased the enthusiasm of the men who created it remained the same. Annually they take part in the Lord Mayor's Show Parade. Each year they participate in the annual St. Bartholomew's Church Bazaar. They never miss the Annual Remembrance Day Service and parade in

In 1975 the Association presented HM Queen Elizabeth the Queen Mother with an oil painting of the Castle of Mey for her 75th Birthday. With Her Majesty are f.l.t.r. F/L Maxwell, S/L Cardew, S/L Meadows, F/L Moody and W/O Cowan.

November. Each year there is an Annual General Meeting and a Squadron Reunion Dinner or Lunch. From time to time combined reunions are organised with No.601 Squadron Association. In October members would meet at the Ladies Night. Some events had to be abandoned, like the monthly evening at the "Flying Horse" pub. It is evident that an Association such as this most lose members. Regular obituaries appear in the Newsletters. Some are recent members, others were with the Squadron when it all started ages ago. One of them was W/C Clennett, who served with the Squadron as an Engineer Officer in North Africa and Italy. From time to time a highlight takes place. Such a one was the Reception the Association held for the Honorary Air Commodore at the Livery Hall of the Worshipful Company of Butchers on 17ᵗʰ April 1980. It was a splendid occasion with 80 members attending.

An important event in the history of the Association took place in November 1981. For many years the Association had gathered to remember friends who had lost their lives during the Second World War. Some of these members had perished after a sortie and never had been identified in a known grave. Four of these were F/O Mike Anderson, F/O Roger Moore and their two air gunners Bert Hawkins and Laurie Isaacs. As reported earlier they had been killed during the raid on Waalhaven aerodrome near Rotterdam on 10ᵗʰ May 1940. It was decided that the Association should accept an invitation to be guests at the launching of a book in which the story of 10ᵗʰ May 1940 was related and for which reason the book had been dedicated to the memory of these men.

On 5ᵗʰ November a party of 33 members and wives, including some guests left for Holland. Jean Aveyard, the late wife of the Association chairman Ray, wrote a story about this visit, which was to become one of the most emotional encounters with the Squadron's past. "We boarded the coach and travelled to Dover – embarking at 1100pm. on the ferry and arriving at Zeebrugge in Belgium at 0400 am. We drove along the motorway to Rotterdam and to our hotel. The first event was a visit to the Royal Yacht "Piet Hein" which had been presented to the Netherlands Veterans Association by Queen Juliana. In the afternoon the first formal event took place when the Association marched behind its Standard to Crooswijk Cemetery where four Squadron members had been laid to rest after the 10ᵗʰ of May attack. While the Netherlands Veterans formed a guard of honour and after one minute's silence had been observed wreaths were laid by W/C Norman Hayes and Ray Aveyard, F/Ls John Wright and Norman Wheeler and Mr. George Isaacs. It was the first time Mr. Isaacs stood in front of the grave of his brother Laurie, one of the four recently identified. A further wreath was laid on behalf of the Netherlands Resistance. After this touching event the Association departed for the town hall of Rotterdam where a formal reception took place with the Deputy Mayor as their host. During the evening the members of the Association were the guests of the town of Barendrecht, where copies of Hans Onderwater's book "And then there was silence" were presented to Ray Aveyard, Mrs. Ann Bennett, Mr. George Isaacs and W/C Norman Hayes by two Dutch boys, dressed as RAF airmen of World War Two. At this function, which took until midnight, a happy atmosphere assured the Association that they were very welcome indeed. The next day the Association left for a civic reception at the townhall of Spijkenisse. Flags were at half mast throughout the town – even the church steeple had a flag flying at half mast. The Mayor received the guests and presented all members with a booklet describing the events in and around Spijkenisse during the days of 1940. Ann Bennett, widow of P/O Anderson, was presented with the buckle of her husband's parachute, a very emotional gift. Then the Association marched to the cemetery. Local people followed in silence. On the way the procession stopped at the "Flame of Remembrance" monument which had been specially lit for this occasion. The Squadron formed up in front of the graves. Flowers were laid by Ann Bennett, and Ray Aveyard laid a wreath with the Squadron badge in the centre. There were wreaths from the town council, Dutch veterans and from many individual people. The silence prevailed all over town while the band played the national anthems of Britain and the Netherlands. Then the Squadron travelled to Piershil, where they honoured P/O Bob Echlin in his lone grave at the rear of the local church. In Piershill even the windmill sails had been draped with black velvet to pay respect to the fallen airman and his visiting comrades. After the ceremony the villagers entertained their guests in the local gymnasium, the only place able to hold such a large group of people. There was tea, there was home-made cake, but above all there was friendship. Maybe this smallest of villages showed the warmest of hospitality. After a farewell dinner at the Amsterdam RAFA club, which ended with marvellous community singing, the Association returned to the hotel.

It had been a visit that no one was likely to forget and, at the same time, a grim reminder of the days when the Squadron paid a very high price. The next day they travelled back to England. As a result 600 Squadron Association and the Dutch Veterans Organisation decided to stay in touch and they have done so ever since.

In October 1982 a group of Association members and their ladies were invited by HRH Prince Bernhard of the Netherlands for an informal meeting at the Royal palace Soestdijk. During the war HRH had met Norman Hayes at RAF Ford and these meetings had been

November 1981. Led by its chairman, now President, Ray Aveyard and escorted by the Mayor of Spijkenisse, His Worship Mr. Jan De Groen (right) and Hans Onderwater (left) the Association and people of Spijkenisse followed the Standard to the Municipal Cemetery to lay wreaths at the graves of F/O Anderson and LAC Hawkins. The caption in the Dutch paper read: "Somewhat older, but still a very proud group of men; No.600 (City of London) Squadron". That year this photo was to become the "Photo of the Year" in Holland.

happy ones as HRH had been able to do some flying from there, in spite of HM Queen Wilhelmina being quite determined to ensure that her son-in-law was not to fly with the chance of being shot down over German-occupied territory.

HRH vividly remembered how he had sought to evade being caught flying operationally. It was a marvellous and very cordial meeting, with HRH happily accepting Honorary membership of the Association and the Squadron tie. In October 1985 the Squadron celebrated its 60th Anniversary with a Jubilee Dinner at the RAF Museum in Hendon. It was a splendid evening that was attended by pre-war, war-time and post-war members of the Squadron. For the pre-war chaps Hendon of course brought back many good memories of the early days of flying when it was such a great adventure every time one became (and stayed) airborne. Before dinner the members had a free run of the Battle of Britain Museum. The dinner was in the Roundel Room of the Museum. The table arrangement consisted of a top table and four sprigs with red of the serviettes against the light blue of the tablecloths and the whole brought to life with the white candles reflecting light from the Squadron silver which was brought out specially for the occasion. The Standard with its battle honours was displayed and floodlit. The Queen Mother sent a message, saying: "I was delighted to receive the kind message from the members of 600 (City of London) Squadron Association meeting together at the Battle of Britain Museum on the occasion of the Diamond Jubilee of the formation of the Squadron. I send to each one of you my greetings and warmest wishes, and I hope you will all have a very enjoyable evening".

Soestdijk Palace 3rd October 1982. His Royal Highness Prince Bernhard of the Netherlands is made an Honorary Member of the Squadron Association. l.t.r. W/C Brian St.Clair RAF, British Air Attaché in Holland, John Wilding, Hans Onderwater, HRH and Air/Cdre C.J. "Micky" Mount, President of the Association.

In May 1990 another visit to the Netherlands took place. Sid Bowen, the Secretary of the Association wrote a story about this visit, a result of the friendship that had grown between veterans of the "Wapenbroeders", the Dutch Veterans Association and 600 Squadron Association. The party assembled at Harwich to embark on the Dutch ferry "Koningin Beatrix". Arriving in Holland on 4th May they were met by a welcoming party at the dockside. May 4th is the Dutch Remembrance Day and at 1pm the Association was to attend a service of Remembrance at the Dutch reformed church at Piershil, where P/O Echlin was buried in May 1940. A similar service took place in Spijkenisse later that day at the graves of F/O Anderson and LAC Hawkins. After a free day on 5th May (Liberation Day) the members went to Rotterdam Crooswijk Cemetery the next day to lay wreaths at the graves of S/L Wells, F/L Moore, Cpl. Kidd and LAC Isaacs. Hosted by Dutch veterans the following days were spent enjoying sight-seeing tours and gatherings. Hospitality was returned in May 1992 when the Association again went to the Netherlands. This time they not only visited the graves of their seven comrades; they also participated in the Liberation parade at Wageningen, where they were met by their second Dutch Honorary Member, HRH Prince Bernhard of the Netherlands. Contacts with No.21 (City of Melbourne) Squadron remained firm, and was again removed when their new CO (S/L Angela Rhodes), visiting England in September 1992, met Association Committee Members at a dinner given in her honour at the RAF Club – a most delightful evening.

In 1992 prominent members of the Squadron passed away, S/L Riseley DSO, S/L Glegg DFC & Bar, and AVM Desmond Hughes CB, CBE, DSO, DFC & Bar, AFC, MA, DL. In 1995 the Association lost men like "Ace" Downing and Victor McAllister who flew during the campaign in North Africa, Sicily and Italy. Old boys like Fred Ryan (1933), Dick Bird (1931) and Norman Wheeler (1933) passed away. Each AGM and Annual Reunion Lunch people from all over England travel to London to join their friends from long ago. Distinguished guests join the members during that lunch. Each year in May a group gathers at St. Barts to remember those who lost their lives in the service of the Monarch and the Country. Each year in June a contingent of the Association takes part in the Annual Parade and Lunch of the City of London Federation of Old Comrades Association. Each year they gather in

600 Squadron Standard laid up in Saint Bartholomew the Great.

October for the Ladies Night at the New Barbican Hotel in London. In November the Association presents itself at the Lord Mayor's Show.

This is the history of No.600 "City of London" Squadron and its Association. Since 1925 it has remained a closely-knit family, prepared to fight for Sovereign and Country, always ready to support its members. A group of dedicated men (and women), still together under the sympathetic and caring command of their Honorary Air Commodore, Her Majesty Queen Elizabeth the Queen Mother. Under their President Ray Aveyard, their life Vice-President Air Commodore "Micky" Mount and an energetic Committee, ably led by Dennis Overton, they intend to stay together until "the last member closes the hangar door". They represent that unique British institution of "Auxiliaries", the **Gentlemen in Blue**.

APPENDIX I

HONORARY AIR COMMODORES

The Rt.Hon. S/L F. Guest
PC,CBE,DSO,MP. 1931 – 1937

The Rt.Hon. Lord Lloyd of Dolobran
PC,GCSI, GCIE,DSO,MP. 1937 – 1941

The Rt.Hon. Sir Archibald Sinclair
Bt, KT,CMG,MP. 1942 -1949

Her Majesty Queen Elizabeth
the Queen Mother 1949 – today

APPENDIX II

ROLL OF HONOUR

Personnel killed while serving with No.600 (City of London) Squadron, 1927 – 1957

DATE	NAME	SITE	AIRCRAFT
07 Jun 30	G.E.Villiers	civil crash UK	unknown
July 34	S/L Collett	nr. Hendon	Hawker Hart
20 Feb 35	F/L Faulds	civil crash UK	unknown
03 Sep 39	P/O Isaac	nr. Hendon	Blenheim IF
16 Nov 39	F/O Vickers	Hornchurch	Blenheim IF
11 Mar 40	Lt Sperling	Manston	Blenheim IF
10 May 40	S/L Wells	Pernis, Holland	Blenheim IF L6616, BQ-R
10 May 40	Cpl Kidd	Pernis, Holland	Blenheim IF L6616, BQ-R
10 May 40	F/O Moore	Waalhaven, Holland	Blenheim IF L1335, BQ-W
10 May 40	Cpl Isaacs	Waalhaven, Holland	Blenheim IF L1335, BQ-W
10 May 40	F/L Anderson	Hoogvliet, Holland	Blenheim IF L1515, BQ-L
10 May 40	LAC Hawkins	Hoogvliet, Holland	Blenheim IF L1515, BQ-L
10 May 40	P/O Echlin	Piershil, Holland	Blenheim IF L1401, BQ-K
24 May 40	F/O Hannay	Channel	Blenheim IF
24 May 40	LAC Short	Channel	Blenheim IF
08 Aug 40	F/O Grice	off Ramsgate	Blenheim IF L8665, BQ-A

DATE	NAME	SITE	AIRCRAFT
08 Aug 40	Sgt Keast	off Ramsgate	Blenheim IF L8665, BQ-A
08 Aug 40	AC1 Warren	off Ramsgate	Blenheim IF L8665, BQ-A
07 Sep 40	Sgt Saunders	Rainham	Blenheim IF L6684
07 Sep 40	Sgt Davies	Rainham	Blenheim IF L6684
03 Oct 40	P/O Hobson	Broadstone Warren	Blenheim IVF L4905, BQ-M
03 Oct 40	Sgt Hughes	Broadstone Warren	Blenheim IVF L4905, BQ-M
03 Oct 40	AC2 Cooper	Broadstone Warren	Blenheim IVF L4905, BQ-M
23 Oct 40	P/O Hurst	Kirkby Malzeard	Blenheim IF L1272, BQ-X
20 Dec 40	Sgt Wilson	West of Richmond	Blenheim IF BQ-W
24 Dec 40	P/O Holmes DFM	died of wounds	Blenheim IF BQ-W
12 Jul 41	P/O Schumer	Predannack	Beaufighter IIF R2317
12 Jul 41	Sgt Smither	Predannack	Beaufighter IIF R2317
22 Aug 41	Sgt Martin	off coast Predannack	Beaufighter IIF R2300
22 Aug 41	Sgt Smith	off coast Predannack	Beaufighter IIF R2300
19 Sep 41	Sgt Lipscombe	Corsham	Beaufighter IIF R2323
29 Sep 41	S/L Scrase	Acton Turville	Beaufighter IIF R2306
Dec 41	F/L Fletcher	Irish Sea	Beaufighter IIF
Dec 41	Sgt Grant	Irish Sea	Beaufighter IIF
09 Dec 41	Sgt Smith	exact location unknown	Blenheim IF L1429

DATE	NAME	SITE	AIRCRAFT
15 Dec 41	F/L Imlay	exact location unknown	Beaufighter IIF R2312
15 Dec 41	Sgt Pierce	exact location unknown	Beaufighter IIF R2312
21 Aug 42	P/O Yielder	at sea	Beaufighter
21 Aug 42	Sgt Peacock	at sea	Beaufighter
14 May 43	F/O Bastow	E of Cap de Garde	Beaufighter X7927
13 May 43	F/O George	E of Cap de Garde	Beaufighter X7927
29 Jan 44	F/O Adam	NW of Anzio	Beaufighter IVF
29 Jan 44	F/O Ditzel	NW of Anzio	Beaufighter IVF
18 Jun 51	F/O Sandeman	Farnborough, crash	Meteor F4
18 Jun 51	Sgt Clarckson	Farnborough, crash	Meteor F4
25 Apr 53	F/O Muntz	Flying accident UK	Meteor F8
13 Feb 54	F/O Bridge	Flying accident UK	Meteor F8

(sources: Operations Record Books & Squadron Diaries.)

Every effort has been made by the author and the Association to find the names, dates and circumstances of the deaths of Squadron members. It is, however, possible that names have been omitted due to lack of information. For this the author wishes to apologise to those concerned.

APPENDIX III

THE SQUADRON BADGES AND AIRCRAFT INSIGNIA.

The oldest badge of the Squadron is the arms of the City of London with the RAF eagle and the words "600 City of London Squadron". It was officially authorised by the Corporation of London, as the majority of the Squadron came from the City offices like Lloyds, the Stock Exchange and the banks. The second badge, showing a crescent moon bisected by a sword and the motto "Praeter sescentos" (More than six hundred) was authorised by His Majesty King George VI in October 1944. It commemorates the Squadron's night-fighter role. The motto, literally translated, is intended to convey the meaning "an immense number" and a redoubtable adversary. No.600 is unique in having two official badges, the original one being authorised by King George VI in March 1951, after the authorisation of the newer badge. Originally the Demons carried the Squadron number on the side of the fuselage below the cockpit. This was soon altered to an official marking comprising interlocking red and white triangles across the upper wing and along the side of the fuselage, each side of the roundels. After the Munich crisis, September 1938, the aircraft were camouflaged and the code letters "MV" carried up to the outbreak of the war in September 1939; they were then changed to "BQ" which was retained until 1943 after which there does not seem to be an official Squadron marking. At one point Beaufighters and Mosquitoes carried the number "6" in place of code letters. Upon reforming after the war the Squadron Spitfires carried the Reserve Command combination "RAG" for identification and the Squadron badge was also painted on the aircraft cowling. Re-equipping coincided with the transfer to Fighter Command and the Meteor F4s received the letter "LJ". The badge and pre-war red/white triangle markings were reinstated in miniature on the nose. Towards the end of 1950, however, the code letters disappeared and the traditional marking was carried each side of the fuselage roundels until disbandment.

APPENDIX IV

CONFIRMED SQUADRON KILLS DURING WORLD WAR II

10 May 40	Ju52	Rotterdam Waalhaven	P/O Hayes – Cpl Holmes
10 May 40	Ju52	Rotterdam Waalhaven	P/O Hayes – Cpl Holmes
10 May 40	He111	Belgium	no names mentioned in ORB
14 Aug 40	2 ˘ Bf110	Manston	Bf110D nr S9+NK collided with Bf110D, S9+MK, of 2/Erprobungs Gruppe 210 after hits by 600 Squadr. 20mm. Cannon. Crew S9+NK: Lt. Brinkmann and 1 NCO †. S9+MK: Uffz Steding †, Gefr Schank POW
16 Sep 40	Ju88	off Bexhill, Waalhaven	F/L Pritchard – P/O Jacobs – Sgt Smith. Possibly F6+HM of 4(F)/122 which failed to return from recce over English coast. Crew (Oblt. Stakloff, Hptm. Lüdke, Uffz Pawletta, Oberarzt Guizetti) MIA
27 Sep 40	Ju88A-1	near Hastings	P/O Denby – P/O Guest. Possibly 3Z+DN

			of 5/KG 77. Oblt Ziel, Fw Niederer killed. Uffz Isensee missing. Gefr. Teichtmayer saved by lifeboat and POW.
Mar 41	He111H-3	Drumshang Farm, Dunore, nr Glasgow	P/O Denby – P/O Guest. He111 H-3 (wrknr 3352) 1/KG100. German crew of four POW
Apr 41	Ju88	Stoke St. Michael, nr. Shepton Mallet	F/O Woodward – Sgt Lipscombe, Bristol Beaufighter T4632. JU88 bombs exploded on impact
Apr 41	He111P	Weston Super Mare	F/O Howden – name of R/O unknown, German aircraft He111P (Werke Nr.1647)
07 May 41	He111P	Farringford Farm Freshwater I.o.W.	F/O Woodward – Sgt Lipscombe, He111P (WNr 2862). Parts of enemy aircraft on display at Tangmere Aviation Museum
07 May 41	He111	Foxwell Farm, Osborne nr. Sherborne, Dorset	S/L Pritchard – Sgt Gledhill. Beaufighter dam. by fire He111H-5 (WNr. 2513) of 7/KG 27, 3 killed, 1 POW
08 May 41	Ju88	over Minehead	(damaged)
16 May 41	Ju88A	Danes Mill, Farm Plymtree Devon	F/L McNeill Boyd – F/O Clegg
09 Jul 41	He111	near Abergavenny	F/O Woodward – Sgt Lipscombe
10 Oct 41	He111	sea off St. Ives	S/L McNeill Boyd – F/O Clegg
02 Dec 41	He111	not mentioned in ORB	??

02 Dec 41	He111	not mentioned in ORB	??
15 Dec 41	He111	not mentioned in ORB	(crew 600 Sq. lost)
25 Jan 42	He111	not mentioned in ORB	S/L McNeill Boyd – F/O Clegg
07 Mar 42	He115	off Lizard Point	S/L McNeill Boyd – F/O Clegg
07 Jun 42	Ju88	off Cornish coast	P/O Harvey and F/O Wicksteed ditched after being hit by return fire. Crew reached Portreath in dinghy.
11 Jul 42	Do217	70 mls SE Predannack	P/O King – P/O Barker
27 Jul 42	He111	50 mls SSE Predannack	S/L Elwell – F/S Burrows
29 Nov 42	CantZ506B	NE. of Nagalite	F/O Hilken – P/O Mason Cant Z506B of No.613 Squadron IAF. The crew: Lt. Pilot Brozzi, Cpl. Pilot Acton, 1st Eng. Bergomi, W/Op Petrella and Cadet Pintus. They survived.
21 Dec 42	He111	NE. of Algiers	Sgt Owen – Sgt McAllister
22 Dec 42	Ju88	N. of Cap Sigh	F/O Ross – P/O Finlay
22 Jan 43	Piaggio108	N. of Philippeville	F/O Thompson – W/O White
23 Jan 43	Ju88	N. of Philippeville	S/L Hughes – F/O Dixon
23 Jan 43	Ju88	N. of Philippeville	S/L Hughes – F/O Dixon
27 Jan 43	He111	NNW. of Philippeville	Sgt Owen – Sgt McAllister
12 Feb 43	CantZ1007	E. of Cap Serratt	S/L Hughes – F/O Dixon The Cant was an a/c of No.262 Bomber

			Squadron IAF. Crew killed (Maj Padovani, Cpl Di Pasquale, Sgt Maj Furlanetto, 1st W/Op Attiani, Gunner Panfichi, 1st Fl/ Eng Guccione).
12 Feb 43	CantZ1007	N. of Cap Negroe	F/L Arnsby – P/O Gillies
21 Feb 43	SM84	N. of Cap Serratt	F/L Arnsby – F/O Lawson. SM84 of No.18 Bomber Squadron IAF. Crew killed (LtCol Gatto , Lt Mengoli, Sgt Sitzia, Sgt Tosolini, 1st W/Op Corsini).
21 Feb 43	SM84	E. of Bone	P/O Thompson – Sgt Gillies. SM84 of No.52 Bomber Squadron IAF. Crew killed (Lt Recagno. Lt Martini, SgtMaj Marcone, Sgt Saltarella, Sgt Moschella).
28 Feb 43	CantZ1007	N. of Bone	Sgt Harrop – Sgt Redmond. Cant Z1007 of No.265 Bomber Squadron IAF. Crew killed (Lt.Abbarchi, Cpl Chinelli, 1st Fl/Eng Modoni, W/Op De Piaggi, 1st AG Bozzano).
01 Mar 43	Piaggio108	NE. of Bone	Sgt Owen – Sgt McAllister
23 Mar 43	Piaggio108	N. of Cap Takouch	F/S Vigar – Sgt Dalfrey
04 Apr 43	Ju88	N. of Bone	F/L Hanus – P/O Eyles
07 Apr 43	Ju88	NE. of Algiers Bay	S/L Horne – F/L Brown

18 Apr 43	Ju88	N. of Algiers Bay	F/O Mellersh – P/O Stanley
18 Apr 43	Ju88	N. of Algiers Bay	F/O Mellersh – P/O Stanley
21 Apr 43	Ju88	N. of Bone	F/L Hanus – P/O Eyles
21 Apr 43	Ju88	N. of Algiers Bay	F/O Paton – P/O McAnulty (1st MkVII AI kill)
21 Apr 43	Ju88	East coast of Sardinia	Sgt Perkinson – F/S Stephens
23 Apr 43	Cant Z1007	N. of Cap Serrat, Tunis	F/O Turnbull – Sgt Fowler. . Cant Z1007 of No.265 Bomber Squadron IAF. Crew killed (Lt Asquer, Cpl Salmasi, Fl/Eng Cucinotta, W/Op Serafini, 1st AG Rocchi).
23 Apr 43	Ju88	NE. of Mateur	F/O Bastow – P/O George
24 Apr 43	Ju88	NW .of Pont du Fahs	F/L Hanus – P/O Thompson
26 Apr 43	Ju88	E. of Tunis	S/L Hughes – F/O Dixon
27 Apr 43	Cant Z1007	NW. of Sousse	F/O Roberts – P/O Thompson. Cant Z1007 of 18 Bomber Squadron IAF. Crew killed (Maj Pitaluga, Sgt Maj Perotti, Fl/Eng Curnis, 1st W/Op De Filipis, A/G Solinas).
27 Apr 43	SM84	N. of Monastir	F/O Roberts – P/O Thompson. SM84 of No.50 Bomber Squadron IAF. Crew killed. (LtCol Bressan, Sgt Maj Micheletti, Fl/Eng Grandi, Gunner

			Janella, W/Op Stabellini).
30 Apr 43	Ju 52	S. of Cagliari	F/S Downing – Sgt Lyons
30 Apr 43	Ju 52	S. of Cagliari	F/S Downing – Sgt Lyons
30 Apr 43	Ju 52	S. of Cagliari	F/S Downing – Sgt Lyons
30 Apr 43	Ju 52	S. of Cagliari	F/S Downing – Sgt Lyons
30 Apr 43	Ju 52	S. of Cagliari	F/S Downing – Sgt Lyons (Downing DFM + US Air Medal)
07 May 43	SM79	10 mls S. of Aegodeon	Sgt Hutton – Sgt Carlan
08 May 43	Ju 52	Menzil – Memine	F/O Mellersh – P/O Armstrong
09 May 43	Ju 52	E. of Cap Bon	F/S Downing – Sgt Lyons
11 May 43	He111	SE. of Tunis	S/L Horne – F/L Browne
24 May 43	He111	E. of Bone	F/O Newhouse – P/O Tate
25 May 43	He111	NE. of Cap Rosa	S/L Horne – F/L Browne
11 Jul 43	Ju88	Augusta Harbour	P/O Turnbull – Sgt Fowler
12 Jul 43	He111	10 mls SW of Syracuse	S/L Horne – F/L Ritchie
12 Jul 43	Do217	Off East coast Sicily	P/O McKinnon – P/O Poole
12 Jul 43	Ju88	5 mls N .of Augusta	W/C Green – F/O Gillies
12 Jul 43	He 111	10 mls SW. of Augusta	W/C Green – F/O Gillies
13 Jul 43	Ju 88	5 mls E. of Augusta	F/O Mellersh – P/O Armstrong
13 Jul 43	Cant Z1007b	SE tip of Sicily	F/O Mellersh – P/O Armstrong. Cant Z1007 of No. 191 Bomber

			Squadron IAF. Crew killed. (SgtMaj Bartali, Sgt Maj Marchesi, Fl/Eng Ghidetti, W/Op Minniti, Gunner Martelli).
13 Jul 43	He111	near Augusta, Sicily	S/L Hughes – F/O Dixon
13 Jul 43	Do 217	into sea	P/O McKinnon – P/O Poole
13 Jul 43	He111	NE of Catania	W/C Green – F/O Gillies – Brig Bowen 1AD
14 Jul 43	Ju88 (dam)	place not in ORB	W/C Green – F/O Gillies
14 Jul 43	Ju88	Millielo area	W/C Green – F/O Gillies
14 Jul 43	Ju88	place not in ORB	W/C Green – F/O Gillies (witnessed by P/O Roberts)
14 Jul 43	Ju88	blew up mid-air	W/C Green – F/O Gillies
14 Jul 43	Ju88	20 mls WSW of Catania	W/C Green – F/O Gillies
15 Jul 43	Ju88	off Cape Possaro	P/O Turnbull – Sgt Fowler
15 Jul 43	Ju88	off Cape Possaro	P/O Turnbull – Sgt Fowler
15 Jul 43	Ju88	off Cape Possaro	P/O Turnbull – Sgt Fowler
15 Jul 43	Ju88	not mentioned in ORB	P/O Roberts – F/S Burraston
15 Jul 43	Ju88	not mentioned in ORB	F/L Hilken – P/O Lushington
16 Jul 43	He111	in Golfo di Noto	P/O Ripley – P/O Thomson
17 Jul 43	He111	Off Augusta, Sicily	P/O McKinnon – P/O Poole
17 Jul 43	He111	not mentioned in ORB	P/O Turnbull – Sgt Fowler

17 Jul 43	He111	15 mls E. of Augusta	Sgt Owen – Sgt McAllister
17 Jul 43	CantZ1007b	20 mls NE. of Augusta	Sgt Owen – Sgt McAllister. Cant Z1007 (?) of No.10 Bomber Squadron IAF. Crew killed (Lt Bonaccorso, Lt Goretta, Fl/Eng Trovato, W/Op Cuccumini, AG Gallitelli) (see also Z1007b by McKinnon and Poole)
17 Jul 43	Ju88	unknown	P/O Turnbull – Sgt Fowler
17 Jul 43	Ju88	near Caltanisetta	P/O Turnbull – Sgt Fowler
17 Jul 43	CantZ1007b	SW of Etna – Biancavilla	P/O McKinnon – P/O Poole (see Cant Z1007b by Owen/MacAllister)
17 Jul 43	He 111	off Augusta	P/O McKinnon – P/O Poole
18 Jul 43	SM84	E. of Augusta	F/O Bates – Sgt Cadman. SM84 of No.241 Bomber Squadron IAF. Crew killed (2Lt Salustri, 2Lt Vetrano, Gunner Gatto, Fl/Eng Adezati, W/Op D 'Isidoro).
19 Jul 43	SM84	in sea off Sicily	P/O Newton – Sgt Ross. SM84 of No.241 Bomber Squadron IAF. Crew killed (Lt Alesini, Sgt Pezzetti, Fl/Eng Astolfi, 1st W/Op Trojse, Gunner Principi)
19 Jul 43	Ju88 (dam)	N. of Syracuse	Sgt Owen – Sgt McAllister

21 Jul 43	Ju88	SW of Cape Correnti	S/L Hughes – F/O Dixon
22 Jul 43	Ju88	W of Catania	P/O Ripley – P/O Thomson
24 Jul 43	Ju88	NE. of Augusta	P/O Newton – F/S Ross
27 Jul 43	Piaggio108	mainland Gulf of Messina	F/S Vigar – F/S Palfroy
30 Jul 43	He111	N. of Etna volcano	F/O Mellersh – P/O Armstrong
01 Aug 43	He111	N. of Etna	F/O Bates – F/O Cadman
04 Aug 43	Ju88	in sea off Sicily	Sgt Owen – Sgt McAllister (Owen 16 kills at VE Day)
04 Aug 43	SM84 (dam)	not mentioned in ORB	F/O Mellersh / P/O Poole
09 Aug 43	Ju88	near Palazzolo	P/O Turnbull – Sgt Fowler
09 Aug 43	Ju88	Syracuse/ Augusta area	P/O Turnbull – Sgt Fowler
10 Aug 43	Ju88	East of Syracuse	P/O Mellersh – P/O Poole
10 Aug 43	Ju88	18 mls N. of Augusta	S/L Hughes – F/O Dixon
10 Aug 43	Ju88	5 mls NW. of Augusta	S/L Hughes – F/O Dixon
10 Aug 43	Ju88	15 mls SE. of Catania	S/L Hughes – F/O Dixon
11 Aug 43	Ju88	8 mls E. of Riposta	W/C Green – F/O Gillies
11 Aug 43	Ju88	3 mls NE of Cassibile	P/O Ripley – P/O Thomson
18 Aug 43	Ju87	N. of Syracuse	S/L Hughes – F/O Dixon
08 Sep 43	Ju88	Gulf of Salerno	F/O Bates – F/S Palfrey
08 Sep 43	Ju88	off Capri	P/O Turnbull – Sgt Fowler
09 Sep 43	Ju88	N of Licosa	F/S Downing – Sgt Lyons

09 Sep 43	Ju88	not mentioned in ORB	F/S Downing – Sgt Lyons
10 Sep 43	He111	N. of Naples	W/C Green – F/O Gillies
10 Sep 43	Ju88	near Foggia	F/O Paton – F/O McAnulty
11 Sep 43	He111	Gulf of Salerno	F/O Newhouse – P/O Tate
12 Sep 43	Ju88	E. of Cape Palinaro	F/O Paton – F/O McAnulty
12 Sep 43	Ju88	Near Cape Licosa	F/O Paton – F/O McAnulty
13 Sep 43	He111	Gulf of Salerno	F/O Newhouse – P/O Tate
13 Sep 43	He111	not mentioned in ORB	F/O Newhouse – P/O Tate
13 Sep 43	Ju88	only "off coast".	F/O Newhouse – P/O Tate (Newhouse awarded DFC)
14 Sep 43	Ju88	near River Sele	F/S Downing – Sgt Lyons
19 Sep 43	Ju88	W. of Cape Camparella	F/O Hanus – P/O Finley
Dec 43	Me 410	Monte Corvino	Captured by 600 Squadron ground staff
24 Jan 44	Ju88	nr Circeo 1915 hrs	F/L Turnbull – P/O Fowler
25 Jan 44	Ju88	N of Anzio 0155hrs	S/L Horne – F/S Cadman
25 Jan 44	Ju88	W of Anzio 0205hrs	S/L Horne – F/S Cadman
25 Jan 44	Ju88	N of Rome 0525hrs	WC Green — F/L Gillies
26 Jan 44	He177	Nw of Circeo 1750hrs	F/O Downing – P/O Lyons
26 Jan 44	He177	Nw of Circeo 1756hrs	F/O Downing – P/O Lyons
26 Jan 44	Ju88	Nw of Anzio 1920hrs	F/O Downing – P/O Lyons (Downing 12 e/a – DFC)

29 Jan 44	Do217	N of Anzio 1805hrs	F/L Hilken – F/O Ritchie
29 Jan 44	Do217	S of R. Tiber 1810hrs	F/L Hilken – F/O Ritchie
30 Jan 44	Do217	WSW of Anzio 1846hrs	W/O Harrop – F/S Redmond
30 Jan 44	Ju88 (dam)	N of Rome 2107hrs	F/S Bamford – Sgt Battersby
06 Feb 44	Do217	N of Rome 0405hrs	F/L Hilken – F/O Ritchie
15 Feb 44	Do217	N of Tiber 1820hrs	W/O Kerr – W/O Wheeler
01 Mar 44	Ju88	N of Anzio 2045	W/O Montgomery – Sgt Robertson . During combat a/c hit in fuselage. Ju88 escaped. On return pilot unable to contact operator. After landing it was found that he had bailed out. Taken prisoner Stalag Luft 3.
01 Mar 44	Ju88	NW of Rome 2249hrs	S/L Bailey – F/O Williams
17 Mar 44	Ju88	Anzio area 2050hrs	S/L Styles – F/O Ritchie
28 Apr 44	He177	NW of Anzio 2335hrs	F/O Branch – F/S Balchin
14 May 44	Ju88	NW Tiber 0441hrs	F/O Rees – F/O Bartlett
02 Jun 44	CR42	Lake Vico 0030hrs	F/O Rees – F/O Bartlett
03 Jun 44	Ju87	??	S/L Bailey – F/O Williams
03 Jun 44	Bf110	??	S/L Bailey – F/O Williams
04 Jun 44	Ju88	Biglio 0320hrs	F/S Cole – Sgt Odd
04 Jun 44	Ju88	NW Frosinone 0335hrs	F/S Cole – Sgt Odd

02 Jul 44	Ju87	NE Trasimeno 2242hrs	W/O Ewing – F/S Chenery
06 Jul 44	Ju88	??	S/L Bailey – Sgt Wint
07 Jul 44	Ju87	Grid R6315 0210hrs	F/O Jeffrey – F/O Brewer
11 Jul 44	Ju87	Lake Trasimeno 0115hrs	S/L Bailey – Sgt Wint (Bailey DFC in September)
27 Jul 44	Ju87	nr Volterra 2245hrs	F/S Waitman – F/S Goss
29 Jul 44	Ju87	Grid R5083 2343hrs	F/L Thompson – F/O Beaumont
01 Aug 44	Ju87	NNE of Arezzo 2113hrs	F/L Thompson – F/O Beaumont
02 Aug 44	Ju87	NE of Pisa 0300hrs	W/O Crooks – Sgt Charles
02 Aug 44	Ju87	SW of Arezzo 2235hrs	P/O Jefferson – P/O Spencer
03 Aug 44	Ju87	E of Arezzo 2245hrs	F/O MacDonald – Sgt Towell
27 Aug 44	Ju87	Florence area 2210hrs	F/L Thompson – F/O Beaumont
29 Aug 44	Ju87	SE of Florence 2115hrs	S/L Styles – F/O Wilmer
03 Sep 44	Ju87	nr Rimini	P/O Judd – F/O Brewer
03 Sep 44	Ju87	nr Rimini	P/O Judd – F/O Brewer
04 Sep 44	Ju87	SW of Rimini	S/L Burke – F/L Whaley
04 Sep 44	Ju87	WSW of Rimini 0305hrs	F/S Cole – F/S Odd
05 Sep 44	Ju87		F/O Rees – F/O Bartlett
05 Sep 44	Ju87		F/O Rees – F/O Bartlett
05 Sep 44	Ju87 (dam)	SW of Rimini 0415hrs	F/L Davidson – P/O Talford
10 Sep 44	Ju87	SW Rimini 0315hrs	F/L Thompson – F/O Beaumont
	Ju87		damaged
	Ju87		damaged
04 Oct 44	Ju87	SE of Cesene 2020hrs	W/C Styles – F/O Wilmer

28 Nov 44	Ju87	Forli-Faenze area	S/L Archer – F/L Barrington. German pilot, 200 sorties veteran, POW
01 Dec 44	Ju87	Forli area 1715hrs	W/O Bait – F/S Lothian
23 Dec 44	Ju87	NW of Forli 2110hrs	F/L Rees – F/O Beaumont
23 Dec 44	Ju87	NE of Forli 2120hrs	F/L Rees – F/O Beaumont
23 Dec 44	Ju87 (dam)		F/L Rees – F/O Beaumont (Rees DFC)
Apr 45	FW190		??

APPENDIX V

DECORATIONS AWARDED TO NO.600 (CITY OF LONDON) SQUADRON DURING WORLD WAR II

George Cross:	F/O Tollemache		
DSO:	W/C Green	P/O Harvey	
2nd Bar to DFC:	S/L Hughes		
Bar to DFC:	W/C Styles	S/L Hughes	F/O Dixon
	F/O Turnbull	F/O Gillies	
DFC:	S/L Pritchard	S/L Boyd	S/L Horne
	S/L Burke	S/L Bailey	F/L Clegg
	F/L Thompson	F/L Paton	F/L Hanus
	F/L Hilken	F/L Whealey	F/L Rees
	F/O Hayes	F/O Dixon	F/O Woodward
	F/O Mellersh	F/O Turnbull	F/O Roberts
	F/O Gillies	F/O Tate	F/O Armstrong
	F/O Newhouse	F/O McAnulty	F/O Downing
	F/O Ritchie	F/O Brewer	F/O Judd
	F/O Beaumont	F/O Bartlett	P/O Kramer
	P/O Lyons	P/O Wicksteed	P/O Denby
	P/O Haine	P/O Thompson	P/O Bailey
	W/O Harrop		
Bar to DFM:	F/S Fowler		
DFM:	F/S Fowler	F/S Downing	F/S Lyons
	F/S Wint	Sgt Parkinson	Sgt Holmes
	Sgt Owen		Sgt McAllister
MBE:	F/L Clennet	W/O Nicholson	W/O Nelson

APPENDIX VI

COMMANDING OFFICERS OF NO.600 (CITY OF LONDON) SQUADRON 1925 - 1957

1925 - 1926	W/C A.W.H. James, MC
1926 - 1931	S/L the Hon F.E. Guest
1931 - 1934	S/L S.B. Collett
Jul 1934 - 1937	S/L P. Stewart
1937 - Dec 1939	S/L Viscount Carlow
Dec 1939 - May 1940	S/L J.M. Wells
May 1940 - Sep 1940	F/L D. de B. Clarke
Sep 1940 - Nov 1940	S/L H.L. Maxwell DSO
Nov 1940 - Jan 1941	S/L Pritchard
Jan 1941 - Dec 1941	W/C G. Stainforth AFC
Dec 1941 - May 1942	W/C H.M. Pearson DFC
May 1942 - Nov 1942	W/C A.G. Miller DFC, Order of Lenin
Nov 1942 - Dec 1942	W/C J.R. Watson
Dec 1942 - Mar 1944	W/C P. Green DSO, DFC
Mar 1944 - Dec 1944	W/C L.H. Styles DFC
Dec 1944 - Aug 1945	W/C A.H. Drummond
Jul 1946 - Jul 1948	S/L T.N. Hayes DFC
Jul 1948 - Aug 1950	S/L D.E. Proudlove
Aug 1950 - Oct 1953	S/L J.P. Meadows DFC, AFC
Oct 1953 - Mar 1957	S/L J. McCormack AFC

APPENDIX VII.

AIRCRAFT FLOWN BY NO.600 (CITY OF LONDON) SQUADRON 1925 - 1957

Oct 1925 - Oct 1929	Avro 504K - De Havilland DH9A
Aug1929 - Jan 1935	Westland Wapiti - AVRO Tutor
Jan 1935 - May 1937	Hawker Hart
Feb 1937 - Apr 1939	Hawker Demon
Jan 1939 - Oct 1941	Bristol Blenheim IF
Nov 1939 - Jun 1940	Bristol Blenheim IV
Sep 1940 - Jun 1941	Bristol Beaufighter 1F
Apr 1941 - Apr 1942	Bristol Beaufighter IIF
Mar 1942 - Feb 1945	Bristol Beaufighter VIF
Dec 1944 - Aug 1945	De Havilland Mosquito XIX
21 Aug 1945	disbanded
Oct 1946 - Nov 1947	Vickers Supermarine Spitfire F.14
Apr 1947 - Nov 1950	Vickers Supermarine Spitfire F.21
Sep 1948 - Mar 1950	Vickers Supermarine Spitfire F.22
Mar 1950 - Apr 1952	Gloster Meteor F.4
Nov 1951 - Mar 1957	Gloster Meteor F.8
10 Mar 1957	disbanded

APPENDIX VIII

AIRFIELDS USED BY NO.600 (CITY OF LONDON) SQUADRON 1925 - 1957

14 Oct 1925	Northolt
18 Jan 1927	Hendon
01 Oct 1938	Kenley
03 Oct 1938	Hendon
25 Aug 1939	Northolt
02 Oct 1939	Hornchurch - detachment at Manston
16 Oct 1939	Rochford
20 Oct 1939	Hornchurch
27 Dec 1939	Manston
16 May 1940	Northolt
20 Jun 1940	Manston
22 Aug 1940	Hornchurch
12 Sep 1940	Redhill
12 Oct 1940	Catterick (detachments at Drem, Acklington and Prestwick)
14 Mar1941	Drem (detachment at Prestwick)
27 April 1941	Colerne
18 June 1941	Fairwood Common (detachment at Predannack)
27 June 1941	Colerne (detachment at Predannack)
06 Oct 1941	Predannack
02 Sep 1942	Church Fenton
14 Nov 1942	Portreath
18 Nov 1942	Blida (Algeria)
07 Dec 1942	Maison Blanche (Algeria)
03 Jan 1943	Setif (Algeria) (dets at Souk-el-Khemis, 'Paddington' (Tunisia), Bone (Algeria) Tingley (Algeria), Monastir (Tunisia).

25 Jun 1943	Luqa (Malta)
26 Jul 1943	Cassibile (Sicily)
30 Sep 1943	Montecorvino (near Salerno - Italy) (detachments at Brindisi, Tortorella (Foggia), Gaudo (South of Salerno), Lago (North of Naples).
02 Feb 1944	Marcianese (North-East of Naples)
22 Mar 1944	Pomigliano (East of Naples)
01 Apr 1944	Marcianese
13 Jun 1944	La Banca (South of Anzio)
19 Jun 1944	Voltone (North of Rome)
05 Jul 1944	Follonica (South of Pisa)
29 Jul 1944	Rosignano (South of Pisa) (detachment at Falconaro (North of Ancona)
25 Aug 1944	Falconaro - detachment at Rosignano, Iesi (West of Ancona), Bellaria
15 Dec 1944	Cesenatico (North of Rimini)
24 May 1945	Campoformido (West of Udine)
26 Jul 1945	Aviano (West of Udine)
21 Aug 1945	disbanded at Campoformido
10 May 1946	Biggin Hill
10 Mar 1957	disbanded at Biggin Hill

APPENDIX IX

TECHNICAL INFORMATION ON SQUADRON AIRCRAFT

Aircraft	Engines	Crew	Speed	Altitude	Range	Weapons
AVRO 504K	1 Monosoupape	1	95mph	16000ft	250mls	-.-
AVRO Tutor	1 Lynx	1	120mph	16200ft	250mls	-.-
De Havilland 9A	1 Liberty	2	114mph	16500ft	400mls	2mg
Westland Wapiti	1 Bristol Jupiter VIIIF	2	135mph	20600ft	360mls	2mg
Hawker Hart	1 Rolls Royce Kestrel	1	150mph	22000ft	450mls	2mg
Hawker Demon	1 Rolls Royce Kestrel	2	155mph	27000ft	400mls	3mg
Bristol Blenheim1F	2 Bristol Mercury VIII	2-3	260mph	27000ft	1125mls	5mg
Blenheim IV	2 Bristol Mercury XV	2-3	270mph	22000ft	1500mls	5mg
Beaufighter IF	2 Bristol Hercules XI	2	320mph	27000ft	1200mls	6mg-4can
Beaufighter IIF	2 Rolls Royce Merlin	2	330mph	27000ft	1470mls	6mg-4can
Beaufighter VIF	2 Bristol Hercules VI	2	333mph	26500ft	1500mls	6mg-4can
Mosquito XIX	2 Rolls Royce Merlin	2	380mph	36000ft	1250mls	4mg-4can
Spitfire F14	1 Rolls Royce Griffon	1	448mph	22000ft	460mls	4mg-2can
Spitfire F21	1 Rolls Royce Griffon	1	454mph	43500ft	515mls	4can
Spitfire F22	1 Rolls Royce Griffon	1	454mph	43500ft	515mls	4can
Meteor F4	2 Rolls Royce Derwent	1	585mph	50000ft	880mls	4can
Meteor F8	2 Rolls Royce Derwent	1	590mph	44000ft	980mls	4can

APPENDIX X

TECHNICAL INFORMATION ON SOME ENEMY AIRCRAFT

Aircraft	Engines	Crew	Speed	Altitude	Range	Weapons
JU 52	3 BMW132 A-3	4	155mph	20000ft	850mls	2 mg
JU87	1 Junkers Jumo 211J	2	255mph	24000ft	1000mls	2mg-can
JU88	2 Junkers Jumo211B	4	275mph	27500ft	1200mls	3 mg
HE111	2 Junkers Jumo211A3	5	275mph	27500ft	1700mls	6 mg
HE 115	2 BMW132K	3	220mph	17500ft	2000mls	2 mg
BF110	2 Daimler Benz DM601	2	375mph	34000ft	800mls	5mg-2can
ME 410	2 Daimler Benz DB603	2	400mph	24000ft	1100mls	4mg-2can
Cant Z506B	3 Alfa Romeo126RC34	5	220mph	25000ft	1750mls	4mg
Cant Z1007	3 Piaggio PXI RC40	5	280mph	28000ft	1250mls	4mg
Piaggio 108	4 Piaggio PXII RC35	6	150mph	28000ft	2100mls	7mg
SM84	3 Piaggio PXI PC40	5	260mph	25500ft	1150mls	4mg
SM79	3 Alfa Romeo126RC34	6	250mph	23000ft	1200mls	4-5mg
Fiat CR42	1 Fiat A74 RC36	1	280mph	31000ft	480mls	2 mg
FW190	1 BMW 801C-1	1	400mph	35000ft	500mls	4mg

mph: miles per hour - ft: feet - mls: miles - mg: machine gun - can: cannon

APPENDIX XI

NO.600 SQUADRON AIRCREW IN COMBAT DURING THE BATTLE OF BRITAIN.

Name	**Rank**	**Remarks**
Aires, E.H.	P/O	
Albertini, A.V.	Sgt	
Atkinson, R.	P/O	† while flying Hurricane P3174 AK-G of No. 213 Squadron (Tangmere) 17 Oct 40
Ayers, D.H.	Sgt	23 Sept 40 in Spitfire P7362, No.74 Sq. Crashed near Southwold. Body found 4 Oct 40
Baker,	P/O	
Barker, G.I.	P/O	† after Battle
Barnard, E.C.	Sgt	
Barnes, J.G.C.	F/O	
Blair, C.E.	P/O	† since Battle
Blake, M.V.	S/L	New Zealand
Booth, J.J.	AC	
Bowring, B.H.	P/O	With No.111 Squadron. Force-landed 5 Sep 40 after hit by Me109s. ✠✠✠
Brown, J.W.	Sgt	† since Battle
Bull, J.C.	P/O	
Burdekin, A.G.	Sgt	
Burley, P.S.	Sgt	
Canham, A.W.	Sgt	
Cave, J.G.	F/O	
Clackson, D.L.	F/L	MBE
Clarke, D. de B.	S/L	CBE

Name	**Rank**	**Remarks**
Clayton,	P/O	
Coombs, R.J.	Sgt	commissioned - DFC
Cooper, C.F.	AC2	† Blenheim BQ-M. Crashed after engine failure 3 Oct 40
Coote, L.E.M.	Sgt	† since Battle
David, J.N.		
Davies, J.W.	Sgt	† Blenheim L6684 crashed at Hornchurch, Sgt Saunders also †
Denby, G.A.	P/O	DFC - † Battle
Dermott,	P/O	
Dixon, L.	AC	commissioned - DFC
Dyer,	Sgt	New Zealand
Edwards, K.C.	Sgt	⚕
Egan, E.J.	Sgt	
Frost, J.L.	P/O	
Glegg, A.J.	P/O	DFC
Graham, K.A.G.	Sgt	† since Battle
Grant, E.J.F.	Sgt	† since Battle
Green, F.W.W.	Sgt	
Grice, D.N.	F/O	DFC † 8 Aug 40 Blenheim L8665, BQ-A, shot down by OLt Sprick, III/JG26.
Haine, R.C.	P/O	DFC
Hardwick, W.R.H.	Sgt	
Hayes, T.N.	F/O	DFC - became OC600 after the war.
Hindrup, F.G.	Sgt	New Zealand
Hobhouse,	P/O	
Hobson, C.A.	P/O	† flying Blenheim BQ-M after engine failure 3 Oct 40
Holland, R.M.	Sgt	
Holmes, G.H.	Sgt	DFM - Commissioned - † Battle
Hopton, B.W.	Sgt	† since Battle
Hough, H.B.L.	P/O	† since Battle
Huckin, P.E.	Sgt	
Hughes, D.E.	Sgt	NZ - † - observer Blenheim BQ-M engine failure 3 Oct 40
Hunter	F/L	† since Battle

Name	Rank	Remarks
Hurst, P.R.S.	P/O	† 23 Oct 40. Blenheim L1272, BQ-X crashed into hill at Kirkby Malzeard
Imray, H.S.	Sgt	
Jacobs, H.	P/O	DFC bar, AFC
Johnson, S.F.	P/O	† since Battle
Juleff, J.R.	P/O	
Keast, F.J.	Sgt	† 8 Aug 40 (for details see Grice)
Kramer, M.	P/O	DFC
Lamb, R.L.	P/O	
Larbalastier, B.D.	Sgt	Commissioned
Le Rougetel, S.P.	F/O	DFC
Lewis, C.S.	Sgt	† 4 Jul 40
Libscombe, A.J.	Sgt	† since Battle
Little, P.	S/L	
Maxwell, H.L.	S/L	CBE, DSO
Moulton, E.W.	Sgt	
Mount, C.J.	F/O	DSO, DFC, CBE ✠
Noble	Sgt	
Owen, A.E.	Sgt	
Pearce, P.G.	AC	Promoted Sgt
Perkins, F.S.	Sgt	
Pritchard, C.A.	F/L	DFC ✠
Rawlence, A.J.	P/O	
Reed, H.	Sgt	
Riseley, A.H.	Sgt	
Ritchie, J.R.	P/O	AFC
Saunders, A.F.C.	Sgt	† 7 Oct 40 (see Sgt J.W. Davies)
Schumar, F.H.	P/O	† since Battle
Scrase, G.E.T.	F/O	
Senior, B.	Sgt	
Smith, A.	Sgt	† since Battle
Smith, E.C.	Sgt	DFC - AFC
Smith, E.S.	F/O	
Smith, St. J.	Sgt	† since Battle
Taylor, E.F.	Sgt	
Tearle, F.J.	Sgt	
Townsend, T.W.	Sgt	
Walker, A.	Sgt	New Zealander

Name	Rank	Remarks
Warren, J.B.W.	AC	† (for details see F/O Grice)
Wheeler, N.J.	P/O	AFC
Whitwell, P.	Sgt	† since Battle
Willis,	Sgt	
Wiseman, W.D.	P/O	
Woodward, R.S.	P/O	DFC - † since Battle

Ϙ = enemy aircraft shot down
† = killed

APPENDIX XII

THE FIRST 100 AUXILIARIES (ORs) OF NO.600 (CITY OF LONDON) SQUADRON

Number	Name	Trade
800.000	W.J. Warrell	Clerk
800.001	W.S. Ashton	?
800.002	E.J. Martin	?
800.003	W.T.J. Wood	Fitter Aero Engines
800.004	F. Greenwood	?
800.005	G. Hibbins	Carpenter/Rigger
800.006	A.S.W. Payne	Fitter Aero Engines
800.007	N.A. Berry	Fitter Aero Engines
800.008	F. Bias	ACH
800.009	F. Bass	Carpenter/Rigger
800.010	A.W. Allen	Fitter Aero Engines
800.011	P.F. England	Fitter Aero Engines
800.012	L.F. Ford	ACH
800.013	N.H. Chester	Carpenter/Rigger
800.014	R.J. Murton	?
800.015	E.S. Leary	Transport
800.016	?	?
800.017	E.M. Ensoll	Carpenter/Rigger
800.018	E. Parker	ACH
800.019	D.G.W. Grainge	Fitter Aero Engines
800.020	F.C.H. Grainge	?
800.021	F.C.H. Witcombe	Fitter Aero Engines
800.022	C. Wickins	Clerk
800.023	A.S.R. Cole	Fitter Aero Engines
800.024	T. Cullinan	Carpenter/Rigger

Number	**Name**	**Trade**
800.025	?	?
800.026	F. Willis	Transport
800.027	G.H.W. Guest	Carpenter/Rigger
800.028	A.H. Watson	Wireless Operator
800.029	S. Shepperdson	ACH
800.030	L. Keegan	ACH
800.031	G. Henderson	ACH
800.032	R.J.H. Hitchin-Kemp	Fitter Aero Engines
800.033	S.V. Nicholson	Fitter Aero Engines
800.034	S.W.H. Egan	Fitter Aero Engines
800.035	A.W. Welham	Wireless Operator
800.036	P. Lawrence	Fitter Aero Engines
800.037	C.J. Cox	Fitter Aero Engines
800.038	V.D. Perrin	Armourer
800.039	A.C. Thomas	Fitter Aero Engines
800.040	J.W.M. Streeter	Transport
800.041	H.A. Laudy	Fitter Aero Engines
800.042	R.R.L. Mitchell	Carpenter/Rigger
800.043	D.A. Litchfield	Wireless Operator
800.044	J.A. Allen	Armourer
800.045	E.E. McGowan	Fitter Aero Engines
800.046	A.J. Stainer	Fitter Aero Engines
800.047	J.E. Lock	Wireless Operator
800.048	D. Dyball	Carpenter/Rigger
800.049	S.A. Haddock	Carpenter/Rigger
800.050	H.H. Edwardson	Carpenter/Rigger
800.051	R.J. Brookes	Wireless Operator
800.052	F. Dewell	Wireless Operator
800.053	J.C. Phipps	Fitter Aero Engines
800.054	G.E. Wren	Fitter Aero Engines
800.055	A. Chantrey	Fitter Aero Engines
800.056	P.E. Hindmarsh	Fitter Aero Engines
800.057	M.G. Pacey	Fitter Aero Engines
800.058	R.J. Ward	Carpenter/Rigger
800.059	R.E. Wilck	Carpenter/Rigger
800.060	R.C. Davies	ACH
800.061	C.N.D. Stewart	Carpenter/Rigger
800.062	R.H.A. Nayler	Fitter Aero Engines
800.063	J.A.G. Everett	Fitter Aero Engines

Number	Name	Trade
800.064	G.J. H. Thomson	Fitter Aero Engines
800.065	H.K. Fearnside	Carpenter/Rigger
800.066	J.H. Gibson	Fitter Aero Engines
800.067	W.R. Kidd	Clerk
800.068	S.E. Lowe	Carpenter/Rigger
800.069	J.S. Thomson	Fitter Aero Engines
800.070	F.C. Assiter	Fitter Aero Engines
800.071	A.S. Bird	Wireless Operator
800.072	R.E. Chaloner	Wireless Operator
800.073	S.W. Musk	Carpenter/Rigger
800.074	J.A. Merchant	Carpenter/Rigger
800.075	W.R. Thorogood	Carpenter/Rigger
800.076	C.D. Hankinson	Armourer
800.077	J.A. Baulk	Armourer
800.078	F.H. Johnson	Carpenter/Rigger
800.079	H.E. Vernon	Fitter Aero Engines
800.080	C.L. Tedder	Armourer
800.081	G.H. Bonner	Carpenter/Rigger
800.082	L.C. Marshall	Fitter Aero Engines
800.083	A.R. Maddox	Carpenter/Rigger
800.084	R. Brownley	Wireless Operator
800.085	?	?
800.086	H.W. Heycock	Armourer
800.087	G. Howard	Carpenter/Rigger
800.088	S. Herbert	Carpenter/Rigger
800.089	J.W. Thorburn	Fitter Aero Engines
800.090	D.G. Broughton	Carpenter/Rigger
800.091	G.D. Lilley	Wireless Operator
800.092	F.C. Sanders	Transport
800.093	A.L. Turner	Carpenter/Rigger
800.094	R. Claringbull	Carpenter/Rigger
800.095	C.G. Jones	Fitter Aero Engines
800.096	S. Moore	Fitter Aero Engines
800.097	H.F. Morris	Fitter Aero Engines
800.098	L.F. Firmin	Fitter Aero Engines
800.099	R.St.J. Collins	ACH

APPENDIX XIII

TOTAL SCORE FOR NO.600 SQUADRON AT THE END OF THE WAR:

Aircraft :	Destroyed - 165	Probably - 13	Damaged - 14	
MT:	Destroyed - 16	N/A.	Damaged - 15	
Railways:	Destroyed - 4 locomotives - 20 trains	N/A.	Damaged - 10 trains	
Shipping:	Destroyed - 1 "I" boat	N/A.	Damaged - 1 "I" boat	6 barges

APPENDIX XIV

AIRBORNE INTERCEPTION; THE EYES OF THE NIGHT-FIGHTER.

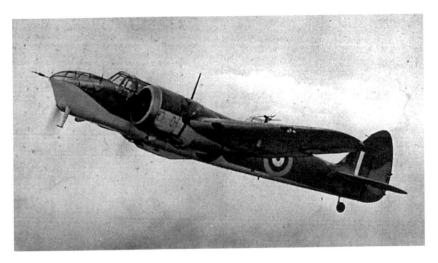

Blenheim Mk.IV with Mk.III AI (note the antennas on the nose and wings).

The first AI (Airborne Interception) in service with 600 Squadron was the Mk.III, an improvement on the Mks.I and II. The first set, the Mk.I, had a transmitter using two triodes TY150, which only gave about 1KW of pulse power and were mounted on a wooden frame. To the horror of Prof. Hanbury Brown, Metro-Vicks had copied the original "bread-board" model even down to the use of wood! The set had two cathode-ray tubes and was horribly unreliable as there had been no time to engineer it properly. The sets were put in the nose of Blenheims Mk.IV or Bolingbrokes, a Canadian version of the Mk.IV. At RAF Northolt ACM Hugh Downing inspected the new device.

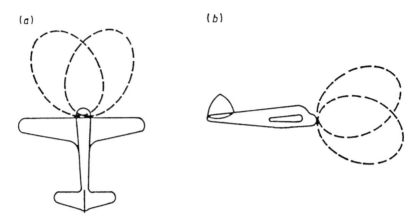

Overlapping antenna patterns used in metric-wave AI

Seeing the cramped position of the operator he was so shocked that he ordered Hanbury Brown to move the whole set to the fuselage, just in front of the air gunner. For Hanbury Brown and his staff it meant an exceedingly tiresome job. The Mk.III was better engineered. The wooden frame was replaced by one of metal. It had a much more powerful transmitter with two air-cooled microwave triodes. These gave about 5KW pulse power and an improved range of ± 15,000 feet. The Mk.IV set was introduced by the end of 1940. It was properly engineered. The set still worked on a wavelength of 1.5 metres. A great improvement was the excellent new modulator, designed by EMI. It gave a minimum target range of 500 feet and a maximum range of 20,000 feet. It used vertically polarised antennas which had cured the troubles of the Mk.III with horizontal polarisation. One thing remaining was the necessity for good Ground Control to get the final kill. Training these men was of the greatest importance.

Ralph Hiscox, Commander of X-Flight, No.600 Squadron was such an expert. Men like Hiscox were able to talk the crew to an enemy aircraft or, as they called it "customers". Only then was it possible to shoot down bombers at night with entirely radar controlled night-fighters. Further it needed expert pilots like John Cunningham to patiently chase the enemy and then close in for the kill. Only when these conditions were met, and after the Beaufighter entered service as a night-fighter did the AI controlled aeroplane become a deadly effective weapon.

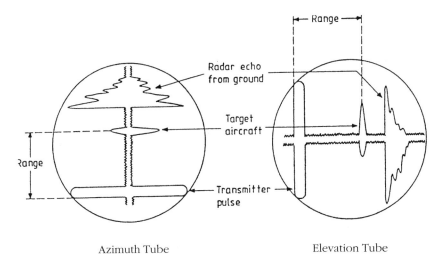

Azimuth Tube   Elevation Tube

The Mk.V still worked on 1.5 metres. It had an operator who placed a strobe on the target echo. This strobe drove an indicator in front of the pilot, with the markings shown in the diagram. It was first fitted in a Mosquito, with pilot and operator sitting next to each other. The Airborne Interception equipment improved during its operational use. Mk.VI was a fully automatic set on 1.5 metres. It had a pilot's indicator similar to the Mk.V, but it was only used experimentally, as Professor Brown remembers, on Defiants and Hurricanes.

The next operational set was the Mk.VIII. The higher frequency gave a better resolution and for some time did not react to the jamming chaff or window interference. Operational use of the Mk.VIII was very similar to the early set except that with the Mk.VIII, GCI would vector the Beaufighter to put it into a position where the enemy aircraft would be crossing in front of the Beaufighter at about 4-5 miles away. Once this contact had been acquired by the Beaufighter operator on his own AI, GCI would make contact with another night-fighter to help him make another interception somewhere else. It was quite common to find oneself vectored onto a "bogie" (unidentified aircraft) to find that it was one of one's own bombers on its way home which had forgotten to switch the IFF (Identification Friend or Foe) on when approaching friendly territory. Night-fighter crews always had to be very sure of themselves and make a positive identification before attacking.

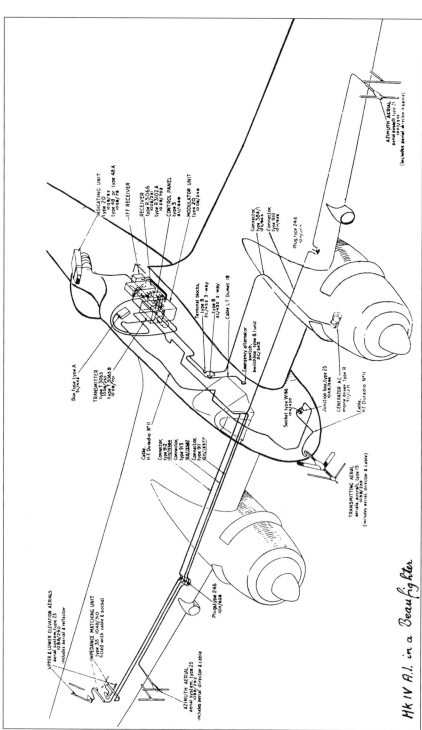

Mk.IV A.I installation in a Beaufighter.

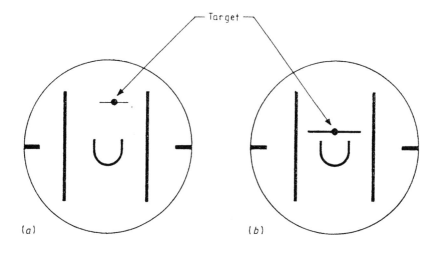

The pilot's spot indicator of a Mk.V AI set. (a) Target at 5,000 feet range, above the fighter and slightly to the right and (b) target at 1,000 feet range, above the fighter and dead ahead, the perfect position for a good kill.

Bristol Beaufighter with Mk.IV AI

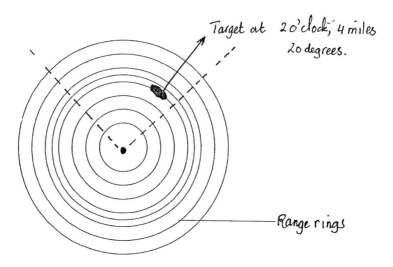

Mk.VIII AI display. The concentric range rings show the distance between night-fighter (centre) and enemy. Here the enemy aircraft is at 2 o'clock, 20 degrees at a 4 miles distance.

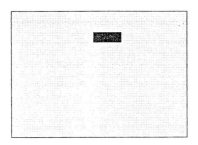

Target
1 o'clock
20°

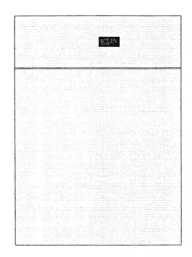

Target at 7mls

AI Mk.X display

The Mk.VIIIs remained in use with the Squadron until December 1944 when the Mosquito night-fighter was introduced, equipped with the Mk.X. In December 1944 No.600 Squadron were sent to Foggia to convert to Mosquitoes whilst the Radar Navigators were sent to Pomigliano to spend two weeks flying around in Wellington flying classroom aircraft fitted with the Mk.X AI This was very much "state of the art" technology and far superior to any AI set which had been used to date. The aerial configuration in the nose of the Mosquito revolved through 360º but the rear 180º of look being blanked off. It could also be moved to nod up and down when required. The receiver monitor consisted of two displays, the one on the right providing Range information only which was provided with a moveable strobe line. When this strobe line was positioned beneath the blip, it would register on the left hand monitor screen as on a clock screen, e.g. 1 o'clock, 20º. The Mk.X set enabled three range scales to be selected, i.e. 100 miles, 10 miles and 1 mile. The 100 miles range was very useful as a navigational aid, when with the aerial dish angled in the downward position, it was possible to make accurate landfalls from the radar map displayed without getting returns from the sea.

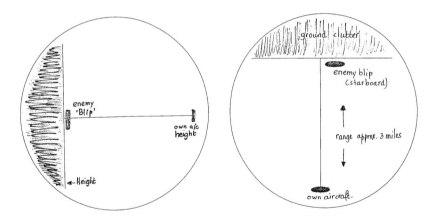

Typical early contact (simplified). The Elevation tube shows an enemy aircraft at the same height as its pursuer, while the Azimuth tube shows its distance at approx. 3 miles and slightly to starboard.

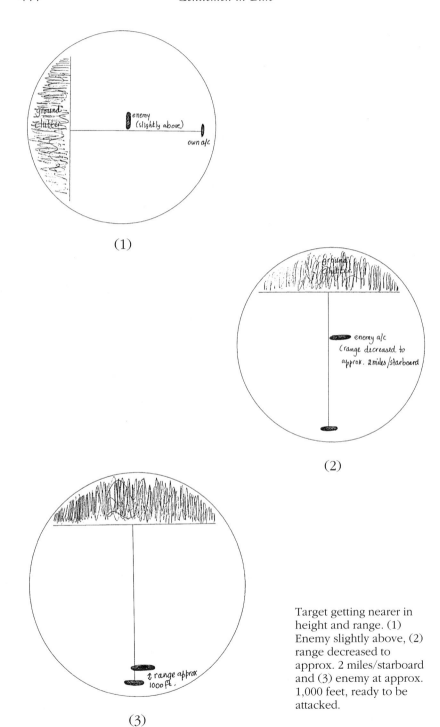

(1)

(2)

(3)

Target getting nearer in height and range. (1) Enemy slightly above, (2) range decreased to approx. 2 miles/starboard and (3) enemy at approx. 1,000 feet, ready to be attacked.

APPENDIX XV

AIRCRAFT OF NO.600 (CITY OF LONDON) SQUADRON - SERIAL NUMBERS/AIRCRAFT CODES

De Havilland DH9a	J8154	J8164	J8165	J8171	J8184/B	J8223/C	
Avro 504N	J8502	J8513	J8515	J8698			
Westland Wapiti IIa	J9601	J9603	J9604	J9606	J9607	J9608	J9609
	J9610	J9613	J9615	J9870	J9871	J9878	K1334
	K1339						
Hawker Hart	K2473	K2979	K2980	K2982	K2983	K2984	K2985
	K2986	K2987	K2988	K3028	K3040	K3045	K3047
	K3848	K3957					
Hawker Hart Trainer	K3147	K5035	K6489				
Hawker Demon	K2846	K2847	K2850	K3982	K4523	K5696	K5697
	K5700	K5701	K5702	K5703	K5704	K5707	K5708
	K5709	K5710	K8190				
AVRO Tutor	K1240	K3391	K3392				
Bristol Blenheim	K7117/L	K7118	K7126	L1111	L1115	L1128	L1164
F (BQ)	L1170	L1179	L1185	L1222	L1240	L1251/Y	L1256
	L1272/X	L1277	L1295/E	L1326	L1335/W	L1397	L1398
	L1399	L1401/K	L1402	L1403	L1404	L1428	L1429
	L1468	L1494	L1513	L1514/N	L1515/L	L1517/O	L1523
	L6608	L6616/R	L6617	L6626	L6671	L6680	L6681
	L6682	L6683	L6684/S	L6685	L6710	L6720	L6786
	L6791	L8363	L8372	L8450/O	L8665/A	L8679/D	L8698/M
	L8723	L8729	L8730				
Douglas Havoc	AW404						
Bristol Blenheim IVF	L4904	L4905/M	L4906	P4825	P4837	P4946/W	T2136
	Z5722						
Bristol Beaufighter IF	R2065	R2070	R2071	R2072	R2074	R2075	R2076
	R2079	R2083	R2088	R2099	R2121	R2133/C	R2158
	R2184	R2185	R2188	R2200	R2256/F	R2259/F	T4628
	T4631	T4632	T4640	X5744			
Bristol Beaufighter IIF	R2272	R2273	R2275	R2276	R2277	R2278	R2279

	R2280	R2282	R2284	R2300	R2302	R2305	R2306
	R2310	R2312	R2317	R2318	R2323	R2325	R2326
	R2327	R2330	R2337	R2374	R2376	R2396	R2451
	R2453	R2477	T3020	T3039	T3044	T3146	
Bristol Beaufighter	V8388/Y	V8393	V8407/A	V6847/P	V8671	V8672	V8692
IVF	V8695	V8697	V8699/A	V8700/F	V8701	V8705	V8712
	V8714	V8716	V8720	V8734	V8755	V8756	V8758
	V8764/J	V8766	V8767	V8771/K	V8811	V8827	V8833
	X7885	X7886	X7887/K	X7888	X7889	X7890	X7892
	X7894	X7920	X7922	X7926	X7927	X7928	X7946
	X7947	X7951	X7958	X7960	X7963	X7967	X8006
	X8008	X8023/I	X8150	X8156	X8213	X8225	X8000
	X8252	X8255	X8258	EL145	EL147	EL148	EL149
	EL150	EL152	EL153	EL156	EL169	EL174	EL178
	EL179	EL186/I	JL704	KV908/K	KV912	KB943	KV972/G
	KW114	MM873	MM876/X	MM877	M884	MM900	MM905
	MM927	MM940	ND139	ND147/Q	ND148	ND162	ND165
	ND170	ND172/B	ND320/R				
DH Mosquito	TA123/H	TA124	TA125	TA126	TA133/X	TA144	TA406
NF XIX	TA407	TA409	TA410	TA413	TA425	TA426	TA433
	TA442	TA444	TA445	TA448			
Spitfire F14 (RAG)	RB165	RM783/G	TX981/X	TZ141/E	TZ175/X		
Spitfire F21	LA192/G	LA223	LA228/N	LA231	LA249/M	LA253/K	LA278/V
	LA299	LA323/H	LA328	LA330	LA331		
Spitfire F22	PK329/G	PK392/U	PK405/Y	PK663/J	PK670/X		
Gloster Meteor	RA379/V	RA423/L	RA428	RA436	VT106/E	VT109	VT171
F4 (LJ)	VT275	VT281/V	VW256/U	VW273	VW300	VW304	VZ411/W
	VZ412/P	VZ414	VZ415	VZ418	VZ429/Q		
Gloster Meteor T7	WA628/S	WA667	WA671	WA672	WA689	WA969	WA723
	WF816						
Gloster Meteor F8	WA869/X	WA933/O	WA962	WA965	WE815/X	WE859	WE975
	WF639	WF683	WF685	WF686/Q	WF706	WF713	WF747
	WF754	WF757	WF759/U	WH253	WH258/P	WH261/Z	WH280
	WH281/V	WH285	WH365	WH424/V	WH465/Y	WH470	WH474/P
	WH505/W	WH975/X	WK671	WK807/W	WK951/Y	WL106	WL108
	WL109	WL162					

APPENDIX XVI

THE MYTH OF THE "MANSTON MUTINY" AND THE TRUTH OF THE MEDITERRANEAN CAMPAIGN.

One episode in the Squadron's proud history would turn into a controversy, when Len Deighton, in his book "Fighter; the True Story of the Battle of Britain" quite wrongfully pictured the Squadron members as cowards, who spent most of the time hiding from the enemy. Deighton painted a scene of "hundreds of airmen cowering in shelters for days, too terrified to move out, even when threatened by officers". He claimed that in one case an officer even had to threaten them with a gun. The members of the Squadron Association were outraged. The Committee even discussed suing Deighton for libel when the book appeared in the shops. Ten years after the book was published F/L Stockman, who had served at Manston, investigated the accusations, writing directly to the author, not receiving any reply but a "thank you" for Stockman's "interest in the book". Nigel Douglas, an officer in the RAFVR(T), a policeman by trade, was asked by Stockman to help him investigate these serious accusations. Squadron members who had been at Manston through the entire period stated that they first heard of the "mutiny" when Deighton's book came out; no one among the Association members had even ever heard about it while they served at Manston. No written evidence was found in official documents. It seemed at first that Deere's mention of "the pilots" of 600 Squadron having been exceptionally courageous "proved" the lack of courage of the others. Deere vigorously denied having had the intention to create a myth. In the Manston Herald F/L Stockman reported on his and Douglas' investigations and replied to every charge made by Len Deighton in "Fighter".

Page 201 - (Monday August 12, 1940)

Here Deighton states that *"Hundreds of airmen took to the shelters and stayed there for days and would not come out 'in spite of threats, orders and entreaties by their officers'."*
    The shelters were there to be used, but only by personnel who did not have essential duty to perform elsewhere. Did airmen take to the shelters for days at a time? During my enquiries, I have been unable to find anyone who heard about such happenings at the time. The late S/L Bill Grout, who had been a Sgt on 600 Squadron, was angered by the accusations which he said were untrue. In "Kent Airfields in the Battle of Britain", he said that the only similar incident that he ever heard about concerned a party of 200 or 300 recruits who were sent from Blackpool. They were to be a labour force helping to fill bomb craters on Manston airfield. Arriving by train under two NCOs they arrived during an air raid. The NCOs ordered the men to march to Manston and got back on the train and returned to Blackpool! Service policemen at the railhead directed the men to take cover in the air raid shelters in the old railway tunnels and caves. They were found to be there still three days later and "their morale shattered, they were sent back to Blackpool". This isolated incident may possibly be the base upon which this particular accusation is founded.

Page 202 - (Monday, August 12)

Deighton alleges that *because the ground crews had gone into shelters and refused to come out, the aircrews of 600 Squadron were the only ones left to refuel and re-arm the visiting Spitfires when they should have been resting after their night operations.* I have never heard about any incident where RAF groundcrews have abandoned their pilots in the face of the enemy, except for this so-called 'Manston Mutiny'. I find it unbelievable. It is possible that some of the 600 Squadron air-crews helped the groundcrews with refuelling and re-arming the Spitfires. Every member of the Squadron with whom I spoke, aircrew or groundcrew, vehemently deny allegations about Manston. S/L Manton, in a letter to me about the so-called 'mutiny', says: "Whilst at North Weald I had heard only that the R&R party at Manston had been shot up but nothing more. Whenever I had operated my Squadron from Manston I had always found the party helpful and efficient. They obviously worked under very great difficulty and strain during the summer, operating from first to last light on long summer days, being bombed night and day and strafed when on duty on the airfield. I would suggest that the whole thing, if it happened, had been blown up out of all proportion; if there had been any real facts severe action would clearly have been taken". Deighton also quoted Alan Deere in this passage as apparently supporting the accusation. In a letter to me about it, Al Deere said: "In fact there was no mutiny, albeit that a few airmen remained in the safety of the shelter when an over-excited technical officer thought they should be working on the aircraft. I did not witness the event, but 'Prof' Leathart did, and he can give you all the facts. I did not know that I was quoted by Len Deighton, and I do not know what he said. In my book 'Nine Lives' I simply recorded the events as told to me by 'Prof' Leathart but the word 'mutiny' was never used, nor should it have been in relation to the ground crew concerned who were superb throughout the difficult days at Manston". On 22 August 1940 signal A/117 was sent to Manston from HQ No.11 Group, saying: GROUP COMMANDER WISHES ALL RANKS RAF, ARMY AND WAAF TO BE CONGRATULATED ON THEIR GOOD DISCIPLINE AND CALM BEHAVIOUR UNDER HEAVY FIRE WHEN ENEMY ATTACKED YOUR AERODROME ON SUNDAY 18TH. GROUND PERSONNEL DISPLAYED THE FINE OFFENSIVE SPIRIT THAT OUR FIGHTER PILOTS HAVE BEEN DEMONSTRATING IN AIR COMBAT

Page 232 - (Saturday, August 24) Allegation:

1.That many airmen had stayed in the shelters since August 12th and the terrified men would not budge.

　　If the men had been cowering in the shelters since August 12, and were still there on the 24th, refusing to come out, how had they survived without any food or drink? And how could they have earned the highest possible praise as reflected in the signal for their behaviour on Sunday 18th?

2. That the accountant officer could not find enough men above the ground to hold a pay parade.

August 24th was a Saturday. A pay parade on a Saturday? This would be a most unlikely event as anyone will confirm who has served in the RAF, and remembers the ritual of Thursday pay parades in the days before bank payments. More to the point, Saturday August 24 was the day when Manston was repeatedly attacked and sustained such damage that it was forced out of the battle for a week. If the accountant officer did try to hold a pay parade it is not surprising that the men were otherwise engaged!

3. That Johnny Leathart only just prevented another officer from going into the shelters to shoot the first man who refused to come out.

This charge is best answered by quoting from a letter to me by Johnny Leathart: As for the mutiny, like the others you mention, I read of it first in Deighton's book - with some surprise I should add. At the time I put it down to sensational exaggeration like the rest of his book, which does little to detract from the author's prowess as a writer of fiction. I, therefore, did nothing about it. However, as OC54 Squadron at the time, we frequently operated from Manston as a forward base. As you know, it was a very hot spot being only 30-40 miles from the Me109 bases. Naturally the refuelling/re-arming party (not 54 Squadron) did not enjoy it, being strafed from time to time, whilst we were airborne. On one occasion, I remember, there had been a strafe shortly before we landed and the men were in the shelter near the dispersal point. There was no one to meet us as there usually was. I went to the shelter with my pistol in my hand (at that time all officers carried pistols) in case of trouble. I was met by the NCO who immediately ordered the men back to work. All was back to normal. There was no mutiny - just that the men were shocked; they gave no trouble at all, and I did not report the matter officially. Had there been a mutiny I certainly would have taken action. If, indeed, this is the incident which inspired Deighton to put in his book, I am at a loss as to know how he heard about it. I have never mentioned it, except, perhaps, in casual conversation at the time.

4. That while the RAF were cowering in the shelters local civilians looted the buildings.

I have been unable to find any reference to civilians looting Manston, nor has any historian or researcher I have consulted.

5. That the civilian workforce, hired specially to make emergency

*repairs to the bomb cratered airfield, were too scared to do their work
and also stayed in the shelters.*

Manston did not have a civilian airfield repair party! We had a
party from the Pioneer Corps. There was nothing to criticise about
their conduct as Gp/Capt Graham Manton observed in his letter to
me: "I cannot close without commenting on the splendid job which
the Pioneer Company did in helping us to fill the bomb holes on
the airfield. They continued their patching during air raid alerts and
worked all through the night whenever there was sufficient moonlight. They came straight from France and their demeanour and
discipline were an example to our young raw airmen". Nigel
Douglas concluded his investigations by saying that there had never
been a mutiny at Manston while No.600 Squadron was there.
Deighton repeated the accusation in another book about the Battle
in 1980, when he said on page 127: "Henceforth, Manston was under
almost continual strafing, and was of limited value to Fighter
Command. Some officers believed that it should have been evacuated, but Dowding declined to give the order for propaganda
reasons. Manston's handful of exceptionally courageous Blenheim
night-fighter pilots of 600 Squadron worked day after day helping
to refuel and rearm fighters that landed there. *Most of the ground
crews who should have been doing the job were hopelessly shaken by
the events of 12 August and after. They went into the shelters and
stayed there, defying all pleas to come out"*. Mr. Deighton never
responded to requests for clarifications. We therefore assume,
considering three events, that, Deighton got mixed up and
constructed one event out of three:

1. The events that took place with the recruits from Blackpool,
   who turned out to be quite unable to perform in a military way.
2. Alan Deere being pleasantly surprised and delighted to see
   pilots assisting in the work to keep the fighters available for
   action.
3. The fact that some people did not act rationally in a large group
   of brave men, out-bombed, out-strafed and outnumbered by
   enemy forces who could reach RAF Manston "on the deck",
   attack and disappear within a matter of 30 minutes. Maybe the
   whole mystification of the so-called "Manston Mutiny" was best
   described by Ray Aveyard and others, who were there all the
   time and who said, when asked about Len Deighton's allegations: "Complete rubbish".

As a "counterbalance" to Deighton the following will show what was written about the Squadron by Air Commodore E.L.Howard-Williams, who witnessed the Squadron while it fought in North Africa, Malta, Sicily and the Italian mainland. Howard-Williams wrote in his book *Now or Never*. "In the afternoon we called upon a night-fighter Squadron with the finest fighting record in the whole great Mediterranean Air Command. They had a name they were intensely proud of "Number 600 City of London, if you please, and don't forget it". As mobile as a hare, they were actually on the move while we were there, leaving their vineyard for more regular quarters some 400 miles away at Monte Corvino, then the most forward airfield in the whole theatre of operations. I was to meet them there a few days later, after they had operated the night before and were landing forward to be ready for the next night's work. They were flying Beaufighters at the time, some of them equipped with the latest devices known to science for bringing down any of the most venturesome German pilots who might essay their worst. The Squadron, its CO a South African, had then knocked down 112 dead certs, and dead is the word. This makes them the top ranking Squadron day or night in the Mediterranean, where they have shot down 95. So great is their skill they have only lost 2 crews in ten months. Their bag adds up to 17 in England, 38 in North Africa, 42 in Sicily and 15 in Italy. Of these the 42 in Sicily were scored in 31 nights. They took all the strength out of the German night bombers' joy. No.600 has an added claim to distinction in that they were chosen to patrol the already famous Churchill-Roosevelt conference at Casablanca. Their overseas story is sufficiently representative to make it worth a word. They landed at Maison Blanche airfield at Algiers shortly after the African expedition had arrived, and left five days later for Bone where they soon found themselves in the throes of defending the harbour against some persistent raids. After the Squadron had shot down ten in one glorious night, as a tribute the Germans stopped their little game with our ports and used low level attacks to go for our ships as they made their way along the shore. Our night-fighters then followed the convoys and stopped the rot. Their next job was to beat the Ju52 "trains" at dusk and dawn, trying to replenish their beleaguered forces in Tunisia. Five of these fell to a Beau in one outing. During two very recent months they made over 1000 battle flights, maintaining their aircraft serviceability above 75 per cent. and moving forward whenever required. Their 400-mile move from Sicily to Italy, of which I was a witness, was completed within three days from the word "go", their operations continuing all the while as the two echelons each played their part. Dakotas flew their ground crews and other important personnel, while 33 lorries took some two hundred men and supplies, by land, sea, and land, from Cassibile and Messina to Salerno and Monte Corvino. Had the need been sufficiently urgent the whole outfit could have been moved by air within the day. The advance party for such a move consists of a detachment called Echelon A, strong enough to lay out a new camp, fix the communications, and refuel the aircraft. All the crews had over 800 flying hours to their credit. One pilot had downed 16fi enemy aircraft. They liked the life. As one of them put it: "There's been more trade out here than at home. Although I must admit it's been dashed slack lately". I learned that over 30 of the airmen at present serving were in the Auxiliary Air Force. The CO was in the Volunteer Reserve.

APPENDIX XVII

EPILOGUE

This book would never have been written without the help and encouragement of the officers and members of No.600 (City of London) Squadron Association. They are a very friendly and active group of people. I first got in touch with them in September 1979, when I was re-searching the events of 10th May 1940 over Waalhaven aerodrome, south of Rotterdam in Holland, when five out of six Blenheims of No.600 Squadron were lost at the terrible cost of seven killed, one very badly wounded and only three members evading capture and returning to England by ship. As a historian and, above all, as a citizen of the country where these men gave their lives, I was rather upset to hear that four Squadron members were still listed "missing in action" on the imposing walls of the Runnymede Memorial. This struck me as unfair and strange at the same time, as four unknown airmen, killed on 10th May 1940, had been buried at Crooswijk and Spijkenisse cemeteries respectively. I considered it my duty to try and do something about it, linking the four victims to the two crashes that occurred on 10th May without a trace of the remains of the crews. To cut a long story short, assisted by authorities in Holland, by friends and eyewitnesses, who made themselves known after articles in the newspapers I believed I have solved the case. I sent the results of my research and the conclusions to the Commonwealth War Graves Commission. They accepted the evidence that I submitted and at very short notice had new headstones put on these graves, with the names of Roger Moore, Laurie Isaacs, Michael Anderson and Bert Hawkins engraved. When the CWGC turned out to be unable to trace the next of kin I contacted Ray Aveyard, Chairman of the Association, who, with admirable diligence informed the next of kin of the results of my research. For reasons of respect and to ensure a private visit to the next of kin the news was kept from the press until my book "En toen was het stil" ("And then it was silent") was launched and the first copies presented to Mr. Ray Aveyard, the Chairman of No. 600 (City of London) Squadron Association. The visit of Association members in November 1980 - especially the presence of Michael Anderson's widow Ann and Isaac's brother and sister in law - was a great honour and made me feel that I had paid back just a tiny part of the interest on the debt we owe to the men of RAF and AuxAF who fought and died, and are now buried in The Netherlands. The Association very graciously made me an honorary member in 1982, a source of great pride and gratitude, also because at the same time HRH Prince Bernhard of The Netherlands was made an honorary member as well, when he received the Association at Soestdijk Palace. It was a marvellous visit, even though HRH was wearing the tie of No.601 (County of London) Squadron. This princely error was soon put right when Air Commodore "Mickey" Mount handed the Prince the No. 600 Squadron tie. In this respect I will never forget His great sense of humour, when I was at a function where HRH was the guest of honour. Both HRH and I wore our No.600 Squadron ties. When Prince Bernhard spotted me, he pointed at his tie and mine, and said: "At least two people here are properly dressed". In 1985 my wife Marjoan and I had the honour of being presented to the Honorary Air Commodore of No.600 (City of London) Squadron, Her Majesty Queen Elizabeth the Queen Mother. Her Majesty graciously accepted a signed copy of my book about Operation Manna/Chowhound, the Allied food drops over Holland from 29th April - 8th May 1945. Her Majesty vividly remembered those days and told me how a very worried Queen Wilhelmina had spoken with HM King George VI about the sufferings of the Dutch people. Ray Aveyard again was a source of inspiration (and translation) when he accepted my request to act as my English tutor and gave great support when reading the chapters I had finished. Each time the chapters were returned I was aware that I was only writing part of the history of this great bunch of men. There are too many people to thank here. Please allow me to make some exceptions. Thank you Air Cdre Mount (and Mrs. Audrey Mount) for continuous hospitality. Thank you Peter Groenveld, faithful and skilful photographer, for doing a great job with the camera. The honorary membership of the "City of London" Squadron Association bestowed on you in

March 1996 is extremely well-deserved. My sincere thanks to my friend Alan Hankinson for patiently checking the manuscript. Thank you, members of the No.600 (City of London) Squadron Association for showing me what comradeship really is. Last but by no means least: Thank you Marjoan, dear wife and "mate" for the last thirty years, for giving me the time to write this book. Yes, the person saying "bye" on his way out to do research in England was I, your husband! Thank you Gerdy and Mark, my daughter and son. I am sure you will not believe me when I say: "It won't happen again . . ."

APPENDIX XVIII

BIBLIOGRAPHY

Aeroplane Monthly	Oct. 1991
The Aeroplane	24 Oct. 1952
Air Mail	Summer 1990
Air Reserve Gazette	Oct 46 - Jul 47 - Aug 47 - Dec 47 - Jan 48 - Feb 48 - Aug 48 - Apr 49 May 49 Jun 49 - Jul 49 - Sep 49 - Oct 49 - Dec 49 - Feb 50 - Aug 50 Nov 50 - Apr 51 - May 51
Flight	Nov 49 - Apr. 50 - Aug. 50 - Feb. 52
Action Stations	Nos. 3 - 5 - 8 - 9
Air Cdre E.L. Howard-Williams	Now or Never
Ray Aveyard	No.600 (City of London) Squadron, a short history.
Chaz Bowyer	Aircraft of the Few
Chaz Bowyer	Fighter Command
Richard Collier	Eagle Day
Gp/Capt Alan Deere	Nine Lives
Len Deighton	Battle of Britain
Norman L.R. Franks	Valiant Wings
Norman Gelb	Scramble; a Narrative Story of the Battle of Britain
Henderson and Jenyns	History of No.600 (City of London) Bombing Squadron
Hough and Richards	The Battle of Britain - The Jubilee History
Leslie Hunt	Twenty-one Squadrons
Ken Sheldon (edit.)	War over the West

C.Shores and C. Williams	Aces High
W/C C.G. Jefford	RAF Squadrons
Peter Lewis	The British Fighter since 1912
Peter Lewis	Squadron Histories RFC, RNAS & RAF
Francis K. Mason	Battle over Britain
Philip J.R.Moyes	The Bristol Blenheim I (Profile Publications 93)
No.600 Squadron Association : Bulletins and Newsletters	Feb 54 - Mar 54 - Sep 54 - Feb 60 - 2/1960 1/1961 - Summer 61 Winter 61/62 - Summer 62 - Winter 62/63 - Summer 63 - Summer 64 Battle of Britain issue 65 - Summer 65 - Winter 65 - Winter 66/67 Winter 68 - Spring 70 - Spring 72 - Summer 73 - Summer 74.
R.H.H. MacAulay	Beaufighter
Newspapers	Times 7 August 1928
	Daily Express 14 August 1928 - 24 July 1934
	Evening News 25 September 1943
Hans Onderwater	En toen was het stil.
Bryan Philpott	RAF Fighter Units Europe 1939-1942
Alfred Price	Battle of Britain Day
Winston G. Ramsey	The Battle of Britain - Then and Now
Richards and St.G.Saunders	RAF 1939 - 1945 (3 volumes)
Anthony Robinson	RAF Fighter Squadrons in the Battle of Britain
Bruce Robertson	British Military Aircraft Serials
Rocky Stockman	The History of RAF Manston
A.G. Taire	Personal Research notes
John Terraine	The Right of the Line
Peter Townsend	Duel of Eagles
Owen Thetford	Aircraft of the Royal Air Force since 1918

F/L R.F. Freeman AE RAuxAF	Auxiliaries; Past and Present (RAFPR Magazine '95)
600 City of London Squadron	Operation Record Books 1927 - 1957 and individual Combat Reports
F/L K.N. Haselwood	Squadron Diaries 1948 - 1951
F/L W. J. Symonds	Squadron Diaries 1950 - 1953
S/L Peter Norman	Squadron Diaries 1953 - 1954

APPENDIX XIX

ACKNOWLEDGEMENTS

J.Atkinson
K.Bamford
S.Bowen
W. Cardew
J.Cox
L.Dixon
K.Edwards
G.Guest,
B.Hills
G.Kirk
P.Lovegrove
J.Meadows
J.Morrison
S.Nicholson
N.Poole
D.Richards
B. Sills
J.Stewart-Garden
T.Tobin
D.Ward
W. Williams
LtCol J.Harrison MBE

W.Atkinson
R.Benns
A.Burdekin
F.J.Cooke
T.Curry
T.Davies
A.Furse
L.C.Hawkes
D. Jennings
B.Larbalastier
J.MacAnulty
P.Montgomery
C.J.Mount
J.Noble
E.Potter
A.Rolfe
C.Spry
T.R.Stokoe
A.Veton
J.Wareing
Maj. Spiteri AFM

R.Aveyard
D.Blackwood
K.Burvill
M.Cowham
G.Curtiss
J.Eames
E. Goodwin
G. Hibbins
L.A. Jones
J.Linford
B.McMahon
E.Mooney
R.Naylor
A.Pickering
D.Proudlove
J.Rosbrook
A.Standing
S.Taylor
J.Walton
N.Wheeler
Martin Scicluna

Public Record Office (London), Imperial War Museum (London),
RAF Museum (Hendon), Air Historical Branch (London),
Commonwealth War Graves Commission (Maidenhead), Embassy of
Malta GC (Brussels, Belgium), Embassy of Germany (The Hague,
Netherlands),Embassies of Italy (Bonn, Germany - The Hague,

Netherlands), National War Museum Association (Valetta, Malta), Headquarters Armed Forces (Luqa, Malta), Adviser Section of the Office of the Prime Minister (Valetta), RAFA Malta Branch (Hamrun, Malta), Bundesarchiv (Koblenz, Germany), the Militärarchiv, (Freiburg, Germany), 5º Reparto, Officia Storica, Stato Maggiore Aeronautica, (Rome, Italy), Air Force Historical Section Royal Netherlands Air Force, (Soesterberg, Netherlands), Air War Documentation Group (Leiden, Netherlands), Documentation Group 1940-1945 (Amsterdam, Netherlands). This book was written and researched with the help and full support of the members of No. 600 Squadron and No.600 Squadron Association, as well as staff of many different institutes and organisations dealing with the history of the RAF and RAuxAF. I was very pleased to receive a lot of help from agencies outside the United Kingdom, like the Embassy of Malta in Brussels, various historical institutes at Malta and the Italian Air Force Authorities in Rome. Unfortunately when contacting them for information about the Squadron in North Africa it proved virtually impossible to get help from the governments of Algeria and Tunisia.

The German archives were helpful, but they insisted that the author travelled in person to their archives in Koblenz, Freiburg and Berlin. This made research costly and time-consuming and had as a consequence that a lot of time was wasted travelling to Koblenz, Freiburg and Berlin. Of course the author takes full responsibility for the contents of this book. If anyone not mentioned claims copyright for photographs supplied to the author he or she is requested to contact the publisher. If any names have accidentally been omitted, the author offers his sincerest apologies.

APPENDIX XX

1995/1996 COMMITTEE NO.600 (CITY OF LONDON) SQUADRON ASSOCIATION.

President : Ray Aveyard, AE
Life Vice President : Air Commodore C.J. "Mickey" Mount CBE, DSO, DFC, RAF (Retd)
Chairman : Dennis Overton
Secretary : Sid Bowen
Treasurer : John Wilding
Asst Secretary : Mike Kempton
Welfare Officer : John Morrison
Members : Bill Williams
 John Rosbrook
 Colin Freeman.

APPENDIX XXI

SPONSORS

The Squadron Association wish to thank all those who donated funds to allow this History of No.600 (City of London) Squadron and Association to be produced:

INDEX

Frankland, The Hon. R.N., 41, 48, 76, 85
Frost, P/O J.L., 430

Galloway, W., 5, 11
Gaudo, 287, 299
George, F/O, 227, 240, 406, 413
Georgeson, Sgt, 157
Gibraltar, 171, 172, 174, 183, 194
Gilbert, Stan, 166
Gillies, Sgt R., 154, 157, 180, 182, 201, 203, 224, 225, 228, 233, 239, 247, 249, 251, 256, 259, 262, 290, 300, 412, 414, 415, 417, 418, 422
Gledhill, Sgt, 145, 146, 147, 410
Glegg, F/O, 147, 148, 154, 155, 157, 158, 400, 410, 422, 430
Goodacre, Charles, 153
Goss, F/S, 312, 420
Graham, Sgt K.A.G., 157, 430
Grant, Sgt E.J., 154, 405, 430
Gray, Cpl G.P., 5
Green, S/L Paddy, 154, 257, 158, 163, 180, 182, 199, 201, 212, 223, 224, 225, 236, 240, 241, 247, 251, 253, 254, 256, 257, 259, 261, 262, 263, 265, 269, 270, 272, 273, 274, 288, 289, 290, 295, 300, 302, 303, 304, 343, 414, 415, 417, 418, 422, 423
Green, Sgt F.W.W., 430
Greenwood, F., 5, 6, 7, 10
Grey, S/L, 11
Grice, F/O D., 121, 122, 404, 430
Grooswijk, 106, 107
Grout, S/L Bill, 448
Guest, G.H.W., 434
Guest, P/O Gilbert, 143, 146, 157, 409
Guest, Rt.Hon. Freddie, PC, CBE, DSO, MP, 1, 9, 11, 13, 14, 17, 21, 22, 23, 28, 57, 58, 423

Hackett, P/O, 8, 11, 14, 16, 17, 35
Haddock, S.A., 434

Haden, Ron, 63
Hadland, G., 48, 381
Haine, P/O Dick, 85, 94, 95, 108, 109, 113, 116, 117, 134, 142, 430
Hale, P/O, 354, 355
Hall, J.J.B., 5
Hall, Wilf, 246, 266
Hammond, S/L, 316
Hanas, F/L Joe, 226, 234, 239, 240, 270, 274, 285, 289, 412, 413, 418, 422
Hankinson, C.D., 435
Hannay, F/O, 76, 115, 404
Hardwick, Sgt W.R., 430
Haresign, Cpl, 266
Harrington, F/L, 369, 370
Harris, Bill, 353
Harrison, Cpl, 200
Harrison, Cpl, 62, 71
Harrop, F/S, 5, 7, 8, 10
Harrop, Sgt, 239, 285, 300, 419, 422
Harvey, P/O, 157, 160, 161, 162, 163, 411
Haselwood, F/O Keith, 333, 334, 338, 341, 342, 345
Haskell, A.B., 5
Hawker, F/L, 354, 355, 383
Hawker, P/O, 371
Hawkes, L.C., 463
Hawkins, Bert, 79, 94, 95, 101, 102, 400, 404, 457
Hayes, P/O R., 62, 76, 94, 111, 112, 113, 114, 115, 140, 144, 326, 327, 338, 349, 389, 396, 397, 397, 409, 423, 430
Hayhoe, 250
Haywood, Cpl, 327
Healy, F/L Tim, 38, 41, 389
Healy, F/L, 302
Hedgecock, Sgt, 200, 218
Henderson, F/O, 2, 6, 7, 8, 10, 11, 15, 18, 20, 384
Henderson, G., 434
Hendon 12, 15, 23, 25, 33, 39, 42, 55, 64, 70, 72
Hennings, S.J., 43, 48